Lecture Notes in Artificial Intellige

Edited by J. G. Carbonell and J. Siekmann

Subseries of Lecture Notes in Computer Science

Danny Weyns   H. Van Dyke Parunak
Fabien Michel (Eds.)

Environments for
Multi-Agent Systems II

Second International Workshop, E4MAS 2005
Utrecht, The Netherlands, July 25, 2005
Selected Revised and Invited Papers

 Springer

Series Editors

Jaime G. Carbonell, Carnegie Mellon University, Pittsburgh, PA, USA
Jörg Siekmann, University of Saarland, Saarbrücken, Germany

Volume Editors

Danny Weyns
Katholieke Universiteit Leuven
Department of Computer Science
AgentWise, DistriNet, 3001 Leuven, Belgium
E-mail: danny.weyns@cs.kuleuven.be

H. Van Dyke Parunak
Altarum Institute
3520 Green Court, Suite 300, Ann Arbor, MI 48105-1579, USA
E-mail: van.parunak@altarum.org

Fabien Michel
Laboratoire d'Etudes et de Recherches Informatiques
Rue des Crayeres, BP 1035, 51687 Reims Cedex 2, France
E-mail: fmichel@leri.univ-reims.fr

Library of Congress Control Number: 2006921545

CR Subject Classification (1998): I.2.11, I.2, C.2.4

LNCS Sublibrary: SL 7 – Artificial Intelligence

ISSN   0302-9743
ISBN-10   3-540-32614-6 Springer Berlin Heidelberg New York
ISBN-13   978-3-540-32614-4 Springer Berlin Heidelberg New York

Springer is a part of Springer Science+Business Media

springer.com

© Springer-Verlag Berlin Heidelberg 2006
Printed in Germany

Typesetting: Camera-ready by author, data conversion by Scientific Publishing Services, Chennai, India
Printed on acid-free paper   SPIN: 11678809   06/3142   5 4 3 2 1 0

Preface

In the past two years the environment in multiagent systems has become increasingly important and is now becoming a focus of research in its own right. Yet, the environment in multiagent systems has been studied before. So the obvious question then is: Why does the environment attract the attention of a broader community of researchers right now?

The answer to this question is manifold. First, current research on environments is built on the *receptive ground* of early work. Pioneers such as Demazeau, Parunak, Ferber, Odell, Omicini and Zambonelli have been stressing the importance of the environment in multiagent systems for almost a decade.

Second, current research on environments is *well organized*. The workshop series on Environments for Multiagent Systems (E4MAS) provides the breeding ground for coordinating research on environments. E4MAS provides an active forum for discussion and exchange of ideas. The constructive atmosphere of the E4MAS workshops and the critical attitude of the attendees stimulate research in the growing community.

Third, researchers interested in environments come from various backgrounds. The notion of environment exceeds specific types of agency. The environment is important for simple ant-like agents as well as for complex cognitive agents. The environment provides a challenging area for *synergetic research* on multiagent systems in general.

And last but not least, the perspective on the role of the environment in multiagent systems has undergone a fundamental change in the last two years. Whereas environment and "infrastructure" are traditionally considered equivalent, recent research considers the environment as a *first-order design abstraction* in multiagent systems. Several researchers have demonstrated that the environment provides a building block that can be used creatively in the design of multiagent system applications. Distinguishing between agent and environment responsibilities supports separation of concerns in multiagent systems, which is a prerequisite for good engineering practice.

This volume collects selected and revised papers of the second E4MAS Workshop, completed with a number of invited papers of prominent researchers active in the domain. The papers represent the full life-cycle of environment engineering, including theoretical analysis, models, mechanisms, architecture and design, and applications. We hope that the work presented in this book stimulates further exploration and exploitation of the environment in multiagent systems.

December 20, 2005

Danny Weyns
Leuven, Belgium

Organization

E4MAS 2005 was organized in conjunction with the 4th International Joint Conference on Autonomous Agents and Multi-Agent Systems (AAMAS 2005), Utrecht, The Netherlands, July 25, 2005.

Program Co-chairs

Danny Weyns   K.U. Leuven, Belgium
H. Van Dyke Parunak   Altarum Institute, Ann Arbor, USA
Fabien Michel   Laboratoire d'Etudes et de Recherches Informatiques Reims, France

Program Committee

Sven Brueckner   Altarum Institute, Ann Arbor, USA
Yves Demazeau   Laboratoire Leibniz, IMAG, Grenoble, France
Marco Dorigo   Université Libre de Bruxelles
Alexis Drogoul   Laboratoire d'Informatique de Paris 6, France
Jacques Ferber   Université de Montpellier II, Lirmm, France
Alexander Helleboogh   DistriNet, K.U. Leuven, Belgium
Tom Holvoet   DistriNet, K.U. Leuven, Belgium
Franziska Klügl   University of Wurzburg, Germany
Marco Mamei   University of Modena and Reggio Emilia, Italy
Fabien Michel   Laboratoire d'Etudes et de Recherches Informatiques Reims, France

James Odell   James Odell Associates, Ann Arbor, USA
Andrea Omicini   Università di Bologna, Italy
H. Van Dyke Parunak   Altarum Instutute, Ann Arbor, USA
Karl Tuyls   Universiteit Maastricht, The Netherlands
Paul Valckenaers   PMA, K.U. Leuven, Belgium
Franco Zambonelli   University of Modena and Reggio Emilia, Italy

Website

http://www.cs.kuleuven.ac.be/~distrinet/events/e4mas/

Acknowledgements

We are grateful to the PC members for their critical review work. We also thank Elke Steegmans, Alexander Helleboogh, Kurt Schelfthout, Tom De Wolf, Koen Mertens, Nelis Boucké and Tom Holvoet for their efforts for E4MAS. A special word of thanks to Tom De Wolf for managing the website.

Table of Contents

Models, Architecture, and Design

Mediated Coordination

Applications

Environments for Situated Multi-agent Systems:
Beyond Infrastructure

Danny Weyns[1], Giuseppe Vizzari[2], and Tom Holvoet[1]

[1] AgentWise, DistriNet, Katholieke Universiteit Leuven, Belgium
{danny.weyns, tom.holvoet}@cs.kuleuven.be
[2] DISCo, Università degli Studi di Milano–Bicocca, Italy
vizzari@disco.unimib.it

Abstract. There is a lot of confusion on what the environment of a multi-agent system (MAS) comprises. Sometimes, researchers refer to the environment as the logical entity of a MAS in which the agents and other resources are embedded. Sometimes, the notion of environment is used to refer to the software infrastructure on which the MAS is executed. Sometimes, environment even refers to the underlying hardware infrastructure on which the MAS runs.

Our research focuses on situated MASs, i.e. MASs in which agents have an explicit position in the environment. In this paper, we propose a three-layer model for situated MASs that considers agents as well as the environment as first-order abstractions. The aim of this model is to clarify the confusion between the concept of the environment and the infrastructure on which the MAS is deployed. The top layer of the model consists of the MAS application logic, the middle layer contains the software execution platform, and the physical infrastructure is located in the bottom layer. Starting from this model, we propose a classification of situated MASs based on the physical infrastructure of the MAS. We illustrate the different classes with examples from the research community and our own practice. We apply the three-layer model to each example. The models show that agents and the environment are abstractions that crosscut the three layers of the model.

1 Introduction

Despite most multi-agent system (MAS) definitions include the term environment (see, e.g., [1, 2]), in general, the environment is not considered as an independent building block in MASs. Typically, the environment is conceived as communication infrastructure, implementing a specific message transfer infrastructure and mechanisms for the management of agent discovery and acquaintance. Sometimes, the notion of environment is used to refer to the software infrastructure on which the MAS is executed. Sometimes, environment even refers to the underlying hardware infrastructure on which the MAS runs. Generally, the environment is only considered as infrastructure and not as a relevant entity at the application level. At the application level, however, several aspects of MASs that conceptually do not belong to the agents themselves should not be assigned to, or hosted inside agents. Examples are the topology of a spatial domain, specification and access management of domain specific resources, or support for indirect coordination. These (and other) aspects should be dealt with explicitly and the

D. Weyns, H. Van Dyke Parunak, and F. Michel (Eds.): E4MAS 2005, LNAI 3830, pp. 1–17, 2006.
© Springer-Verlag Berlin Heidelberg 2006

environment is the natural candidate to encapsulate these aspects. In practice however, such aspects are typically integrated implicitly in MASs, or implemented in an ad-hoc manner. This indicates that in general, the MAS research community fails to treat the environment as a *first-order abstraction*, i.e. the environment is not considered as an independent building block that encapsulates its own, clearly defined responsibilities within the MAS, irrespective of the agents [3].

The importance of the environment as a first-order abstraction is particularly apparent for situated MASs. Situated MASs are characterized by the presence of an explicit spatial structure in which agents are placed. Generally, situated MASs are also characterized by specific perception and interaction mechanisms based on contextual properties, such as agents' relative positions. Situated MASs typically provide a means for indirect coordination, e.g., with digital pheromones [4] or gradient fields [5]. The domain specific stipulation of environmental markers, the management of the coordination infrastructure, and the actual implementation of these mechanisms should not be delegated to agents, but are instead typical responsibilities of the environment.

In this paper, we introduce a three-layer model for situated MASs that considers agents as well as the environment as first-order abstractions. The main goal of this model is to analyze relationships among agents, the environment, and the MAS deployment infrastructure, aiming to bring clarity in the confusion between the concept of the environment and MAS infrastructure.

This paper is structured as follows. Section 2 discusses a three-layer model for situated MASs that considers agents and the environment as first-order abstractions. We use this model to propose a classification of situated MASs based on the physical infrastructure the MAS is built upon. Section 3 illustrates the different classes with practical examples. Finally, in Sect. 4 we draw conclusions.

2   A Three-Layer Model for Situated MASs

The term environment is generally included in most agent and MAS definitions, but there is much confusion on relationships between the concept of environment and the deployment infrastructure of a MAS. In this section, we describe a three-layer model for situated MAS that aims to bring clarity in this confusion. Starting from this model we then propose a classification of situated MASs based on the physical infrastructure on which the MAS is deployed. We conclude with a discussion of related work. In the next section we apply the three-layer model to three applications that belong to different classes.

2.1   Three-Layer Model

The proposed model is a standard deployment model for distributed applications (see, e.g., [6]) applied to situated MAS-based applications. The model for situated MAS is depicted in Fig. 1.

The model is made up of the following three layers:

- The *multiagent system (MAS) application* layer at the top (i.e., the application logic and the MAS framework);

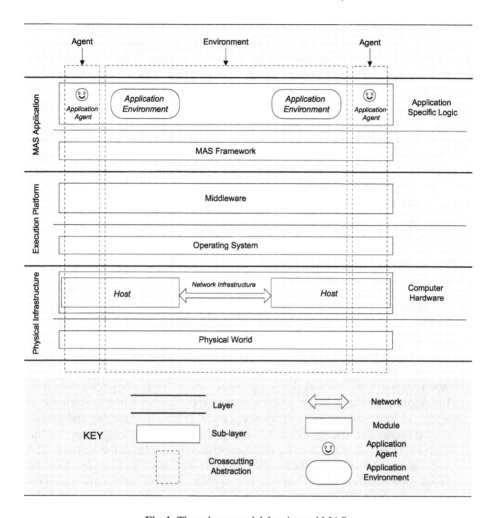

Fig. 1. Three-layer model for situated MASs

- The *execution platform* layer (i.e., middleware infrastructure and the operating system);
- The *physical infrastructure* layer at the bottom (i.e., processors, network infrastructure, etc.).

Below we elaborate on each layer and illustrate that the abstraction of the environment as well as the agents, crosscut the three layers in the model. Before that, we introduce a simple file searching system in a peer-to-peer (P2P) network [7] that we use as a running example to illustrate the different layers of the three-layer model. The idea of this application is to let mobile agents act on behalf of users and browse a shared distributed file system to find requested files. Each user is situated in a particular node (its base). Users can offer files at their base and can send out agents to find files for them. Agents can observe the environment, however, to avoid network overload, agents can perceive the environment only to a limited extend, e.g. 2 hops from the agent's current position. An agent can perceive nodes and connecting links, bases on nodes, and files available on nodes. Agents can also sense signals. Each base emits such a signal. The intensity of the signal decreases with every hop. Sensing the signal of its base enables an agent to "climb up" the gradient, i.e. move towards its base or alternatively "climb down", i.e. move away from it. Finally, agents can sense pheromones. An agent can drop a file-specific pheromone in the environment when it returns back to its base with a copy of a file. Such a pheromone trail can not only help the agent later on when it needs a new copy of the file, it can also help other agents to find their way to that file. Pheromones evaporate, thereby limiting their influence over time. This is an important property to avoid that agents are misled when a file disappears from a certain node.

We now zoom in on each layer of the three-layer model.

Multiagent System Application Layer. The *MAS Application* layer consists of two sub-layers:

- The *Application Specific Logic* layer, which comprises the *Application Agents* and the *Application Environment* of the MAS, which represent the solution for the specific problem context. The Application Agents are the autonomous entities in the MAS, the Application Environment provides an application specific representation of the domain to Application Agents. The Application Environment enables Application Agents to interact with domain resources and with other Application Agents. The Application Environment offers a domain specific abstraction to Application Agents, hiding the complexity of resource access, interaction handling and consistency management. The Application Agents in the P2P file searching system are the logical entities that are created by the users to search for files in the network. The Application Environment is the logical entity that represents the space in which the Application Agents perform their job. The Application Environment offers a representation to the Application Agents of the neighboring nodes and connecting links of the network. The Application Environment also represents the available files, the gradient fields emitted by the bases, and the file-specific pheromones dropped by the agents.
- The *MAS Framework* layer: the Application Specific Logic is typically deployed on top of a *MAS Framework*. The latter supplies predefined MAS abstractions, such as a particular engine for agent's decision making, support for communication, a model for action, etc. These abstractions can be reused over different applications. In the P2P file searching system, the MAS framework layer likely provides a pheromone infrastructure and infrastructure for gradient fields. Another example is support for mobility of the agents.

Execution Platform. The Execution Platform is in turn subdivided in two sublayers:

- A *middleware* layer which serves as the glue between (distributed) components. It provides support for remote procedure calls, threading, transactions, persistence, load balancing, generative communication, etc. In general, middleware offers a software platform on which distributed applications can be executed. An example of middleware support in the P2P file searching system is a distributed tuple-space infrastructure that provides a basic substrate for the pheromone and gradient field infrastructure.

- An *Operating System* layer that enables the execution of the application on the physical hardware and it offers basic functionality to applications, hiding low-level details of the underlying physical platform. The Operating System manages memory usage and offers transparent access to lower level resources such as files, it provides network facilities, it handles the intervention of the users, it provides basic support for timing, etc. The operating system provides many basic functions, one example is the file system.

Physical Infrastructure. The Execution Platform runs on top of the Physical Infrastructure, which can is generally divided in two parts:

- The *Computer Hardware*, which contains the *Hosts* with processors and the connecting *Network Infrastructure*. In the P2P file sharing system, the physical infrastructure consists of a computer machine on each node and a connecting network. Each machine is a possible access point to the system for a user.
- The *Physical World*, which refers to the physical parts of the MAS, if present in the application. In the P2P file sharing system this aspect is not relevant, and thus this layer is empty.

Agent and Environment Crosscutting Abstractions. Situated MAS applications typically comprise all three layers, although some sub-layers may be empty, e.g. when the MAS application is built from scratch, the MAS Framework layer is empty. Agents and the environment span the three layers of the three-layer model, this is graphically depicted in Fig. 1 with the dashed vertical rectangles. An agent, first of all, is composed of an application specific part, i.e. the Application Agent located in the MAS Application layer. The realization of this Application Agent may be based on a generic MAS Framework that, in turn, exploit an underlying Middleware and the Operating System services. Finally, the agent software is hosted and executes on a physical system that is part of the Physical Infrastructure layer. Analogously, the environment consists of an application specific part that corresponds to the Application Environment, located in the MAS Application layer. The Application Environment is typically built on top of a MAS Framework that is supported by generic Middleware and Operating System services. As for the agents, the environment software executes on a physical system, that includes Hosts provided with processors and an interconnecting Network Infrastructure.

The proposed three-layer model promotes the environment to a first-order abstraction, on the same level as the agents. Considering the environment as a first-order abstraction urges researchers to deal with responsibilities of the environment explicitly, and also promotes the modelling, design and implementation of concepts like perception, action handling, and locality in comprehensive ways. In particular, it must be noted that one of the responsibilities of the environment is to provide situated agents with proper perceptions, which may include information of the physical world obtained

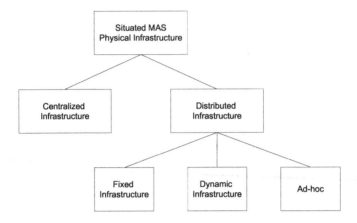

Fig. 2. A classification of situated MASs based on the physical infrastructure

through sensors. On the other hand, agents' actions may have effects which extend over the software environment and may cause modification on the physical world via actuators. The three-layer model also stresses the need to consider the "vertical" relationships among different layers.

2.2   Classification of Situated MASs

Starting from the three-layer model, we now present a classification of situated MASs based on the physical infrastructure on which the MAS is deployed, see Fig. 2. The goal of this classification is to further clarify the relationship between the agent and environment abstractions and the MAS infrastructure. The structural aspects of the environment are particularly relevant for situated MASs, as agents are deeply influenced by their position, which generally determines their perceptions and (inter)actions.

The physical MAS infrastructure can be centralized (*Centralized Infrastructure*), i.e., deployed on a single computer, or distributed, i.e., deployed on a set of computers that are connected through a computer network (*Distributed Infrastructure*). Distribution can be a constraint of the application, or a well-considered architectural decision. In a centralized MAS infrastructure, the environment is an encapsulated software entity deployed on a single computer. In a distributed MAS infrastructure, the distributed environment is a logical entity that physically consists of a set of software entities deployed on different nodes that are connected through a network. In a centralized setting, agents experience the environment as one shared entity that is locally accessible. In a distributed setting, agents can be aware of distribution or distribution may be transparent to agents. Distribution of an environment is supported by generic middleware infrastructure.

Besides the distinction between centralization or distribution, we further distinguish between the dynamics of the distributed infrastructure. The distributed infrastructure of a MAS can be static or change dynamically. In a static infrastructure, the number of computers and the layout of the connecting network does not change over time (*Fixed Infrastructure*). A topology of a dynamic infrastructure changes over time due to newly added nodes or nodes that disappear (*Dynamic Infrastructure*). In other cases, the environment is not based on a predefined notion of adjacency, but generates ad-hoc spatial relationships reflecting for instance the positions of physical agents in an actual environment (*Ad-hoc*).

The complexity related to the design and implementation of hardware/software infrastructures related to agents and the environment grows in distributed scenarios, especially in cases that do not provide a fixed predefined infrastructure for the arrangement of agents and the environment.

2.3   Related Work

To our best knowledge, no deployment models for MASs were previously proposed that explicitly discusses the position of agents and the environment. However, several layered models for MAS infrastructure are discussed in literature. Here we look at three representative examples: Retsina, Jade and TOTA.

Retsina (Reusable Environment for Task-Structured Intelligent Network Agents) is a well-known MAS infrastructure [8]. Retsina is an open MAS infrastructure that supports communities of heterogeneous agents. The Retsina MAS infrastructure is built up in several layers. The bottom layer contains the operating environment that provides the platform on which the infrastructure components and the agents run. Retsina supports a broad range of execution platforms and it automatically handles different types of network transport layers. The operating environment corresponds to the Physical Infrastructure layer in the three-layer model presented in this paper. On top of the operating environment, Retsina defines eight different layers. The communication infrastructure layer provides communication channels for message transfer between peers, and multicast that is used for a discovery process to let the agents find infrastructural components. The ACL infrastructure layer provides an ontology and a protocol engine with a protocol language. The MAS management services layer offers tool support to monitor the activity of the agents and to launch the applications. The security layer supports agent authentication, secure communication and integrity of the Retsina infrastructure components. The ANS (Agent Name Services) layer provides a means to abstract away from physical locations by mapping agent identifiers to network addresses. The Matchmakers layer provides a mapping between agents and services. Service providers can advertise their services at the matchmakers and agents can request the matchmakers to get contact information of relevant providers. Finally, the Retsina-OAA InterOperator on top of the Retsina MAS infrastructure bridges the Retsina MAS infrastructure with the OOA platform (Open Agent Architecture). These eight layers provide middleware and MAS specific services that conceptually belongs to the Middleware layer and the MAS Framework layer in the three-layer model presented in this paper.

Jade (Java Agent Development Environment) [9] is a pure Java, middleware platform intended for the development of distributed multiagent applications based on peer-to-peer communication. Jade includes Java classes to support the development of application agents and the "run-time environment" that provides the basic services for agents to execute. An instance of the Jade run-time is called a container, and the set of all containers is called the platform. The platform provides a middleware layer that hides from agents the complexity of the underlying execution system. Jade includes a naming service ensuring that each agent has a unique name, and a yellow pages service that can be distributed across multiple hosts. Agents can dynamically discover each other and communicate by exchanging asynchronous messages. Jade provides a set of skeletons of typical interaction protocols. The Jade platform also supports mobility of code, enabling agents to stop running on a host, migrate to a different remote host and restart execution from the point they stopped. The Jade middleware layer corresponds to the MAS Framework layer in the three-layer model presented in this paper. The Jade layer executes on top of a Java Virtual Machine layer that provides generic middleware support for Web services, distributed communication, threading, transaction management, security, etc.

In [10], Mamei and Zambonelli introduce the notion of "spatial computing stack" and apply it to the TOTA (Tuples On The Air) middleware. The spatial computing stack defines a framework for spatial computing mechanisms at four levels: the physical level at the bottom, the structure level above it, then follows the navigation level, and finally the application level at the top. The "physical level" deals with how components find each other and start communication with each other. In the case of TOTA, a node detects in-range nodes via one-hop message broadcast. The "structure level" is the level at which a spatial structure is built and maintained by components in the physical network. In TOTA, a tuple can be injected from a node. A TOTA tuple is defined in terms of a content and a propagation rule. The content represents the information carried on by the tuple and the propagation rule determines how the tuple should be propagated across the network. Once a tuple is injected it propagates and creates a centered spatial structure in the network representing some spatial feature relative to the source. At the "navigation level" components exploit basic mechanisms to orient their activities in the spatial structure and to sense and affect the local properties of space. TOTA defines an API to allow application components to sense TOTA tuples in their one-hop neighborhood and to locally perceive the space defined by them. Navigation in the space consists of agents acting on the basis of the local shape of specific tuples. At the "application level", navigation mechanisms are exploited by application components to interact and organize their activities. TOTA enables complex coordination tasks in a robust and flexible way. An example is a group of agents that coordinate their respective movements by following locally perceived tuples downhill or uphill resulting in specific formations. The spatial computing stack model extends over the three layers of the model presented in this paper. The physical level is situated in the Physical infrastructure, the structure and navigation level are situated in the Middleware layer, and the application level finally is situated in the MAS Application layer.

3   Applying the Three-Layer Model for Situated MASs

In this section, we apply the three-layer model for situated MASs to three MAS applications with different physical infrastructures. First we look at a multiagent-based simulation application that is deployed on a centralized infrastructure. Then we look at a MAS-based control system that is deployed on an ad-hoc infrastructure. Finally, we zoom in on a mobile MAS application that is deployed on a dynamic infrastructure.

3.1 MMASS-Based Crowd Simulation

In this section, we discuss an application that simulates a crowd adopting a situated MAS [11] approach. In particular, the application supports the modelling and study of crowds and pedestrian behaviour in large rooms, e.g., lecture halls. According to the classification proposed in Sect. 2.2, this application is classified as *centralized infrastructure*. The goal of the simulation is to support architects and designers of large rooms in their decision making activities, for instance to determine the number and positions of emergency exits. Given a design and specific starting conditions, the architect can then obtain an indication of the behaviour of a crowd, for example in an evacuation situation.

There are several approaches to this problem which adopt a Cellular Automata (CA) based model (see, e.g., [12]), but they generally relax the basic CA model and allow action–at–a–distance. Moreover these approaches typically model only homogeneous behaviour of the simulated entities by means of cell states and transition rules that also include the local state of the environment and the laws that regulate its dynamics. In this way, the environment and the embedded entities are mixed up, causing large cell states and very complex transition rules. The MAS approach instead provides a clean separation between the environment and the entities which inhabit it, and also allows to model heterogeneity of agents in a more convenient way.

For the application, the Multilayered Multi Agent Situated System (MMASS) [13] model was adopted to support the design and development of the crowd simulation application. MMASS provides an explicit spatial representation of the environment and an interaction model strongly related to the agents' context. In MMASS, agents can (1) interact through a reaction with adjacent entities, (2) emit fields that are diffused in the environment, and (3) can be perceived by other agents. Fig. 3 depicts the three-layer model for situated MASs, applied to the MMASS simulation application.

MAS Application Layer. The crowd simulation system is composed of a set of Pedestrian Agents situated in a Lecture Hall (i.e. a virtual environment that represents a bidimensional abstraction of a physical space). Pedestrians (and other relevant elements of the environment) generate fields that can be perceived by pedestrians according to specific diffusion and perception mechanisms. The perception of these fields, and their local state, influences pedestrian behaviors. In critical situations, the pedestrians can use the perceived fields to move towards emergency exits.

All the application specific elements are built on top of the MMASS Framework. The MMASS Framework offers a set of basic components for applications that use the MMASS model. In particular the framework supports: the definition of the *spatial structure* of the environment by means of basic elements (i.e. nodes and edges); *interaction* among agents by means of field based mechanisms and though the reaction among adjacent agents; and support the definition of domain specific agents through *agent templates*, which define the fundamental elements common to all MMASS agents.

Execution Platform. The MMASS framework, that is based on Java technology, exploits some basic library for XML file access for configuration matters. Facultatively,

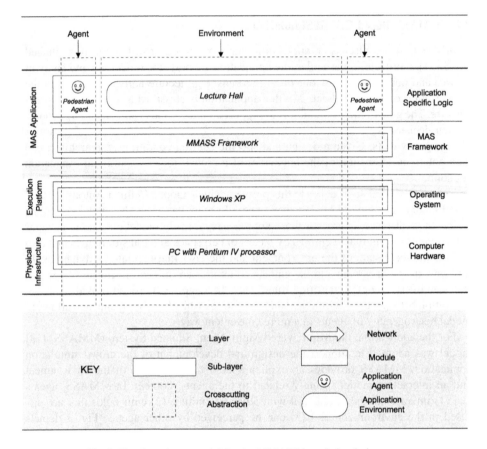

Fig. 3. The three-layer model for the MMASS based simulation case

the simulator is able to generate a 3D visualization by means of 3D Studio Max, a commercial 3D modelling and visualization tool[1]. For reasons of performance, the application can be distributed, however, in this specific case, a centralized approach is used, so there is no need for supporting middleware.

The crowd simulation runs on the Windows XP operating system.

Physical Infrastructure. The physical infrastructure of the application consists of a single PC provided with a Pentium IV processor.

3.2   Automated Guided Vehicles Coordination

In this section, we apply the three-layer model to a real-world application that uses a situated MAS to the control of an automatic guided vehicle (AGV) transportation system [14]. This application is classified as *ad-hoc* infrastructure in the classification

---

[1] http://www4.discreet.com/3dsmax/

proposed in Sect. 2.2. The application is developed in the context of a R&D project between the AgentWise research group and Egemin[2], a manufacturer of industrial auto-mated logistic service systems. Traditionally, AGV transportation systems use a central server that controls the system. Although efficient, the centralized architecture lacks flexibility. In the project we investigate the feasibility of a decentralized architecture aiming to improve flexibility.

An AGV transportation system uses unmanned vehicles to transport loads through a warehouse. Typical applications are repackaging and distributing incoming goods to various branches, or distributing manufactured products to storage locations. AGVs can move through a warehouse, guided by a laser navigation system or by magnets or cables that are fixed in the floor. AGVs are provided with a battery as energy source.

The main functionalities of an AGV transportation system are: (1) perform transports: transports are generated by client systems (warehouse management system, operator, etc.) and have to be assigned to AGVs that can execute them; (2) collision avoidance and deadlock prevention; (3) when an AGV is idle it has to park at a free park location; (4) when an AGV runs out of energy, it has to charge its battery at one of the charging stations. The low-level control of the AGVs in terms of sensors and actuators (staying on track on a segment, turning, and determining the current position, etc.), is handled by the low-level AGV control software called E'nsor[3].

Fig. 4 depicts the three-layer model for the AGV transportation system.

MAS Application Layer. The situated MAS consists of an environment and two kinds of agents, *Transport Agents* and *AGV Agents*. Transport Agents are located at transport bases, a transport base may host one or more Transport Agents. A transport base is a computer system that is in charge to manage the transports of a particular area in the warehouse. Together, the transport bases, connected through a wired network, cover the whole layout of the warehouse. AGV Agents are located on mobile AGV machines that are situated on the factory floor. With each AGV there is one AGV Agent associated.

Transport bases receive transport requests from client systems, i.e. typically a ware-house management system, but it can also be another logistic machine or even an opera-tor. For each new transport request, a new Transport Agent is created that is responsible to assign the transport to an AGV and to ensure that the transport is completed cor-rectly. The Transport Agent also determines the priority of the transport. The priority of a transport depends on the kind of transport, the pending time since its creation, and the nature of other transports in the system. Transport agents interact with other related transport agents to determine the correct priority over time. AGV Agents are responsible for executing the assigned transports.

Since the physical environment of a factory is very constrained, it restricts how agents can use their environment. Therefore a Virtual Environment has been introduced for the agents to live in. This Virtual Environment offers an application specific medium that Application Agents can use to exchange information and coordinate their behavior. One example of the use of the Virtual Environment are road signs. The Virtual Environ-ment provides a logical map consisting of nodes and segments that corresponds with

[2] http://www.egemin.com/

[3] E'nsor ® is an acronym for Egemin Navigation System On Robot.

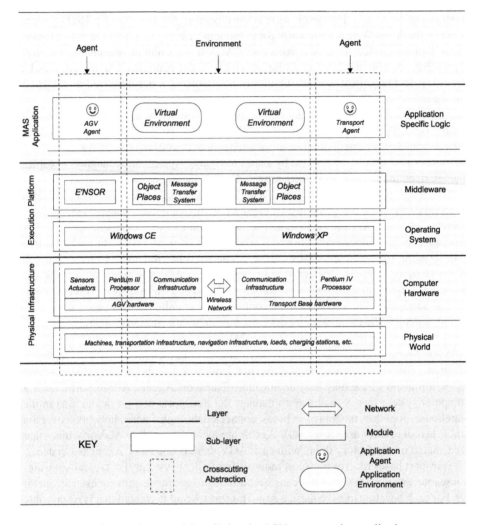

Fig. 4. Three-layer model applied to the AGV transportation application

the physical layout of the factory floor. At each node in the map, a sign in the Virtual Environment represents the cost to a given destination for each outgoing segment. The cost per segment is based on the average time it takes for an AGV to drive over the segment. This cost has a static part that depends on the length and the properties of the segment, and a dynamic part that depends on the recent traffic load on the segment. The Virtual Environment maintains the dynamic part of the cost of a segment according to the time AGVs are delayed on the segment. The AGV Agent perceives the signs in the Virtual Environment, and uses them to determine which segment it will take next. Transport Agents use the Virtual Environment to find AGV agents to assign the transports, and to follow the progress of the assigned transports. To assign the transport, the Transport Agent negotiates with AGV Agents of idle AGVs near to the location of the load. Once the transport is assigned, the awarded AGV handles the transport.

Execution Platform. The *Message Transfer System* enables agents to send messages to each other. The E'nsor software that deals with the low-level control of the AGVs is fully reused. As such the AGV Agents control the movements of the AGVs on a fairly high level.

Since the only physical infrastructure available to the agents is a wireless network to communicate, the Virtual Environment is necessarily distributed. In effect, each AGV and transport base in the system maintains a local Virtual Environment, which is a local manifestation of the Virtual Environment. Synchronization of the state of the local Virtual Environment with local Virtual Environments of neighboring AGVs and transport bases is supported by the ObjectPlaces [15] middleware. The local Virtual Environment uses the ObjectPlaces middleware by sharing objects in a tuplespace-like container, called an *objectplace*. Each AGV and each transport base has one objectplace locally available. Objects in objectplaces on remote AGVs and transport bases can be gathered using a *view*. A view specifies (1) which objectplaces need to be included in the view (e.g. the objectplaces of all AGVs within a specific range), and (2) what objects need to be included in the view (e.g. positions of AGVs).

The AGV software runs on Windows CE, the Transport Base software runs on Windows XP.

Physical Infrastructure. The AGV machines are equipped with a Pentium III processor. AGVs can interact with the physical infrastructure via sensors, actuators and communication infrastructure. Transport bases are equipped with a Pentium IV processor and provides communication infrastructure for Transport Agents to communicate. Communication between AGVs and transport bases happens via a wireless communication network. The factory floor consists of navigation infrastructure for the AGVs, the transportation system infrastructure, the loads that AGVs have to transport, etc.

3.3   TOTA: A Mobile Computing Application

As a final example, we discuss an application that supports visitors of a museum to retrieve information about art pieces, to orientate in the museum, and to meet each other in case of organized groups [5]. This mobile computing application is deployed on top of the TOTA [16] middleware. The application is classified as *dynamic infrastructure* in the classification we have proposed in Sect. 2.2.

Visitors are provided with PDAs, and further it is assumed that the museum is provided with a dense distributed network of computer-based devices, associated with rooms, art pieces, alarm systems, climate conditioning systems, etc. The topology of this network dynamically changes when visitors enter, leave or move through the museum, or also when art pieces are moved, e.g., for special exhibitions. The activities of visitors are typically contextual, i.e., related to the environmental setting (rooms, types of art pieces, members of a group, etc.).

The museum application is build on top of the TOTA middleware (see also Sect. 2.3). TOTA enables the interaction among a network of possibly mobile nodes, each running a local version of TOTA. Each node holds a reference to a limited set of neighboring nodes. The structure of the network is automatically updated by the nodes to support dynamic changes (nodes that enter, move or fail). Entities that live in this dynamic space are able to inject tuples on each node. A TOTA tuple is defined in terms of a content and a propagation rule. Tuples injected in a node are spread by the middleware according to the propagation rule. This rule can also defines how the content of the tuple changes during propagation. In this way it is possible to implement spacial related coordination mechanisms, such as fields, removing the burden of coordination from the agents. A detailed study of TOTA can be found in [16].

Fig. 5 depicts the three-layer model applied for the museum application.

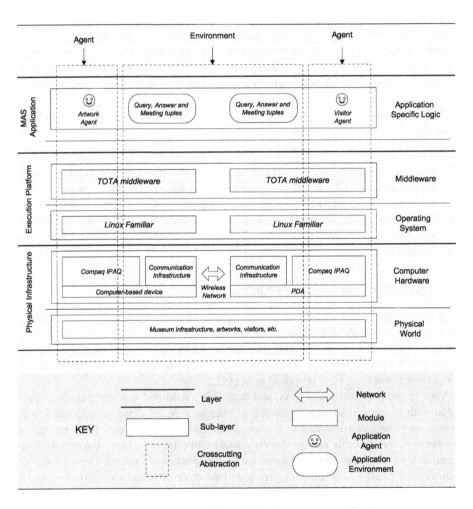

Fig. 5. The three-layer model applied to the museum application

MAS Application Layer. The situated MAS consists of two basic types of agents, Artwork Agents and Visitor Agents that are associated with active entities in the museum. Each agent is able to inject and perceive application specific tuples in their environment. Besides, the MAS consists of system nodes that provide support for tuple propagation (not depicted in Fig. 5). A Visitor Agent can inject a Query tuple in the TOTA infrastructure to indicate his/her interest for a particular art piece. Such a tuple creates a gradient field leading to the queried art piece. The corresponding Artwork Agent react to the Query tuple by injecting an Answer tuple. This Answer tuple can reach a tourist even while he/she is moving. Thus, the gradient fields guide the interested visitors towards the source of interest. If a visitor is interested in locating a specific artwork, its Visitor Agent senses the field generated by that artwork, that guides him toward the artwork [4].

Visitor Agents can also express their interest for a group meeting. Therefore the tourists inject Meeting tuples in the TOTA infrastructure. Tourists then have to follow downhill the gradient field generated by the farther other tourist in the group. This way tourists will move toward each other, to meet in their barycenter room.

Artwork and Visitor Agents are examples of Application Agents, while Query, Answer and Meeting tuples and their corresponding gradient fields are domain specific objects that are part of the Application Environment.

Execution Platform. TOTA is a generic middleware infrastructure that supports mechanisms for the management of field diffusion (i.e. transmission of fields among TOTA peers) and the management of dynamism in the structure of the TOTA network. TOTA offers support to develop application specific tuples as well as agents. For example, the Meeting tuple in the museum application is based on the generic Gradient tuple and Downhill tuple defined by TOTA, and the Artwork Agent is based on the generic AgentInterface also provided by the TOTA middleware.

The museum application runs on the Familar distribution of Linux.

Physical Infrastructure. The museum application is hosted on Compaq IPAQ PDAs, equipped with 802.11b wireless network devices. A similar kind of equipment must be associated with the other nodes of the network, including the artworks that host Artwork Agents.

3.4   Discussion

The three example applications clearly illustrate how agents and the environment cross-cut the three layers of the MAS model. In the MMASS application, the MAS Application (i.e., Application Agents and the Application Environment) runs on top of a dedicated MAS Framework, while in the AGV and the TOTA applicaton the MAS Application directly runs on top of generic middelware infrastructure. In general, applications of the class *distributed infrastructure* are candidates to be supported by generic middleware.

In the MMASS and the AGV application, the Application Agents experience the Application Environment as a common shared entity. In the TOTA example, the Application Agents are aware of the network topology, changes in the context are reflected in

---

[4] We have simplified the explanation of this example, for a detailed discussion see [5].

modifications of perceived gradient fields. An interesting research issue is the relationship between the way Application Agents experience the Application Environment and the underlying executing platform and the physical infrastructure.

All the discussed applications reify elements of the physical environment. All of them also augment this environment with additional elements (gradient fields, marks, etc.) to enable the situated agents to better exploit the environment. Such additional support for indirect interaction has consequences on different layers of the applications, typically the two top layers of the model. This additional support for indirect interaction illustrates how the environment, as a first-order abstraction, can be used creatively in the design and implementation of the problem solution.

4   Conclusion

Generally, the environment is not considered as a first-order abstraction in the MAS research community. Often, the environment in MASs is confused with the infrastructure on which the MAS is deployed. As a consequence, the functionality of the environment is mostly integrated in the MAS in an implicit or ad-hoc manner. To clarify the confusion between the concept of the environment and the infrastructure of the MAS, we have presented a three-layer model for situated MASs. The three-layer model promotes the agents as well as the environment as first-order abstractions. The MAS application logic is located on top, the middle layer consists of the software infrastructure, and the bottom layer of the model represents the physical infrastructure. Agents and the environment crosscut the three layers of the model.

Starting from this model, we have proposed a classification of situated MASs based on the physical infrastructure. We have applied the three-layer model to three applications that represent different classes of the classification.

The major conclusion are:

1. Environment and infrastructure are no synonyms; more than that, the Application Environment as well as the Application Agents exploit infrastructure of the MAS.
2. The Application Environment is a powerful instrument that can be used creatively in the design of a MAS solution, helping to manage the complexity of engineering real-world applications.

An interesting track for future research in to study the relationship between the structure of the environment at the MAS Application layer (as experienced by the Application Agents) and the underlying execution platform and physical infrastructure.

Acknowledgements

This research is supported by the K.U.Leuven research council (AgCo2) and the Flemish Institute for Advancement of Research in Industry (EMC^2), and was partially funded by the Italian Ministry of University and Research within the FIRB project Multichannel Adaptive Information Systems.

References

1. Wooldridge, M., Jennings, N.: Intelligent agents: Theory and practice. The Knowledge Engineering Review **10** (1995) 115–152
2. Ferber, J.: Multi–Agent Systems, An Introduction to Distributed Artificial Intelligence. Addison–Wesley (1999)
3. Weyns, D., Parunak, V., Michel, F., Holvoet, T., Ferber, J.: Environments for Multiagent Systems State-of-the-Art and Research Challenges. In: E4MAS. Volume 3374 of Lecture Notes in Computer Science., Springer (2005)
4. Brueckner, S.: Return from the Ant, PhD Dissertation. Humboldt-Universitat Berlin, Germany (2000)
5. Mamei, M., Zambonelli, F., Leonardi, L.: Programming Pervasive and Mobile Computing Applications with the TOTA Middleware. In: 2nd IEEE International Conference on Pervasive Computing and Communication (Percom2004), IEEE Computer Society (2004)
6. Couloris, G., Dollimore, J., Kindberg, T.: Distributed Systems: Concept and Design (3rd ed.). Addison Wesley (2001)
7. Weyns, D., Steegmans, E., Holvoet, T.: Towards Active Perception in Situated Multi-Agent Systems. Applied Artificial Intelligence **18** (2004) 867–883
8. Sycara, K., Paolucci, M., Velsen, M.V., Giampapa, J.: The RETSINA MAS Infrastructure. Autonomous Agents and Multi-Agent Systems **7** (2003) 29–48
9. Bellifemine, F., Poggi, A., Rimassa, G.: Jade, A FIPA-compliant Agent Framework. 4th International Conference on Practical Application of Intelligent Agents and Multi-Agent Technology (1999)
10. Mamei, M., Zambonelli, F.: Spatial Computing: the TOTA Approach. Self-* Approaches to Distributed Computing, Lecture Notes in Computer Science Hot Topics Series (2005)
11. Bandini, S., Manzoni, S., Vizzari, G.: Situated Cellular Agents: A Model to Simulate Crowding Dynamics. IEICE Transactions on Information and Systems: Special Issues on Cellular Automata **E87-D** (2004) 669–676
12. Schadschneider, A.: Cellular automaton approach to pedestrian dynamics. In: Pedestrian and Evacuation Dynamics. Springer-Verlag (2002) 75–98
13. Bandini, S., Manzoni, S., Simone, C.: Dealing with Space in Multi–Agent Systems: A Model for Situated MAS. In: Proceedings of the First International Joint Conference on Autonomous Agents and Multiagent Systems, ACM Press (2002) 1183–1190
14. Weyns, D., Schelfthout, K., Holvoet, T.: Design and evolution of autonomic application software, DEAS, St. Louis, USA, 2005. (http://www.cs.kuleven.ac.be/~danny/deas_2005.pdf)
15. Schelfthout, K., Weyns, D., Holvoet, T.: Middleware for protocol-based coordination in dynamic networks. In: MPAC '05: Proceedings of the 3rd international workshop on Middleware for pervasive and ad-hoc computing, New York, NY, USA, ACM Press (2005)
16. Mamei, M., Zambonelli, F., Leonardi, L.: Tuples On The Air: A Middleware for Context Aware Computing in Dynamic Networks. In: International ICDCS Workshop on Mobile Computing, IEEE Computer Society (2003)

Holonic Modeling of Environments for Situated Multi-agent Systems

Sebastian Rodriguez, Vincent Hilaire, and Abder Koukam

Université de Technologie de Belfort-Montbéliard,
Systems and Transports Laboratory,
90010 Belfort Cedex, France
Tel.: +33 384 583 837, Fax: +33 384 583 342
sebastian.rodriguez@utbm.fr

Abstract. In a Multi-Agent Based Simulation (MABS) special attention must go to the analysis, modeling and implementation of the environment. Environments for simulation of real world problems may be complex. Seeing the environment as a monolithic structure only reduces our capacity to handle large scale, real-world environments. In order to support this type of environments, we propose the use of an holonic perspective to represent the environment and the agents. In our approach, agents and environment are represented by holons. The environment defines a holarchy. Each agent belong to a specific holon in this holarchy following its needs.

Keywords: Holonic modeling, environment of MAS, simulation.

1 Introduction

It is generally accepted that multi-agent systems (MAS) operate within an environment [23, 19]. In a Multi-Agent Based Simulation (MABS), special attention must go to the analysis, modeling and implementation of the environment [20]. Indeed, it simulates a real-world environment and agents represent acting entities in this environment.

Environments for simulation of real world problems may be complex. Indeed, a real world problem, as the one we present in this paper, is frequently characterized by an environment composed of heterogeneous and numerous entities. However, current practice of MABS modeling and simulation tends to consider the environment as a monolithic structure. This approach, even if useful in certain situations, limits our capability to develop large scale agent based simulations.

In order to support large scale, real world environments, we propose to use a holonic perspective to represent both the environment and the agents. The interest of a holonic view of the environment is that it provides a scalable multi-level model to express real-world environments. The designer is able to represent different levels of detail, from a high-level coarse-grained view of the system to a low-level fine-grained one.

D. Weyns, H. Van Dyke Parunak, and F. Michel (Eds.): E4MAS 2005, LNAI 3830, pp. 18–31, 2006.

Defined by Koestler [15] as entities that can not be considered as wholes nor parts in an absolute sense, Holons provide a possible answer to this problem. According to Koestler, a holon is a self-similar structure that consists of several holons as sub-structures. The hierarchical structure composed of holons is called holarchy. Holonic systems have already been used to model a wide range of systems, Manufacturing systems [3] Transportation [4], Adaptive Mesh Problem[30] and Cooperative work[1], to mention a few.

In order to show how holonic concepts can be applied to model and simulate large environments, we present in this paper a holonic based model for the traffic network of an important industrial plant of the east of France. The Peugeot SA (PSA) plant is located near two towns and directly connected to the highway and the railway. Within a surface of over 250 hectares, the plant produces more than 1700 cars per day. The plant can be seen as a small town with a high density of traffic that needs to be regulated. A simulator was built to detect possible bottle-necks and evaluate the plant's design. In order to produce a scalable and reliable traffic simulator, we must carefully model this environment to be both efficient and realist. The results we obtained from the simulations aimed first at identifying groups of buildings with an important product exchange and second at evaluate plant structure modifications. These results are not in the scope of this paper so we do not present them.

The use of holons to model both, environment and agents, is the natural consequence of seeing the environment as an active entity, and not merely as a passive component modified by agents at will. The environment is seen as an active entity, capable of interacting with agents and able to enforce the environmental principles [23].

The paper is organized as follows : section 2 introduces our framework for holonic multi-agent systems. Section 3 discusses the holonic environment model and simulation principles. Section 4 presents related works and, eventually, section 5 concludes.

2   Holonic Multi-agent Systems

Before discussing the holonic model of the environment, we introduce in this section the terminology used to address the holonic structure and the composition of holons. More importantly, we present a brief overview of our holonic framework [30].

We distinguish two main aspects that overlap in a holon. First, the status of the members (or sub-holons) in the composition of the higher level holon (or super-holon). Second, the coordination mechanism used by the sub-holons to achieve a goal or task. In other terms, the interactions undertaken by the member to exchange information, distribute tasks, etc.

In order to provide a clear distinction between these two aspects, the framework is based upon an organizational approach. While the framework offers means to model both aspects, in this paper we will limit the discussion to the organization used to model the structure of a super-holon. This organization will

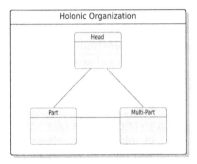

Fig. 1. Holonic Organization

provide a terminology that make it easier to discuss about the holonic model proposed for the environment in the next section.

The behavior of the members of a holon and their interactions are described in terms of roles. These roles represent the "status" of the holon inside a specific super-holon. From the super-holon's point of view, a member may play three roles : Head, Part and Multi-Part. To model this organization we have selected the Role-Interaction-Organization (RIO) model [14]. The choice of RIO is justified by the possibilities offered by this approach (eg animation and proofs). This organization, called *Holonic Organization*, is presented using a RIO diagram in figure 1.

Our approach is based in an HMAS as a moderated group, where the head represents the members of its super-holon with the outside world [9]. Different ways to select this representative can be stated, eg. voting, authority, predefined holon, etc. However, selecting the most suited one remains problem dependent.

In a complex system, multiple holarchies can be identified. A holarchy should be seen as a "loose hierarchy" in the sense of [33], where there are no subordination relation.

As the representative, the holon plays the *Head* role. According to the objective and rules of the super-holon, the *Head*'s responsibilities and rights may range from merely administrative tasks to being able to take decisions concerning all members. The head role may be played by several member simultaneously.

Members not playing the *Head* role may play either the *Part* or *MultiPart* role. The *Part* role is played by those members belonging to a single super-holon and the *MultiPart* role by those members belonging to more than one holon. These members may confer a certain degree of authority to the *Head* role player when they join the super-holon. Its autonomy is then reduced because of its obligations towards the super-holon. The degree of this autonomy lost may variate according to the holon's purpose.

The *MultiPart* Role is a special case of the Part Role. This role is played by holons belonging to more than one Holon. Interesting possibilities are available when a holon is shared. For instance, we can now see this holon as a gateway between super-holons, allowing message forwarding. Imagine that holon a is

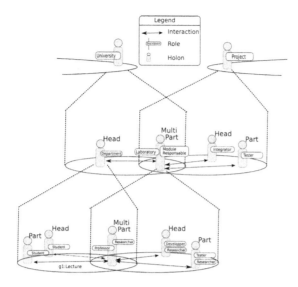

Fig. 2. University Example holarchy

shared by h_1 and h_2. Suppose that h_1 confers to a the authority to accept new members coming from h_2. Now a can not only forward requests among members of different super-holons, but also act as an ambassador of h_1 inside h_2. This can be used to reduce the administrative load to the Head of h_1, but also to provide means for members of h_2 to enter a new holarchy. Other possibilities are present like trust mechanism based on recommendations of shared members, translation of messages in different languages, etc.

These roles represent a generic framework describing high-level behaviors and interactions between components of Holonic Multi-Agent System.

Lets consider the case of an university to illustrate the use of these roles. If we consider the university as a holon, it can be model as being composed of *Departments* and *Research Laboratories*. In turn a department holon can be consider to be composed of professors and students. A professor may, in addition to the lectures given inside a department, be a member of a research laboratory. In this case, the professor is a *MultiPart* role player. This holarchy is depicted in figure 2. "Pawns" represent holons / agents. Each pawn / holon may be decomposed by dashed lines into sub-holons. We show in superscript the holonic roles and in subscript the application dependent roles.

The way member will interact with holons outside its super-holon should be specified in the holon's creation. Depending on the goal of the holon different ways to interact with the "outside" world are possible. It is important to keep in mind, that *Head*, *Part* and *MultiPart* are roles and they describe the "status" and interactions of members of a holon. Evenmore, holons may change the roles they play at runtime.

This framework has been formalized using the RIO Model and properties concerning self-organization have been prooven [31]. The formal specification

is based upon the OZS formalism [10], which is a component of the RIO
model.

3   A Holonic Model for Traffic Networks

Multi-agent Systems operate within an environment [23, 19], and therefore, in
an Agent Based Simulation (MABS) special attention must go to the analysis,
modeling and implementation of the environment [20].

We propose the use of holarchies for the modelling of environments. In the
PSA example we want to simulate the traffic within the plant. The environment
of this simulation is defined by the topology of the plant. The agents will be the
different vehicles driving through the plant.

The environment will be represented by a holarchy. This holarchy defines
the organizational and topological structure in which agents will evolve. Each
environmental holon will enforce contextual physical laws and represent a specific
granularity level of the real plant topology. This holarchy is predefined as it
represents the real plant environment. Indeed, the latter can't evolve and the
physical laws we need to enforce are known *a priori*.

3.1   Environment Model

In order to represent the geographical environment of the plant as a holarchy,
we have to find recursive concepts which represent the plant's components. The
concepts we have chosen are described in the figures 3 and 4.

Figure 3 shows that a road is divided into links. A link represents a one way
lane of a road. A segment is composed of two exchange points, called input and
output exchange points, and, at least, one link. Exchange points let vehicles pass
from one link to the other. And they are always shared by at least two segments.

Figure 4 presents the hierarchical decomposition of the environment of the
plant. We can see that the industrial plant is composed of a set of zones, that

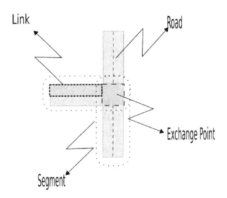

Fig. 3. Roads, Segments, Links and Exchange Points

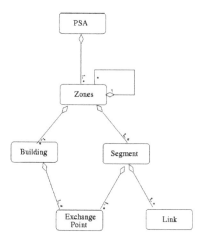

Fig. 4. Conceptual view of the plant

contain Buildings and Segments. Buildings and Segments can also communicate through shared exchange points. Usually, an exchange point represents a cross-road, but it can also represent an entrance used by trucks to access buildings. A zone may also be recursively decomposed into smaller zones.

ExchangePoints are always shared by two segments or one segment and a building. As we can see the exchange point is a "special" role from the "holonic point of view" since the role is actually shared by more than one super-holon (Segment or Building) by definition.

Such a hierarchical decomposition of environments is based on the idea of Simon, who defines a nearly decomposable system (NDS) [33] as presenting two distinctive characteristics. The first characteristic is that the short-run behavior of each sub-component is approximately independent of the short-run behavior of other components. The second characteristic is that in the long run the behavior of any one of the components depends only in an aggregate way on the behavior of the other components. Based on this definition, we can define a Nearly Decomposable Environment (NDE) as the environment where we can find a decomposition that respects the propositions stated for NDS. Traffic Networks can be seen as a NDE, since in the short-run the behavior and phenomena that may exhibit a zone of the traffic remains independent of the behavior of other components. Indeed, phenomena like congestion, jams and others, remain localized in a zone before spreading.

This model presents several advantages when compared to a global representation. First, no size limit is imposed by the model. This enables us to use the same environment decomposition to simulate the traffic inside a city or a (much) smaller industrial plant. If required, semantic information can be introduced; so instead of zones, we will represent quarters, blocks, etc. [7].

Another interesting characteristic is that all necessary information to simulate the traffic inside a link is local (other vehicles, roadsigns, etc). This makes the model easier to distribute in a network and leaves the door open to Real-Time applications as well as Virtual Reality implementations.

In this work we have concentrated in the traffic network, but the decomposition of the environment may continue to provide a higher level of detail. For instance, a building can be decomposed in Rooms and Exchange Points(doors). The model provides a simple and flexible way to decompose different types of environments. Even more, it offers means for these different environments to coexist in the same simulation.

In situated MAS, the environment contains its own processes that may change its state independently of the embedded agents [36]. These active processes are in charge of enforcing the environmental laws (in our case physical laws). In large scale simulation, hundreds, or even thousands, of agents may be present in the environment. As a possible solution, we advocate for the decomposition of the environment into regions capable of locally computing the proper reaction to agents' influences. However, each region is not self-contained but approximately independent in the "short-run". In the long run these region must be considered as parts of a whole, larger environment. This basic idea has been applied, in this paper, to the modeling of a traffic network.

Holonic MAS can be used to model and implement such an environment. This allow us to maintain multiple levels of granularity and to see each one of these regions as a holon.

On the other hand, this type of decomposition imposes a highly hierarchical and decentralized representation of the environment. This could present some disadvantages when the environment presents some global "variables" accessible to all agents.

3.2   Agent-Environment Interaction

The need to make a clear distinction between the body and the mind of the agent has been acknowledged by many MAS researchers [37, 19]. In this section we describe how this distinction is taken into account and how the agent interacts with the environment it is in.

Inside an industrial plant, different types of vehicles coexist (cars, trucks, etc). Furthermore, the drivers do not necessarily behave the same way. In an unorganized traffic scenario, the psychology of the driver is of great importance [24]. In our model, the driver is able to change a set of variable that affect the vehicle's state. The environment ensures that the environmental rules are respected. The model of a vehicle, and the relation between *body* and environment, has been influenced by the work presented in [19]. We consider the vehicle as composed of three fairly independent modules, figure 5.

Physical Characteristics. Contains physic related contants like maximal speed, maximal acceleration/deceleration, etc. and a set of variable that the agent can modify at will, like acceleration.

Control Logic. Provides a façade that maps driving logic commands, like "speedup", to values that can be assigned to the physic characteristics variables.

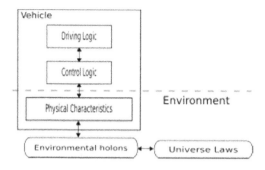

Fig. 5. Vehicle Model

Driving Logic. Encapsulates the actual behavior of the agent, including Route Planning.

In the real world, the driver (encapsulated in the *DrivingLogic*) does not control the vehicle's speed directly. He actually changes the speed by accelerating/decelerating. This fact is modeled by letting the driver modify only certain variables of the *PhysicalCharacteristics*. These variable are later used by the environment to adjust the vehicle's speed according to the environmental principles.

The *PhysicalCharacteristics* Module presents a standardized representation of the Vehicle's state to the environment. Every simulation loop the environment will take in consideration this state, the environment's state and the environmental principles, and generates the appropriate responses.

In order to provide an easier implementation of different driving logic, the *ControlLogic* module translates driving commands, like "speedup" or "slow down", into the precise values of acceleration. This approach enable a rapid prototyping of different behaviors using a high-level description.

Vehicles can query their current link to obtain information about road sign, traffic lights, maximal speed, etc. They can also request information about adjacent link to the exchange points.

3.3 Simulation

As presented in section 3.1, the environment is modeled as a holarchy. Each environmental holon represents a specific context. In the PSA example, it is a specific place in the plant. These places have different granularity levels according to their level in the holarchy. During the simulation, vehicle agents move from one holon to another and the granularity is chosen using execution or simulation constraints.

The dynamic choice of the environment granularity level during the simulation must be transparent for the agents. In order to do this, agents use our holonic framework and specifically *ExchangePoint* holons which enables the communication between holons of the same level and connected in the plant

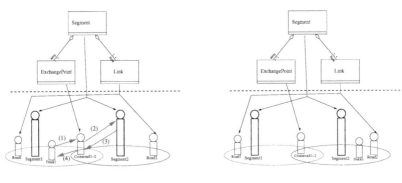

Fig. 6.   **Fig. 7.**

topology. Figure 6 describes the sequence of messages exchanged between the *ExchangePoint*, a vehicle and the Segment's Head. The truck agent is moving along segment 1 and requests the exchange point to forward a merging request. The exchange point forwards the request and receives a reply. The reply is then forwarded to the truck. If the reply is positive the truck can merge with the segment 2 holon as shown in figure 7. These interaction sequences are a mean to represent the influence/reaction model [8]. Indeed, the agent emits influences in asking to merge with a specific holon. The environment is able to determine the eventual answer according to jams or environment properties.

This approach enables one to describe the environment with multiple levels of granularity examples are given in figures 8 and 9. In figure 8 we can view the simulation of several roads, crossroads and buildings. The figure 9 is a more fine grain simulation of a crossroad. Nevertheless the simulation of the rest of the plant is always running in the two cases. Each level stores pertinent information

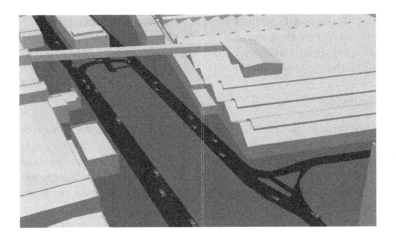

Fig. 8. View of different crossroads and buildings

Fig. 9. Crossroad close up

about the topology, characteristics and environment laws such as adjacent links, road signs, etc. These different granularity levels can coexist during a simulation. The advantages of this approach is threefold. First, it enables the decomposition of the complexity of the environment in an holarchy of components with only pertinent aspects at each level. Second during the simulation the pertinent level of detail can be automatically chosen to be more efficient.

Finally, in order to support real-time application with high density of agents, the environmental rules can be assigned by zone or region. This lets us regulate the behavior of the system according to the simulation requirements. For instance, in a Virtual Reality simulation, a high level of precision is required in the surroundings of the avatar[1]. On the other hand, in distant regions, certain environmental rules can be relaxed or annulled, such as collision detection.

4 Related Works

Considering the importance of traffic flow simulation, it is not surprising that a vast number of models and simulators can be found. Although presenting a full survey of all these approaches is out of the scope of this work, in this section we present some of the most important models and their implementations.

Mainly two different approaches are used in traffic simulation, Macro and Micro Simulations. Macroscopic models [13] describe the traffic from its observable global behavior. They describe the system with a set of global variables like flow rate, flow density and average speed. Such macroscopic representations

---

[1] Virtual representation of the human user.

are based on hydrodynamic theory [18, 27] and queuing models [12, 38]. One important advantage of this type of model is the low computational resource required (compared to microscopic simulation). On the other hand, these models ignore any individual behavior. Various simulators, like NETSTREAM [35] or METANET [16] implement macroscopic models.

Microscopic models, on the other hand, intend to provide a precise simulation of the traffic state. Different approaches have been proposed, Cellular Automata [29, 22, 17], Particles [21], etc. It is in this type of models that ABS has emerged as a powerful tool for traffic simulation[28, 5, 2, 26, 32]. ABS offer the possibility to introduce individual behaviors, and simulate how their difference may influence traffic flow [24].

The Smartest project [34] provides an extensive survey of microscopic traffic simulators. These simulators where conceived with different purposes and aiming different types of traffic and networks (Urban, Free way, etc.).

The main difference between these simulators and our approach is in the scope and intentions of the developed systems. While those systems concentrate solely on traffic and its analysis, we include the possibility to analyze and understand its impact in depending activities. Even if the plants objects is to optimize its production traffic lays in the very heart of the system. Our model offers a modular design letting the responsibles concentrate in specific aspects without neglecting the consequences of their modifications in the infrastructure and/or functioning of the site.

5   Conclusion

In this paper we have presented an approach for the modelling of environments for situated multi-agent based simulations. The modelling is based upon holonic concepts. The environment is represented as a holarchy. Each holon models an environment part which may be decomposed in sub-entities. This approach presents several advantages when compared to a global representation.

First, no size limit is imposed by the model, this enables us to use the same environment decomposition to simulate the traffic inside a city or a (much) smaller industrial plant.

Second, the granularity may evolve during the simulation according to performance and precision needs.

Third, the distribution on a network of the simulation can be done easily by choosing which part of the holarchy could be executed where [30].

Using this approach we have simulated the traffic within the PSA plant and we have observed plant emergent properties such as functional exchange between buildings, traffic density, jams, etc. However, using the concept of Nearly Decomposable Environment, we can identify other types of environments that result as suitable candidates for a holonic modeling. In general terms, we can say that a specific environment is suitable for a holonic modeling, if we can divide the "global" environment into sub-components where the environmental processes can locally compute the response of the environment to agents actions / influences.

This type of hierarchical decomposition of the environment has already been successfully applied in several applications, mainly in the field of Virtual Reality [6, 7]. We can find a set of self-similar components to describe the environment in the model proposed by [25].

Future research will consider new simulation cases in order to extract a methodology from our approach. We are developping a formal specification model for the concepts we have presented which may enable verification and validation [31]. An API in JAVA using the MadKit platform [11] has been developed. In addition, we intend to further deepen the concepts of NDS and NDE for situated MAS simulation.

Acknowledgments

The authors would like to thank the three anonymous reviewers of the E4MAS workshop for their valuable remarks that helped improve the presentation of this work. This paper has also benefited from the discussions with other members of the SeT Laboratory, specially Nicolas Gaud.

References

1. Emmanuel Adam, Rene Mandiau, and Christophe Kolski. *Une Méthode de modelisation et de conception d'organizations Multi-Agents holoniques*, chapter 2, pages 41–75. Hermes, 2002.

2. E. Bonakdarian, J. Cremer, J. Kearney, and P. Willemsen. Generation of ambient traffic for real-time driving simulation. In *1998 Image Conference*, pages 123–133, August 1998.

3. H. Van Brussel, J. Wyns, P. Valckenaers, L. Bongaerts, and P. Peeters. Reference architecture for holonic manufacturing systems: Prosa, 1998.

4. H.-J. Bürckert, K. Fischer, and G.Vierke. Transportation scheduling with holonic mas - the teletruck approach. In *Proceedings of the Third International Conference on Practical Applications of Intelligent Agents and Multiagents*, 1998.

5. Nurham Cetin, Adrian Burri, and Kai Nagel. A large-scale agent-based traffic microsimulation based on queue model. In Tristan Chevroulet and Aymeric Sevestre, editors, *Swiss Transport Research Conference 2003 - STRC 03*, 2003.

6. Stéphane Donikian. How introduce life in virtual environments: a urban environment modeling system for driving simulation. Technical report, Institut de Recherche en Informatique de Toulouse, octobre 1996.

7. N. Farenc, R. Boulic, and D. Thalmann. An informed environment dedicated to the simulation of virtual humans in urban context. In *Proc. Eurographics '99*, Milano, Italy, 1999.

8. Jacques Ferber and Jean-Pierre Müller. Influences and reaction: a model of situated multiagent systems. In *ICMAS'96*, december 1996.

9. Christian Gerber, Jörg H. Siekmann, and Gero Vierke. Holonic multi-agent systems. Technical Report DFKI-RR-99-03, Deutsches Forschungszentrum für Künztliche Inteligenz - GmbH, Postfach 20 80, 67608 Kaiserslautern, FRG, May 1999.

10. Pablo Gruer, Vincent Hilaire, Abder Koukam, and P. Rovarini. Heterogeneous formal specification based on object-z and statecharts: semantics and verification. *Journal of Systems and Software*, 70(1-2):95–105, 2004.
11. Olivier Gutknecht and Jacques Ferber. The MADKIT agent platform architecture. In *Agents Workshop on Infrastructure for Multi-Agent Systems*, pages 48–55, 2000.
12. D. Heidemann. A queuing theory approach to speed-flow-density relationships. In *Proceedings of the 13th International Symposium on Transportation and Traffic Theory*, pages 103–118, Lyon - France, July 1996.
13. Dirk Helbing. Theoretical foundation of macroscopicnext term traffic models. *Physica A: Statistical and Theoretical Physics*, 219:375–390, 1995.
14. Vincent Hilaire, Abder Koukam, Pablo Gruer, and Jean-Pierre Müller. Formal specification and prototyping of multi-agent systems. In Andrea Omicini, Robert Tolksdorf, and Franco Zambonelli, editors, *Engineering Societies in the Agents' World*, number 1972 in Lecture Notes in Artificial Intelligence. Springer Verlag, 2000.
15. Arthur Koestler. *The Ghost in the Machine*. Hutchinson, 1967.
16. A. Kotsialos, M. Papageorgiou, C. Diakaki, Y. Pavlis, and F. Middelham. Traffic flow modeling of large-scale motorway networks using the macroscopic modeling tool metanet. *Intelligent Transportation Systems, IEEE Transactions*, 3(4):282–292, 2002.
17. Hideki Kozuka, Yohsuke Matsui, and Hitoshi Kanoh. Traffic flow simulation using cellular automata under non-equilibrium environment. In *IEEE International Conference on Systems, Man, and Cybernetics (SMC'2001)*, pages 1341–1345, October 2001.
18. M. J. Lighthill and G. B. Whitham. On kinematic waves. ii. a theory of traffic flow on long crowded roads. In *Proc. Roy. Soc. London. Ser. A. 229*, pages 317–345, 1955.
19. Fabien Michel. *Formalisme, méthodologie et outils pour la modélisation et la simulation de systèmes multi-agents*. PhD thesis, Université de Montpellier II, 2004.
20. Fabien Michel, Abdelkader Gouaich, and Jacques Ferber. Weak interaction and strong interaction in agent based simulations. In *The 4th Workshop on Multi-Agent Based Simulation MABS'03 at AAMAS 2003*, Melbourne, Australia, july 2003. to appear in a LNCS volume.
21. Kai Nagel. Particle hopping models and traffic flow theory. *Physical Review E.*, 53(5):4655–4672, 1996.
22. Kia Nagel. Traffic at the edge of chaos. In *Artificial Life IV*, pages 222–235, 1994.
23. James Odell, H. Van Dyke Parunak, Mitch Fleischer, and Sven Breuckner. Modeling agents and their environment. In F. Giunchiglia, James Odell, and Gerhard Weiss, editors, *Agent-Oriented Software Engineering (AOSE) III*, volume 2585 of *Lecture Notes on Computer Science*, pages 16–31, 2002.
24. Praveen Paruchuri, Alok Reddy Pullalarevu, and Kamalakar Karlapalem. Multi agent simulation of unorganized traffic. In *International Joint Conference on Autonomous Agents and Multi-Agent Systems*, Bologna, Italy, 2002. ACM.
25. L.S.C. Pun-Cheng. A new face-entity concept for modeling urban morphology. *Journal of Urban and Regional Information Systems Association*, 12(3), 2000.
26. Bryan Raney and Kai Nagel. An agent-based microsimulation model of swiss travel: First results. In Tristan Chevroulet and Aymeric Sevestre, editors, *Swiss Transport Research Conference 2003 - STRC 03*, March 2003.
27. M. Rascle. An improved macroscopic model of traffic flow: Derivation and links with the lighthill-whitham model. *Mathematical and Computer Modelling*, 35:581–590, 2002.

28. Michel Resnick. *Turtles, Termites and Traffic Jams. Explorations in massively parallel microworlds.* MIT Press, 1997.
29. M Rickert, K Nagel, M Schreckenberg, and A Latour. Two lane traffic simulations using cellular automata. *Physica A*, 1996.
30. Sebastian Rodriguez, Vincent Hilaire, and Abderrafiâa Koukam. Towards a methodological framework for holonic multi-agent systems. In *Fourth International Workshop of Engineering Societies in the Agents World*, Imperial College London, UK (EU), 29-31 October 2003.
31. Sebastian Rodriguez, Vincent Hilaire, and Abderrafiâa Koukam. Fomal specification of holonic multi-agent system framework. In *Intelligent Agents in Computing Systems - The Agent Days in Atlanta*, Lecture Notes in Computer Science. Springer-Verlag, 2005. to appear.
32. Paulo C. M. Silva. Buses in miroscopic traffic simulation models. Technical report, University of London, Centre for Transport Studies, May 1997.
33. Herbert A. Simon. *The Science of Artificial.* MIT Press, Cambridge, Massachusetts, 3rd edition, 1996.
34. Project Smarttest. Smartest. final report. Technical report, Smartest Project, 2000.
35. E. Teramoto, M. Baba, H. Mori, Y. Asano, and H. Morita. Netstream: traffic simulator for evaluating traffic information systems. In *IEEE Conference on Intelligent Transportation System*, pages 484 – 489, Boston, MA USA, 1997.
36. Danny Weyns, H. Van Dyke Parunak, Fabien Michel, Tom Holvoet, and Jacques Ferber. Environments for multiagent systems: State-of-the-art and research challenges. Technical report, The First International Workshop on Environments for Multiagent Systems, 2004.
37. T. Wittig. *ARCHON: An Architecture for Multi-Agent Systems.* Ellis Horwood, 1992.
38. Tom Van Woensel and Nico Vandaele. Queuing models for uninterrupted traffic flows. In *PROCEEDINGS of the 13th Mini-EURO Conference. Handling Uncertainty in the Analysis of Traffic and Transportation Systems*, Bari, Italy, June 2002.

An Environment-Based Methodology
to Design Reactive Multi-agent Systems
for Problem Solving

Olivier Simonin and Franck Gechter

Laboratoire SeT (Systèmes et Transports),
Université de Technologie de Belfort-Montbéliard,
90010 Belfort cedex, France
{olivier.simonin, franck.gechter}@utbm.fr
http://set.utbm.fr/membres/simonin/

Abstract. Even if the multi-agent paradigm has been evolving for fifteen years, the development of concrete methods for problem solving remains a major challenge. This paper focuses on reactive multi-agent systems because they provide interesting properties such as adaptability and robustness. In particular, the role of the environment, which is effectively where the system computes and communicates, is studied. From this analysis a methodology to design or engineer reactive systems is introduced. Our approach is based on the representation of the problem's constraints considered as perturbations to stabilize. Agents are then defined, in the second place, as a means of regulating the perturbations. Finally, the relevancy of our proposition is justified through the development of two solving models applied to real and complex problems.

1 Introduction

Even if the multi-agent paradigm has been evolving for fifteen years, the development of concrete methods for problem solving remains a major challenge. This paper addresses this problem by proposing a methodology aimed at designing reactive multi-agent solutions. Such systems rely on reactive agents, which are simple entities that behave following their perceptions [14]. We focus on reactive systems because they present interesting features such as self-organization/emergent phenomena, robustness, adaptability, simplicity and redundancy of the agents (and consequently low cost agent design). It has been shown that this approach is efficient for tackling complex problems such as life-systems simulation/study [31] [21] [26], cooperation of situated agents/robots [38] [27] [9] [26], problem/game solving [8] [10],...

However, it is difficult to extract a generic method to build reactive-based solutions facing (distributed) problems. This difficulty is due to the complexity of such systems where agents and interactions are numerous and where global dynamics are complex to control and/or predict.

As it has been emphasized in [31] and [28], the environment plays an important role in reactive multi-agent systems (MAS). It is the main place where

D. Weyns, H. Van Dyke Parunak, and F. Michel (Eds.): E4MAS 2005, LNAI 3830, pp. 32–49, 2006.
© Springer-Verlag Berlin Heidelberg 2006

the system computes, builds and communicates. In the problem-solving framework, it is clear that one reactive agent can neither handle a representation of the problem nor compute its solution. The resolution is obtained from numerous agent-agent and agent-environment interactions [14] [31] [21]. Agent interactions are reactions to perceptions, they participate directly in the solving processes, but they do not provide a means to express the problem. So, the representation of the problem can only be defined through the environment model. In this paper we re-examine the role played by each element in collective systems, by focusing on the environment. This work is motivated by the necessity of clarifying the common points used in different environment-based techniques and reactive agent-based MAS. Thus we present a synthetic view on reactive systems by considering existing collective solving systems such as the pheromone-based approach and the eco-resolution model. This analysis allows us to propose a methodology aimed at building environment-based solving systems.

The proposed methodology establishes the link between the representation of the problem, expressed as environmental constraints, and agent behaviors, which are regulation items of the environmental perturbations. This method contrasts with classical approaches that involve defining agents and interactions by following the expected organization (as proposed in [27] [28]). In our case, agents are defined in the second place, and build as regulation processes depending on the problem model. The environment is clearly defined as a first-class entity of the multiagent system ([42] as shown the importance of such an approach in multiagent conception).

The paper is structured as follows. Sect.2 presents a re-examination of reactive MAS from an automatic control point of view and classical collective models are analyzed. In Sect.3 the four main points of the methodology are introduced, first with a general point of view and then in detail considering a concrete use. This section ends with a comparison to related work. Section 4 illustrates the methodology through two examples of applications: the satisfaction-altruism model for decentralized cooperation between situated agents and a Physics based model for localization and target tracking. Finally, in Sect.5, we conclude on the proposed methodology and present some future work.

2   Examination of Collective Processes

2.1   Expression of Reactive MAS Within the Automatic Control Approach

As opposed to the socio or bio inspired approaches, we propose a more pragmatic engineering method for defining reactive agent-based problem solving systems. Our approach is closely tied to the standard regulation loop defined in automatic control. The goal of the problem solving is to build a solution, stable in time and space, considering the formulation of a problem that has its own topology (i.e. how the problem is structured in space) and dynamics (i.e. how the problem evolves). Thus, the MAS can be considered as a regulation (or filtering) process. As a consequence, solving a problem leads to defining the parameters of the

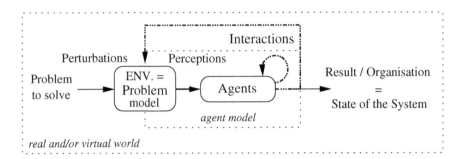

Fig. 1. Environment based solving principle

regulation loop in order to obtain a stable output (solution level) considering the variations of the input (problem level).

The environment is defined as the input layer of the regulation loop, see Fig.1. It translates the variations and the topology of the problem and presents them to the agents. The organization is the output layer of the system. It represents the state of the system on a spatial and temporal level. The regulation mechanism is defined by the agents' actions and their interactions. These interactions have been divided into two categories. The first characterizes the agent-agent interactions, which compose the direct branch of the regulation loop that is considered, in automatic control, as amplification. This can be compared to positive feedback defined by Muller in [28]. The second, called the negative feedback, is the regulation loop carried out by agents-environment interactions (these different kind of interactions are detailed in Sect. 3.2). The environment is modified by both the problem and regulation dynamics.

2.2   Analysis of Classical Collective Solving Models

In this section, we re-examine two widespread techniques of collective problem solving: the eco-resolution and the pheromone-based models. This re-examination considers the automatic control point of view exposed in the previous paragraph. The goal of this section is to evaluate the place of the environment and of the regulation mechanisms in these methods.

Eco-Resolution. The eco-resolution model [13][8] relies on the agentification of all the elements of the problem. As a consequence the environment is divided in a set of agents (for instance in the Towers of Hanoï problem, the disks and the stacks will be defined as agents). Each agent is defined by the same reactive model (the eco-agent model). An eco-agent has only 3 possible states: satisfied, dissatisfied and attacked. It has 3 possible behaviors: (i) searching a place to flee when attacked, (ii) attacking the agents that hinder its actions, (iii) running an action to be satisfied. The resolution relies on the fact that when an agent is attacked, it has to search a place to flee. If such a place does not exist it has to attack its hinderers.

In this model each agent has to be satisfied to consider the problem solved, corresponding to the achieving of a stable state (the solution representation). An agent tries to move when attacked by another agent. This attack represents a perturbation in the environment. The model then ensures that the attacked agent tries to flee in order to regulate this perturbation (local interaction). If this locate regulation cannot be performed, due to the presence of hinderers, the attacked agent propagates the perturbation by attacking new agents. This "recursive" process corresponds to the generation of a collective process, i.e. a solving process at the macro level, leading to the whole solution (details in [13]). However, this model can presents instable processes such as loops or oscillations. It is then necessary to enhance agents' perceptions and/or introduce knowledge on the system state, as presented in [10] for the N-Puzzle solving.

Pheromone-Based Algorithms. The well known pheromones-based algorithms are typical environment-based solving systems. Agents drop artificial pheromones in the environment in order to create shared information (these pheromones are chemical substances diffusing and evaporating). Here we illustrate the principle on the construction of an optimal path between a nest and a resource place. The problem is represented by the nest, the resource and an obstacle that define two possible paths of different length (as presented in [7]). Agents drop pheromones as they move, then the pheromone is initially distributed along the two possible paths (probabilities to choose one of them are equal). For the agents this repartition of pheromones represents an absence of information. The resulting state of the environment, and consequently of the problem, can be considered to be totally perturbed.

In order to allow the emergence of the optimal path, a reinforcement mechanism is defined by a simple agent behavior. Agents move preferentially towards directions with the maximum amount of pheromones. Consequently ants concentrate pheromones on the shortest path (details in [7]). This concentration involves a reduction of the initial perturbation of the environment state. The reinforcement mechanism leads, in time, to a stable state where only one path is built and used between the nest and the resource. This state is characterized by equilibrium between the problem dynamics, made material by the diffusion/evaporation phenomenon, and the resolution dynamics induced by the agents.

In the case of pheromone-based algorithms, the emergent organization is particular. It is not included in the agents states but directly in the environment itself (areas concentrating pheromones).

3   Methodology for Building an Environment-Based Solving System

3.1   General Description of the Methodology

Existing environment-based solving techniques are generally presented by referring to a set of implicit or explicit concepts (such as biological behaviors, emergence principles, regulation loops, etc). Defining a methodology allows to clarify the implicit methods used for the construction of many environment-based systems. The two previous sections establish the role of the environment that can be considered as the place where the problem constraints are expressed and the multi-level resolution of these constraints thanks to agent behaviors. This analysis leads to define a conception methodology for environment-based solving processes, which is composed of four main steps:

1. **Defining the problem's model, i.e. the environment.** It has to represent the problem to solve on both a topological and dynamic level (details in next section). Modeling an environment implies also for the designer to define almost an environment structure (for spatial representation, which can be discrete or continuous) and the laws that govern its dynamics (as analyzed in [42]). Note that the environment can be totally a virtual one or include elements of the real world. In this last case, the environment can be considered as an enhanced real world.

2. **Defining agent perceptions.** Agents must be able to perceive the environmental perturbations modeling the problem. They have to detect states and dynamics that are considered as problem constraints, in order to solve them. Means of perception abilities are tackled in the next section.

3. **Defining agents' interaction mechanisms** in order *to reduce the perturbations*. These mechanisms are defined in 3 levels:
   (a) Provide individual and local reactions to the perceived constraints, i.e. actions from agent to the environment.
   (b) If these local actions are inefficient in some situations or can lead to conflicts, even considering their combination, provide direct interactions (agent-agent(s)) that enable cooperative processes. They have to reduce conflicts/constraints perceived by agents and to perform complex tasks (involving several agents).
   (c) Provide actions to regulate the previous processes (local and cooperative) when they present instability risks (amplifications, loops, etc..)

4. **Measuring/Observing the result as an emergent structure**, in terms of agents (position, dynamics,...) or in terms of environment (structure, topology,...) as defined in [29]. This structure is the consequence of the two dynamics of the solving principle (i.e. the dynamics of the problem on one side and the resolution dynamics on the other). This result can only be measured and/or observed at a macroscopic level. Measuring organization in reactive MAS is a recurrent problem. The next section gives some clues in order to tackle with this issue.

A fifth optional step may be considered. It consists to iterate on the third step after the measuring/observing phase. Indeed, the designer can discover, while measuring/observing the resolution, that it neglected some constraints or that instable behaviors are not taken into account (these ones are generally difficult to forecast). Modifying agents' interaction can then improve the system efficiency (it is the parameter settings phase of the system). This phase can be a process of trail and error and/or learning/optimization process with specific algorithms such as gradient descent methods.

3.2   Detailed Points on the Methodology

The previous section describes the general meaning of the proposed methodology. The goal of the current section is to give some clues in order to cope with each point of the methodology. The key principles given are not necessarily exhaustive but they represent the main directions that a designer can follow in order to build up a reactive MAS solving process.

How to Build Up a Problem's Model?   Two main characteristics have to be taken into account to build up an environment representing the problem's model: its topology and dynamics (as emphasized in [42]).

As for the *topology*, there are two main possibilities whether the problem's topology must be discretized or not. In fact, this choice depends also on what kind of approach is used to deal with the agents' decision processes and moves. Indeed, if the agents have to follow a probability law to compute their next position, the choice of a discrete representation is more relevant. For instance, if pheromones [33] or Markov models [5] are key elements for the agents' decision process, using a discrete environment is the best choice. By contrast, if the moves are computed considering Physics based force fields [17], [25], the environment has to be continuous to better fit to agents' behaviors.

Two main methods are widespread in order to deal with the *dynamics*. One is a bio-inspired method using digital pheromones [33], [34]. In this case, the dynamics of the environment is tied to the evolution of the amount of pheromone (evaporation, aggregation, diffusion,...). The second is a Physics based approach and is linked to artificial potential fields [1] or force fields (gravitational or electrostatic) such as these used in Co-Fields [25].

How to Perceive the Problem's Constraints?   The perception of the problem's constraints that take place in the environment depends strongly on their representation. Yet, we can use generic models such as the model for active perception proposed in [41]. This is composed of 3 main modules (sensing, interpreting, filtering) that can be adapted to specific application. As for the proposal of this paper, since only reactive agents are taken into account, the last two modules (interpreting and filtering) are reduced to their minimum. Hence, the key point is the definition of the constraints' sensing. This can be direct thanks to a definition of an artificial vision-like ability (or smelling-like ability if it concern pheromones) or indirect when the agents sustain the influences of fields present in the environment.

Which Kind of Interaction Models for Reactive Agents?   Basically, interactions in MAS can be defined considering two orthogonal axes [14]. On one side the type of the interaction (which can be direct or indirect) and on the other side its nature (cooperation or competition).

Concerning the type of the interaction, indirect ones are usual in reactive systems because, due to the limit of each entity, the environment is used as a shared memory. Agents have indirect "communication" via their changes of the environment (for instance dropping a mark [37], a pheromone [31], etc.). Such an approach is very efficient to self-organize numerous entities and enable stigmergy processes [6][26]. It is well suited to steps 3-b and 3-c of the proposed methodology.

Direct interaction, involved in particular in step 3-a of the methodology, can take three forms: (i) one agent that physically acts on the environment (that can possibly produce an environment-agent reaction), (ii) an agent-agent interaction (which can be a physical interaction or a message/signal exchange) and (iii) one agent interacting simultaneously with several others (through a signal emission, its physical presence, etc.).

The nature of the interaction can be abstracted in two categories: cooperation and competition. Generally cooperative interaction/actions are defined to solve conflicts or to perform difficult tasks that cannot be performed by only one agent. Reactive coordination can be placed in this category [14]. By contrast, competitive interaction or attacking actions can be defined as direct influences (as for instance in [8] [35]). Such interaction can express conflicts between agents and trigger some behaviors solving them such as the escape behavior in Eco-Resolution [13].

How to Measure the State of Balance of the System? The characterization of the equilibrium of the system is a complex issue from both a theoretical and practical point of view. In the context of problem solving, two kinds of situation have to be considered depending on whether the problem is static or dynamic. The difficulty of expressing equilibrium in complex systems is similar to that encountered in biology for stable organisms. To avoid the static connotation of the term equilibrium, the notion of homeostatic process is used to qualify a stable organization/entity whatever its dynamics [6].

In the case of a static problem, where the constraints do not change in time, the equilibrium of the solving system can be characterized by a stable state in which the agents stop interacting. This is the simplest case to consider.

When the problem is dynamic, the task is much harder because the state of balance of the system depends on whether there is equilibrium between two dynamics (the problem and the solving process). Thus, state of balance cannot be considered only as a measure of the interaction activity of the agents. Consequently, a measure of the equilibrium (and by translation, a measure of the organization) has to be designed. Much of the related work deal with the issue of the measurement of the organization. In many cases, this measure is closely tied to the intrinsic nature of the problem [17]. Another solution consists of designing a measure based on the mechanisms of the system. For instance, the entropy can be one of these measures. Entropy can be considered as a global estimation of the organization of the system on a global topological level [2], as a local consideration of the dynamics of each agent [32] or both of the two methods [20]. None of the propositions in the related literature deal with the nature of the local mechanisms, however.

The issue of measuring the organization of a MAS is central when deploying a problem solving application. Indeed, it is not only required characterizing the state of balance of the system but also for evaluating its performance and, by extension, the way of improving it by using learning algorithms for instance.

3.3   Related Work

Cybernetics Work. Cybernetics was defined by Weiner ([39]) as the study of control and communication in the animal and the machine. During 1940's cybernetics introduced the feedback principle, or retroactive loop. With such a loop, a system can adapt its actions to its own outputs. This approach is well suited to stabilizing a system towards a predetermined goal. Although this approach concentrated on the development of individual entities, its influence on the swarm approach was important. Indeed, it emphasized that social insects are also machines and that regulation loops exist at the colony level. Work of the last decade has developed the study of social systems involving numerous entities (social insects, collective robots, particle systems). In particular, such work has shown the importance of the loop in linking agents to the environment ([31][28]). This main loop, allowing collective solving, is present in our representation of an environment-based solving system (Fig. 1). In a sense, this loop is similar to that defined in cybernetics for one agent. We apply a similar approach in that we consider regulation at the agent level but also at the macro/collective level.

MAS Methodologies. The multiagent community has proposed a set of methodologies for the design and the analysis of MAS, such as Gaia [43], Adelfe [3], Promotheus [30]. Most of these methodologies focus on agent definition and their interactions, especially on deliberative agent architectures. For instance, Adelfe methodology aims at designing adaptive MAS [3] considering the AMAS agent architecture (for adaptive MAS). This one relies on agent's attitude, competences, beliefs and interactions language. Then the "cooperation failures" activity, defined as the A7-S2 step of the Adelfe methodology, is defined following social attitudes, such as incomprehension, ambiguity, uselessness, which are not suitable to our reactive-based approach.

One particularity of our methodology is to focus on the problem-solving framework considering collective systems. In existing works, methodologies are generally devoted to software engineering, using object-oriented methodologies [3] and organizational concepts such as role and group.

Nevertheless, an extended version of Gaia methodology presents interesting elements in relation to our proposition. In particular, this methodology defines the environment as a primary abstraction of MAS [44]. Authors propose to first define the environment by considering resources that can be sensed and consumed by agents. They point out the possibly constraints induced by their accessibility. In the first step of our methodology, we let the designer defining the constraints' representation, and then defining agent resources can be a way to model them. The second phase of the environmental modeling proposed in [44] concerns agents perception. As for us it is emphasized that they depend on both the environment model and the concerned application. Next phases of this methodology do not focus on reactive-based solving processes.

Concerning methodologies devoted to reactive-based systems our approach can be compared to the constructivism method, exposed in [15]. The constructivism methodology aims at designing reactive Multi-Agent Systems for the solving of spatially defined problems (such as features extraction in images, cartographic generalization and spatial multi-criteria decision processes). This technique, which is specific to spatialized problems (i.e. defined by a map or a picture), is based on the interpretation of the position and state of the agents. Consequently, it is not well adapted to dynamic problems. Nevertheless, as we have exposed in our proposition, the problem constraints are defined and represented in the environment. By contrast, authors deal with problems where the form of the solution is known in advance and then use it to define constraints on the agents' organization. However, [15] gives some interesting clues as to the definition of spatially defined problem constraints.

4   Application

This section presents two applications following the *four steps* of the proposed methodology.

4.1   The Satisfaction-Altruism Model

This model aims at providing a means of cooperation and of conflict solving to reactive agents working in the same environment. As agents are simple, intentionality does not exist in their behaviors, and only intelligent collective processes can be considered at a macro level. So, in order to provide intentional interactions while keeping collective properties, the model extends such an approach. The *artificial potential fields* (APF) model is considered because of its efficiency for collective and individual tasks (such as individual and team navigation). This technique relies on the perception of attractive elements and obstacles present in the agents' close environment (details in [22] [1] [26]). The satisfaction-altruism model relies on this extension and on the definition of satisfaction states inspired by the homeostatic behavioral model of C. Hull [19].

1. In order to express agent intentions, the satisfaction-altruism model [35][36] introduces *new artificial fields* in the environment. These fields are *dynamically* and intentionally generated by agents thanks to the emission of attractive and repulsive *signals*. Agents broadcast such signals in order to influence their close neighbors. Repulsive signals express constraints/conflicts between agents (expression of a part of the whole problem) and positive signals express cooperative calling. Fig. 2 shows the application of the model to the foraging task. Over the working area a surface is drawn to represent the enhanced environment (i.e. obstacles plus signals). Cooperative signals are represented as hollows and repulsive signals as peaks (the latter ones are added to fields generated by obstacles). These artificial fields augment the information present in the environment in order to express agent goals and constraints. The next steps show that agents are designed to reduce these artificial perturbations.

2. To cooperate and to solve conflicts, agents must be able to perceive the signals and the presence of other agents. The key idea of the model is that agents

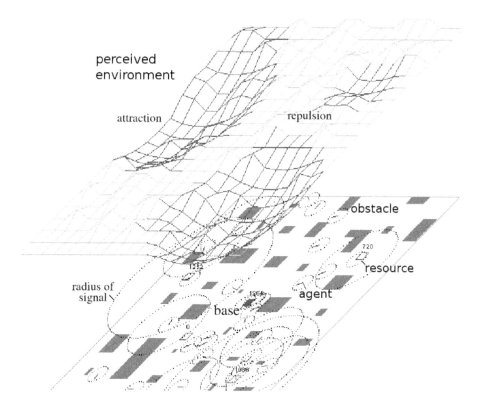

Fig. 2. Application of the satisfaction-altruism model to the foraging task (snapshot simulation step 497). On top, representation of attractive and repulsive signals as environment distortions (= the environment perceived by agents).

evolve in the perceptual environment drawn in Fig. 2. So agent perceptions are limited to the detection of physical obstacles and to the reception of attractive and repulsive signals.

3. Interactions consist of agents carrying out cooperative reactions to signal reception. One interesting application of this model is the distributed resolution of access conflicts in constrained environments (several robots/agents trying to navigate in narrow passages, as represented in Fig. 3.a). In this problem there are two kinds of constraints: the presence of static obstacles and other agents (which are moving obstacles).

   – (a) *Individual level* : the perception of local obstacles is used as stimulus to avoid them (a simple avoidance behavior is defined).
   – (b) *Cooperative level* : If several agents are blocked, i.e. a deadlock due to the environment's topology (cf. Fig. 3.a), simple avoidance behavior will be inefficient. A cooperative mechanism, based on the emission of repulsive signals, is then added. Agents measure their local constraints, i.e. elements surrounding them, to broadcast a level of dissatisfaction (agents and walls do not have the same weight, see [35]). The cooperative

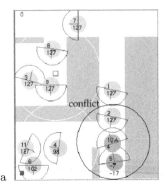 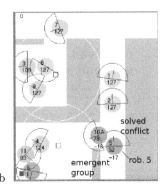

Fig. 3. Snapshots of simulated individual robots based on the satisfaction-altruism model. Example of conflict resolution. Each robot is represented by its range of perception, id number, current satisfaction and possible emitted signal value.

reaction, which is called *altruism*, forces the less dissatisfied agents to move away in order to unlock the situation. Thanks to this mechanism, signals are propagated to all agents involved in the blocking. Fig. 3.a shows an example of a column of blocked agents where the less dissatisfied ones are at the top.

- (c) *Regulations* : Signal propagation can lead to oscillatory and cyclic behaviors (as in the eco-resolution model). To avoid oscillations, the notion of persistence is added to the emission of repulsive signals: a blocked agent emits its initial dissatisfaction while it is not totally free (see agent number 5 in Fig. 3.b). This behavior illustrates the necessity of regulation mechanisms in cooperative processes.

4. The observed solution is equilibrium between the problem dynamics and agent interactions. For the navigation application, the solution is characterized by coherent displacements of all the agents (note that immobilized agents express a conflicting situation). For conflicts involving several agents, repulsive signals are passed from agent to agent. As a consequence, we observe the emergence of groups of agents moving in the same direction as a coherent entity (see details in [24]). It is the case in Fig. 3.b for the two robots freeing from the conflict, noted emergent group.

This model has been applied to different simulated problems such as collaborative foraging [36], navigation in constrained environments, box-pushing [12] and validated with real robots in conflict problem solving [24].

4.2   A Physics-Based Reactive Model

Localization, with mobile or fixed sensors, is a very difficult but required task to control mobile robots in an indoor dynamic and uncertain environment. This task can be defined as finding the position of an object, mobile or not, in a well known referential. The localization is composed of two methods: localization with on board sensors (also called self localization) and localization with external sensors. The algorithms used generally stem from signal or image processing, or from the stochastic methods based on Markov Decision Processes (MDP) [16]. So, the standard localization algorithms are extremely dependent on the nature of the used sensors and deal only with one single target. There are no multi-agent based localization and tracking devices except with specialized cognitive agents [11]. Some related work, such as environment mapping and data fusion deals also with cognitive agent-based methods. In this way, tracking is considered to be a collection of temporally and spatially coherent localizations. As a means of localization, the tracking algorithms stem from the signal processing. Among the most spread out we can point out the Kalman filter, the optical flow algorithms and the particle filtering [23]. The main difficulty in designing such systems for localization and tracking is to take into account the characteristics of the used sensors while obtaining properties such as robustness and adaptation to the variation in the targets' kinetics. Considering these required properties, using a reactive multi-agent system to solve this problem seems to be adapted.

Before detailing the physics based model following the methodology exposed in Sect.3, a description of the problem is required. For this, both the topological and the dynamic point of view have to be considered.

Localization and tracking are based on the use of sensors that are spread out in the environment. The topology of the problem is tied to the gathering range of the sensors. This can be considered as an area, observable by the sensors, where the targets are expected to move. The dynamics of the problem depend on the dynamics of the targets.

These can (i) *appear*, i.e. they arrive in the observation field of the sensors, (ii) *move*, i.e. they go from one observable point of the real world to another observable point, (iii) *disappear*, i.e. they go out of the observation field.

With this description in mind, the constraints of the problem can be formalized. The topology has to take into account the range of each sensor and the topology (obstacles, walls, doors, ...) of the observed area. The dynamics of the problem have to take into account those of the targets. The structure of the model is shown in Fig. 4. From here, the proposed methodology can be applied.

1. To start with, an *environment model* has to be defined in order to represent the problem and its constraints. For the localization and the tracking, the chosen representation is an *occupancy grid* that represents the areas of the real world observable according to the range of the sensors. The obstacles are labeled as unreachable areas of the grid. As for the dynamics, these have been translated into two main trends. First, *accumulation* of the sensing information deals with the appearance of the targets. This accumulation leads to the construction of a plot that represents a possible position for a target. This construction can be considered as a deformation of the environment that has to be perceived by the agents. Second, *evaporation* of the plot has been designed. This deals with the disappearance of the targets. It also prevents the persistence of bad information in the environment. This evaporation tends to reduce the deformation involved in the accumulation. These

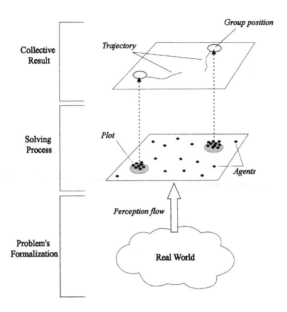

Fig. 4. Architecture of the Physics based reactive model for the localization and the tracking

two trends take into account the targets' movements. The movement of a target to a place near its last position can be considered as the appearance of this target in a place near from its last position. Since the evaporation tends to reduce the out-dated plots, this last position will disappear.

2. Then, the *perceptions of the agents* have to be defined. Without any information the agents' environment is flat. The deformation of the environment, induced by the accumulation, can be considered as a perturbation. This Physics based model has been designed for the perception of this kind of perturbation. The agents perceive the plots through the environment by means of an *attraction* force. This force is induced by the appearance of a plot and depends on its size. Thus, the agents are mass particles in a force field.

3. As for the *interaction mechanisms*, they have to be defined considering individual and collective levels and the required regulation.

   (a) *Individual level*: The agents are expected to compensate the perturbations in the environment. Since they are already attracted by the plots, a behavior has to be designed to reduce the plot when the agents are on it. So, a *consumption* behavior has been introduced.

   (b) *Cooperative level*: Two situations have to be considered. The first characterizes the system in its stable initial state (i.e. when there is no information given by the sensors). In this case, the agents have to be as far as possible from each other in order to better prevent the arrival of information. So, a *repulsion* behavior has been defined. This behavior is based on a Model inspired by Physics as the attraction is. In the second case, the agents have to deal with the information that deforms their environment. If the agents are expected to cooperate in the consumption of the information, they must be allowed to be near each other. So the repulsion mechanism is inhibited when the agents are consuming considering their respective potential energy. This value is computed considering the level of the plot where the agent is.

(c) *Collective and local regulation*: As it has been defined, the environment is physically coherent (i.e. all the behaviors have been defined following mathematical formulations based on Newtonian Physics). Nevertheless, it is still conservative since the speed of an object moving in the environment, without any interaction, remains constant. Consequently, a *fluid friction force* has been introduced in order to regulate the movements of the agents.

4. Then, the *emerging collective organization* has to be observed. This is both a gathering of the agents on the percepts, which leads to a *group construction*, and a homogenous repartition of them in the information less areas. Each group can thus be considered as a localized target. The output of the system is stable when equilibrium is established between the refreshing and the resolution dynamics. Fig.5 shows of the localization and tracking solving process using the automatic control point of view applied in the proposed methodology.

From an application point of view, this device has been successfully applied in simulation and with real targets. It shows relevant properties compared to classical localization and tracking algorithms such as anticipation of the targets' moves, independence from the number of information sources (information sources can be added and/or remove in run time), independence from the number of targets,... (see [18] or [17] for detailed results).

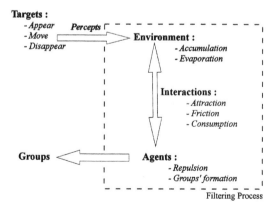

Fig. 5. Representation of the solving process as a filter

5   Conclusion

This paper presents an environment-based methodology for building reactive multi-agent systems aimed at dealing with the problem solving issue. Considering the limitation of simple entities, the environment appeared to be the main element involved in a reactive-based solving problem system. First, it models the problem to solve and its constraints. Second it establishes the link between the problem on one side and the reactive solving process on the other. Finally, in some cases, it can also characterize the emergent organization.

Our approach contrasts with classical emergentist or artificial life works that define agents and interactions by following the expected emergent organization. Our proposition can be seen as a bottom-up methodology based on the representation of the problem, where constraints are translated into perturbations in the environment. These have to be regulated through agent behaviors. The originality of our methodology is the fact of starting the building of the solving system by focusing on the environment instead of focusing on the agents, their knowledge and their behaviors as it is done in the classical approach.

The fourth step of the methodology claims that the global solution emerges from the solving process and can be characterized when the system reaches a stable state. Such a state must be measured or observed by an external agent. It is a complex task that remains an open problem. However, we propose in Sect.3.2 some clues about the characterization of this stable state.

Two detailed examples illustrate the application of the methodology: (i) a generic kernel for cooperation and conflict solving between situated agents, which is based on an extension of the APF approach (ii) a model for localization and target tracking using a Physics based approach. It appears to us that describing these models following the construction steps is a good way for their presentation/understanding.

The proposed methodology is currently applied to features extraction in image processing by using agent based active shapes that respect the B-Spline formalism. The methodology is also applied to the facilities location issue. On the theoretical level, we plan to develop some keys for the definition of the environment model as expressed in the first point of the methodology.

Acknowledgments

The authors would like to cordially thank Anna Crowley for the correction of the English writing of the paper.

References

1. Arkin R.C.: Behavior Based Robotics. The MIT Press (1998)
2. Balch T.: Hierarchic Social Entropy: An Information Theoretic Measure of Robot Group Diversity. Atonomous Robots, vol.8, n°3, July (2000)

3. Bernon C., Gleizes M-P., Peyruqueou S., Picard G.: ADELFE, a methodology for adaptative multi-agent systems engineering. in Third International Workshop on Engineering Societies in the Agent World (ESAW-2002), Madrid, sept (2002)
4. Bonabeau E., Dorigo M., Theraulaz G.: Swarm Intelligence: From Nature to Artificial Systems. New York, Oxford University Press (1999)
5. Buffet O., Dutech A., Charpillet F.: Adaptive Combination of Behaviors in an Agent. Proceedings of the Fifteenth European Conference on Artificial Intelligence (ECAI'02), .48-52, Lyon, France, (2002)
6. Camazine S., Deneubourg J.L., Franks N.R., Sneyd J., Theraulaz G., Bonabeau E.: Self-Organization in Biological Systems. Princeton studies in complexity, Princeton University Press (2001)
7. Colorni A., Dorigo M., Maniezzo V.: Distributed Optimization by Ant Colonies. in proceedings of ECAL91, European conference on artificial life, Paris, Elsevier, p 134-142 (1991)
8. Drogoul A., Ferber J., Jacopin E.: Pengi: Applying Eco-Problem-Solving for Behavior Modelling in an Abstract Eco-System. in Modelling and Simulation: Proceedings of ESM'91, Simulation Councils, Copenhague, 337-342 (1991)
9. Drogoul A., Ferber J.: From Tom-Thumb to the Dockers: Some Experiments with Foraging Robots. in From Animals to Animats II, MIT Press, Cambridge, 451-459, (1993)
10. Drogoul A., Dubreuil C.: A Distributed Approach to N-Puzzle Solving. Proceedings of the Distributed Artificial Intelligence Workshop, Seattle (United-States) (1993)
11. Ealet F., Collin B., Sella G., Garbay C.: Multi-agent architecture for scene interpretation. SPIE'00 on Enhanced and synthetic vision, Orlando, USA, (2000)
12. Chapelle J, Simonin O, Ferber J.: How Situated Agents can Learn to Cooperate by Monitoring their Neighbors' Satisfaction. Proc. 15th European Conference on Artificial Intelligence, 68-72 (2002)
13. Ferber J., Jacopin E.: The framework of ECO-problem solving. in Decentralized AI 2, North-Holland, Yves Demazeau and Jean-Pierre Müller Eds. (1991)
14. Ferber J.: Multi-Agent System: An Introduction to Distributed Artificial Intelligence. Harlow: Addison Wesley Longman (1999)
15. Ferrand N., Demazeau Y., Baeijs C.: Systèmes multi-agents réactifs pour la résolution de problèmes spatialisés. Revue d'Intelligence Artificielle, Numéro Spécial sur l'IAD et les SMA, 12(1):37-72, january, (1998)
16. Gechter F., Charpillet F.: Vision Based Localisation for a Mobile Robot. In 12th IEEE International Conference on Tools with Artificial Intelligence ICTAI'2000. 229-236 (2000)
17. Gechter F., Chevrier V., Charpillet F.: A Reactive Multi-Agent System for Localization and Tracking in Mobile. In 16th IEEE International Conference on Tools with Artificial Intelligence - ICTAI'2004, 431-435 (2004)
18. Gechter F., Chevrier V., Charpillet F.: Localizing and Tracking Targets with a Reactive Multi-Agent System. In Second European Workshop on Multi-Agent Systems - EUMAS'04 (2004)
19. Hull C.: Principles of Behavior. New York: Appleton-Century-Crofts, (1943)
20. Kanada Y., Hirokawa M.: Stochastic Problem Solving by Local Computation based on Self-Organization Paradigm. IEEE 27th Hawaii International Conference on System Sciences, 82-91 (1994)
21. Kennedy J., Eberhart R.C.: Swarm Intelligence. Morgan Kaufmann Publisher 2001 ISBN 1-55860-595-9 (2001)

22. Khatib O.: Real-Time Obstacle Avoidance for Manipulators and Mobile Robots. Proceedings of IEEE International Conference on Robotics and Automation, 500-505 (1985)

23. Kwok C., Fox D., Meila M.: Real-Time Particle Filters. Proceedings of the IEEE, 92(2),Special Issue on Sequential State Estimation (2004)

24. Lucidarme P, Simonin O, Liegeois A.: Implementation and Evaluation of a Satisfaction/Altruism Based Architecture for Multi-Robot Systems. Proc. IEEE Int. Conf. on Robotics and Automation, 1007-1012 (2002)

25. Mamei M. , Zambonelli F.: Motion Coordination in the Quake 3 Arena Environment: a Field-based Approach, International Workshop on Environments for Multi-agent Systems Postproceedings of the Workshop on Environments for Multi-agent Systems (E4MAS 2004), Springer, LNAI 3374 264-278 (2005)

26. Mamei M., Zambonelli F. Programming stigmergic coordination with the TOTA middleware Proceedings of the fourth international joint conference on Autonomous agents and multiagent systems ACM Press New York, 415-422 (2005)

27. Mataric M. J.: Designing and Understanding Adaptative Group Behavior. Adaptive Behavior 4:1, 51-80 (1995)

28. Müller J-P., Parunak H.V.D.: Multi-Agent systems and manufacturing. IFAC/INCOM'98, Nancy/Metz (1998)

29. M.R.Jean: Emergence et SMA. 5eme Journées Francophones sur l'Intelligence Artificielle Distribuée et les Systèmes Multi-Agents, AFCET, AFIA, La Colle-sur-Loup, Quinqueton, Thomas, Trousse (eds), 323-342 (1997)

30. Padgham L., Winikoff, M.: Promotheus : A Methodology for Developing Intelligent Agents. 3th Agent-Oriented Software Engineering Workshop, Bologna (2002).

31. Parunak H.V.D.: Go to the Ant: Engineering Principles from Natural Agent Systems. Annals of Operations Research 75, 69-101 (1997)

32. Parunak H.V.D., Brueckner S.: Entropy and Self-Organization in Multi-Agent Systems. Fifth International Conference on Autonomous Agents, 124-130 (2001)

33. Parunak H.V.D. , Brueckner S., Sauter J.: Digital Pheromones for Coordination of Unmanned Vehicles. Postproceedings of the Workshop on Environments for Multi-agent Systems (E4MAS 2004), Springer, LNAI 3374 246-263. (2005)

34. Ramos V., Almeida F.: Artificial Ant Colonies in Digital Image Habitats. A Mass Behaviour Effect Study on Pattern Recognition ANTS'2000, Brussels Belgique, 113-116 (2000)

35. Simonin O, Ferber J.: Modeling Self Satisfaction and Altruism to handle Action Selection and Reactive Cooperation. in proceedings SAB 2000 The Sixth International Conference on the Simulation of Adaptative Behavior, vol. 2, 314-323 (2000)

36. Simonin O., Liégeois A., Rongier P.: An Architecture for Reactive Cooperation of Mobile Distributed Robots. DARS'2000 5th International Symposium on Distributed Autonomous Robotic Systems in Distributed Autonomous Robotic Systems 4, L.E. Parker G. Bekey J. Barhen (Eds.), Springer, 35-44, (2000)

37. Simonin O.: Construction of Numerical Potential Fields with Reactive Agents. in AAMAS'05 proceedings The Fourth International Joint Conference on Autonomous Agents and Multi Agent System, ACM-SIGART, 1351-1352 (2005)

38. Steels L.: Cooperation between distributed agents through self-organization. in Workshop on Multi-Agent Cooperation, 3-13, North Holland, Cambridge, UK (1989)

39. Weiner, N.: Cybernetics, or Control and Communication in Animals and Machines. Wiley,New York (1948)

40. Welch G., Bishop G.: An introduction to the kalman filter. Technical Report TR 95-041, Computer Science, University of North California at Chapel Hill, Chapel Hill, NC (2003)
41. Weyns D., Steegmans E., Holvoet T.: Towards Active Perception In Situated Multi-Agent Systems Applied Artificial Intelligence 18(9-10) 867-883 (2004)
42. Weyns D., Parunak V., Michel F., Holvoet T., Ferber J.: Environments for Multiagent Systems, State of the art and research challenges Post-proceedings of the first International Workshop on Environments for Multiagent Systems, LNAI vol 3374 (2005)
43. Wooldridge M., Jennings N.R., Kinny D.: The Gaia Methodology for Agent-Oriented Analysis and Design. Autonomous Agents and Multi-Agent Systems, 3, Kluwer Academic Publisher, 285-312 (2000)
44. Zambonelli F., Jennings N.R., Wooldridge M.: Developing multiagent systems: The Gaia Methodology. Transactions on Software Engineering and Methodology, 3(12), ACM Press (2003)

An Architecture for MAS Simulation Environments

Renee Steiner, Gary Leask, and Rym Z. Mili*

The University of Texas at Dallas,
Department of Computer Science,
Box 830688, Richardson, TX 75083-0688, USA
rsteiner@utdallas.edu, gary.leask@student.utdallas.edu,
rmili@utdallas.edu

Abstract. In this paper, we discuss the model of an environment for a geographically based simulation system. The environment is structured as a graph in which nodes represent locations and edges represent paths between locations. The space is decomposed into a network of cells which are managed by cell controllers. In order to visualize location information at various levels of abstraction, we define the environment as a cell hierarchy.

1 Introduction

In MAS development, it is common for designers to couple agents and environment. Agents are embedded in their environment, and the environment is merely considered in terms of the agents it supports. Hence, one cannot separate the two entities without crippling or destroying both. In addition, passive entities, which are neither agent nor environment, are often embedded in agent architectures. Linking the passive entities with agents causes limitations in the extensibility of MAS architectures. Moreover, it is common for environments to play the role of *Message transport facilitators* [1] whose responsibilities centers around the communications between agents through a message transport service or a broker infrastructure. The communication can be direct [2, 9], or indirect [10, 17]. Our work is based on the idea that, by separating the agent from its environmental responsibilities, both the environment and the agent are more robust and adaptable. Such a clear separation of duties and responsibilities leads to a reduction in unnecessary coupling and a more understandable, extensible, reusable architecture. New multi-agent simulation tools make use of this principle [18,19].

Conversely, we subscribe to the idea that agents and environment play an equally important role, and propose a definition for Agent-Environment Systems (AES). The AES concept is particularly useful when a) the environment is dynamic and distributed, b) the environment includes entities that are not agents, and c) agents cannot have a complete view of the environment at any

---

* Correspondence author.

D. Weyns, H. Van Dyke Parunak, and F. Michel (Eds.): E4MAS 2005, LNAI 3830, pp. 50–67, 2006.
© Springer-Verlag Berlin Heidelberg 2006

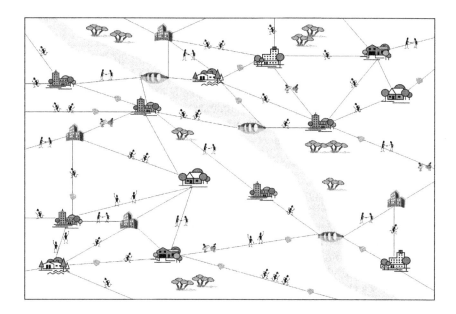

Fig. 1. Geographical Simulation Environment

point in time. As such, AES are subsets of MAS and supersets of agent simulation tools. We illustrate our concepts through the DIVAs environment. DIVAs (or *Dynamic Information Visualization of Agent systems*) is a social simulation tool in which the environment is a geographical map consisting of a graph whose nodes indicate places, and whose edges represent pathways between places (see Figure 1). DIVAs' environment system allows the creation of environments, and the execution of a simulation.

In section 2, we begin by defining Agent-Environment Systems (AES) and propose a general AES architecture. In section 3, we introduce the DIVAs framework and in section 4, we examine our implementation of the environment.

2   Agent-Environment Systems

In this section, we define Agent Environment Systems and discuss agent and environment characteristics.

2.1   Definition

We define an AES as a MAS composed of

1. a set of interacting agents;
2. a distinct environment in which these agents are situated (not embedded);
3. a mechanism for agent to environment interactions.

In an AES,

1. an *agent* is a software entity which
   (a) is driven by a set of tendencies in the form of individual objectives;
   (b) can communicate with other agents and the environment;
   (c) possesses resources of its own; a resource is a consumable commodity;
   (d) has a partial view of this environment;
   (e) possesses the ability to perform tasks and can offer services;
   (f) is mobile in an environment.

   An agent's behavior tends towards satisfying its objectives, taking into account the resources and abilities available to it, and depending on its perception and the communications it receives [20].

2. an *environment* is a software entity which
   (a) is driven by a set of tendencies in the form of individual objectives;
   (b) can interact with other environment entities and agents;
   (c) possesses resources of its own; a resource is a consumable commodity;
   (d) has a partial view of the agent population;
   (e) possesses the ability to perform tasks and can offer services;
   (f) includes a set of objects; objects are passive entities that are not consumable but can be perceived, modified or destroyed by agents.

   An environment's behavior tends towards satisfying its objectives, taking into account the resources and abilities available to it, and depending on its perception, interactions and events it receives.

It is important to note that the ordering of these characteristics is intentionally presented to emphasize the commonalities inherent in the agent and environment. However, even though the characteristics are similar at a high level, at the application level they diverge.

In the following subsection, we compare and contrast the characteristics exhibited by agents and environments using an embodiment of an AES.

2.2   Example

DIVAs is a geographical based simulation system which implements the AES concepts [21, 23]. Agents represent social entities that move, act, use resources and interact with each other (see Figure 1). Every action by every agent produces a change in the state of the environment. When the simulation involves a few hundred thousand agents, it is impractical to model the environment as a single component. Hence, to mitigate the processing overhead, we decompose the environment into smaller, more manageable partitions that we call *cells* (see Figure 2). In DIVAs, the environment is a graph, G in which nodes represent locations and edges represent paths between locations. Agents move in the environment using the map specified by G (see Figure 3).

As discussed in the previous section, environment cells and agents have similar characteristics, however, these characteristics are realized differently in an application.

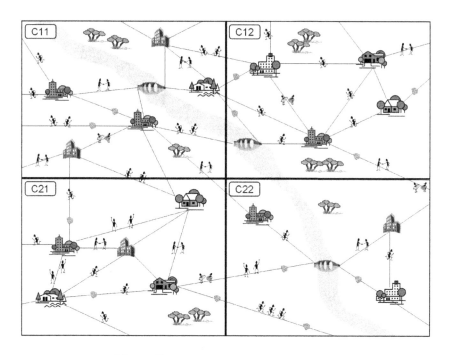

Fig. 2. Environment partitioned into cells

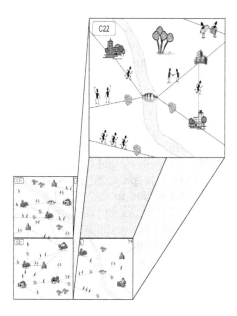

Fig. 3. Representation of the Environment

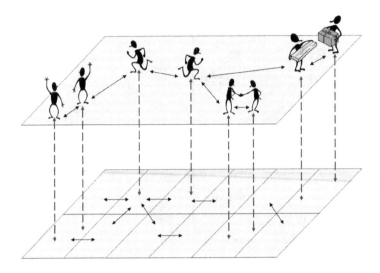

Fig. 4. Communication illustration for AES

1. *Objectives.* Both agents and environments have goals to satisfy. Agent goals are goals in the traditional sense whereas the goal of a environment's cell is to maintain a stable state for the situated agents. For example, a cell's goal might be to recover a path in the shortest period of time following the occurrence of an external event that simulates a natural phenomenon. If a path is unusable following a flood event, the cell makes every effort to recover a near approximation to the original path in the shortest time.

2. *Communication and Interaction.* Both agents and environments communicate. We distinguish between three types of communications: agent to agent, cell to cell, and agent to cell (see Figure 4).

   - *Cell to cell communication.* This type of communication centers around exchanging information that may affect the state of another cell. For example, if two adjacent cells c_1 and c_2 share a path, and c_1 receives an external event to remove the path, c_1 will act on its portion of the path and propagate the information to c_2.

   - *Agent to cell communication.* Agents communicate with cells to obtain a vision of their immediate surroundings as well as to inform the cell of a state change incurred by them. For example, as an agent enters a cell, it passes its *business card* to the cell. The agent's business card symbolizes the minimal amount of information needed by the environment. This includes the agent's id, position, etc.

   - *Cell to agent communication.* Cells communicate with agents to impart changes to the state of the cell that may affect an agent's plan. For example, if a path is removed from a cell's graph, the agents within the cell are informed so that they may replan their trip if necessary.

3. *Resources.* Both cells and agents possess resources. A cell's resource aids its survival (air, water, sun, etc), while an agent's resource aids the fulfillment of its tasks (money, time, hammer, etc.).

4. *Partial View.* Cells have a partial view of the agent population and agents have a partial view of the environment. A cell is aware only of those agents within the cell's boundaries; there is no need to know about agents that cannot affect its state. An agent is only aware of the state of the cell in which it is situated; there is no need to know about cells that it cannot see.

5. *Tasks and Services.* Both cells and agents can perform tasks and offer services. A cell's tasks are completed in the process of maintaining a stable state. For example, the environment has the ability to perform the task of repairing a path. Once repaired, the cell offers notification services communicating the state changes to all affected cells and agents. An agent's tasks entirely are dependent on its goal for a specific application and agent services are likewise application-centric (ie. they vary based on the needs of the application and its specific implementation).

Therefore, it can be concluded that an agent and an environment cell possess many of the same qualities even though they realize those qualities in different manners. As such, an environment can be considered a first class entity. Hence, having developed a basic understanding for AES, in the following section we discuss the details of the DIVAs architecture.

3   DIVAs Architecture

DIVAs [21]consists of four main components (see Figure 5). The *AES* component creates the environment and populates it with agents; the *Data Management System* extracts information about emergent structures through data mining and clustering techniques. The *Visualization System* uses graph drawing algorithms to visualize the dynamics of a large number of agents; the *Prediction System* generates prediction models when data is sparse or incomplete.

As discussed in the previous section, the environment is partitioned into a network of *cells* where each cell is a single environment entity. A cell $c_{i,j}$ is related to cell $c_{i,j+1}$ if $c_{i,j}$ and $c_{i,j+1}$ share nodes or paths. Cell information is managed by individual controllers. A cell controller is responsible for informing its local agents about changes in the location graph, hence providing them with a vision of their surroundings. It is also responsible for informing neighboring cells of any changes that may affect them.

In addition, because we are interested in visualizing location information at various levels of abstraction, the environment is defined as a hierarchy. The information contained in cells and location graphs is refined as the level of granularity increases. Hence, in order to manage the environment as a whole, each cell has to manage its connections with the cells it is linked to at the same level (i.e., horizontally), as well as at the upper and lower levels (i.e., vertically).

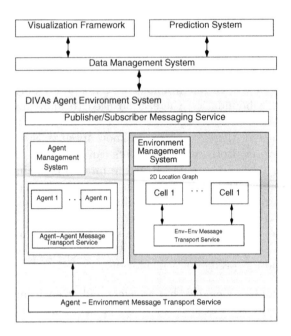

Fig. 5. DIVAs Architecture

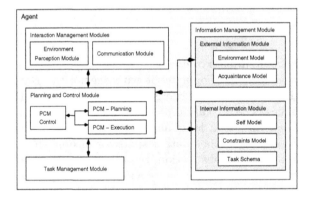

Fig. 6. DIVAs Agent Architecture

As alluded to in section 2.1, DIVAs' cell structure is very similar to the agent's structure (see Figure 6). The cell includes four main components [24,23]: the *Interaction Management Module*, the *Information Management Module*, the *Task Management Model*, and the *Planning and Control Module*. These modules are shown in Figure 7. In the following section, we will elaborate upon these modules by first discussing their purpose followed by a brief description of the implementation as shown in, Figure 8, the class diagram.

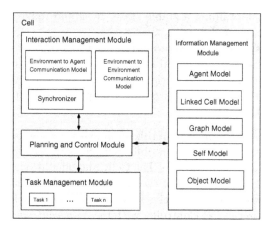

Fig. 7. Environment Architecture

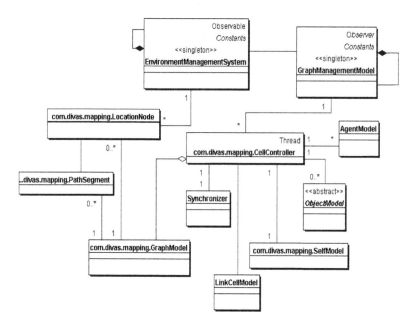

Fig. 8. DIVAs Environment Design Data Model

3.1   Planning and Control Module (PCM)

Description. This module is the "brains" of the environment. It maintains interfaces to all the other modules and is responsible for the planning, task execution, monitoring and decision making. It is responsible for determining the next course of action (i.e., new cell state). As such, its main responsibility is to satisfy its goal of maintaining a stable state. It should make no decisions that compromise, or are in conflict with, that goal.

The PCM is responsible for determining what a "stable state" is. When the environment is initialized, its initial state is set and the Information Management Module is populated. This initialization is an external event (and the first such event) on the environment. From this point on, the PCM has a goal of maintaining that state.

Implementation. The main class of this module is the CellController. The Cell-Controller has access to the external information via a facade implemented by the InformationManagementModule. The CellController also holds a reference to the InfluenceModel which is part of the *Environment to Agent Communication Module*. In this way, it is able to receive influences via a callback mechanism. The callback is handled in the CellController with the *envEvent(event)* method which is called by the InfluenceModel. When the CellController has any environment events that it wishes to propagate, it calls the InfluenceModel's *producePerception()* method.

3.2   Interaction Management Module

The Interaction Management Module is responsible for handling environment-to-environment and environment-to-agent communications, expressed in KQML, which is delivered by the Message Transport Service (MTS). This module is subdivided into the *Environment to Environment Communication Model*, the *Environment to Agent Communication Model* and the *Synchronizer*.

The Environment to Environment Communication Module (EE-CM). This module is responsible for the environment-to-environment communications. Since processing for these events occur in a *asynchronous* manner, there is no need to involve a synchronizing mechanism.

The Environment to Agent Communication Model (EA-CM). This model is responsible for handling the environment-to-agent interactions. It produces *influences* caused by events within the environment. Internal events are generated as a result of activities being performed by the agents or the environment. External events are triggered by the system user. Once triggered, events cause influences in the environment and these influences will cause a reaction, or a change in state, by the environment. Influences carry content to the interested agent(s).

This module receives *EventInfo* messages from the agents and forwards them to the PCM. It also receives the *EnvInfo* message from the PCM and forwards it to the agent to be received as perceptions. It interfaces with the Synchronizer by receiving *SyncReaction* messages and sending *EndOfReaction* messages back to the Synchronizer.

Implementation. This model is composed of several classes foremost of which is the InfluenceModel class. It holds references to the Synchronizer Model, as well as an indirect reference to the CellController in the form of a callback method. Since the Controller has an instance of the InfuenceModel, it is able to directly send the *EnvInfo* message to the InfluenceModel which will then format the perception for the agent and send an *EnvInfo* message to the agent. The InfluenceModel will also receive *EventInfo* messages from the agent which it will then pass to the CellController via the callback mechanism using the EnvironmentEvent class. Likewise, the InfluenceModel receives a callback in the form of an InfluenceEvent from the HeartbeatPublisher when a *SyncReaction* message triggers in the HeartbeatPublisher. In these ways, it is able to send and receive all messaging for events.

Synchronizer. This component implements mechanisms to synchronize the processing of the agents perception of the cell with their actions since communication from the agents occurs in an *asynchronous* manner while processing must be *synchronous*. It enables agents' perception of the environment and the environment's reaction to influences generated by agents' actions, to occur at a specified rate and time.

Implementation. This module is implemented following a publish/subscribe pattern using the Java Messaging Service which allows the asynchronous messaging that agent-environment communications require. All an agent needs to do upon entering the cell is register for that cell's events. Several classes make up the Synchronizer Module. HeartbeatPublisher is the class that is responsible for pulsing out events. Events, not content, are transmitted by the synchronizer module. The HeartbeatPublisher is responsible for receiving *EndOfAction* events from agents and passing those to the InfluenceModel in the form of a *SyncReaction* message via a callback mechanism. Once the InfluenceModel has finished responding to the agent's action, it sends a *EndOfReaction* event to the HeartbeatPublisher. The HeartbeatPublisher then fires an *SyncPercept* event to all agents in the cell.

3.3   Information Management Module

Description. The Information Management Module (IMM) manages the *minimal* data a cell needs to function. Since a cell may be subjected to several external events, and may contain a large number of agents at any point in time, it is necessary to not overload it with unnecessary information so as to optimize its processing and interaction functions. A cell is composed of the following models:

- *Agent Model.* This model contains minimal information about the agents within environment such as id and location.
- *Linked Cell Model.* This model contains information about the neighboring cells to the environment such as cell id and path id of any shared paths.
- *Graph Model.* This model contains information regarding the nodes and edges in the cell. This is done in order to maintain a localized mapping of the graph. It is discussed in detail in section 4.4.

- *Self Model.* This contains information regarding the characteristics of the environment such as the cell's id and its boundaries. It also includes information about the resources available for the cell. A resource is a commodity (e.g., time, energy) that is used during the execution of tasks.
- *Object Model.* This includes information detailing the *Physical Objects* that are situated in the environment including id, position and description.

Implementation. The CellController instantiates a list of AgentModels, the GraphModel of the cell and a list of LinkedCellModels. It also instantiates the SelfModel and a list of all ObjectModels in the environment.

3.4 Task Management Module

Description. This contains information regarding tasks that can be performed by the environment. This serves as a "database" containing the detailed description of each atomic level task, or operation, that the environment is capable of performing.

Implementation. The CellController has an instance of the TaskManagement-Module. It provides all the information that the PCM needs to schedule activities. It contains the currentTask as well as an array of possible tasks.

3.5 Event Handling

Having discussed the modules that make up the core of the environment framework, we will illustrate the key interactions that environments handle. There are three types of events in DIVAs: *Environment↔Environment*, *Environment ↔Agent*, and *External*. Each event type has its own characteristics and, by necessity, must be handled differently by the cell.

External events, generated by the user, are unidirectional and include, but are not limited to, *objectAdded*, *objectMoved*, *objectRemoved*, *pathAdded*, *pathRemoved*, *locationNodeAdded*, and *locationNodeRemoved*.

Environment↔Agent events are bidirectional and include *influences* and *perceptions*. Influences may include *welcomeToCell*, *objectAdded*, *objectMoved*, *objectRemoved*, *pathAdded*, *pathRemoved*, *locationNodeAdded*, and *locationNode-Removed*. Perceptions may include *enteredCell*, *exitedCell*, *objectAcquired*, *objectReleased*, *agentMoved*,

Environment↔Environment events are bidirectional and include, but are not limited to, *pathAdded* and *pathRemoved*.

4   Creating and Managing DIVAs Environment

In this section, we discuss the implementation of version 1.2 of DIVAs environment [25].

4.1   Cell and Level Specification

The DIVAs Environment allows the user to pre-configure the levels of abstraction that can be viewed in the visual space. The Environment can be configured to view multiple levels of increasing detail. Each level is configured as a grid. The grid is defined by a longitude and a latitude or the number of increments along the x and y axis. The longitude and latitude are further divided into a smaller cell divisions producing the grid displayed to the user.

Each level of abstraction is built on the cells defined in the previous level. For example, if a level is defined to have a longitude of 100 and a latitude of 100 with a cell division of 10. The grid would display as a square with division lines every 10 degrees. The next level then must be defined in terms of the previous. Therefore, the next level must have a longitude 10 and a latitude of 10. It can then select it owns subdivision of these dimensions for the new visual space (See Figure 9). The relation between the neighboring abstractions is necessary, because when the user selects to view a specific cell at a specific abstract level, the new visualization needs to reflect the area chosen.

4.2   Creating the Graph

The DIVAs Environment implementation is an embodiment of a Graph Model. The Environment Management System (EMS) provides an interface between external events and the Environment Management Module (EMM). The Environment supplies a User Interface (UI) to seed or initialize the Environment. Once locations have been added through the UI or a configuration element, they can be viewed in the environment on the visual plane.

A user can add additional locations and connections between the locations to initialize the environment as needs arise. Locations are the nodes of the graph. They indicate places or destinations, within the environment. The nodes are specified using longitude and latitude positions. It is important to note that a node belongs to only one cell. For example, a node at an intersection of, 95.0 longitude and 30.0 latitude is contained in the cell defined by 95 to 94.00000001 west longitude and 30.0 30.999999 north latitude. The relationships that connect nodes together form the arcs in the graph. These connections may represent paths along which agents can travel between locations.

The UI for the environment aids in plotting the locations at longitude and latitude positions. The references between the locations can be established between the nodes through the user interface as well. The DIVAs system uses a 2D graph model to represent the Environment. The complete environment is constructed from grouping the nodes of each of cells into a cell Graph Model. The graph plots the nodes and represents the connections as lines between the nodes, creating the graph. The graph is then plotted onto the environment visualization.

The user interface provides a means to list the locations of nodes and their connections. The UI also provides the ability to add new nodes and connections between new nodes and/or existing nodes. The connections can also be manipulate by adding new connections or removing current ones.

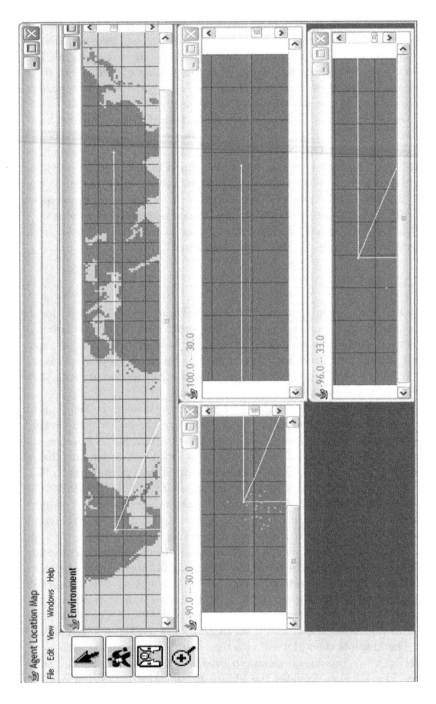

Fig. 9. Tool illustrating environment at three layers of abstraction

4.3   Managing the Environment

The process of adding a new node to the Environment involves the UI notifying the Environment Management System that a change has occurred or, specifically, a node had been added. The system, using the Environment Message Transport Service (EMTS), a publish/subscribe messaging service, broadcasts a message to the Environment Management Module, which in this case is the Graph Management Module (GMM) - a 2D management system for the graph model. The Graph Management Module maintains a list of the active cell controllers. When it receives a message that a node is to be added, the Graph Management Module determines if there is already an active cell controller for the location of the node. If there is an active controller, the exact position of the node is sent to the cell controller to update it's Graph Model. If there is no active cell controller for the node's location, a new cell controller is created and added to the GMM. The newly created cell controller is then notified of the node addition and updated.

The process of adding new connections to a node through the user interface is similar to that of adding a node. The UI notifies the Environment Management System that a change has occurred affecting the environment. The EMS notifies the Graph Management Module that a request has been made to connect two nodes together. The Graph Management Module acquires the cell controller of the originating node and sends node connection information to the cell controller for processing. The cell controller, using helper classes, determines the segment of the arc that lies within its boundaries. The remaining portion of the line is sent back to the Graph Management Module to be processed by subsequence cell controllers. The process terminates when a cell controller determines that the termination of the line is within its cell boundary. Each cell controller determines the segment of the entire line that resides with in its boundaries and is responsible for the management of only that portion of the line. The removal of nodes and connections uses the same logic to update the cell controllers which are responsible for the management of the node or line segment. Once the information has been updated in each of the cell controllers, the appropriate cell controller then adjusts its view of the environment accordingly. This may be reflected in the removal or addition of a line segment within the boundaries of its control.

The real power of separating the Environment Management System from the visualization is that different types of EMMs, such as a 3D model, can be plugged into the Environment Management System and be notified of an environment change and act accordingly. The EMMs, can then display a different type of visualization and various levels of abstraction for each type of Environment Model. The Graph Management Model simply groups the number of cell controllers to be displayed and shows them at different levels of detail.

4.4   Design

The design diagram for a cell in Figure 8 illustrates the classes needed to implement the functionality of the various modules included in the Environment Module (EM) with the exception of the Env-Env Message Transport Service.

The Environment Management System (EMS) acquires the location nodes from a data source and, once the data has been initialized, notifies the Environment Management Module (EMM) to create the Cell Environments Modules. The CellController class implements the Environment Module (EM) in the DIVAs project. The EMM or GraphManagementModel class is responsible for dividing the environment into manageable partitions. In a world environment, this would equate to a division along longitude and latitude demarcations. The demarcation depends on the granularity with which the user wants to visualize the world.

The CellController is coupled with the Information Management Module (IMM) for state maintenance. Thus, the CellController contains references to the following classes: SelfModel, AgentModel, and a concrete ObjectModel representing the Passive Entity Model. It also aggregates the LinkedCellModel as well as the GraphModel.

The AgentModel monitors the minimal information about agents within the cell, such as its last known location. It also broadcasts to the Synchronizer when the agent leaves the cell. The GraphModel class describes paths available in the environment. The GraphModel consists of nodes and edges connecting the nodes. A LocationNode describes a physical location in the two-dimensional environment denoted by an x and y component. In the broad sense, edges link two nodes together. In the small, however, an edge can span many cells. Therefore, a conceptual physical edge is divided in to path segments that are controlled by the individual CellControllers through which it passes. Thus, the instantiation of the PathSegment class can be one of three different varieties; a source segment, a sink segment or a line segment. A source segment is a PathSegment that has its origin within the cell (this assumes that the edges are directional or at least have an initiator of the line indicating direction such as a line of communication). A sink segment is a PathSegment that has its destination within the cell. A line segment is a PathSegment that either passes completely through the controller, in which case the cell considers the end points to be on the cell boundaries, or the PathSegment begins and ends within the cell. The PathSegment is defined by its origin (x; y; cellid) and its destination (x1; y1; cellid). The cellids are identifiers of the linked cells from which the link entered or exits. If the line segment is completely contained within the cell, then both ids reference the cell's SelfModel. The LinkedCellModel class associates the controller with its neighboring cells. There are, at most, eight neighboring cells and, depending upon location in the cell network, there are as few as three.

The ObjectModel serves the same purpose as the AgentModel but its focus is on monitoring objects (passive entities). The SelfModel class describes the identification of the controller. It contains a unique identifier as well as a parameterized boundary constraining its height and width.

5   Conclusion

In this paper, we have defined the concept of Agent-Environment Systems (AES), proposed that agents and environments have much in common, and presented a highly flexible and adaptable architecture for AES realized by DIVAs. Through examination of DIVAs, we established the environment as a legitimate, first-class entity whose responsibility is to maintain a stable state in which agents exist.

To demonstrate our concepts of AES, we have implemented all environment functionality using Java. In its current version, DIVAs allows the creation of a geographical world and the partitioning of that world into cells governed by their controller. The current functionality also includes the creation of the graph of cities and streets that maps onto the geography, as well as the implementation of algorithms which process external events injected into the environment. We have populated the world with agents, who mimic people, who interact with each other and the environment to preform basic functions while attempting to complete their goals. Through our 2D visualization, using the environment perspective, we can monitor people as they move from city to city. We can observe these people at a high, course-grained level, as if viewing the world's activities or, by opening new levels of visual abstraction, we can observe them at the finest grain as they walk the streets.

Several definitions of environments at various conceptual levels exist in the literature. Weyns et al. [1] propose a classification of environments in three major categories: *inter-agent facilities*, *agent-environment interaction*, and *environments in agent oriented methodologies*. Our work falls in the second category since it is based on the influence-reaction model. More specifically, DIVAs belongs to the class of *metric environments*, i.e., environments that use a grid-like structure, and are based on cellular automata concepts. Two recent multi-agent systems follow the same ideas. AKIRA [26], whose environment can be represented metrically, has rules and dynamics that can be used to model it as a simple agent. While the environment is responsible for simple system functions, it appears to be implemented as a single daemon. DIVAs differs from AKIRA's centralized nature of sharing messages via a blackboard, by having the cell controller dynamically manage the agent's perception of the environment.

Another work has been presented that offers agents and environment as a set of environment logical processes (ALPs and ELPs)[27]. The shared state of the environment is assigned to a group of special logical processes called *Communication Logical Processes* (CLPs), and the distribution of the state is performed dynamically in response to events generated by agents and environment. The CLPs form a tree where the ALPs and the ELPs are the leaves, and each CLP maintains a subset of the shared state associated with the children ALPs/ELPs. At the conceptual level, our work has some commonalities with this model since we also consider agents and environment as parallel logical processes, and we do allow dynamic state information sharing among the various entities. Our work diverge at the detailed design and implementation levels. Experiments have to be run to determine the efficiency of the CLP tree structure, versus the DIVAs cell network architecture.

The version of the DIVAs environment presented in this paper is undergoing change. We are currently re-implementing the Environment Specification Tool using the Eclipse Framework version 3.1 and Eclipse Rich Client Platform (RCP) version 3.1.0. Two views of the environment will be offered: the *Levels Map View*, and the *Environment View*. These views characterize the main perspective used in the tool and are implemented by extending *org.eclipse.ui.perspectives*. Each view is implemented by extending *org.eclipse.ui.views*. We will also be adding a 3D visualization to the capabilities of the Visualization Framework. It is interesting to note that the addition of a new visualization will not cause any change to the DIVAs AES structure since the AES architecture is decoupled from the visualizations. Also, we plan on testing the efficiency of the MTS on different sized populations of agents, and determining the limits of the current architecture.

References

1. Weyns, D., Parunak, H.V.D., Michel, F.: Environments for multiagent systems: State-of-the-art and research challenges. In: Post-Proceedings of the First International Workshop on Environments for Multiagent Systems. Volume 3374., Springer-Verlag (Spring 2005)
2. Bellifemine, F., Poggi, A., Rimassa, G., Turci, P.: An object-oriented framework to realize agent systems. Technical report, Universit di ParmaArizona, Italy (2000)
3. Howden, Ralph Ronnquist, A.H., Lucas, A.: Jack summary of an agent infrastructure. In: 5th International Conference on Autonomous Agents. (2001)
4. Chauhan, D.: JAFMAS: A Java-Based Agent Framework for Multi-Agent Systems Development and Implementation. PhD thesis, University of Cincinnati (1997)
5. Sycara, K., Paolucci, M., Van-Velsen, M., Giampapa, J.: The retsina mas infrastructure. special joint issue of Autonomous Agents and MAS **7** (2003)
6. Nwana, H., Ndumu, D., Lee, L.: Zeus: An advanced tool-kit for engineering distributed multi-agent systems. In: Proceedings of PAAM98, London U.K. (1998) 377–391
7. Rogers, T., Ross, R., Subrahmanian, V.: Impact: A system for building agent applications. Journal of Intelligent Information Systems **13** (1999)
8. Sloman, A., Poli, R.: SIM AGENT: A toolkit for exploring agent designs. Lecture Notes in Computer Science **1037** (1996) 392
9. Technologies, B.: Cougaar architecture document. Available from BBN Technologies over the Internet (accessed November 2005) http://www.cougaar.org.
10. Cabri, G., Leonardi, L., Zambonelli, F.: Mars: A programmable coordination architecture for mobile agents. In: IEEE Internet Computing. (2000)
11. Sun Microsystems, Inc: The JavaSpaces v1.2.1 Specification. (2002)
12. Schelfthout, K., Holvoet, T.: An environment for coordination of situated multi-agent systems. In: First International Workshop on Environments for Multiagent Systems, New York, USA (2004)
13. Julien, C., Roman, G.: Egocentric context-aware programming in ad hoc mobile environments. In: 10th International Symposium on the Foundations of Software Engineering, Charleston, USA (2002)
14. Mamei, M., Zambonelli, F., Leonardi, L.: Tuples on the air: A middleware for context-aware computing in dynamic networks. In: ICDCS Workshop. (2003)
15. Murphy, A., Picco, G., Roman, G.: Lime: a middleware for physical and logical mobility. In: 21st International Conference on Distributed Computing Systems, 21st International Conference on Distributed Computing Systems (2001)

16. Mamei, M., Leonardi, L., Zambonelli, F.: Co-fields: Towards a unifying approach to the engineering of swarm intelligent systems. In: Lecture Notes in Artificial Intelligence. Volume 2577., Berling Heidelberg New York (2003)

17. Brueckner, S.: Return from the Ant. PhD thesis, Humboldt-Universitt, Berlin Germany (2000)

18. Collier, N.: Repast: An extensible framework for agent simulation. Available from RePast Group over the Internet (accessed November 2005) http://repast.sourceforge.net/.

19. Luke, S., Cioffi-Revilla, C., Panait, L., Sullivan, K.: Mason: A new multi-agent simulation toolkit. In: Proceedings of the SwarmFest Workshop, Michigan, USA (2004)

20. Ferber, J.: Multi-Agent Systems: An Introduction to Distributed Artificial Intelligence. Addison Wesley (1999)

21. Mili, R.Z., Oladimeji, E., Steiner, R.: Design of the divas simulation system. Technical Report UTDCS-11-05, University of Texas at Dallas, USA (2005)

22. Oladimeji, E., Mili, R., Shakya, U.: Towards an abstract agent architecture for mas simulation systems. Technical Report UTDCS-12-05, University of Texas at Dallas, USA (2005)

23. Mili, R., Leask, G., Steiner, R., Oladimeji, E.: Architecture and design viewpoints for agent-environment systems. Technical Report UTDCS-43-04, University of Texas at Dallas, USA (2004)

24. Mili, R., Leask, G., Shakya, U., Steiner, R., Oladimeji, E.: Architectural design of the divas environment. In: Proceedings of 1st workshop on Environments for Multiagent Systems, New York, USA (2004)

25. Leask, G.: Two dimentional environment for the divas multi-agent system. Master's thesis, University of Texas at Dallas, USA (2005)

26. Pezzulo, G., Calvi, G.: Designing and implementing mabs in akira. In Davidsson, P., Logan, B., Takadama, K., eds.: Multi-Agent and Multi-Agent-Based Simulation - Joint Workshop MABS 2004, Revised Selected Papers, New York, NY, USA, Springer, Lecture Notes in Computer Science Series (July 2004) 49–64

27. Lees, M., Logan, B., Minson, R., Oguara, T., Theodoropoulos, G.: Distributed simulation of mas. In Davidsson, P., Logan, B., Takadama, K., eds.: Multi-Agent and Multi-Agent-Based Simulation - Joint Workshop MABS 2004, Revised Selected Papers, New York, NY, USA, Springer, Lecture Notes in Computer Science Series (July 2004) 25–36

Indirect Interaction in Environments for Multi-agent Systems*

David Keil and Dina Goldin

University of Connecticut, Storrs, CT, USA
{dkeil, dqg}@engr.uconn.edu

Abstract. The E4MAS community is leading an effort to accept environments of multi-agent systems as a first-class entity, distinguishing *indirect interaction* via the environment from the environment's role in message transport. This paper defines classes of interaction (sequential and multi-agent, direct and indirect) and environments (physical and virtual, persistent and amnesic, dynamic and static). These notions provide an underpinning for proper acknowledgement of the roles of MAS environments and for powerful MAS design techniques that use indirect interaction. We explore the limitations of MAS models that are restricted to message passing and suggest research directions for constructing more powerful models.

1 Introduction

In situated multi-agent systems (MAS), the environment is independently active, in effect providing a shared memory, and making possible decentralized coordination [41]. For these reasons, research in multi-agent systems has begun to accept the environment of a MAS as a first-class entity. The E4MAS community [7] is at the forefront of this effort, pointing out how agents may use the environment in coordinating their activities.

The CFP for E4MAS 2005 distinguishes interaction via message transport from interaction via the environment, and points toward the more active conception of the environment in the latter case. *Indirect interaction* is precisely the nontrivial use of the environment in the way that the E4MAS CFP suggests. The trivial use of the environment for message transport is a case of what we call *direct interaction*.

Currently accepted models of concurrency explicitly represent only direct interaction (message passing). A major challenge for MAS research is to break out of the restricted framework that limits the environment to the role of message transport. Meeting this challenge entails providing a theoretical underpinning for indirect interaction among agents via the environment. To support research in multi-agent systems and their environments, new formalizations are required that explicitly represent indirect interaction.

---

* Supported by NSF award 0545489.

D. Weyns, H. Van Dyke Parunak, and F. Michel (Eds.): E4MAS 2005, LNAI 3830, pp. 68–87, 2006.

After surveying of research in environments for multi-agent systems, we outline steps toward formalizations that will address the needs of MAS research. We make a formal distinction between use of the environment for message transport and use of it for indirect interaction, and define a useful taxonomy of environments. In particular, we categorize environments along three dimensions:

- *persistent* vs. *amnesic*
- *dynamic* vs. *static*
- *physical* vs. *virtual*

Persistent environments have memory of past interactions with agents; persistence is a prerequisite for indirect interaction. Dynamic environments change their responses to agents over time; as a result, agents in dynamic environments may need adaptive behavior to meet utility criteria. Physical environments are ones in which situated agents operate; these environments can offer the greatest challenges, having memory with which to counter-adapt and lacking the predictability of computing entities.

Research in indirect interaction via the environment points to the computational power of this form of interaction. For example, natural systems of extremely simple agents, such as amoebae and ants, perform complex tasks via indirect interaction, also known as *stigmergy* (Sect. 3.3). Indirect interaction offers a powerful tool for MAS design (Sect. 4.3). The limitations of the standard models of concurrency, which are based on message passing (direct interaction), prevent them from modeling this form of interaction (Section 5.3).

Our work is part of an effort within the theory community to account for and to model interactive forms of computation [40,12,38], analogous to the successful modeling of *algorithmic* computing [19] with Turing machines [36]. We believe that new models of multi-agent interaction, based on indirect interaction, are needed to adequately underpin research in multi-agent systems.

Outline. In Sect. 2 we survey environments in MAS research, provide a definition of the notion of an environment, and classify environments. As a foundation for formal discussion of MAS environments, we offer in Sect. 3 a set of definitions of interactive computation, the environment of a single computing agent, persistence in environments, and direct and indirect interaction. Properties of indirect interaction and examples of it in E4MAS research are presented in Sect. 4. In Sect. 5, we highlight the limitations of the message-passing model of Milner. Sect. 6 sums up and points to related work and future research challenges.

2   MAS Environments

In this section, we survey E4MAS research (Sect. 2.1). This research has produced a number of characterizations and definitions of the term "environment." Based on this survey, and on our own work in models of interaction, we formulate a unifying definition of MAS environments (Sect. 2.2). We also provide a taxonomy, i.e., a set of dimensions along which to classify MAS environments

(Sect. 2.3). Our definitions apply to physical environments of embedded agents as well as virtual environments of software agents.

2.1   Environments in E4MAS Research

Research in environments for multi-agent systems has produced many examples of environments, with some common features.

A web site may be described as an environment for agents that visit it via HTTP. Its spatial structure is defined by pages hyper-linked together. Users move through this environment; hence linking and unlinking to a page is a form of mobility. The Multilayered Multi-Agent Situated Systems (MMASS) model [3] represents such an environment as an undirected graph where pages are vertices and links are edges. Since multiple clients may visit the same web site concurrently, and may change the state of data stored at the site, it is possible not only for agents to interact with the site, but also for agents to interact with each other via the site.

The web site here is an environment via which clients interact with each other, not by passing messages to each other, but anonymously and without handshake. This research is recognized as pointing to "a new form of interaction" among simultaneous visitors to a web site [3]. Traditional discourse about web-based interaction focuses on direct file transfers between servers and individual clients (browsers viewing pages).

An environment may be specifically the *physical* (analog) setting in which agents are situated. Alternatively, it may be a *virtual* (digital) setting for agents, subject to being shaped by system designers. Indirect interaction via the physical environment is also known as *stigmergy*. MAS-based manufacturing control serves as an example of stigmergy and of *self-organization*, the attribute of a *decentralized* MAS that displays behavior at a global level that is more than the composition of the behaviors at the lower level, of subcomponents. The Product-Resource-Order-Staff Architecture (PROSA) [37] supports self-organization by agents.

In a MAS of situated agents, the environment of each agent is often a combination of virtual and physical. An example of such a combination is the system of automatic guided vehicles (AGVs) that transport loads through a warehouse, adapting flexibly to changing conditions [42]. The application described supports a *local virtual environment* for each vehicles, which constitute a decentralized system. These virtual environments contain three types of information: *static* (e.g., layout of factory floor); *observable* (from other local virtual environments; e.g., position of an AGV); and *shared* (modifiable in two local virtual environments concurrently; e.g., traffic map). When a nearby load (located in the physical environment) requires transport, the location of that load is communicated to the AGV via its virtual environment; agents can also communicate with each other with the help of their local virtual environments.

Another example is a PDA-based museum-visitor scenario for access to museum information [43]. Visitors may interact with the museum environment and may also interact via a shared environment of tuples, such as when expressing the desire for a group meeting, Artwork and visitor agents may enable human visitors to move toward art pieces of interest, or toward other visitors for group meetings.

Sometimes, however, situated agents may live in a purely virtual environments, such as the the distributed ant algorithm framework of [22].

It is possible to view the virtual environment as (non-agent) entities *in* a MAS that affect agents [34,41]. Often, it is a single software entity with individual objectives, which communicates with the agents in the MAS. Unlike the agents, it is an independent and self-supporting entity, offering support services to the agents, including services of mediation between agents [39].

Seen as an *organizational layer*, a MAS environment may be designed to impose *constraints* on agent behavior. A common constraint is that of *locality*; that is, agents in a MAS each have their own *local* environment, and their interaction is limited to this environment. This notion of locality adds a *spatial* aspect to a MAS environment [41].

Some discussion of environments refers to *software or hardware platforms* as "environments," and other discussion refers to entities that interact with systems of agents as their "environments." Consider a MAS running as an application on a computer. We may say that the MAS's environment is the set of entities with which the agents interact, or we may alternatively say its environment is the computer and its operating system, and all the data streaming through ports of the computer. These are completely different senses of the word "environment."

Sometimes, a MAS environment is referred to as *application environment*. The application environment may be defined as "the logical entity that represents the space in which the Application Agents perform their job." This notion of environment can be contrasted with the execution infrastructure of a MAS, sometimes referred to as its *execution environment*; examples are those provided by Jade, LIME, JavaSpaces, or Retsina. The term "Distributed Agent Environment" (DAE) has been used to refer to the support infrastructure [43].

Both notions of the environment are meaningful, but to use the same word for both within the same field of research presents a conflict and risks being highly misleading. Our interest in this paper lies only with application environments; we will not be considering execution environments.

2.2   Defining Environments

As researchers in models of interactive computation, we suggest ways to unify and reconcile the various descriptions of environments presented in Sect. 2.1. This work is aimed towards providing foundations for new models of multi-agent interaction. We also suggest below some dimensions of a taxonomy of multi-agent system environments.

The following concise definition emerges from the examples in Sect. 2.1:

Definition 1. *An* environment *of a multi-agent system is a* physical *or* virtual *setting that acts as the producer of the system's inputs and consumer of its outputs. The environment of a single computing agent is simply the environment of the multi-agent system that consists only of this agent.*   □

Our approach to conceptualizing environments positions them as a *relative* notion that is defined by *interaction*. An environment of a system is identified with the set of agents or other entities with which it interacts, and the environment of an agent is identified likewise. Suppose that agents in a multi-agent system interact with each other and with the system environment; then, these agents are part of each other's environment, though they are not part of the system's environment. In fact, if the system were to consist of two agents that interact exclusively with each other, then each would *be* each other's environment. This underscores the relative nature of the concept of environment.

It might be objected that environments and agents are distinct because agents are *active* and environments may be *passive*. But consider the standpoint of agent A that interacts with a "passive" entity B, which also interacts with agent C. Then as observed by A, B changes its state autonomously (when C changes B's state); hence from A's perspective, B does not behave passively. Thus, to agents such as A, passive environmental entities may be indistinguishable from active agent entities.

When two agents share the same environment, or have overlapping local environments (see Sect. 2.1), it follows naturally that these agents may end up affecting each other, by reading from and writing to their common environment. We say that they interact *indirectly* via their environment; it is this form of interaction that is of particular interest to us.

2.3   A Taxonomy of Environments

We focus on some *properties* of environments that help establish a taxonomy of MAS environments. In their popular textbook on artificial intelligence [31], Russell and Norvig have listed the following dimensions of environments, among others: *dynamic versus static, accessible* versus *inaccessible*; *deterministic* versus *non-deterministic*; *discrete* versus *continuous*.

We suggest here the dimensions of *persistent versus amnesic, dynamic versus static*, and *physical versus virtual* as the basis for a taxonomy of agent environments [17]. Other dimensions to be considered include *centralized versus decentralized* [16,9].

We begin with the *static/dynamic* dimension in our taxonomy of MAS environments:

Definition 2. *An environment E is static with respect to an agent A if A's inputs from E are strictly dependent on A's outputs to E. A dynamic environment is one that is not static.* □

For example, a lamp that lights dependably when plugged in and goes out when unplugged defines a static environment w.r.t. the agent operating the lamp. A lamp with a light sensor, which lights when plugged in only if the room is dark, defines a dynamic environment with respect to the agent.

Dynamic environments are characterized by their capacity to change autonomously. If agents A and C are both interacting with an entity B (but not with each other), and C's interaction with B affects B's behavior, then B is a dynamic environment with respect to A. Clearly, an environment that is static is more predictable than a dynamic one.

We now define a class of environments that *can* remember from previous interactions:

Definition 3. *An environment is* persistent *if its outputs depend not only on its immediately preceding inputs, but also on earlier inputs. An environment is* amnesic *if it is not persistent.*   □

For example, an electric light with a button switch, that lights when it is off and the user presses the button, but turns off when it is on and the user presses the same button, defines a persistent environment. A piece of paper defines a persistent environment w.r.t. a person writing on the paper. The air is amnesic w.r.t. a person singing to it, and persistent w.r.t. a person spraying perfume into it.

A persistent virtual environment can be viewed as a *reactive system* [21]; so can *intelligent agents* (as opposed to *reflex agents* [31]). When systems of intelligent agents operate in persistent environments, their design is concerned with utility maximization, rather than with satisfaction of predicates as in the design of functional systems [45].

When an environment is persistent, it is sometimes modeled as a Markov decision process (MDP); when it is also dynamic, it is modeled as a partially observable Markov decision process (POMDP); see [14].

Our taxonomy distinguishes real-world environments from the digital environments of finite computing devices:

Definition 4. *A* physical *environment is one observable only by analog sensors. A* virtual *environment is accessed digitally.*   □

Note that our definition of environments (Definition 1) is general enough to encompass both virtual and physical environments. When an agent's environment is physical (the real world), the kinds of input and output are different from those in virtual environments. In artificial intelligence, these inputs and outputs are known as *percepts* and *actions*, respectively. An example is an automatic car [8], whose percepts consist of video camera snapshots, and whose actions consist of turning the wheel or pushing on the brake pedal. According to our definition, the road constitutes the environment of an automatic car.

Since we are interested in indirect interaction, our special concern is with environments that have persistence, a necessary precondition for indirect interaction. The notion of persistence is consistent with Piaget's definition of *behavior*, whose purpose is to change the state of the environment in a way favorable to a species or organism [29]. Persistence enables a higher long-term expectation of reward from the environment, not just a higher immediate reward.

The environment in which we drive a car is dynamic, persistent, and physical. It changes with respect to the car whenever we cause the car to move. Cars, pedestrians, and other potential obstacles appear and vanish in a way that our actions determine.

Not all dynamic environments are *persistent*, in the sense that they "remember" what happens to them, and this influences their later input to agents. Consider the environment of a theater stage, with either a play or a comedy routine; the audience is the agent. Both the play and the comedy routine are dynamic. The play is amnesic, in that the viewers' reaction cannot affect its progress. By contrast, the comedy routine is persistent, in that the comedian may make comments about audience members, or change his jokes in response to audience reaction.

3   Interactive Computation

As we have suggested, identifying the environment of an agent or system of agents presupposes the existence of *interaction*. In this section, we formalize the notion of interaction, making the possibility of mutual *causality* a condition for applying it (Sect. 3.1). We then distinguish two forms of interaction, *direct* and *indirect* (Sect. 3.2), with examples (Sect. 3.3).

3.1   Sequential and Multi-agent Interaction

Interaction is a form of concurrent computation where communication is viewed as occurring *during* the computing process, rather than *before* or *after* it [13].

Definition 5. Interactive computation *is the ongoing exchange of data among the participants (agents or their environment) such that the output of each participant may causally influence its later inputs.*   □

Exchange of data that never affects the actions of the recipient, and never has a later effect on the inputs of the sender, is not true interaction between them. A person who responds to what is shown on a television screen, by talking to or shouting at the television, is not interacting with it. A microphone and an amplifier do not interact unless *feedback* is present. Research in cybernetics fifty years ago recognized feedback or mutual influence as a feature that distinguishes an important kind of coupling of systems, both natural and artificial ones [44,2,32].

We consider feedback essential to interaction. One-way communication without feedback should be distinguished from interaction; likewise, input alone is not interaction. Interaction must allow mutual causality, hence the semantics of interaction demand that feedback be present.

Note that the outputs of two agents may causally influence their later inputs without the agents communicating directly; they may communicate via an intermediary. In that case the causality and interaction are *indirect* (Sect. 3.2).

In interactive computation, the role of the environment is heightened, relative to the role of the environment in the execution of an algorithm. An *algorithm* is a description of the steps for effectively transforming an input to an output, so that the output is a (computable) function of the input [19]. Once the environment determines the input value passed to an algorithm, its job is done. By contrast, the environment participates *throughout* an interactive computation.

For algorithmic (function-based) computation, captured by Turing machines, the properties of an environment are of no consequence, because one execution of an algorithm simply computes a function on whatever single input arrives from the environment. For interactive computation, on the other hand, how an action by a computing agent will change its environment can be crucial to the choices made by the agent.

The simplest form of interactive computation is when the communication between a system and its environment takes place via a single stream (channel or interface). This type of interaction is referred to as *sequential*:

Definition 6. Sequential interactive computation *is interaction involving two participants, at least one of which is a finite computing agent (machine, device).*
□

By definition, the other participant in sequential interactive computation serves as the environment of the first.

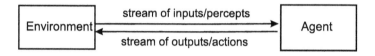

Fig. 1. Agent and environment

In sequential interaction, there is a single input stream and a single output stream between the computing entity and its environment (see Fig. 1). The temporal interleaving of these two streams creates a single *interaction stream* that consists of pairs of input and output tokens. In a physical environment, the notion of *sensing* by a computing agent corresponds to *getting input*, and the notion of *actuating* corresponds to *emitting output*. Sequential interactive computation has been formalized by *Persistent Turing Machines* (Sect. 5.1).

As we explain in Sections 3.2 and 4.2, persistence of state in an environment makes possible indirect interaction among agents, which in turn facilitates *systems* of agents, i.e., MASs. Sequential interaction with its single interaction stream is distinguished from *multi-agent interaction*, where multiple autonomous streams may exist simultaneously between the system and its environment. This is illustrated in Figure 2; the dashed box indicates the boundary between the system and the external environment.

We define multi-agent interaction as follows:

Definition 7. Multi-agent interaction *is interactive computation involving* more *than two agents; the agents are assumed to be* asynchronous.   □

It is conjectured that models of multi-agent interaction such as the *multi-stream interaction machine* (MIM) are more expressive than models of sequential interaction [40]. The remainder of this paper focuses on multi-agent interaction and MASs.

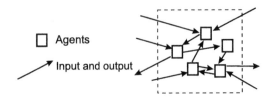

Fig. 2. Multi-agent interaction

3.2 Direct and Indirect Interaction

It is commonly thought that interaction is the same as communication, associated with the notion of *message passing* [26] or *targeted send/receive* (TSR) [10]. We refer to this form of interaction as *direct*:

Definition 8. Direct interaction *is interaction via messages, where the identifier of the recipient is specified in a message.* □

Message passing is appropriate when two entities possess identifying information about each other and have the intent to communicate with each other. However, entities may also interact without knowing about each other, and without even having any intent to communicate. This happens when they share a common environment, and the changes made by one of them to the environment can be observed by the other. This second category of interaction is known as *indirect*, originally defined in [15]:

Definition 9. Indirect interaction *is interaction via persistent, observable changes to a common environment; recipients are any agents that will observe these changes.* □

Note that the acts of making changes (output) and of observing those changes (input) are decoupled in time; persistence of the environment allows the change to endure, allowing for a lapse of time before it is observed. Furthermore, the identity of the observer(s) may not yet be determined when the environment is changed, allowing for *anonymous* interaction. In fact, the change need not be motivated by the need to communicate, but may occur as a byproduct of the first agent's computation.

While indirect interaction differs significantly from direct interaction (communication), both clearly satisfy the definition of interaction (Definition 5). However, in computing, indirect interaction seems to be treated as a poor cousin of the direct form, as it is not supported by current models of interaction.

Indirect interaction deserves the same level of recognition and the same attention from the theoretical community as does direct interaction. It is not by accident that multi-agent systems occurring in nature often rely on indirect interaction to "get their job done." Likewise, indirect interaction via work in progress, shared writing, pictures, and publicly viewed symbols of all kinds, is the basis for most forms of human production and for shared culture and markets of all kinds. Some examples of such multi-agent systems are presented next.

3.3   Examples of Indirect Interaction

In this section, we discuss several examples of indirect interaction via the environment. The first three are based on naturally occurring multi-agent systems: ant trails [4,5], termite piles [30], and slime molds [18]. The last is a classic example of distributed computation, the *Dining Philosophers* problem [6].

Most of us have seen a column of ants forming a busy highway on our floor or our counter top. Ant colonies solve the problem of efficiently foraging for food sources by a decentralized approach involving multi-agent indirect interaction, where each ant deposits *pheromones* (slowly evaporating scent chemicals) as it carries food, and each ant follows pheromone trails as it searches for food. The pheromone trail to a food source gets reinforced over time, turning into a highway. Once the food source is exhausted, the trail is no longer reinforced, and it evaporates over time. Without a plan, the ants find paths to the food that tend toward optimality.

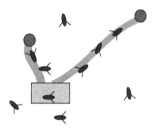

Fig. 3. Ant trails

The problem of building an ant hill or a termite pile is likewise solved in a decentralized fashion, relying on indirect interaction. In the StarLogo termite simulation [33], the termites build a single circular pile of wood chips, despite having no capacity for planning or coordination, and with minimal ability to perceive. They continuously apply a simple protocol: move at random, pick up a chip whenever one is encountered, and put it down when the termite bumps into another chip. Eventually, a single pile emerges. Remarkably, the termites accomplish this task without having an internal representation of their eventual goal.

Another naturally occurring multi-agent behavior that depends on indirect interaction is the formation of *slime molds*. When their food is scarce, *slime mold* amoeba organisms emit a "distress" chemical that causes them to gravitate to one another. The chemical signal is relayed among these microscopic organisms, and they migrate in a spiral toward the center of such signals, eventually aggregating in huge numbers into a single crawling slug-like organism that is large enough to see with the naked eye. Again, aggregate behavior emerges from individual behavior through indirect interaction, without centralized direction.

In each of the above examples, the global behavior of the population is more than the composition of the individual behaviors. No one in that population ever decides where the trail will lie, where the pile will be located, or where the slime mold slug will raise its head. Individually, these organisms are too simple to have an "understanding" of such complex phenomena, yet their behavior as an aggregate predictably results in these phenomena. *Emergent behavior* occurs in such complex systems, which exhibit *self-organization.*

The classic *Dining Philosophers* problem is another example of indirect interaction. In this problem, philosophers sit at a circular table, with one chop-stick between each pair of diners. Each one occasionally interrupts her thinking to pick up two chop-sticks – first one, then another – and eat, then put them down, repeating these steps when hungry. The problem is to avoid starvation by deadlock; if each diner simultaneously picks up the left chop-stick, for example, and holds it until the other one is available, then all will starve. One solution involves *exogenous coordination* by managing *channels* [1].

Fig. 4. Dining Philosophers

This problem is often formulated in terms of concurrent communicating processes that share common resources. The objective is to define a protocol for a ring-shaped arrangement of processes, each communicating only with its two neighbors, such that all processes are allowed to move forward under the constraint that no two adjacent ones may execute simultaneously. Yet in the original problem, the philosophers never communicate with each other; in fact, it is not even clear that they are aware of each other, as they sit deep in thought or search hungrily for their chop-sticks. Despite the lack of direct communication, each philosopher's behavior is affected by the others, since she cannot eat while her neighbor is eating. This is due to indirect interaction; the philosophers communicate *indirectly* via the chop-sticks.

4   Indirect Interaction and Multi-agent Systems

Indirect interaction is ubiquitous. In this section, we discuss the use of indirect interaction in research in environments for multi-agent systems (Sect. 4.1). We then focus on the properties of indirect interaction, which include *name decoupling* (anonymity), *time decoupling* (asynchrony), *space decoupling* (locality), and *non-intentionality* (Sect. 4.2) and sketch an approach to MAS design that makes use of indirect interaction (Sect. 4.3).

4.1   Indirect Interaction in MAS Research and Beyond

The examples in Section 3.3 have inspired the design of MAS systems based on indirect interaction. *Digital pheromones*, which are data structures inspired by the insect model, have been used for coordination of autonomous vehicles [28]. A related approach is to use *force fields* [20], which are generated by the agents, propagated via some embedded infrastructure, and perceived locally by those agents in the vicinity of the field.

MAS's for manufacturing control are an example of indirect interaction, where the environment is "a first-class abstraction" [37]. Rather than communicating only with each other, the various agents involved (resources, orders, products, etc.) all interact with the common factory environment and adjust their behavior according to what they observe in that environment.

In another example, a web site serves as a shared environment for the agents that visit it via HTTP. Its spatial structure is defined by pages hyper-linked together. Users move through this environment; hence linking and unlinking to a page is a form of mobility. Since agents can both write to, and read from, the web pages, it is possible not only for agents to interact with the site, but also for agents to interact with each other indirectly, via the site. This interaction is anonymous, without handshake. This research is recognized in [3] as pointing to "a new form of interaction"; we can now see that this refers to indirect interaction.

[42] introduces a virtual persistent environment for situated MASs of autonomous guided vehicles (AGVs) that is an alternative to the approach of [28]. The virtual environment is alongside the physical environment; it is distributed over physical agents and synchronized using middleware. It maintains a shared memory of the agents, and its role is to set rules of dynamic relationships among agents. This is in effect *exogenous coordination* [1].

From the above examples it is clear that creation of a persistent virtual environment, adequate for supporting indirect interaction, is useful for engineering certain applications. We also believe that for some forms of system behavior, indirect interaction is not only useful but necessary; direct interaction is not sufficient.

Indirect interaction, where agents (organisms) interact via their *shared environment* rather than by exchanging messages directly, is ubiquitous outside of MAS research as well. In addition to above examples, there are many others, both within and outside computer science. Here is a sampling from various fields:

- *Operating systems:* Processes exchange information via semaphores in shared memory;
- *Programming languages:* The Linda language uses tuple spaces to enable coordination by indirect interaction [10];
- *Anatomy:* Cells exchange information via hormones in the bloodstream;
- *Social biology:* In stigmergy, social insects interact indirectly by leaving trails of pheromone chemicals [35];
- *Sociology:* Most group dynamics consist of actions or percepts whose destinations or sources are other than one's immediate partner in a communication;

- *Multi-agent systems:* Agents communicate indirectly either through intermediary agents or through changes in the environment;
- *Economics:* the storage and publication of stock market listings enables large
numbers of buyers and sellers to interact indirectly to negotiate prices.

In the next section, we discuss indirect interaction in multi-agent systems at
greater depth, focusing on its properties.

4.2   Properties of Indirect Interaction

Several characteristics of indirect interaction distinguish it from message passing
(direct interaction):

- *time decoupling* (asynchrony): due to persistence of the environment, there
may be a delay between the state change and its observation;
- *anonymity:* the observer's identity need not be known to the originator of
the state change;
- *late binding of recipient:* the identity of the observer of changes to the environment may be determined dynamically by events occurring after the
change is made;
- *space decoupling* (locality): indirect interaction of mobile agents need not
imply co-location; one may leave after making state changes, and the second
state may arrive later to observe them;
- *non-intentionality:* indirect interaction does not require an intent to communicate;
- *analog form:* the medium of indirect interaction may be the real world, e.g.
for embedded or situated agents (robots, sensors).

Asynchrony in indirect interaction follows from time delay due to the persistence of the observable changes in the environment. By contrast, message passing
is synchronous; synchronization occurs when one process stops and waits until the
other has reached a certain point in the computation or interaction. Synchronization by handshake enables processes to begin communicating with each other.

Examples of synchronous interaction are conversations and the TELNET
protocol. Asynchronous interaction includes exchanges of email and communication among ants via pheromone trails. Message queues enable asynchronous
communication when interaction is direct.

Anonymous interaction occurs when computing entities interact without
knowledge of each other's identities. In indirect interaction, anonymity is not
only possible but often necessary, when the identity of the observer (recipient) is
not determined until after the change to the environment has been made. When
an ant leaves a pheromone trail, it is not yet known which of the ants milling
nearby will be the one to pick up this scent. Similarly, after a termite drops a
wood chip, many things can happen that will eventually determine which termite
will pick it up.

The Dining Philosophers problem also exhibits the above characteristics. This
problem has the properties of (1) *locality*, because diners can only see neighboring

chop-sticks; (2) *anonymity*, because diners need not know each other's names or even whether their neighbors exist; (3) *asynchrony*, because a diner doesn't necessarily pick up a chop-stick as soon as it is put down; and (4) *non-intentionality* of communication, because diners pick up (put down) chop-sticks so as to eat (think), not to communicate.

A *mobile* version of the Dining Philosophers problem can also be defined, where the philosophers may leave to go sleep, then come back to occupy the first empty chair they can find. This mobile version exhibits the additional property of *late binding of recipient*, since the identity of one's neighbor cannot be known ahead of time.

4.3   Indirect Interaction and MAS Design

While indirect interaction serves as a valuable communication paradigm for all types of agency, its properties make it ideal for the design of large complex systems from small simple agents. Ants, termites, and slime molds from the previous section are all examples of such systems that occur in nature.

In II-MAS, it is assumed that the agents are much simpler than their environment; in the extreme case, agents are finite-state automata (single-celled organisms), while the environment is the real world. The agents in II-MAS are therefore expected to lack the cognitive abilities to observe and act on the state of the complete environment. As a result, they must limit themselves to a small part of their environment that we call their *locality*, where locality may be either physical or virtual. In either case, if the locality of an agent may change during the computation, we refer to the agent as *mobile*. As a result of mobility, the recipient of indirect interaction need never share the same locality as the initiator of that interaction; this is what we call *space decoupling*.

In an II-MAS, each agent's protocols for its interaction with the environment are simple and repeatable. While there may be more than one type of ant (worker, drone, etc.), there is no need to provide a unique program for each ant or termite. The agents in II-MAS are not concerned with other agents, except as those agents make changes to their shared environment. There are no issues of scalability or redesign if agents are added to, or removed from, the system during the computation.

Anonymity ensures that agents in II-MAS are interchangeable, while asynchrony allows systems to be adaptable. Unlike algorithms, where a single deviation from the plan means an incorrect result for the computation, II-MAS can be designed to withstand dynamic changes in the agent population, or to the environment. If the food source moves, the ant trails will eventually lead to the new location; if the wood chips are disturbed, the termites will eventually reassemble them.

5   Modeling Multi-agent Systems and Their Environments

Just as a gap has been observed between the *theory of computation* and *concurrency theory* [13], we also see a gap between research in *multi-agent systems* and the modeling of *concurrent distributed systems*. Whereas indirect interaction via the environment can play a key role in MASs, the traditional message-passing model of concurrency provides no first-class representation of indirect interaction.

Below we present a model of sequential interaction (Sect. 5.1) as well as Robin Milner's model of concurrency, based on message passing (Sect. 5.2), and highlight their limitations with respect to MAS research (Sect. 5.3).

5.1   A Formal Model of Sequential Interaction

Multi-agent interaction (Definition 7) has to date been modeled as as a set of concurrent instances of sequential interactions (Definition 6). Let us begin with a model of sequential interactive computation based on Turing machines, the *Persistent Turing Machine* (PTM) [11,12]. The PTM is a Turing machine with three special features that distinguish it from a TM:

- The TM's executions are *iterated* so that the PTM performs an infinite series of TM computations;
- the input/output semantics of the PTM differ from those of the TM in that input and output are dynamically generated *streams*; where later input tokens to the PTM may depend on its earlier output tokens;
- The PTM has a *persistent* tape, which retains its contents between one execution of the TM and the next.

A PTM is a nondeterministic 3-tape Turing machine (N3TM) with a read-only input tape, a read/write work tape, and a write-only output tape. Upon receiving an input token from its environment on its input tape, a PTM computes for a while and then outputs the result to the environment on its output tape, and this process is repeated forever. A PTM performs *persistent computations* in the sense that a notion of "memory" (work-tape contents) is maintained from one computation step to the next, where each PTM computation step represents an N3TM computation.

Persistence extends the effect of inputs. An input token affects the computation of its corresponding macrostep, including the work tape. The work tape in turn affects subsequent computation steps. If the work tape were erased, then the input token could not affect subsequent macrosteps, but only "its own" macrostep. With persistence, an input token can affect all subsequent macrosteps; this property is known as *history dependence*.

The treatment of PTMs has proceeded along the following lines. Our team first formalized the notions of interaction and persistence in PTMs in terms of the persistent stream language (PSL) of a PTM. Given a PTM, its persistent stream language is coinductively defined to be the set of infinite sequences (interaction streams) of pairs of the form (w_i, w_o) representing the input and output strings of a single PTM computation step. Persistent stream languages induce a natural, stream-based notion of equivalence for PTMs. *Decider PTMs* are an important subclass of PTMs; a PTM is a *decider* if it does not have divergent (non-halting) computations.

Our team defined the class of *amnesic* PTMs and a corresponding notion of amnesic stream language (ASL). In this case, the PTM begins each new computation with a blank work tape. It was shown that the class of ASLs is strictly contained in the class of PSLs, and that ASL-equivalence coincides with the equivalence induced by considering interaction-stream prefixes of length one, the bottom of our equivalence hierarchy; and that this hierarchy collapses in the case of amnesic PTMs. ASLs are representative of the classical view of Turing-machine computation. One may consequently conclude that, in a stream-based setting, the extension of the Turing-machine model with persistence is a nontrivial one, and provides a formal foundation for reasoning about programming concepts such as objects with static attributes.

In an analogous fashion to the Church-Turing Thesis, our team hypothesized that anything intuitively computable by a sequential interactive computation can be computed by a persistent Turing machine. This hypothesis, when combined with other results, implies that the class of sequential interactive computations is more expressive than the class of algorithmic computations, and thus is capable of solving a wider range of problems.

5.2 Milner's Model of Concurrency

Robin Milner is a pioneer of models of interaction, winner of the 1992 Turing award. Milner observed that *reactive* systems are unlike *algorithmic* ones in that they do not compute *functions* [23]. His Calculus of Communicating Systems (CCS) formalized some notions about interaction, including the notion of *concurrent composition* in which systems are composed (placed in communication), equivalent to the notion that they *observe* each other [24]. Alongside (mutual) observation, a second fundamental idea of the CCS was *synchronized communication*. Thus under Milner's theory, communication is *sequential interaction* between *two* agents.

Milner's π-calculus is a successor to CCS that leaves unchanged the basic assumption that interaction is reducible to binary communication. Agents take turns emitting and receiving data, synchronized by a *handshake*. When agents lack handshake protocol (as, for example, virtually throughout nature), they may use *buffers* to avoid loss of data. Models mentioned by [24] as alternatives to synchronized models include the Actor Systems of Hewitt and the model of Kahn and McQueen based on unbounded buffers and queues.

In Milner's model, communication is in the form of *messages*, where the emitting agent knows the identifier of the receiving agent. Hence this form of communication is sometimes called *targeted send/receive* (TSR). This assumption is explicitly stated in [25].

Milner has consistently made clear that interaction between agents via their environment is to be modeled by treating shared memory as *processes*: "I also insisted that memory registers be modeled as processes..." [26]. In this way, the underlying assumption is maintained that all interaction is message passing between mutually identified processes.

A higher development of this theory occurred with the π-calculus, created to model *mobility*, i.e., the dynamic creation or breaking of links between pairs of processes in a multi-agent system. The mobility of π-calculus was motivated in [27] by positing the case where one agent (*source*) wishes to send a value to a second (*destination*) via a third (*intermediary*). The model supports this indirect but targeted communication by enabling the source to send to the intermediary both the data intended for the destination, and a reference or link to the destination.

While adding mobility, π-calculus does not deviate from CCS's original philosophy of modeling all interaction as *synchronized* communication via *message passing* from agents to *pre-identified recipients*. In the next section, we challenge this approach.

5.3 Limitations of the Message-Passing Model

Can message passing simulate indirect interaction, as concurrency theory assumes? Is it always possible to replace the environment, via which agents in a MAS interact indirectly, with a mere transport medium for direct interaction (message passing)?

The assumption that all multi-agent interaction is modeled adequately by message passing has never been proved. [25], for example, does not assert that a message-passing model is suitable for interaction in general. Rather, it assumes that shared variables constitute the only alternative to direct interaction, and shows how a finite number of discrete shared variables can be replaced by corresponding communicating processes.

The most obvious criticism of this model is its limited *expressiveness*. In particular, it excludes situated and embedded systems, whose environments are physical (real-world), or a combination of virtual and physical. Physical environments are *continuous* and *analogue*; in the case of the real world, they may be infinite as well. No finite set of shared discrete variables can adequately represent all possible observations over such environments.

In fact, we believe that it can be shown that message passing is not as expressive as indirect interaction. That is, any model based on message passing can be simulated by a model based on indirect interaction. On the other hand, there exist stigmergic systems not captured by any model based on message passing.

Another criticism concerns the *scalability* of direct interaction, especially in the context of very large systems of very simple agents (Sect. 4.3). Assume that the size of the system (the number of agents) increases, while the complexity of each agent remains fixed. By representing the communications within the system by a graph, we see that this graph must either continue increasing its density (average number of links adjacent on any single agent) and/or its diameter (average number of links between any pair of agents). It can be shown that either of these cases results in a gradual increase in the agents' cognitive load. Since the complexity of agents is fixed, the system must eventually reach a crisis point where it can no longer carry out its job.

The final criticism is on more aesthetic grounds. Models based on direct interaction simply fail to explicitly capture the properties of indirect interaction. Indirect interaction has several properties that distinguish it from direct interaction, such as dynamic binding, anonymity, and asynchrony (Sect. 4.2). A formalization of indirect interaction must explicitly reflect these properties; models of interaction as message passing do not.

The Dining Philosophers problem (Sect. 3.3) serves as an illustration. This problem can be modeled as direct interaction between philosophers and chop-sticks, as in the original solution; each chop-stick is a process, which communicates with the two philosophers on either side of it. In this problem, however, chop-sticks are not autonomous computing entities, like philosophers; they are passive, initiating no action. Their only roles are to reflect the states of the philosophers next to them. The semantics of the problem are of indirect interaction among diners, not direct interaction between diners and utensils.

6 Conclusion

Communication (direct interaction) is not the only type of interaction. A multitude of indirect interaction examples exist. Indirect interaction is appropriate for MAS design, as evidenced by examples in E4MAS research, including cases of agents interacting via web sites, warehouse-floor transport, and PDA-based coordination of human activity in museums. We introduced a design strategy, II-MAS, that uses agents that are much simpler than their environments but that use their environments to interact as components of highly-adaptive multi-agent systems.

We have shown that indirect interaction via the environment is a distinct and useful part of multi-agent systems operation, meriting formalization via definitions and models. The notions of *dynamism*, *persistence*, and *physicality/virtuality* of environments are part of a taxonomy of environments for multi-agent systems that feature indirect interaction.

In assessing current models of multi-agent interaction, we showed that *message-passing* cannot adequately model multi-agent interaction, which includes both direct and indirect interaction. Therefore, we showed, a model of multi-agent interaction that is adequate for reasoning about, and providing an underpinning for, multi-agent systems, cannot limit itself to representing message passing (direct interaction), but must explicitly include indirect interaction within its scope.

New formalisms are required that incorporate indirect interaction explicitly, supporting the notion of environments as first-class entities in multi-agent systems, rather than just as transport media. They must also support the notions of *anonymity, asynchrony, locality, non-intentionality*, and *mobility*.

Future research challenges include:

- formalizing multi-agent systems in a way that explicitly incorporates indirect interaction;
- formally proving the greater expressiveness of models that allow indirect interaction over those that do not.

References

1. Farhad Arbab. Reo: A Channel-Based Coordination Model for Component Composition. *CWI Report SEN-0203*, 2002.
2. W. Ross Ashby. *An Introduction to Cybernetics*. University Paperbacks, 1964.
3. Stefania Bandini, Sara Manzoni, and Giuseppe Vizzari. Web Sites as Agents' Environments: General Framework and Applications. In *Second International Workshop on Environments for Multiagent Systems (E4MAS)*, 2005.
4. Eric Bonabeau, Marco Dorigo, and Guy Theraulaz. *Swarm Intelligence: From Natural to Artificial Systems*. Oxford Univ. Press, 1999.
5. Eric Bonabeau and Guy Theraulaz. Swarm Smarts. *Scientific American*, pages 72–74, March 2000.
6. Edsger Dijkstra. Hierarchical Ordering of Sequential Processes. *Acta Inform.*, 1:115–138, 1971.
7. Environments   for   Multi-Agent   Systems   2005   (E4MAS). *http://www.cs.kuleuven.ac.be/ distrinet/events/e4mas/2005/*.
8. Eugene Eberbach, Dina Goldin, and Peter Wegner. Turing's Ideas and Models of Computation. In *Christof Teuscher, ed., Alan Turing: Life and Legacy of a Great Thinker, Springer*, 2004.
9. Jacques Ferber. *Multi-Agent Systems: An Introduction to Distributed Artificial Intelligence*. Addison Wesley Longman, 1999.
10. D. Gelernter and N. Carriero. Coordination Languages and Their Significance. *CACM*, 35(2):97–107, 1992.
11. Dina Goldin. Persistent Turing Machines as a Model of Interactive Computation. *in: K-D. Schewe and B. Thalheim (Eds.)*, Foundations of information and knowledge systems, First Int'l Symposium (FoIKS'2000), *LNCS 1762*, pages 116–135, 2000.
12. Dina Goldin, Scott A. Smolka, Paul Attie, and Elaine Sonderegger. Turing Machines, Transition Systems, and Interaction. *Information and Computation Journal*, 194(2):101–128, Nov. 2004.
13. Dina Goldin and Peter Wegner. The Church-Turing Thesis: Breaking the Myth. In *Proc., CiE 2005, Amsterdam, June 2005 LNCS 3526, Springer*, pages 152–168, 2005.
14. C.V. Goldman and S. Zilberstein. Decentralized Control of Cooperative Systems: Categorization and Complexity Analysis. *Journal of Artificial Intelligence Research*, 22:143–174, 2004.
15. David Keil and Dina Goldin. Modeling Indirect Interaction in Open Computational Systems. *TAPOCS Workshop, Proc. WET ICE 03*, 2003.
16. David Keil and Dina Goldin. Indirect Interaction and Decentralized Coordination. *Extended draft, http://www.cse.uconn.edu/ dqg/papers/indirect.pdf* 2004.
17. David Keil and Dina Goldin. Adaptation and Evolution in Dynamic Persistent Environments. In *Proc. FInCo2005, Edinburgh*, 2005.
18. James Kennedy and Russell Eberhart. *Swarm intelligence*. Morgan Kaufman, 2001.
19. Donald E. Knuth. *The art of computer programming, Vol. 1: Fundamental algorithms*. Addison-Wesley, 1968.
20. Marco Mamei, Franco Zambonelli, and Letizia Leonardi. Distributed Motion Coordination with Co-Fields: A Case Study in Urban Traffic Management. In *Proceedings of the The Sixth International Symposium on Autonomous Decentralized Systems (ISADS'03)*, 2003.

21. Zohar Manna and Amir Pnueli. *The Temporal Logic of Reactive and Concurrent Systems: Specification.* Springer Verlag, 1992.
22. Koenraad Mertens and Tom Holvoet. CSAA: A Distributed Ant Algorithm Framework for Constraint Satisfaction. In *FLAIRS Conference 2004.*
23. Robin Milner. Processes: A Mathematical Model of Computing Agents. *H. E. Rose and J. C. Shepherdson, Eds., Logic Colloquium '73, North-Holland,* 1975.
24. Robin Milner. *A Calculus of Communicating Systems.* LNCS 92, Springer, 1980.
25. Robin Milner. *Communication and Concurrency.* Prentice Hall, 1989.
26. Robin Milner. Elements of Interaction. *Comm. ACM,* 36(1):78–89, 1993.
27. Robin Milner. *Communicating and mobile systems: the π-calculus.* Cambridge Univ. Press, 1999.
28. H. Van Dyke Parunak, Sven Brueckner, and John Sauter. Digital pheromone mechanisms for coordination of unmanned vehicles. In *Proceedings of the first international joint conference on Autonomous agents and multiagent systems Bologna, Italy,* 2002.
29. Jean Piaget. *Behavior and evolution.* Pantheon, 1978.
30. Mitchel Resnick. *Turtles, Termites, and Traffic Jams.* MIT Press, 1994.
31. Stuart Russell and Peter Norvig. *Artificial Intelligence: A Modern Approach.* Addison-Wesley, 1995.
32. Herbert Simon. *The Sciences of the Artificial.* MIT Press, 1970.
33. Starlogo site at MIT Media Lab. *http://starlogo.www.media.mit.edu / people / starlogo.* 2000.
34. Renee Steiner, Gary Leask, and Rym Z. Mili. An Architecture for MAS Simulation Environments. In *E4MAS,* 2005.
35. G. Theraulaz and E. Bonabeau. A Brief History of Stigmergy. *Artificial Life,* 5:97–116, 1999.
36. Alan Turing. On Computable Numbers with an Application to the Entscheidungsproblem. *Proc. London Math Society,* 2(DK: GET PUB):Reprinted in Martin Davis, Ed., The Undecidable, pp. 173–198, 1936.
37. Paul Valckenaers and Tom Holvoet. The Environment: an Essential Abstraction for Managing Complexity in MAS-based Manufacturing Control. In *E4MAS,* 2005.
38. Jan van Leeuwen and Jiri Wiedermann. The Turing machine paradigm in contemporary computing. *In B. Enquist and W. Schmidt, Eds., Mathematics unlimited – and beyond, Springer-Verlag, 20,* 01, 2001.
39. Mirko Viroli, Andrea Omicini, and Alessandro Ricci. Engineering MAS Environment with Artifacts. In *E4MAS,* 2005.
40. Peter Wegner. Why Interaction is More Powerful Than Algorithms. *Communications of the ACM,* 40(5), 1997.
41. D. Weyns, H. Parunak, F. Michel, T. Holvoet, and J. Ferber. Environments for Multiagent Systems: State-of-the-Art and Research Challenges. In *Proc., E4MAS,* 2004.
42. Danny Weyns, Kurt Schelfthout, and Tom Holvoet. Exploiting a Virtual Environment in a Real-World Application. In *E4MAS,* 2005.
43. Danny Weyns, Giuseppe Vizarri, and Tom Holvoet. Environments for Situated Multi-Agent Systems: Beyond Infrastructure. In *E4MAS,* 2005.
44. Norbert Wiener. *Cybernetics, or control and communication in the animal and the machine, 2nd Ed.* MIT Press, 1961.
45. M. Wooldridge. On the Sources of Complexity in Agent Design. *Applied Artificial Intelligence,* 14(7):623–644, 2000.

The Governing Environment

Michael Schumacher[1] and Sascha Ossowski[2]

[1] Artificial Intelligence Lab,
Ecole Polytechnique Fédérale de Lausanne (EPFL), Switzerland
michael.schumacher@epfl.ch
[2] Artificial Intelligence Unit, Universidad del Rey Juan Carlos, Spain
sascha.ossowski@urjc.es

Abstract. Whenever a multiagent system is designed, many dependencies in the system are identified and must be solved in a correct way. Coordination deals with the management of such dependencies. For that, two complementary viewpoints can be distinguished: *subjective coordination* manages intra-agent aspects while *objective coordination* essentially deals with inter-agent aspects. On the basis of this separation of concerns, the paper discusses the need of infrastructures for objective coordination. As in usual agent software platforms, this can be done by offering implicit support for objective coordination, by establishing the conditions necessary for running agent programs and maintaining agent interactions. Other infrastructures such as Electronic Institutions go one step further and shape the governing aspects of objective coordination. However, this is usually done through dedicated middle-agents that belong to the institution. An alternative approach is to transfer the governing or regulating responsibility from institutional agents to the *environment* of a multiagent system. A promising way of doing this is to view the environment as a rule-based infrastructure that defines reactions to events. This has the advantage of allowing for the definition of laws that not only regulate agent interaction (as most work in governed interaction), but *any* action within the environment. We illustrate this approach by several examples in different domains of laws.

1 Introduction

The interest for multi-agent systems (MASs) has grown increasingly in the last years. These systems are used in a great variety of applications such as process control, manufacturing, electronic commerce, patient monitoring, or games. MASs present very attractive means of more naturally understanding, designing and implementing several classes of complex distributed and concurrent software. The main reason resides in their unique paradigm of combining populations of autonomous active entities (agents) within a shared structured entity (the environment).

An autonomous agent is classically seen as *a system situated within and a part of an environment that senses that environment and acts on it, over time, in pursuit of its own agenda and so as to effect what it senses in the future* [13]. This description stresses the importance of the environment as the

D. Weyns, H. Van Dyke Parunak, and F. Michel (Eds.): E4MAS 2005, LNAI 3830, pp. 88–104, 2006.

living medium, the condition for an agent to live, or the first entity an agent interacts with [39,8]. Thus an agent is part of the environment. However, it remains autonomous, so that the environment may not "force" the agent integrity. Franklin and Graesser's definition shows that the environment is strongly related to the notion of *embodiment*, which refers to the fact that an agent has a "body" that delineates it from its environment in which the agent is situated. It is in this environment that an agent senses and acts. The acting of the agent on the environment is done autonomously; it directly influences its future sensing, because the environment is changed by the agent actions.

This view of the importance of the environment originally comes from Behavior Based AI (also named Bottom Up AI), which considers interaction with an environment as an essential feature for intelligent behavior. In this field, the main work has been done in systems that interact with a physical environment such as robots. This has influenced many research efforts within the software agent community, which deal with logical environments. However, most approaches in agent research have viewed the environment as something being modelled in the "minds" of the agents, thus using a minimal and implicit environment that is not a first-order abstraction, but rather the sum of all data structures within agents that represent an environment. This is a typical *subjective view* of the multiagent system inherited from distributed AI, which contrasts with an *objective view* that deals with the system from an external point of view of the agents [33,29].

Whenever a multiagent system is to be implemented and deployed, an underlying *infrastructure* becomes essential [26]. It offers to the MAS basic services to be used by the agents. Example functionalities are agent communication, naming or life-cycle management. The abstractions provided by such infrastructures are essential for agent-oriented software engineering, as they should be as close as possible to the concepts used for analysis and design.

Today's infrastructures primarily offer agent-related abstractions for the programming of agent architectures using for instance libraries for BDI agents [16], thus supporting subjective coordination. But they also offer implicit support for objective coordination (which we consider as *enabling* aspects), as they establish the conditions necessary for running agent programs (e.g. life-cycle management) and for setting the basic interaction means (e.g. message-enabled middleware between agents). However, current infrastructures have a main drawback. The used abstractions are not adapted for open systems, where participating agents may have totally different architectures, goals and interests, thus possibly behaving in a non-benevolent manner.

An appealing way to exert the necessary level of control over an agent in a truly open system is through an adequate MAS infrastructure. The type of services provided by the infrastructure, and the way in which these services are enacted, limit the set of possible actions (or modify their preconditions and/or effects). For that, a MAS designer can use a *governing infrastructure* to structure and shape the space of (inter-)action within a MAS in an open environment [26]. This governing perspective of objective coordination mainly allows to manage agent interactions from an external point-of-view. This has the strong advantage that agents may be defined independently, and that some control is overtaken externally. In the area of virtual organizations, the Electronic Institutions (EI) approach [25] does this by defining so-called *governors* which are middle agents that mediate all (communicative) actions within a MAS [1]. This solution has, however, important disadvantages. Providing each agent with a governor puts a heavy computational burden on the infrastructure. But, more importantly, middle agents do not capture a natural design for the functionality they are expected to fulfill, i.e. mediation of communication. The governing or regulating responsibility should be transferred from specialized middle agents to the environment of a MAS, calling for the *environment as a governing infrastructure*. This can be done with the idea of a *programmable coordination medium* [9], which essentially defines *reactions to events* happening in an environment. This schema has the strong advantage to allow the definition of laws that not only regulate agent interactions, but also any happening within an environment. The paper proposes different domains of laws that can be identified with this idea. Overall, we expect that viewing the environment as a governing infrastructure dramatically simplifies the design and deployment of open multiagent systems.

The paper is organized as follows. Section 2 introduces objective and subjective point of views in modelling MASs. On the basis of this separation of concerns, the paper discusses infrastructures for objective coordination in Sect. 3, elaborating on enabling and governing aspects. Following the idea to transfer governing responsibility within the environment using a *programmable coordination medium*, Sect. 4 presents environment entities and events to be considered for defining laws as *reactions to events*. It then lists law domains to be used as a taxonomy. Section 5 concludes the paper.

2   Objectivity Versus Subjectivity

The interaction between agents is absolutely essential in a MAS, because it enables the MAS to exist. If agents are not able to interact with one another, no global behavior in the MAS is possible. One has therefore to model the interaction setup of the multitude of agents participating in the MAS. If this is not done, this typically leads to an *agent-oriented* view of a MAS [7]. This agent-oriented view models a MAS by describing the intra-agent aspects, such as the agent's representation of the world, its beliefs, desires, intentions, and by neglecting the description of the agent interaction means and of the space where these interactions take place.

This necessity for a clear identification of the interaction setup in a MAS naturally calls for a separation between the design of the individual tasks of each agent and the design of their interactions. This can be done at two different levels, according to the types of dependencies.

Indeed the modelling of the setup of multiple agents into a MAS leads to the detection of many dependencies of different nature. On one side, these dependencies rely on the result of the external composition of multiple agents into an

---

[1] All actions that the EI approach accounts for are communicative by nature.

ensemble; on the other side, they result from the individual or peculiar point of view of each agent interacting with other agents. Two types of dependencies can thus be distinguished and, as coordination is defined as *managing dependencies between activities* [21], two corresponding types or levels of coordination [33]:

- Agents have *subjective dependencies* which refer to intra-agent aspects. The management of these subjective dependencies refers to what we call *subjective coordination*. Thus, subjective coordination treats dependencies in an agent's *model*, its perception of the environment.
- A MAS is built by *objective dependencies* which refer to inter-agent aspects, namely the configuration of the system in terms of the basic interaction means, agent generation/destruction and organization of the environment. We refer to the management of these dependencies as *objective coordination*, because these dependencies are external to the agents. Thus, objective coordination acts directly on the dependencies in an environment.

Subjective coordination is dependent on objective coordination, because the first is based on and supposes the existence of the second. The mechanisms that are engaged to ensure subjective coordination must indeed have access to the mechanisms for objective coordination. If this is not the case, no subjective coordination is possible at all. This does not mean that objective coordination belongs to the intra-agent view, but only that the access mechanisms have a subjective expression in the agent. This is essentially the case for mechanisms like sending or receiving information.

Not differentiating the two levels of coordination leads to MASs that resolve objective coordination with subjective coordination means, i.e. by using intra-agent aspects for describing system configurations. For instance, a MAS intended at modelling the hierarchy in an organization would model this hierarchy internally in each agent by means of knowledge representation of the hierarchy, and would not describe it by establishing the communication flows that represent it.

2.1   Subjective Coordination

We distinguish two types of subjective coordination: *explicit* and *implicit* subjective coordination. They differentiate themselves in the explicit or implicit treatment of the management of subjective dependencies.

The research in distributed artificial intelligence (DAI) has proposed several coordination techniques [20,18,30] that deal with explicit subjective coordination. These techniques typically consider coordination as *the process by which an agent reasons about its local action and the (anticipated) actions of others to try and ensure the community acts in a coherent manner* [20]. Thus, these techniques are qualified as subjective coordination, because they try to resolve subjective dependencies by means of intra-agent structures that often involve high-level mentalistic notions and appropriate protocols. We characterize these techniques as explicit, because they explicitly handle coordination.

Agents may also coordinate themselves implicitly, without having explicit mechanisms of coordination. This may be, for instance, the case in the framework of collective robotics [3,22,23], in which robots act on the base of the result of the work of other robots. Thus, this result, which is locally perceived through the sensors, allows to resolve a subjective dependency, namely the necessity to sense a specific information in order to act. This kind of coordination, which is also named *stigmergic* coordination, literally means an *incitement to work by the product of the work* [3].

2.2   Objective Coordination

Objective coordination is mainly concerned with the organization of the world of a MAS. This is achieved in two ways: i) by describing how the environment is organized, and ii) by handling the agent interactions. In the following, we address these two points.

The organization of the environment varies according to the space the MAS wants to integrate. We thus propose to distinguish between implicit and explicit environment organizations. An *implicit organization* does not explicitly model the environment, because it is given or imposed by the underlying logical structure or space organization on which a MAS evolves. This is, for instance, the case for network-aware agents roaming on the World Wide Web, where the environment is structured by the nodes of the network. An *explicit organization*, however, establishes a model of an environment that does not necessarily reflect the intended logical structure. This can be done by realizing an approximation of the target. When, for instance, one wants to simulate a continuous physical space, he will not be able to keep the continuity and will have to render the space discrete.

More importantly, the environment allows the arising of the interactions between the agents. Handling agent interactions asks for the description of the interactions between an agent and its environment, and the interactions between the agent themselves. As the environment also has a container function, it can be used to interact. Indeed, an agent has a relation with its environment by means of its perception. Furthermore, it can influence the state of its environment with specific actions. The interaction with the environment can then be understood and used to interact: all information is transmitted within the environment. Interaction thus becomes an action that changes the state of the environment.

Consider, for instance, the case of an insect-like robot dispersing in the environment information similar to pheromone. This information can be sensed by another robot that notices it as a trace of the roaming of the first agent.

In summary, we consider that agent interaction is always dealt through the environment. This is even the case in usual message-passing mechanisms that use agent-communication languages. We thus consider objective coordination as the way to *organize the environment*.

3   Infrastructures for Objective Coordination

Agent software platforms are a key element for the effective implementation and deployment of multiagent systems, as they provide the "interface" between the agents and their environment. They can be seen as an *infrastructure* for MAS, providing basic resources and critical services to the agents, thus shaping their environment as part of a MAS [2]. Such MAS infrastructures are of foremost importance for Agent-Oriented Software Engineering, as the abstractions provided by them need to be as close as possible to the concepts used for analysis and design.

Any infrastructure for MAS needs to provide some services to allow agents to effectively *interact*, either directly by means of message-passing, or indirectly by leaving "messages" in shared data containers. Therefore, it is obvious that coordination in a multiagent system ultimately relies on the services provided by the infrastructure.

Today's infrastructures essentially provide (different levels of) support for programming a collection of individual *agents* in a multiagent world. So, from this perspective, they primarily render a certain level of support for *subjective* coordination. The more powerful the agent-related abstractions provided by the infrastructure, the higher their level of support for (and potential influence on) the instrumentation of subjective coordination mechanisms. For instance, if an infrastructure offers libraries for the implementation of BDI-type agents [16], the mechanisms for subjectively detecting dependencies, and reacting to them, will most probably be realized in these terms.

Although this is usually not made explicit at a conceptual level, agent platforms such as JADE[4] also provide some implicit support for *objective coordination* as they establish the *conditions* necessary for running agent programs and maintaining agent interactions. Other infrastructures, such as RICA-J [34], increase this level of support, as they provide the abstractions (and their software counterparts) to structure the space of interaction in a MAS. Finally, infrastructures based on the notion of Virtual Organizations or Electronic Institutions shape the *governing* aspects of objective coordination. In the sequel, we will elaborate on these points.

3.1   Enabling Aspects

Most current MAS platforms constitute essentially *enabling infrastructures*, as they provide agents with the means to interoperate. The services provided by FIPA-compliant infrastructures, for instance, refer to services such as agent communication, security, naming, location, etc., which are necessary preconditions that make it possible for agents to "live", "coexist", and interact within a MAS [26]. Other aspects relevant for achieving a basic level of objective coordination, such as the management of concurrency, are usually left to the agent designer. In essence, all but the most basic functionalities are to be dealt with subjectively, from the point of view of the agents (or: agent programmers).

The support for objective coordination by enabling infrastructures is not only determined by the *functionality* of the services that enable the co-existence of agents in a MAS. It is also affected by the conceptual abstractions in terms of

---

[2] The notion of infrastructure is fundamental for complex systems in general, not only in computer science and engineering, but also in the context of organizational, political, economical and social sciences [26]. Agent software platforms can be conceived as embodiments of this concept in the multiagent domain.

which they are modelled and/or accessed. By shaping these abstractions one exerts influence over the way in which individual agents are designed and deployed. There is a growing awareness that *organizational abstractions* (types of roles, interactions, etc.) are adequate candidates to this respect. In fact, it is tempting to maintain a tight coupling between a MAS, and the relevant features of the (human) organization that it models, during the whole design process. Several authors have put forward conceptual frameworks that conceive MAS in organizational terms [11,19,35].

Software frameworks that directly support such models shall still be conceived as enabling infrastructures, as they provide a basic set of computational abstractions that agent may make use of. Still, they provide an increased level of support for objective coordination. This is not only true because these computational abstractions are coarser grained. Infrastructures such as AGRE [12] or RICA-J [34] also allow for an "extension" of the infrastructure, e.g. by creating new types of interactions as a specialization of others, and thus providing the means for customizing basic services.

Agent programmers may benefit from using the computational abstractions provided by the infrastructure in order to simplify subjective coordination mechanisms, and the agent programs that instrument it. However, notice that agent programmers are not *forced* to do so – they may still decide to directly act upon the outside world instead of or use other lower-level services.

3.2   Governing Aspects

As of today, MAS infrastructures exploit only a minimal part of the potential of organizational abstractions. This is especially true with respect to the *coercive* facets of these abstractions. However, the increasing complexity and articulation of MAS application scenarios call for a more effective engineering support. In particular, designs must account for increased levels of openness (not only with respect to semantic interoperability but also, and maybe even more importantly, respecting the spectrum of different agent interests and goals), and decreased levels of predictability of (and control over) agent behavior. The former part of this requirement is exemplified by the work outlined in [30] where different types of behavioral restrictions (limitations to the set of possible actions of an agent in a given state of the world), operationalized in terms of "prohibitions" and "permissions", are used to bias the (macro-level) outcome of the interaction of autonomous (self-interested) "problem-solving" agents in a desired direction. However, the approach still assumes the possibility to "hand-wire" compliance with these restrictions into the agents' behavior strategies.

An appealing way to exert the necessary level of control over an agent in a truly open system (without relying on unrealistic assumptions on agent behaviors that limit their autonomy) is through an adequate definition of the MAS infrastructure. The type of services provided by the infrastructure (and/or the infrastructure agents that offer them), and the way in which these services are enacted, limit the set of possible actions (or just modify their outcome). Thus, such *governing infrastructures* can be used by the MAS designer to structure and shape the space of (inter-)action within a MAS in an open environment [26].

Again, from the standpoint of an engineer concerned with designing mechanisms for objective coordination, infrastructures need to incorporate suitable abstractions for the *governance* of interaction. Coercive organizational abstractions, especially the different conceptualizations of the notion of *norms* or , are of foremost importance here. Upon the normative background of a MAS, the agents' social actions create (social) facts and, in turn, these facts constrain (or, at least, modify the outcome of) future behavior options. From this perspective, governing MAS infrastructures refer to the software that embodies and enacts the instititional aspects of Virtual Organizations.

Electronic Institutions (EI) [25], conceived as a particular instantiation of a Virtual Organizations, are of particular interest to this respect. EIs focus on the dialogical aspects of open MAS, and provide abstractions to shape the interactions of the agents participating in it. Agents play different roles in the (sub-)protocols that, together with additional rules of behavior, determine the legal sequences of illocutions that may arise within a particular instance of a *scene*. Scenes, in turn, are interconnected and synchronized by means of transitions within a *performative structure*. Instances of EI abstractions are meant to be of both descriptive and coercive nature. Specific institutional agents, called *governors*, assure that the latter is effectively implemented: in EIs, all relevant (communicative) action of agents is mediated through the corresponding governors. In fact, software tools that support the implementation of EIs [10] are (among the few existing) examples of governing MAS infrastructures.

To provide each agent with a governor puts a heavy computational burden on the infrastructure. An alternative approach is to incorporate the governance functionality into the infrastructure. This approach allows for a much more natural modelling of what the governors are expected to fulfill. It is then the proper infrastructure services that make sure that agent (inter-)actions are compliant with institutional norms. For instance, a governing infrastructure's basic communication service may filter out certain messages or automatically add context information to others. From this perspective, norms or laws are nothing but means to configure and customize the behavior of infrastructure services. As such, they can be conceived as the key component to instil objective coordination in open MAS.

4   The Environment as a Governing Infrastructure

To capture the idea of norms and laws in MASs, we propose to consider the environment as a regulating system. This is best shown by important elements of a definition of environment that were identified at the plenary session of E4MAS 2005[3]:

- The environment is a *first-class entity* [39]. It should be taken into account since the very first phase of modelling.

---

[3] http://www.cs.kuleuven.ac.be/~distrinet/events/e4mas/

– The environment provides the *situation* for the existence of the agents and the interactions within the MAS. The situation mainly significates the conditions of existence, i.e. creation/destruction mechanisms, supplier and organization of the living space, and time management.
– The environment *regulates*. This regulation can be weak or strong, in the sense that the environment may control weakly or strongly what happens in and through it. This may be done by control mechanisms that cannot change at runtime, or by some laws that may be adapted at runtime.

Those descriptive elements of a MAS environment belong to the design of a MAS application. Therefore, the environment should be directly supported as an infrastructure. And for a MAS to provide law definitions, its supporting infrastructure should include rule-based mechanisms. Among research efforts that have tackled governed interaction [24,9,17,37,2], a programmable coordination medium [9] is a good candidate to realize an environment as a governing infrastructure.

4.1   Programmable Coordination Medium

Reactive coordination models [6,31] allow reactions associated to specific communication events to be programmed, leading to the notion of *programmable coordination medium* [9]. For that, this family of coordination models integrates an event mechanism into shared data space models, which show to be very useful to capture the idea of laws or norms in environments. This can be done by considering a tuple space as being reactive in the sense that the space can react to communication events rather than to the communication state changes only. Thus, from the point of view of the coordination medium, the observability is shifted from the tuples to the communication operations over the tuples. When a communication operation is executed, a reaction catching the event produced atomically executes a sequence of operations which usually have access both to the space and the information associated with the event. The idea of a programmable medium can be found for instance in TuCSoN (*Tuple Centers Spread Over Networks*) [27] [28].

LAW-GOVERNED LINDA [24] is also a model that follows the notion of programmable media. The basic motivation of LAW-GOVERNED LINDA is the inherent security problems of LINDA [15,5]. In order to control each exchange of tuples through the tuple space, the model forces every process to adopt specific laws that control each exchange of tuples through the tuple space. For achieving this goal, LAW-GOVERNED LINDA attaches a *controller* to every process. Each controller, which is in charge of regulating the exchange of tuples, has a copy of the law, and only allows a communication if it conforms to the law. This law regulates the occurrence of so-called *controlled events* that occur at the boundary between a process and the medium. It determines the effect of an event using a prescription, which is the *ruling* of the law, realized with a sequence of primitive operations. An example for the ruling of the law controlling an out could be to transform the corresponding tuple by concatenating some useful information.

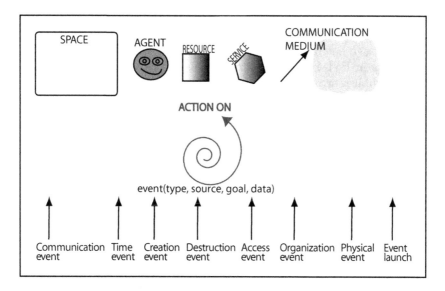

Fig. 1. Law definitions on events

4.2   Mechanisms for Environment Laws

Programmable coordination media can elegantly support the programming of laws regulating the environment in a MAS. The main reason is that their underlying mechanism can be used to support regulation not only of interaction, but also of *any* action in the environment. We therefore propose to extend their basic scheme to support ruled environment systems, i.e. which define laws as reactions to events. These reactions apply actions on environment entities (Fig. 1). In order to support such a definition of laws, the MAS infrastructure should thus be able to define as first-class entities all environment entities, all events happening in an environment, and law mechanisms.

We consider as being part of the environment the following entities:

- *Resources* are passive data being shared within the environment. Conditions of access and modifications are defined by the environment.
- *Services* offer functionalities within the environment, which again control their acting and the access of other entities to them. Services are different from resources, because they are activated and are not purely passive as data resources.
- *Spaces* are a logical organization of agent groups, resources and services. Furthermore, they make locality and localization possible, for instance offering encapsulation of events (e.g. for catching them) or allowing agents to move from one place to the other. Spaces are the most straightforward entity that make situatedness[4] of agents possible.

---

[4] We refer with this notion to the function of the environment to provide the situation.

– *Communication medium* are abstractions that allow interaction between agents. They can be mainly classified as point-to-point connections, using some message-based middleware (as in JADE [4] or explicit communication canals (as in IWIM [1]); or shared-data interaction where a blackboard is used to publish or retrieve information.

When considering agents from external point of view (i.e. as embodied entities), laws may also be applied on them. Consider for instance laws that have influence on agent creation/destruction.

As Fig. 1 shows, an event is a specific data that is launched at a specific moment within the environment and that may be catched to create a reaction to it. An event may include information such as the type (of event), the source (entity), the goal (entity) and a specific data.

Table 1. Events

Communication	Access to communication means (get, put, ...), configuration changes, communication breaks, ...
Time	Time period change, time exceeded, ...
Creation	Creation, re-launch or arrival of entities
Destruction	Destruction, pause or departure of entities
Access	Access to the entities
Organization	Density (population within a space), location change
Event Launch	At each event

Different types of events can be differentiated in a MAS (see also Tab. 1):

– *Communication events* belong to the most important one, because they give information on all access to communication means. They provide therefore the main source for laws. Examples are access to communication means (get, put, ...), configuration changes, or communication breaks.
– *Time events* are straightforward. Examples are time period change or time excess.
– *Creation or destruction events* of all kind of entities. These events may be general or specific to some types of agents or resources. Examples are creation, re-launch or arrival of entities in a specific space.
– *Access events* are launched whenever a specified entity is accessed.
– *Organization events* are mainly related to the space. For instance, they can be fired whenever a specific agent population density is reached or there is a location change of an agent.
– *Event launch* capture the idea that every event (whatever its type) is itself an event, which may be useful for logs.

The set of events tries to be as general as possible. We estimate that it should be part of an infrastructure offering environment laws for MASs. At a higher abstraction, application specific events are needed in each MAS application.

4.3   Law Domains

On the basis of the regulation capacity of a MAS infrastructure, a catalogue of possible laws helps the definition of the environment responsibilities in each case. We therefore propose a categorization that is based on events. Actually, each kind of event defines different types of laws. We will explain one by one the law domains. This list should be further completed.

- *Security laws* (Fig. 2a) are mainly related to interaction between agents and accesses to resources or services. They can change communicated data for encryption; or they can add some identification information. Access to resources/services may be restricted by some UNIX-like rights. Communication may be forbidden to specific agents.
- *Communication laws* (Fig. 2b) regulate interaction between agents at two levels. They can change transmitted data (such as cast data if it is of a

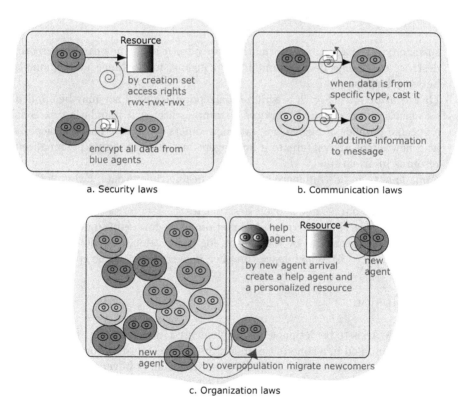

Fig. 2. Example of law domains: a. security laws: i) change resource access rights; ii) or, for all agents of a special type, encrypt communicated data; b. communication laws: i) When the data is from a specific type, cast it to another type; ii) or add time information to all messages in the space; c. organization laws: i) if population exceeds a specific number of agents, migrate newcomers to an alternative space; ii) or, at a new agent arrival, create a help agent and corresponding personalized resource information

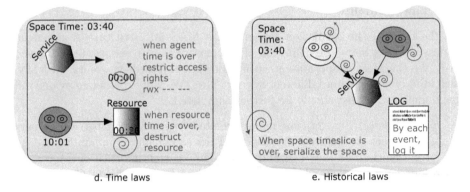

d. Time laws   e. Historical laws

Fig. 3. Example of law domains: a. time laws: i) when agent time is over, restrict access rights to a specific service; ii) or when resource time is over, destruct the resource; b. historical laws: i) By each event, log it (creation, destruction, arrival, departure, etc.); ii) When space timeslice is over, serialize the space

specific type, or add time information), or filter it out. They can also create, destruct or change new communication means, for instance new channels between agents.

– *Organization laws* (Fig. 2c) regulate space populations. They may be applied on agents or on resources/services. Examples are: i) if population exceeds a specific number of agents, migrate newcomers to an alternative space. ii) at a new agent arrival, create a help agent and corresponding personalized resource information.
– *Time laws* (Fig. 3d) influence entities at specific time events. Examples are: i) When an agent's time is over, restrict its access to resources and services; ii) When a resource time is over, destruct it.
– *Historical laws* (Fig. 3e) provide functionalities for loging and serializing spaces. Examples are: i) by each event, log it (creation, destruction, arrival, departure, etc.); ii) When space timeslice is over, serialize the space.

5   Conclusion

Whenever a MAS is to be designed and implemented, dependencies are identified and must be handled in a coherent manner. Subjective coordination solves those raised from intra-agent aspects. Objective coordination, however, manages those that are related to inter-agent aspects. The environment, as a first-class entity, is the main place for objective coordination.

A MAS should both tackle subjective and objective coordination. For that, the use of an adequate infrastructure is essential. Indeed, in order to support implementation and deployment, MAS infrastructures play a central role, because they enable agent existence and interoperability. Usual agent software platforms provide a basic infrastructure for MAS by shaping the enabling aspects for objective coordination (e.g. middleware services for agent communication). Other infrastructures such as Electronic Institutions go one step beyond by governing agent interactions, which is particularly relevant in open systems where the designer has limited or no control of the internal dynamics of agents. Electronic Institutions make use of institutional middle agents that assure compliance with *communication* laws. Still, if the infrastructure become the agents' only means to access the environment, then *all* types of relevant actions can be regulated *directly* by the infrastructure. In a nutshell: the environment is conceived as a governing infrastructure.

Among research efforts that have tackled governed interaction [24,9,17,37,2], a programmable coordination medium [9] is a good candidate to realize an environment as a governing infrastructure. The reason is its basic functionality to define reactions to environment events. This has the advantage to cope with other aspects as "only" ruling agent interactions. Laws become a general tool to describe in high-level terms any *reactions to events*. Thus, more complex inner dynamicity of the environment can be expressed and controlled by environment laws. This is shown by the different proposed domains of laws.

We expect future infrastructures to integrate means for supporting environment laws. For that, several issues can be considered. The first one is related to the expression of laws. It is an advantage to have a language that allows a higher-level law expression [36,14]. In some cases business rules such as DROOLS[5] may offer the sufficient functionality. But additionally, some applications in open systems would benefit to let their agents inspect the rules in order to adapt their own behavior. An agent with special rights may even change a law at runtime [32]. This may be achieved with an interpreter for the law language or through specific law objects that apply on environment entities.

Acknowledgments

This paper reports on work that has been partially supported by the Spanish Ministry of Education and Science (MEC) under grant TIC2003-08763-C02-02.

References

1. F. Arbab. Coordination of Massively Concurrent Activities. Technical report, CWI, Computer Science Department, Amsterdam, The Netherlands, 1995. CS-R9565.
2. S. Bandini, S. Manzoni, and G. Vizzari. A spatially dependent communication model for ubiquitous systems. In Weyns et al. [38], pages 74–90.
3. R. Beckers, O.E. Holland, and J.L. Deneubourg. From local actions to global tasks: stigmergy and collective robotics. In R.A. Brooks and P. Maes, editors, *Fourth Workshop on Artificial Life*, Boston, MA, USA, 1994. MIT Press.
4. F. Bellifemine, A. Poggi, and G. Rimassa. JADE – a FIPA-compliant agent framework. In *4th International Conference and Exhibition on The Practical Application of Intelligent Agents and Multi-Agent Technology (PAAM'99)*, pages 97–108, April 1999.

---

[5] http://drools.org

5. N. Carriero and D. Gelernter. Linda in Context. *Communications of the ACM*, 32(4):444–458, 1989.
6. N. Carriero and D. Gelernter. Coordination Languages and Their Significance. *Communications of the ACM*, 35(2):97–107, February 1992.
7. P. Ciancarini, A. Omicini, and F. Zambonelli. Multiagent engineering: the coordination viewpoint. In J. R. Nicholas and Y. Lespérance, editors, *Proceedings of the 6th International Workshop on Agent Theories, Architectures, and Languages (ATAL'99)*, pages 327–333, Orlando (FL), July 15–17 1999.
8. D. Weyns and H. Van Dyke Parunak and F. Michel and T. Holvoet and J. Ferber. Environments for Multiagent Systems, State-of-the-art and Research Challenges. In Danny Weyns, H. Van Dyke Parunak, and Fabien Michel, editors, *Environment for Multi-Agent Systems - Post-proceedings of the First International Workshop on Environments for Multiagent Systems*, volume 3374 of *Lecture Notes in Computer Science*. Springer Verlag, 2005.
9. E. Denti, A. Natali, and A. Omicini. Programmable Coordination Media. In D. Garlan and D. Le Metayer, editors, *Proceedings of the Second International Conference on Coordination Models, Languages and Applications (Coordination'97)*, number 1282 in LNCS, pages 274–288. Springer Verlag, September 1997.
10. Marc Esteva, Bruno Rosell, Juan A. Rodríguez-Aguilar, and Josep Ll. Arcos. AMELI: An agent-based middleware for electronic institutions. In *Proceedings of the Third International Joint Conference on Autonomous Agents and Multiagent Systems*, volume 1, pages 236–243, 2004.
11. J. Ferber and O. Gutknecht. A meta-model for the analysis of organizations in multi-agent systems. In Y. Demazeau, editor, *ICMAS'98*, pages 128–135. IEEE Press, 1998.
12. J. Ferber, F. Michel, and J.-A. Báez-Barranco. Agre: Integrating environments with organizations. In Weyns et al. [38], pages 48–56.
13. S. Franklin and A. Graesser. Is it an Agent or just a Program? A Taxonomy for Autonomous Agents. In J.P. Muller, M.J. Wooldridge, and N.R. Jennings, editors, *Proceedings of ECAI'96 Workshop (ATAL). Intelligent Agents III. Agent Theories, Architectures, and Languages*, number 1193 in LNAI, pages 21–35, August 1996.
14. A. Garcia-Camino, P. Noriega, and J. A. Rodriguez-Aguilar. Implementing norms in electronic institutions. In *AAMAS '05: Proceedings of the fourth international joint conference on Autonomous agents and multiagent systems*, pages 667–673, New York, NY, USA, 2005. ACM Press.
15. D. Gelernter. Generative Communication in Linda. *ACM Transactions on Programming Languages and Systems*, 7(1):80–112, 1985.
16. M. P. Georgeff and A. S. Rao. The Semantics of Intention Maintenance for Rational Agents. In *Proceedings of the International Joint Conference on Artificial Intelligence (IJCAI)*, number 1202 in LNAI, pages 704–710, 1995.
17. A. Gouaich, F. Michel, and Y. Guiraud. Mic: A deployment environment for autonomous agents. In Weyns et al. [38], pages 109–126.
18. L. Lee H.S. Nwana and N.R. Jennings. Co-ordination in Multi-Agent Systems. In H. S. Nwana and N. Azarmi, editors, *Software Agents and Soft Computing*, number 1198 in LNAI. Springer Verlag, 1997.
19. J. Fred Hübner, J. Simão Sichman, and O. Boissier. Using the moise+ for a cooperative framework of mas reorganisation. In *Advances in Artificial Intelligence - SBIA 2004*, pages 506–515, 2004.
20. N.R. Jennings. Coordination Techniques for Distributed Artificial Intelligence. In G.M.P. O'Hare and N.R. Jennings, editors, *Foundations of Distributed Artificial*. John Wiley and Sons, 1996.

21. T.W. Malone and K. Crowston. The Interdisciplinary Study of Coordination. *ACM Computing Surveys*, 26(1):87–119, March 1994.
22. A. Martinoli and F. Mondada. Collective and Cooperative Group Behaviours: Biologically Inspired Experiments in Robotics. In *Proceedings of the Fourth Symposium on Experimental Robotics ISER-95*, Stanford, USA, June 30- July 2 1995.
23. M.J. Mataric. From Local Interactions to Collective Intelligence. In L. Steels, editor, *The Biology and Technology of Intelligent Autonomous Agents*, pages 275–295. NATO ASI series, Hillsdale, NJ, USA, 1995.
24. N.H. Minsky and J. Leichter. Law-Governed Linda as a Coordination Model. In *Proceedings of the ECCOP Workshop on Models and Languages for Coordination of Parallelism and Distribution*, LNCS, Berlin, 1994. Springer Verlag.
25. P. Noriega and C. Sierra. Electronic institutions: Future trends and challenges. In Matthias Klusch, Sascha Ossowski, and Onn Shehory, editors, *Cooperative Information Agents VI*, volume 2446 of *Lecture Notes in Computer Science*. Springer Verlag, 2002. 6th International Workshop (CIA 2002), Madrid, Spain, September 18-20, 2002. Proceedings.
26. A. Omicini, S. Ossowski, and A. Ricci. Coordination infrastructures in the engineering of multiagent systems. In Federico Bergenti, Marie-Pierre Gleizes, and Franco Zambonelli, editors, *Methodologies and Software Engineering for Agent Systems: The Agent-Oriented Software Engineering Handbook*, chapter 14, pages 273–296. Kluwer Academic Publishers, June 2004.
27. A. Omicini and F. Zambonelli. TuCSoN: a Coordination Model for Mobile Agents. In *Proceedings of the First Workshop on Innovative Internet Information Systems*, pages 183–190, Pisa, Italy, June 1998.
28. A. Omicini and F. Zambonelli. Tuple Centres for the Coordination of Internet Agents. In *Proceedings of Fourteen ACM Symposium on Applied Computing (SAC'99). Special Track on Coordination, Languages and Applications*, pages 183–190, San Antonio, Texas, USA, February 28 - March 2 1999. ACM Press.
29. Andrea Omicini and Sascha Ossowski. Objective versus subjective coordination in the engineering of agent systems. In Matthias Klusch, Sonia Bergamaschi, Peter Edwards, and Paolo Petta, editors, *Intelligent Information Agents: An AgentLink Perspective*, volume 2586 of *LNAI: State-of-the-Art Survey*, pages 179–202. Springer-Verlag, March 2003.
30. S. Ossowski. *Co-ordination in Artificial Agent Societies – Social Structure and Its Implications for Autonomous Problem-Solving Agents*. Number 1535 in LNAI. Springer Verlag, 1999.
31. G.A. Papadopoulos and F. Arbab. Coordination Models and Languages. In M. Zelkowitz, editor, *Advances in Computers, The Engineering of Large Systems*, volume 46. Academic Press, August 1998.
32. A. Ricci, A. Omicini, and E. Denti. Activity Theory as a framework for MAS coordination. In Paolo Petta, Robert Tolksdorf, and Franco Zambonelli, editors, *Engineering Societies in the Agents World III*, volume 2577 of *LNCS*, pages 96–110. Springer-Verlag, April 2003. 3rd International Workshop (ESAW 2002), Madrid, Spain, 16–17 September 2002. Revised Papers.
33. M. Schumacher. *Objective Coordination in Multi-Agent System Engineering - Design and Implementation*. Number 2039 in LNAI. Springer Verlag, 2001.
34. J. M. Serrano, S. Ossowski, and S. Saugar. Reusability issues in the instrumentation of agent interactions. In *Third International Workshop on Programming Multi-Agent Systems: Languages and Tools (ProMAS'05)*, Utrecht, Jul 2005.

35. J.M. Serrano, S. Ossowski, and A. Fernández. The pragmatics of software agents – analysis and design of agent communication languages. In Klusch et al., editor, *Intelligent Information Agents – The AgentLink Perspective*. Springer-Verlag, 2003.
36. J. Vazquez-Salceda. *The Role of Norms and Electronic Institutions in Multi-Agent Systems*. Whitestein Series in Software Agent Technologies. Springer-Verlag, Berlin, 2004.
37. D. Weyns and T. Holvoet. A formal model for situated multi-agent systems. *Fundam. Inform.*, 63(2-3):125–158, 2004.
38. D. Weyns, H. V. D. Parunak, and F. Michel, editors. *Environments for Multi-Agent Systems, First International Workshop, E4MAS 2004, New York, NY, USA, July 19, 2004, Revised Selected Papers*, volume 3374 of *Lecture Notes in Computer Science*. Springer, 2005.
39. D. Weyns, M. Schumacher, A. Ricci, M. Viroli, and T. Holvoet. Environments for Multiagent Systems. *Knowledge Engineering Review*, 2005. to appear.

Enriching a MAS Environment with Institutional Services

Andreia Malucelli[1,2], Henrique Lopes Cardoso[1], and Eugénio Oliveira[1]

[1] LIACC – NIAD&R, Faculty of Engineering, University of Porto,
R. Dr. Roberto Frias, 4200-465 Porto, Portugal
[2] PUCPR – Pontifical Catholic University of Paraná,
R. Imaculada Conceição, 1155, 80215-901 Curitiba PR, Brazil
{malu, hlc, eco}@fe.up.pt

Abstract. Most environments for multi-agent systems limit themselves to providing message transport and white/yellow page services. While these are generic facilities, in some domains other services are necessary, which may map real-world services provided by institutions. The Electronic Institution concept represents the virtual counterpart of real-world institutions, and one of its benefits is to provide a regulated and trustful environment by enforcing norms and providing specific institutional services. This paper presents some of such institutional services. Ontology-based services are provided to assist agent interaction, making the establishment of business agreements more efficient. After the establishment of an agreement through an appropriate negotiation process, it is necessary to verify the execution of the resulting contract. For this, we introduce an institutional normative environment based on the concept of institutional reality and norms.

1 Introduction

Multi-agent systems (MAS) applications include two different kinds of approaches. Some problems require system architectures including cooperative agents developed so as to accomplish an overall goal. On the contrary, in other situations agents may represent independent self-interested entities, with no presupposed cooperation besides mere interaction efforts. While the former types of problems may be addressed through a centralized design, the latter comprise open environments where agents interact and may, through negotiation, establish further cooperation commitments.

Although decentralized and dynamic systems are much more appealing, they must be handled with hybrid approaches. A minimum set of requirements is necessary to allow for heterogeneous and independently developed agents to successfully interact. One way of achieving such a common milieu is by defining communication standards, such as those proposed by FIPA [13], which have been implemented in several agent development platforms, such as JADE [18]. However, in terms of agent's interaction, such frameworks typically limit themselves to providing message transport and white/yellow page services [31].

D. Weyns, H. Van Dyke Parunak, and F. Michel (Eds.): E4MAS 2005, LNAI 3830, pp. 105–120, 2006.
© Springer-Verlag Berlin Heidelberg 2006

This paper describes a set of additional services – provided in an *Electronic Institution* (EI) framework – that facilitate agent interaction enabling the establishment of a normative environment.

Our background scenario is the domain of e-business automation, comprising not only the use of information gathering and filtering agents but also the establishment and operation of business relationships. Furthermore, we are interested in the process of Virtual Organization (VO) formation and operation, through which agents representing different business units or enterprises come together to address new market opportunities by combining skills, resources, risks and finances no single partner can alone fulfill [10]. In order to be trustful a VO needs to be regulated by appropriate norms.

One of the key factors influencing the adoption of agent-based approaches in real-world business scenarios is trust. When attempting to automate the creation and operation of business relationships, the behavior of agents must be made predictable, by creating a regulated environment that enforces agents' commitments. The notion of an EI [9, 20] is proposed as a means to provide such a regulated and trustable environment, by enforcing norms and providing specific services.

One of the topics presented in this paper is the ontology-based services, which are important when addressing open environments, that is, situations in which a centralized design is neither possible nor desirable. Such services are also proposed by FIPA, although most MAS platforms seem to ignore them. In our EI environment, such services are provided with the intent of enabling the utilization of negotiation protocols by agents using different domain ontologies.

A protocol for negotiating VO formation can be found in [28]. This protocol is used in an institutional negotiation mediation service. A successful negotiation process must result in an explicit contract that can be monitored. We describe the role of the EI in providing a normative environment that can be used as a means to verify agents' compliance with their established commitments. The EI acts as a trustable third-party providing such a monitoring and enforcement service.

The rest of the paper is organized as follows. Section 2 details ontology-based services, describing the integration of JADE and OWL. Moreover, it presents an ontology interaction protocol based on the contract-net protocol. In section 3 we explore the notion of an institutional normative environment. We present our approach including the representation of institutional reality and norms, which are monitored within the environment. Section 4 concludes the paper.

2   Institutional Ontology-Based Services

The Electronic Institution (EI) concept represents the virtual counterpart of real-world institutions, and one of its benefits is to provide institutional services. Besides enforcing norms, institutional services should be provided to assist the coordination efforts between agents using heterogeneous domain ontologies which, representing real-world entities, interact with the aim of establishing business relationships. The ontology-based services proposed and implemented are essential to support agent interaction (suppliers and customers) as a coordination framework, making the establishment of business agreements more efficient.

We have created a set of services (ontology-based services) embedded in the environment in order to ensure an effective, meaningful negotiation. The provided services are [23]: (i) currency conversion service, (ii) unit measure conversion service, and (iii) matching terms service.

The currency conversion service may be useful in the calculation of prices when agents are dealing with different currencies. Similarly, the unit measure conversion service may be useful when agents are dealing with different measure units. The currency conversion and unit measures conversion services are provided as web services. The user may choose the preferences for the currency and unit measures (International System of Units (SI), UK Imperial System or US System) in which he prefers to negotiate.

The matching terms service is required when some of the agents does not understand the content of a message, e.g. an item (product/service) under negotiation. This service is implemented based on lexical and semantic similarity measures. We have integrated three different similarities matching, which are: (i) calculating an n-grams [8] value for the attributes and relations of the concepts; (ii) calculating an n-grams value for the description of the concepts, and (iii) applying the LCH method [3] based on WordNet [25] to detect semantic similarity between both concepts.

Afterwards, if at least two of the three methods deliver a result, a final result is calculated using weighting in order to make a statement if the compared concepts (products or services, in the context of this work) have the same meaning. Furthermore, a classification according to the correspondence values, based on an established threshold is done.

Ontology-based services are important to allow negotiation to take place. The mapping between two heterogeneous domain ontologies is done dynamically when an agent requests this service, after a not-understood CFP (Call for Proposal). When agents get their ontology terms matched (i.e., they achieve a common understanding), they identify a business opportunity and may negotiate towards the establishment of a contract.

As agents need to be able to communicate with other agents and perceive the environment, a number of interaction languages, tools and platforms have been developed [17]. It is necessary to be aware of the potency as well as the impact of each language, tools and platforms, and select the appropriate form according to the requirements of the problem domain.

In [31], the authors argue that some popular frameworks such as JADE reduce the environment to a message transport system or broker infrastructure, and even in the FIPA specifications it is hard to find any functionality for the environment beyond message transport or broker systems. The objective would be not to restrict interaction to inter-agent communication because it neglects a rich potential of possibilities for the paradigm of Multi-Agent Systems (MASs).

However, if there exists already an effort to develop platforms, tools and languages, and they have been used successfully in the MAS area, it seems reasonable to integrate and improve them in order to explore the full potential of environments.

To address the problem of how to create agents with heterogeneous ontologies using an automated and integrated approach, we developed a new methodology, since we were faced with the problem of creating JADE agents with disparate ontologies. First, we created the ontologies using the ontology editor Protégé [16], from Stanford University, and produced a set of OWL (web ontology language) [27] files. Then, we transformed the ontological information into an object-oriented language format suitable for JADE.

If our agents shared a common ontology, it would have been possible to use the JADE's built-in approach. However, in open MAS, as we are considering, the JADE's built-in approach is not applicable, since it does not provide support for the integration of different ontologies.

The implemented platform allows both scenarios. The first one is the case when all agents share the same hard-coded ontology which is by default supported by JADE. It was implemented to explore the JADE's features in order to find out how to use ontologies in JADE. The second case, and the most relevant to work, uses the Jena [19] model interface, which has been used to extract information from the ontologies to implement a transparent mapping mechanism from ontologies to agents. This approach has also the advantage of allowing the use of Protégé as a tool to update the ontologies; otherwise updating an ontology would implicate generating Java sources with the protégé BeanGenerator [2] plug-in and recording portions of the agents source code.

Moreover, the implementation of our negotiation process combines the FIPA Contract Net Interaction Protocol with an additional protocol called Ontology Interaction Protocol (OIP). The former represents the general scenario of agents trading goods or services proposed by FIPA. The latter implements the protocol necessary for solving the interoperability problems, when agents are interacting with the environment requesting the ontology-based services [24].

2.1 Combining Ontologies and Agents Technologies

In order to communicate, agents need to use a common language – a language with an unambiguous syntax, well-defined semantics or meanings and expressive power. Thus, JADE agents exchange ACL (Agent Communication Language) messages that are in a standard and FIPA-compliant form to ensure interoperability by providing a standard set of ACL message structure, and, to provide a well-defined process for maintaining this set [13].

Inside of an agent, ontological information is represented as Java objects, but in the content slot of an ACL message, this ontological information is represented as a string or a sequence of bytes. To achieve translations between these two different types of representation, JADE provides a number of classes structured in several packages, known as the Content Reference Model (CRM) [4]. To create an ontology, the CRM contains the classes: Predicates, Concept and AgentAction, that have to be instantiated. "Predicates" are expressions that say something about the status of the world and evaluate to true or false, "Concepts" are expressions that indicate entities that exist and that agents talk and reason about, and "AgentActions" are expressions that indicate something that can be executed by some agent.

The total of all classes make up our ontology and every single agent involved in a negotiation process has to use these classes. This means that there must be prior agreement not only about the name used to identify the ontology but as well about sharing the ontological classes. We have compensated this limitation for agents using heterogeneous ontologies creating a shared top-level ontology while each agent has its own private domain ontology.

Top-Level and Domain Ontology. We profit from JADE's support to build in hierarchies in ontologies as a way to combine ontologies, thus facilitating code re-usage. We have created two types of ontologies using Protégé: a generic one named *Institutional Ontology* and other ones fitting in the Car Assembling domain named *Car Assembling Ontology* and *Automobile Assembling Ontology*.

Institutional Ontology is considered as a top-level ontology, while *Car Assembling Ontology* and *Automobile Assembling Ontology* are considered as a domain ontology. The *Concepts*, *AgentActions* and *Predicates* defined in the top-level ontology describe the basic concepts and relationships invoked when any information in an e-commerce context is expressed in natural language, and therefore, are not only related to the domain of *Car Assembling*. The domain ontology contains the elements a car consists of.

Figure 1 graphically points out the hierarchy (UML representation) in the ontologies. Every agent who wishes to negotiate with others must be acquainted with the ontological classes ("CLS" in the figure) whose objects are used to fill the content of an ACL message. Both, the Customer Enterprise Agent (CEAg) and the Supplier Enterprise Agent (SEAg) are able to interpret unambiguously the messages exchanged. To indicate this, they register the name of the ontology they use. *Institutional Ontology* and *Car Assembling Ontology* are recognized as Java classes.

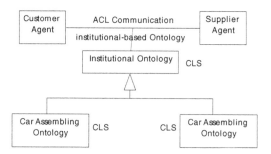

Fig. 1. Agents communicating with the same Domain Ontology

However, with agents using heterogeneous ontologies – but designed to describe the same domain of discourse - there are no classes that can be shared. A merging of two or more ontologies might not be an adequate solution in a competitive context since it presumes that every enterprise fully reveals its ontology.

To solve this problem, our approach uses a different way to access the information contained in the ontology of any agent and to search for the required information. The implementation partially abstains from the ontological classes, but choosing another format to provide the knowledge. In this way, the model tries to compensate the platform's incapability to deal with agents using different ontologies. Figure 2 shows this scenario.

Every agent taking part in a negotiation process shares the *Institutional ontology* and additionally each one explores its own, more specific ontology for the domain of

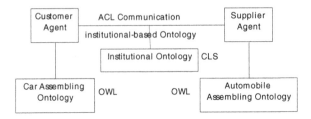

Fig. 2. Agents communicating with heterogeneous Domain Ontology

Car Assembling (in the example *Car Assembling Ontology* and *Automobile Assembling Ontology*). The *Institutional Ontology* is an ontology that is represented in a suitable way for JADE agents, that is, a set of Java classes. The domain ontologies rely on Web Ontology Language (OWL) files and to handle the OWL files we are using JENA.

Sharing the institutional ontology on the one hand ensures that the agents know exactly the meanings of the messages they are sending and receiving. On the other hand, since agents are able to use their own domain ontology, uniformity is not enforced and consequently the semantic interoperability problem may occur. To solve such problems the ontology-based services are required.

2.2 Ontology Interaction Protocol (OIP)

The implementation of a negotiation process combines the FIPA Contract Net Interaction Protocol with an additional protocol called Ontology Interaction Protocol (OIP), as presented in figure 3. The former represents the general scenario of agents trading goods or services proposed by FIPA. Alike other interaction protocols, it structures complex tasks as aggregations of simpler ones. The latter implements the message flow necessary for solving the problems of interoperability, including the interaction of customer and supplier agents when requesting/receiving a service. We have agentified the services with the purpose of facilitating the interaction between the agents and services.

In our scenario, the Customer Enterprise Agent plays the role of the initiator while the Supplier Enterprise Agent is the participant. The initiator wishes to have some task performed and further wants to optimize a function that characterizes the task. This characteristic is commonly expressed as the price, but could also be soonest time to completion, fair distribution of tasks, etc. [14].

For a given task, the participants may respond with a proposal or refuse. Negotiations then continue only with the participants that proposed. The initiator selects among all proposals the best one, based on its own criteria defining what "best" is, and replies, telling if it accepts the proposal or not. In the former case, once the Supplier Enterprise Agent has completed the task, it sends a message to the Customer Enterprise Agent in the form of an INFORM-DONE or a more explanatory version in the form of an INFORM-RESULT. However, if the participant fails to complete the task, a FAILURE message is sent.

This sequence diagram (figure 3) of the FIPA Contract Net Protocol shows how contracts in general accomplish. JADE provides classes that are implementation of the FIPA Contract Net Protocol.

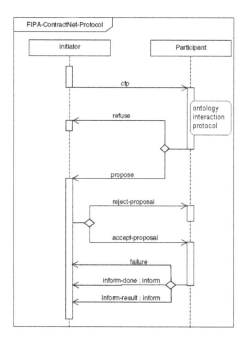

Fig. 3. FIPA Contract Net Interaction Protocol and Ontology Interaction Protocol

The agent responding to a CFP (Call for Proposal) performative should answer with a proposition giving its conditions on the performance of the action. The responder's conditions should be compatible with the conditions originally contained in the CFP, e.g., the CFP might seek proposals for an offer for a set of tires, with a condition that the currency is euro. A compatible proposal in reply would be "500 euros for a set of 4 Michelin tires". An incompatible proposal, for example, would be to use South African rand as currency.

The sequence diagram in figure 4 represents the implemented ontology interaction protocol (OIP), which intends to find correspondent concepts in two heterogeneous ontologies. The ontology-based services are provided by the Ontology-based Services Agent (OSAg). The Customer Enterprise Agent (CEAg) and the Supplier Enterprise Agent (SEAg) will interact with the OSAg.

Negotiation proceeds as follow, the numbers in brackets refer to the messages exchanged as depicted in the figure 4.

After having received a CFP (1) as part of the FIPA Contract Net Protocol and not being able to interpret the requested item, the SEAg sends a message with the performative NOT_UNDERSTOOD to the OSAg (2), acquainting who sent the CFP and the name of the unknown item.

The OSAg sends the name of the item it has just received to the CEAg (3) in order to get further information about it. The CEAg will analyze that request and send back attributes of the concept, their types, price and the description, i.e. all the information about this item (4). The price is taken from its pricelist.

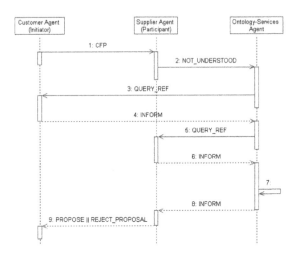

Fig. 4. Ontology Interaction Protocol

(5) and (6) refer to the pre-selection process. As the name suggests, the pre-selection process aims at getting candidate concepts, which could be the correspondent for the requested product and therefore reducing the target quantity. After having received (4), the OSAg knows the price of the product under negotiation and sends it to the SEAg (5). The process selects among all products the ones whose price value is in the range between 75% and 125% of the received value. This process results in a list of product candidates that is returned to the OSAg, including their names, the characteristics and their description in natural language.

Applying the pre-selection process, we reduce the set of potential matching concepts, which is absolutely essential in huge ontologies defining many entities. Otherwise the number of pairs, meaning concepts that have to be compared, would be too high.

The currency conversion service provided by the OSAg might be needed and can be requested if the SEAg's pricing of items uses a different currency from the requested product. After the selection, the SEAg answers with a list containing names, documentation and attributes of potential correspondent concepts (6).

After receiving all the information about the item under negotiation and a list of possible corresponding items, the OSAg is able to apply methods in order to match the terms (7).

These ontology mapping methods aim at detecting syntactic and semantic similarity of terms. Every term of the proposed, potential correspondent item is compared to the requested term.

In step (8), the OSAg informs the SEAg about the result of the comparisons delivered from the ontology mapping methods, i.e. it informs the name of the correspondent item or an appropriate message if this could not be discovered.

The SEAg is then able to respond to the CEAg (9), either with a PROPOSE or with a REJECT_PROPOSAL that is part of the FIPA Contract Net Interaction Protocol again.

3 Normative Environment

As exposed before, one of the main aims of the EI is to provide a level of trust through an enforceable normative environment. Norms can play an important role in open artificial agent systems, where they improve coordination and cooperation [6] and allow for the development of trust and reputation mechanisms. As in real-world societies, norms provide us a way to achieve social order [5] by controlling the environment and making it more stable and predictable.

Since we are concerned with the possibility of commitment creation at run-time through the establishment of contracts, our environment has a flexible normative structure. Contractual norms are used to represent agents' commitments. It is the EI responsibility to maintain the normative state of the environment, taking into account the compliance or non-compliance of agents regarding their applicable norms.

Having norms is not sufficient by itself, since agents will not voluntarily submit themselves to associated penalties in case of deviation. Therefore, appropriate mechanisms are needed to enforce norm compliance. The normative environment [22] provides such mechanisms. Therefore, while other institutional services are meant to further facilitate agent interaction (namely the ontology-based services and negotiation mediation), the normative environment comprises an active service that can change the state of the system independently of agents' actions [26]. This is because norm violation can simply be caused by the absence of a certain action, and the occurrence of an associated deadline.

Our EI conceptualization contrasts with other approaches, namely [11], where the EI is seen as a constraining infrastructure implementing a predefined protocol, in which agents are not allowed to violate norms. In our perspective, to enforce norms is not the same as preventing their violation. This approach allows us to maintain the autonomous nature of agents, while influencing their decision making by ensuring that certain consequences will hold in case of non-compliance.

3.1 Institutional Reality

In order to provide a trustable environment, the EI must have a means to register what is going on. The notion of "institutional reality" embraces the collection of the facts that make it possible to provide norm monitoring services.

Constitutive Rules. Part of this institutional reality is achieved by registering events acknowledged by the EI as having occurred. For this we took some inspiration on Searle's theory on "the construction of social reality" [29]. We distinguish between *brute facts* and *institutional facts*. The latter are obtained from de former, through rules defining "counts-as" relations (*constitutive rules*, according to Searle). Brute facts refer to agents' illocutions.

Constitutive rules make a connection between what is said and what is taken for granted, by taking into account a set of *institutional roles* enacted by agents providing specific services. Therefore, some institutional facts may come into existence only if agents performing certain institutional roles utter appropriate illocutions. Authoritative relations are thus established between roles and institutional reality: an agent performing a given role is said to be empowered to achieve the effects expressed in its role-related constitutive rules.

For illustration purposes, consider the following simple representation schemes:

- brute facts: `illocution(<Sender>, <Content>)`
- institutional facts: `ifact(<IFact>, <Timestamp>)`
- roles: `agentRole(<Agent>, <Role>)`

Constitutive rules are important to allow the recognition of action execution. This includes the fulfillment of contractual obligations through the realization of certain transactions. Consider that we want to certify an action corresponding to a certain payment obligation. Although the debtor agent may claim to have paid its debt, that does not make it the case. We would instead trust an agent providing a banking service:

```
illocution(?B, payment(?Ag1, ?Amount, ?Ag2, ?Time)) ∧
agentRole(?B, bank)
→ ifact(payment(?Ag1, ?Amount, ?Ag2), ?Time)
```

If we need to certify product delivery, we may rely on a delivery tracking service:

```
illocution(?DT, delivery(?Ag1, ?I, ?Qt, ?Ag2, ?Time)) ∧
agentRole(?DT, delivery_tracker)
→ ifact(delivery(?Ag1, ?I, ?Qt, ?Ag2), ?Time)
```

If message delivery recognition is a must, a messenger role may provide such a service. This may also be provided as an extension to the message transport service of any agent development platform.

By defining institutional roles instead of institutional agents providing their associated services, we emphasize the open and distributed nature of our institutional environment. Therefore, we may have several agents performing the same institutional role, and thus providing the same institutional service. By "institutional" we mean that those agents are certified by the EI as being trustworthy.

Institutional Rules. The purpose of providing an enforceable normative environ-ment must consider other elements, besides institutional facts, that compose the reality to be monitored, and that do not depend directly on brute facts. Taking into account the norms to be monitored, we must consider pending obligations, their fulfillment and violation. The passage of time is also important. All these elements may have interdependencies that may be made explicit by defining *institutional rules*. These rules work on institutional reality elements to produce new elements.

Examples of institutional rules include those that allow us to detect when certain obligations are fulfilled or violated. For illustration purposes, consider the following simple representation schemes for further institutional reality elements:

- obligation: `obligation(<Agent>, <IFact>, <Deadline>)`
- fulfillment: `fulfilled(<Agent>, <IFact>, <Timestamp>)`
- violation: `violated(<Agent>, <IFact>, <Timestamp>)`
- time: `time(<Timestamp>)`

The `<Agent>` tag refers to the bearer of the given obligation. We assume that an institutional procedure generates `time` elements whenever they are relevant for the application of a certain institutional rule.

We may define a rule for verifying the fulfillment of an obligation:

```
ifact(?IFact, ?T) ∧
obligation(?Agent, ?IFact, ?Deadline) ∧ ?T<?Deadline
→ fulfilled(?Agent, ?IFact, ?T)
```

The rule states that if an institutional fact prescribed by an obligation is achieved before its deadline, then that obligation is fulfilled.

We may also define a rule for detecting the violation of an obligation:

```
ifact(time, ?Deadline) ∧
obligation(?Agent, ?IFact, ?Deadline) ∧
¬fulfilled(?Agent, ?IFact, ?)
→ violated(?Agent, ?IFact, ?Deadline)
```

The rule states that if a deadline referring to an obligation was reached, and such obligation was not fulfilled, then a violation occurred.

Institutional rules may also point to procedures not amenable to a declarative representation. Examples include rules that trigger notification procedures whenever obligations arise, or rules that impose a reputation update when violations occur.

Figure 5 illustrates the relation between constitutive and institutional rules.

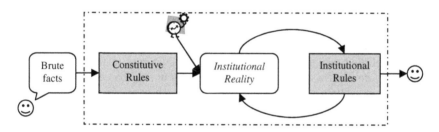

Fig. 5. Constitutive and Institutional Rules

This approach to the creation of institutional reality is closely related to the notion of influence and reaction [12]. In our case, influences comprise agents' illocutions (brute facts), through which they try to modify the state of the normative environment, trying to convince the EI that certain events took place. The environment then reacts to such influences by applying the constitutive and institutional rules (the "laws of the world" [12]) and producing institutional facts. However, ours is an asynchronous action model, since agents can run asynchronously and independently of the environment itself (closer to the model in [32]). The next subsection addresses the issue of norms and their relationship with institutional rules.

3.2 Norms

A norm-aware environment can operate either preventively (making unwanted behavior impossible) or reactively (detecting violations and reacting accordingly) [30]. In order to cope with the autonomous nature of agents, our approach considers norms as regulations that agents may or may not abide to.

Norms prescribe the expected behavior of agents, specifying states of affairs that *must* be brought about by an agent before a certain deadline. Therefore, we consider *obligations* as the means to express the prescription of behavior norms. Instead of dictating the exact action an agent must perform, obligations prescribe the institutional fact that he must bring about. This fits our model of institutional reality, where we specify by means of constitutive rules how an institutional fact may be accrued.

Just as with institutional rules, norms work on institutional reality elements. The distinguishing feature of norms is that they prescribe obligations when certain conditions are met.

Example Norms for a Purchase Contract. A simple set of norms governing a purchase contract is shown below. Contract specific information include the starting time ?S, the vendor ?V, the customer ?C, the item ?I, and the price ?P.

```
→ obligation(?V, delivery(?V, ?I, ?C), ?S+2)

fulfilled(?V, delivery(?V, ?I, 1, ?C), ?TDeliv)
→ obligation(?C, payment(?C, ?P, ?V), ?TDeliv+3)

violated(?V, delivery(?V, ?I, ?C), ?Dln)
→ obligation(?V, delivery(?V, ?I, ?C), ?Dln+5) ∧
   obligation(?V, payment(?V, 10%*?P, ?C), ?Dln+5)

violated(?C, payment(?C, ?P, ?V), ?Dln)
→ obligation(?C, payment(?C, ?P*110%, ?V), ?Dln+15)
```

These norms state that the contract starts with a delivery obligation on the vendor, that when fulfilled triggers the obligation on the customer to make the associated payment. The contract also includes two sanctioning norms (based on the violation of obligations), indicating what are the penalties for each case of non-compliance. The institutional rules presented in subsection 3.1 are fundamental for enabling the chaining of obligations within a contractual relationship. They establish a connection between the institutional facts that are added and the pending obligations, verifying their fulfillment or violation, and allowing the applicability of further norms.

Normative Framework. Besides the simple norm representation presented above, we consider that a normative environment should be embodied with a set of norms applicable in the absence of further information. An important concept in contract law theory is the use of "default rules" [7], which exist with the intent of facilitating the formation of contracts, allowing them to be underspecified by defining default clauses or default values. The most useful case for this is in defining contrary-to-duty situations (i.e., sanctions), which typically should be not likely to occur. Default regulations provide a normative background in which agents can rely to build their contractual commitments.

Furthermore, taking into account our stated goal of providing assistance to VO formation, we developed a normative framework [21] that considers three hierarchical layers of norms: *institutional, constitutional* and *operational*. While institutional norms may be applicable to all agents inside the EI, constitutional norms apply to agents taking part in a VO, and operational norms specify the operationalization of such organizations. Default norms may be defined for each of these layers.

To deal with an environment where a potentially large number of contracts (and VOs) need to be monitored, each of which may include many norms, our formalism considers the use of contextualized norms [22], allowing us to organize them. Also, elements of institutional reality have a context referring to the contract they belong to.

This normative framework, while getting inspiration from law systems in the real-world, comprises a valuable enrichment of MAS environments that need to be regulated.

3.3 Implementation

Not surprisingly, our rules and norms are amenable to a rule-based implementation. Also, the normative environment is based on the occurrence of events. We therefore chose a forward-chaining production system as the basis for implementation.

Our normative environment prototype is implemented using the Jess shell [15]. Our knowledge base consists of rules and norms, while the working memory includes institutional reality elements.

Jess also includes the possibility of using frame-based approaches, allowing us to easily aggregate and use contractual information. Jess also has a built-in concept of modules, which we use to organize norms within the system and to employ the default reasoning of the normative environment.

4 Conclusions

We have described our approach towards an Electronic Institution that defines a framework for agent activities by adding services to those proposed by agent platforms, building on JADE. The proposed services aim at enriching the MAS environment and point to the creation of organizations of agents through commitments. These are made explicit in contracts that a normative environment is responsible to monitor.

In our open and distributed environment where agents representing different enterprises come together to address new market opportunities, problems as interoperability and trust may happen. In order to help in solving these problems we have presented the ontology-based services and an approach towards the development of a normative environment.

We have implemented a platform integrating agents and ontologies technologies. JADE was used as a communication platform and a taxonomy was applied as a way to combine ontologies to facilitate code re-usage. For the domain ontology creation we used the Ontology editor Protégé with a plug-in, which enables us to store and load our ontology in OWL format. The generic *Institutional ontology* was proposed to ensure that the agents know exactly the meanings of the messages they are sending and receiving, although using their own domain ontology.

The adaptation of the negotiation process combines the FIPA Contract Net Protocol with an additional protocol called Ontology Interaction Protocol, which helps on solving the interoperability problems.

A key factor towards the adoption of agent-based approaches in real-world business scenarios is trust. Therefore, assisting the establishment of agreements is the first step in managing a business relationship. The negotiation process must result in a contract that can be enforced by a third-party. We have presented our approach towards the development of a regulated environment that makes explicit the contractual commitments in order to enforce them.

The agent technology roadmap [1], by AgentLink III, identifies as key problem areas the development of infrastructures for open agent communities, as well as the need for trust and reputation mechanisms. Electronic institutions, together with ontologies and related services, address the needed infrastructures. Norms, electronic contracts and their enforcement are pointed out as means to achieve trust in open environments. Our work is motivated by the need to develop services to assist the coordination efforts between agents which, representing different real-world entities, interact with the aim of establishing business relationships.

Acknowledgements

The work reported in this paper is supported by the FCT (Fundação para a Ciência e a Tecnologia) Project POSC/EIA/57672/2004.

References

1. AgentLink III, Agent Technology Roadmap: Overview and Consultation Report. http://www.agentlink.org/roadmap/index.html, December (2004)
2. Beangenerator Plug-in, http://acklin.nl/page.php?id=34, October (2004)
3. Budanitsky, A., Hirst, G.: Semantic distance in WordNet: An experimental, application-oriented evaluation of five measures. Proceedings of the Workshop on WordNet and Other Lexical Resources, Second Meeting of the North American Chapter of the Association for Computational Linguistics. Pittsburgh, USA (2001)
4. Caire, G.: Application-defined Content Languages and Ontologies. JADE Tutorial. TILab S.p.A.. June (2002)
5. Castelfranchi, C.: Engineering Social Order. In: Omicini, A., Tolksdorf, R., Zambonelli, F. (eds.): Engineering Societies in the Agents World Springer (2000) 1-18
6. Conte, R., Falcone, R., & Sartor, G.: Introduction: Agents and Norms: How to fill the gap?. Artificial Intelligence and Law, 7(1) (1999) 1-15
7. Craswell, R.: Contract Law: General Theories. In: Bouckaert, B., De Geest, G. (eds.): Encyclopedia of Law and Economics, Volume III: The Regulation of Contracts. Edward Elgar, Cheltenham (2000) 1-24
8. Damashek, M.: Gauging Similarity via N-Grams: Language-independent Sorting, Categorization, and Retrieval of Text, Science 267 (1995) 843-848.
9. Dignum, V., Dignum, F.: Modelling agent societies: co-ordination frameworks and institutions. In: Brazdil, P., Jorge, A. (eds.): Progress in Artificial Intelligence: Knowledge Extraction, Multi-agent Systems, Logic Programming, and Constraint Solving, LNAI 2258 Springer (2001) 191-204
10. Dignum, V., Dignum, F.: Towards an Agent-based Infrastructure to Support Virtual Organizations. In: Camarinha-Matos, L. M. (ed.): Collaborative Business Ecosystems and Virtual Enterprises Kluwer (2002) 363-370

11. Esteva, M., Padget, J., Sierra, C.: Formalizing a language for institutions and norms. In: Meyer, J.-J., Tambe, M. (eds.): Intelligent Agents VIII Springer (2002) 348-366
12. Ferber, J., Muller, J.P.: Influences and Reaction: a Model of Situated Multiagent Systems. 2nd International Conference on Multi-agent Systems, Japan, AAAI Press (1996)
13. FIPA ACL Message Structure Specification. SC00061G. FIPA TC Communication, http://www.fipa.org/specs/fipa00061/SC00061G.html, March (2004)
14. FIPA Contract Net Interaction Protocol Specification, SC00029H, 12/03/2002, http://www.fipa.org/specs/fipa00029/SC00029H.html, March (2004)
15. Friedman-Hill, E.: Jess in Action. Manning Publications Co. (2003)
16. Gennari, J., Musen, M.A., Fergerson, R.W., Grosso, W.E., Crubézy, M., Eriksson, H., Noy, N.F., Tu, S.W.: The Evolution of Protégé: An Environment for Knowledge-Based Systems Development, Technical Report. SMI Report Number: SMI-2002-0943 (2002)
17. He, M., Jennings, N.R., Leung, H.-F.: On Agent-Mediated Electronic Commerce, IEEE Transactions on Knowledge and Data Engineering. Vol. 15(4) July/August (2003) 985-1003.
18. Java Agent DEvelopment Framework, http://jade.tilab.com
19. Jena Semantic Web Framework, http://www.hpl.hp.com/semweb/jena.htm, October (2004)
20. Lopes Cardoso, H., Malucelli, A., Rocha, A.P., Oliveira, E.: Institutional Services for Dynamic Virtual Organizations. In: Camarinha-Matos, L. M., Afsarmanesh, H., Ortiz, A. (eds.): Collaborative Networks and Their Breeding Environments – 6th IFIP Working Conference on Virtual Enterprises (PRO-VE'05) Springer. (2005) 521-528
21. Lopes Cardoso, H., Oliveira, E.: Virtual Enterprise Normative Framework within Electronic Institutions. In: Gleizes, M.-P., Omicini, A. & Zambonelli, F. (eds.): Engineering Societies in the Agents World V Springer. (2004) 14-32
22. Lopes Cardoso, H., Oliveira, E. Towards an Institutional Environment using Norms for Contract Performance. In: Pechoucek, M., Petta, P., Varga, L. Z. (eds.): Multi-Agent Systems and Applications IV – 4th International Central and Eastern European Conference on Multi-Agent Systems (CEEMAS 2005). Springer (2005) 256-265
23. Malucelli, A., Oliveira, E.: Using Similarity Measures for an Efficient Business Information-Exchange. In: Skowron, A., Barthes, J-P., Jain, L, Sun, R., Marizet-Mahoudeaux, P., Liu, J., Zhong, N. (eds): 2005 IEEE/WIC/ACM International Conference on Intelligent Agent Technology. IEEE Computer Society, Los Alamitos, California (2005) 234-237
24. Malucelli, A., Palzer, D., Oliveira, E.: Ontology-based Services to help solving the heterogeneity problem in e-commerce negotiations. To be published in Journal of Electronic Commerce Research and Applications - Special Issue Electronic data engineering: the next frontier in e-commerce. Vol. 5(3) Elsevier (2006)
25. Miller, G.: WordNet:A Lexical Database for English. Communication of ACM, 38(11) (1995) 39-41
26. Odell, J., Parunak, H.V.D., Fleischer, M., Breuckner, S.: Modeling Agents and their Environment. In: Giunchiglia, F., Odell, J., Weiss, G. (eds.): Agent-Oriented Software Engineering III. Lecture Notes in Computer Science, Vol. 2585. Springer-Verlag, Berlin Heidelberg New York (2002)
27. OWL – Web Ontology Language, http://www.w3.org/TR/owl-features/, October (2004)
28. Rocha, A.P., Lopes Cardoso, H., Oliveira, E.: Contributions to an Electronic Institution Supporting Virtual Enterprises' Life Cycle. In: Putnik, G., Cunha, M.M. (eds.): Virtual Enterprise Integration: Technological and Organizational Perspectives Idea Group, Inc. (2005) 229-246

29. Searle, J. R.: The Construction of Social Reality. Free Press, New York. (1995)
30. Vázquez-Salceda, J., Aldewereld, H., Dignum, F.: Implementing norms in multiagent systems. In: Lindemann, G., Denzinger, J., Timm, I. J., Unland, R. (eds.): Multiagent System Technologies, Springer. (2004) 313-327
31. Weyns, D., Holvoet, T.: A Formal Model for Situated Multi-agent Systems. Formal Approaches for Multi-Agent Systems, Special Issue of Fundamenta Informaticae, 63(2) (2004)
32. Weyns, D., Van Dyke Parunak, H., Michel, F., Holvoet, T, Ferber, J.: Environments for Multiagent Systems, State-of-the-art and Research Challenges. In: First International Workshop on Environments for Multiagent Systems, LNAI, Vol. 3374 (2005)

Overhearing and Direct Interactions: Point of View of an Active Environment

Eric Platon[1], Nicolas Sabouret[2], and Shinichi Honiden[1]

[1] National Institute of Informatics, Sokendai,
2-1-2 Hitotsubashi, Chiyoda, 101-8430 Tokyo
[2] Laboratoire d'Informatique de Paris 6, 8, Rue du Capitaine Scott, 75015 Paris
{platon, honiden}@nii.ac.jp, nicolas.sabouret@lip6.fr

Abstract. Overhearing has been proposed recently as a model of indirect interactions in Multi–Agent Systems. Overhearer agents receive messages that were not primarily sent to them, as when someone hears a conversation among others. Overhearing has been modeled essentially as message broadcasting, but this approach raises several issues of scalability and appropriateness of the mental state of overheard agents.

In this paper, we motivate and propose a model of overhearing that copes with these issues by introducing an *explicit environment entity* to handle overhearing. We define key notions with focus on the environment perspective, model them and their relations, and detail an algorithm that describes the environmental process for agent interactions. We finally illustrate our approach with an electronic market scenario.

1 Introduction

The design of software environments in Multi–Agent Systems (MAS) originates from the need for an explicit representation of the 'world' in computer simulations [7,6]. Design is now evolving to broader use in an expanding variety of systems where the environment yields new solutions—and new challenges—as can be observed in the literature [25]. In particular, agent interactions leverage conceptual and concrete advantages from the environment, for instance in the case of *indirect interactions* [19,5,12]. Stigmergy is a notable case that leads to novel ways to design systems and algorithms [19,3], and *overhearing* recently appeared as relevant and promising [12,2,14]. When an agent 'overhears an interaction', it receives information about the interaction that is not primarily addressed to it. For instance, one can listen to a conversation between two friends without being part of their dialog.

Although overhearing (OH) is natural for humans, it remains exceptional in software systems. Multi-party discourse analysis shows nonetheless that OH is a required communication type to model group interactions among artificial agents [5]. Moreover, recent agent systems were developed with OH and they have validated advantages as for improving group awareness [14], group communication [2], or monitoring [12]. However, this work models OH as 'message broadcasting' and it does not address several issues relative to the environment.

D. Weyns, H. Van Dyke Parunak, and F. Michel (Eds.): E4MAS 2005, LNAI 3830, pp. 121–138, 2006.

In this paper, we argue that overhearing should be *processed* by an explicit and active environment. The environment approach is supported by related work in the agent community but we think several issues remain to be clarified. What is the very nature of OH, classified indistinctly as communication or interaction? And how does the environment contribute to the OH concept? In order to address these questions, we describe a model of agent environments that mediates and manages homogeneously 'traditional' direct communications and OH.

After motivating this research in section 2, section 3 describes the concepts involved in this work from the *point of view of the software environment*. Section 4 introduces our preliminary model of environment in supporting overhearing. Section 5 illustrates our approach with an example scenario. Finally, we discuss the status of this work in section 6 and conclude in section 7.

2   Motivations and Related Work

In early work, overhearing was modeled and implemented as message broadcasting or multi–casting [12,2,14,20]. This is a straightforward way to represent and exploit OH owing to the available infrastructures, technologies, and design usage. However, broadcasting and multi–casting suffer from several issues. First, broadcasting seems lacking scalability in open and large MAS. If all agents are to broadcast any message to all reachable agents, communication infrastructure would be rapidly overwhelmed, without guarantee to effectively reach agents. Second, multi–casting contradicts some intuitive features of OH since it requires that the sender agent knows how to reach addressees (*e.g.* diffusion list), whereas an overhearing agent *is not* directly contacted, but indirectly informed. That is, sender and receiver agents cannot always be in appropriate mental states, *e.g.* when an agent does not *expect* to yield information by overhearing. Third, multi–casting often supposes all recipients have the same status of 'addressee' in the discourse, whereas OH requires two 'roles' of addressee and overhearer as defined in multi-party communication [5]. The two roles could be modeled with multi–casting (*e.g.* the *cc.* field for emails for the 'OH role'), but it emphasizes that the sender knows how to reach overhearers and it is not usually the case since the sender is not always aware of each overhearer[1]. Consequently, multi–casting implies an addressing concern in open MAS. It cannot model sending a message to unknown agents that enter the system if the new comers do not explicitly inform the sender about their arrivals. For instance, a conversation on the street seems hard to overhear by multi–casting, because speaker and addressees do not usually know dynamically how to reach 'pedestrians that walk nearby'. Such argument leads to the idea that OH should be mediated, since an explicit link between the sender and the overhearer is missing. That is the reason of the interest in an *active environment*.

---

[1] In [5], the authors distinguish overhearers (known by the speaker) from eavesdroppers (unknown by the speaker). We confound the two roles into overhearer, due to looser hypothesis than multi–party discourse: conversing on a street, the speaker knows the presence of pedestrians who are potential eavesdroppers.

Beyond this result, the environment enacts a panel of properties that could not be achieved with broadcasting only. For example, broadcasting does no guarantee that agents comply with overhearing, *i.e.* that agents effectively send messages to overhearers. If a system designer wants to enforce overhearing, broadcasting has to be imposed by coding into each agent, which is not a likely hypothesis in open systems where agents are supposed heterogeneous. The environment is however external to agents and it can mediate communication to enforce overhearing independently from agents.

The environment has already been investigated as candidate for the missing link in indirect interactions among agents. Balbo *et al.* developed the ESAC bus fleet management system whereby agents interact by annotating messages with delivery directives the environment has to execute [1]. Such directives define receivers by properties (closest agent, bus agent, agent on line n, *etc.*), so that OH is possible since messages are delivered to all agents verifying the properties whether they are addressees or not. However, ESAC yields the control of the environment to agents. Although ESAC benefits from this decision at design and implementation time, we think the concept is counter–intuitive and the engineering may be neither portable nor reusable. Indeed, the environment should be a first class–entity in MAS [26], *i.e.* its existence should be independent and complementary to agents. Directives from agents should be instead *preferences* (or perhaps *influences* [7]) they express about messages, in the way we direct our head toward the addressee to allow our voice better traveling to its destination. In this case, OH is performed by the environment that uses such preferences to determine the adequate execution independently from agents.

In MIC*, interactions are represented by 'interaction objects' (IO) that evolve in a deployment environment independently from agents, which only produce or consume IOs [11,10]. Once produced by agents, IOs become a responsibility of the environment that manages their life cycle and delivery. In addition, the notion of interaction space is developed to express that IO propagation is framed into physical or virtual areas. A model of OH is thus possible where IOs are delivered in an interaction space at least defined with the speaker, addressees and overhearers. However, the algebraic model of IO unifies all classes of interactions as one concept. From the point of view of the environment, we think different interaction types should be distinguished to deal with both concrete and epistemic situations. If both are confounded, it is unclear how the bits representing a 'paper IO' (a newspaper) and 'discussion IOs' (pronounced words) should be composed. It seems possible to 'overhear the paper IO' in this model, and we think such semantical issues should be more carefully handled.

Coordination fields and TUCSON share similar concepts dealing with typed tuples and programmable tuple centers, respectively [17,16,18,21]. These technologies provide implementation frameworks for overhearing by letting designers configure entities distinct from agents—that form an environment—to define how interactions propagate into the system. 'Message tuples' in coordination fields seem particularly adapted to model OH [16], and the 'mailbox' developed upon TuCSoN in [21] shows another possible implementation. The design of applications with TuCSoN is based on the notion of 'coordination artifact' [21]. This entity in–between agents and their environment supports the idea of separation of concerns and responsibilities. Nevertheless, we think an agent does not interact the same way with another agent and with a 'non–agent' (to be defined in 3.1) and it has consequences on modeling OH with an environment that is not represented with coordination fields or artifacts. Although it might be achieved with two different kinds of coordination artifacts, guidances are required and this is a corollary theme of this paper.

3   Concepts

In this section, a series of definitions is compiled to present elements exploited in our approach of overhearing. We adopt the *point of view of the environment* in these definitions. That is, we focus on the traits in the elements that are related to the environment. In particular, the definitions emphasize the interactive aspects of the elements.

3.1   MAS Concepts from the Environment Viewpoint

Transfer, Interaction, and Communication. Toward a definition of over-hearing, we first distinguish the notions of transfer, interaction, and communication, where Fig.1 depicts a graphical notation to represent the definitions. The term 'entity' refers to the active elements involved in the definition and will be detailed in the next definition. First, we define transfer and interaction.

A *transfer* is a process whereby information is transfered among entities;
   An *interaction* is a transfer whereby the state of involved entities is modified [15].

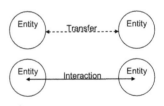

Fig. 1. Transfer and Interaction

Transfers exist *in–between* entities as 'information carriers'. We represent transfers with a dashed arrow that terminates at entity boundaries, as shown on the upper part of Fig. 1. Transfers can be *direct* from a sender to a receiver entity, or *indirect* when the receiver is not an intended target of the transfer.

Interaction is a transfer that changes the internal state of entities and so our representation is a plain arrow that 'crosses' boundaries of the entities on the figure to show that some effects happen.

We further separate two types of interactions. *Tangible* interactions modify the correlated states of environment and involved entities. In this case, the environment mediates the interaction and its state is changed in accordance with the states of involved entities. Properties of tangible interaction are that they are *only direct* and their effects are *evaluated* by the environment. Examples come from natural interactions such as pushing a physical object where the effect is the modification of the object shape or position in the environment. Other examples in a virtual context are the update of a database or the exploitation of a web–service whereby 'tangible' reactions occur (*e.g.* service execution).

Intangible interactions are communication. The environment only mediates the interaction and its state is uncorrelated to the effect. Intangible interaction effects can be *direct or indirect* and they are *not evaluated* by the environment, but by some entities (see next definition). A typical example is a speech act whereby one can influence someone without apparent result. In agent–based auction systems, auctioneers send descriptions of an item to sell, but decisions from bidders are in their internals. Replies can only be expected by the auctioneer.

In consequence of these definitions, the involvements of the environment and entities in the different types are summarized in the following Table 1.

Table 1. Environment Involvement

		Environment	Entities
Transfer		X	
Tangible Interaction	Transfer aspect	X	
	Effect	X	X
Intangible Interaction	Transfer aspect	X	
(Communication)	Effect		X

Transfer is performed by the environment to mediate information among entities, in both types of interactions. Tangible interactions involve environment and entities, where the role of the environment is to ensure valid states in the execution of interaction effects. In contrast, intangible interactions depend on entities and the environment has no responsibility in their effects. The role of the environment is limited to the transfer of information.

Agent and Non-agent. From the point of view of the environment, we now identify the entities that can interact. We first define an agent as follows.

An *agent* is an autonomous and knowledgeable entity that can engage in all types of interactions, *i.e.* tangible and intangible.

The definition emphasizes the interaction aspect of agents. It remains a compatible version of classical definitions [7,22], but only the interactive parts matter from the point of view of the environment.

The second type of entities are *elementals*[2], or 'non–agents'.

> An *elemental* is an entity that can participate in tangible interactions.

Such an entity participates in tangible interactions with other entities, but it cannot participate in intangible interaction, *i.e.* in communication. In addition, it cannot *engage* interactions. It is passive, by contrast with the activity of agents due to their autonomy. For instance in a software simulation, two stones interact in a physical meaning when a collision occurs (tangible in the environment), but they cannot decide the interaction.

Agents have the property to verify the definition of elementals, so that they can *act as elementals*. Various reasons motivate this statement, such as considering an agent interacting with an elemental, or two agents interacting out of the scope of the language (*e.g.* with senses, or pushing one another). In the first case, an agent can only act on an elemental through a tangible interaction, and from the environment, we consider this interaction involves two elementals.

From the environment perspective as shown in table 1, agents and elementals are similar, since they both participate in transfers and tangible interactions. Agents can also engage in intangible interactions, but this is concretely an information transfer for the environment. However, overhearing is a case of *indirect intangible interaction*. It requires that the environment can distinguish agent from elemental, since elementals cannot process such type of transfer.

Overhearing. Before defining overhearing in the perspective of the environment, we present a generally accepted definition based on [12,14,5]: 'Overhearing is an indirect interaction whereby an agent receives information for which it is not an addressee.' For instance, one can overhear a discussion on the street just by listening to the involved agents. Our definition in this paper is as follows.

> *Overhearing* is an agent–specific *indirect transfer* whereby an agent receives information for which it is not addressee.

This definition highlights that the sole function of the environment toward overhearing is to *carry* information and *deliver* it according to environmental configuration (*e.g.* delivery to all nearby agents in the 'air environment', to none in the 'water environment'). The consequence of the delivered information is out of the environment responsibilities.

3.2   An Environment for Overhearing

In relation with Table 1, Fig. 2 depicts the environment perspective on agent communication and interaction.

Only transfer and tangible interaction are completely processed by the environment (upper figure). However, the effect of intangible interactions is out

---

[2] Initially, we chose the term 'object' to label this concept, but the meaning inherited from object-oriented programming cannot easily be redefined. Consequently the term elemental should be understood as an alternative in the frame of this paper, independently from its legal meaning.

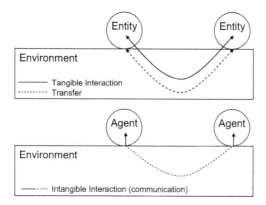

Fig. 2. Environment Perspective on communication, interaction, transfer, and entities

of the environment responsibilities, so that the environment processes this type of interaction as a simple transfer, represented by a dashed line prolonged with plain arrows to highlight the difference with other cases on the lower figure.

In order to handle the different cases of 'traditional' direct interactions and indirect interactions related to OH, the environment needs to deal with the concepts introduced above and it should address:

What to process? A mean to distinguish transfer from tangible interaction. Intangible interactions are out of the scope of the environment.

For Who? A list of agents and elementals that lie in the environment. The population evolves in open systems, but also in 'closed' systems where mobility is possible. Thus, the environment must catalog who is present to react appropriately.

Where to direct the process? A mean to address agents and elementals. The environment manages the propagation of transfers, and it must determine direct and indirect targets.

How to process? A mean to specify the types of transfer that are allowed. Different environments have different properties: air and water do not permit the same propagation laws and affect the processing of OH.

In conclusion to this conceptual part, the environment we identify for direct interaction and OH is a *structured information transfer carrier* that *facilitates* interactions among agents and elementals, and *obeys* to configurable *environmental rules*.

4   Model

The conclusive statement of section 3 declares that the environment is a well-defined entity of MAS. The environment has a proper *interface* to let agents and elementals deal with it, and to distinguish them. Also, it must maintain a *population list* that lies and can therefore interact. The addressing relative to the presence of entities deals with a mean to structure and situate targets of communication/interaction. Consequently, we refer to a *topology* of the environment. Finally, environmental rules can be compiled in a configuration *policy* that defines how the environment must process its activity.

Hence, we model the environment as the hereafter formula and the following parts aim at detailing the different elements constituting this representation.

$$ENV = (Topology, Policy, Interface) \tag{1}$$

4.1   Model Development

Population Management and Topology. The environment must maintain a list of entities in accordance with a topology to retrieve them. Consequently, we define the tuple:

$$Topology = (Transpace,\ Pop\_Ag,\ Pop\_Ele) \tag{2}$$

Transpace is a pair ({TS}, *Relations*) referring to a set of *Transfer Spaces* (TS) and their relations to structure the environment. TS are subsets of the environment that serve to representing virtual or physical spaces, such as a room or a network domain. *Pop_Ag* and *Pop_Ele* reference agent and elemental populations that are present in the environment, out of any transfer space.

Each TS is a tuple:

$$TS = (TS\_Pop\_Ag,\ TS\_Pop\_Ele,\ TS\_Rules) \tag{3}$$

TS_Pop_Ag and *TS_Pop_Ele* reference agents and elementals respectively in the TS. *TS_Rules* is a set of environmental rules applied in the TS only, and it is explained later in this section. For example, an agent can be in the concrete room of a house (a TS) and obeys to the 'air rule' whereby transfer is propagated in all directions. Another example is a 'virtual room' (another TS) defined by a phone call, where agents obey to the line configuration.

In our approach, the structure of the environment depends on agents and elementals that can belong simultaneously to several TS. *Relations* represents the organization of TS as a hierarchical structure. A link between two TS means there exists an agent or elemental that belongs to both. For example, an agent may be in a room TS and a phone call TS at the same time, so that these two TS are connected. In such situation, transfer involving agents in the intersection are ruled by both TS. In the case where TS_1 is included in TS_2, *i.e.* all agents in TS_1 are in TS_2, TS_1 overrules TS_2 for all transfers in TS_1. For example, agents attending a party TS can have a 'private TS' discussion. In particular, each TS overrules the default policy of the environment.

Relations in *Transpace* can be represented as a tree where the root is the environment and leafs are TS depending on their relations. TS with partial or no intersection appear at the same hierarchical level, and nested TS appear as children. An example of topology is presented on Fig. 3.

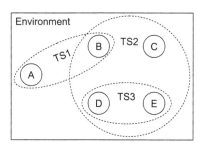

Fig. 3. An environment topology

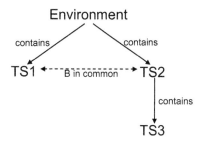

Fig. 4. Relations between TS

On this figure, we consider that plain rounds are agents, dashed ovals are TS, and the rectangle delimits the environment. This situation then means:

$$Topology = (\{TS1, TS2, TS3\},\ \emptyset,\ \emptyset)$$
$$TS1 = (\{A, B\},\ \emptyset,\ TS\_Rules_1)$$
$$TS2 = (\{B, C\},\ \emptyset,\ TS\_Rules_2) \tag{4}$$
$$TS3 = (\{D, E\},\ \emptyset,\ TS\_Rules_3)$$

For instance, A, and B can communicate through TS1 under the condition TS_Rules_1, and TS1 and TS2 are connected through B. A cannot interact with others than B since they are not in a common TS.

In this example, the structure of TS has the tree representation on Fig. 4. TS1 and TS2 are directly contained in the environment and they share agent B, so that they are at the same level with a 'B in common' relation to state the two TS are joint. Interactions with B are ruled by both TS. TS3 is included in TS2, and this is represented by placing TS3 one level lower as child of TS2.

Environmental Policies. Policies rule the environment process in *Policy* and transfer spaces in *TS_Rules*. We define them commonly as a set of rules:

$$Policy = (list\ of\ rules) \tag{5}$$

In our approach, a policy is a list of formulas named rules that define the reactions of the environment for transfer processes[3]. The structure and variety of rules depend on environmental needs, and we chose two types in this paper: *overhearing* to enforce OH so that all agents in the environment or TS receives all transfers, and *none* to only authorize direct interactions. Other applications may define refinements such as a range of communication or variable OH.

---

[3] Other approaches might define rules for different functions of the environment instead of only transfers, for example for tangible interactions (*e.g.* Laws of Physics). We focus on transfers in this paper for the case of overhearing.

The formulas for our two cases are as follows, in a first–order predicate logic syntax:

$$overhearing : \forall x \in Agent, \ \forall m_x \in Mes : \ (\forall y \in Agent, \ deliver(m_x, y)) \ \wedge$$
$$((\neg \exists z \in Agent, target(x, z)) \ \Rightarrow \ deliver(fail, x))$$
$$none : \forall x \in Entity, \ \forall m_x \in Mes : \ \ \ \ \ \ \ \ \ \ \ (6)$$
$$(\forall y \in Entity, \ target(x, y), \ deliver(m_x, y)) \ \wedge$$
$$((\neg \exists z \in Entity, target(x, z)) \ \Rightarrow \ deliver(fail, x))$$

The formula of *overhearing* is restricted to agents, where *Agent* represents an agent population (either *Pop_Ag* or *TS_Pop_Ag*). Any message m_x from agent x is delivered to all other agents y in the space, including the addressees of the message. If there is no such a y, a failure message is sent to x.

The formula for *none* can be applied to agents and elementals. Any message m_x from agent x is delivered to addressees y if they exist. Otherwise, a fail message is returned to x.

Environment Interface. The interface of environments features similarities with tuple–spaces [9]. Only two operations are however defined, namely *in* and *out*. The *read* action is not needed in our case due to our definitions: tuples vanish once they are transmitted and we think the environment should not maintain them (*e.g.* the air does not maintain our words). 'Persistent tuples' should be elementals in our approach (*e.g.* a book, a note, a recorder) and so 'reading' them becomes a tangible interaction with it through the environment.

In addition, the environment interface exposes specific elements to deal with the communication spaces. Agents can indeed create TS, or enter and exit existing TS—actions that can be related to mobility.

The in/out operation set has two forms depending on agents and elementals. The two forms are aimed to indicate to the environment when to deal with transfer or tangible interaction, and process them accordingly. Consequently, we define the environment interface as a tuple:

$$Interface = (Env\_in\_ag, \ Env\_out\_ag, \ Env\_in\_ele, \ Env\_out\_ele,$$
$$NewTS, \ Enter, \ Exit) \ \ \ \ \ \ \ \ \ \ (7)$$

Each element of *Interface* specifies an interface of the environment by defining what agents or elementals have to comply with. The first four elements of *Interface* define how entities interact. *Env_in_ag* allows the environment to send an information to an agent. Its signature is $Env\_in\_ag(to, from, message)$ with *to* the identity of the intended recipient of the *message* and *from* the identity of the sender. The *to* parameter is relevant when the environment delivers the message to an agent that is not addressee, which is a case of overhearing. *Env_out_ag* defines the operation where an agent sends a message. The signature is similarly $Env\_out\_ag(from, to, message)$. Typically, *Env_in_ag* and *Env_out_ag* fit agent communication language such as FIPA–ACL [8].

Env_in_ele and *Env_out_ele* are equivalent operations for elementals, with the same signatures. For example, *Env_in_ele* and *Env_out_ele* can be procedure calls such as SOAP [23]. Agent can also use elemental interfaces when they 'act as elementals' in tangible interactions.

The three remaining elements of $Interface$ define how agents interact with the environment itself. Elementals were defined as passive entities and cannot engage in such interactions. $NewTS$ is a special communication from an agent A to the environment, asking for the creation and maintenance of a new TS. Its signature requires the agent identity and the intended rules. In case of successful creation, the environment first adds the TS to the $Relations$ tree as child of the current space of A. In the example of Fig. 4, TS3 was created from TS2. Second, the environment informs all agents about the new space, so that others are aware of the creation. In case of failure (that could be due to an environmental rule), A is informed about it. To destroy a TS, all agents must leave it. This permits the TS to be independent of any agent, especially its creator.

Finally, $Enter$ and $Exit$ are communications asking respectively for entering or exiting a TS. They have similar signatures and we describe the case of $Enter(x \in self \cup Elementals, s \in \{TS\} \cup \{Environment\})$. First, the subject of the entrance is either $self$—the agent itself—or an elemental. An agent can decide to enter a TS or to introduce an elemental. However, an agent cannot force the entrance of another agent in our model. Second, s is the identity of the aimed TS or the environment itself to enter the system. The exit of a TS is guided by the topology structure maintained in the $Relations$ of $Transpace$. When an agent succeeds in exiting a TS, it 'returns' to the parent TS in the hierarchy. From the example of Fig. 4, an agent that exits TS3 returns to TS2, and an exit from TS2 ends in the environment out of any TS. If the exit concerns the environment itself, the agent leaves the system. $Enter$ and $Exit$ events are also propagated by the environment in the current space, so that all agents are aware of the presence of others.

4.2   Environment Internal Algorithm

We describe in Algorithm 1 an environmental process to handle direct interactions and OH, relying on our model. All transfers are mediated by the environment, so that agents have no other ways to interact with each other.

Algorithm 1 is an infinite loop that lasts while the system is running. The loop contains two parts. First, line 2 is the input of the environment. It receives

---

Algorithm 1. Environment Internal Algorithm

1: **loop**
2:    operations ← {entities output}
3:    **repeat**
4:       process_agent_transfers(operations)
5:       process_elemental_transfers(operations)
6:       manage_transfer_spaces(operations)
7:    **until** operations=∅
8: **end loop**

---

requests from agents and elementals to be processed. Second on lines 3–7, a loop repeats three sub–procedures to process the requests depending on their types, namely agent and elemental transfers, or TS management (line 4–5–6 respectively). Once the current operations list is emptied (line 7), the algorithms continues by reading new inputs in the next iteration. The code of the sub–procedures is commented in appendix (process_agent_transfers and process_elemental_transfers are similar so only the former, more complex, is detailed).

5   Illustrative Scenario: A Market Place

5.1   System Description

A market place is a regulated open system where agents can trade goods. Several types where developed so far such as [28,13], without an explicit and active environment.

Our market place is based on an environment that provides the system foundations whereon agents trade (interact), and it enforces overhearing to produce some real market conditions such as expected for fish markets or stock exchange.

Our system has the following specification:

1. The system is open, built on an explicit environment.
2. The system mediates interactions through the environment.
3. The environment default policy is to enforce direct interactions ('none' rule).
4. There exists only one transfer space in the environment. This TS is the market place itself.
5. The market place policy is set to 'overhearing'.

The above specification describes the settings of the system. Openness means that agents are free to enter or leave the environment and the market place. We assume interoperability issues to be 'solved', notably protocols and ontologies are known.

5.2   Scenario

Two Seller and one Buyer agents exist in the system and trade the same kind of goods, for instance appliance. Our scenario has two consecutive frames:

First frame. Seller S_1 offers an appliance price of 10. All in the market place receive this information. Seller S_2 desires being attractive before buyers reactions and offers for the same appliance a price of 9. The buyer B does not react to these offers.

Second frame. S_2 decides to exit the market place and asks B to do so as well. S_1 expresses its disagreement. B exits and there, S_2 offers the appliance for a price of 10 with a special guarantee that B accepts.

Fig. 5 shows the settings of the system for this scenario in its initial state, and Fig. 6 shows the final state.

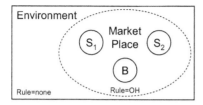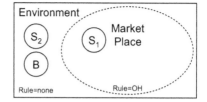

Fig. 5. Scenario Environment (initial)   **Fig. 6.** Scenario Environment (final)

Agents are represented by circles with a letter to label them, namely B, S_1, and S_2. The only transfer space is the dashed–lined oval that delimits the market place where OH is enforced. Out of the transfer space, agents are in the 'default environment' (the outer rectangle) where the none rule is enforced.

5.3 Model Exploitation

The diagram on Fig. 7 shows the evolution of the scenario with our model as a sequential diagram (UML notation [24]).

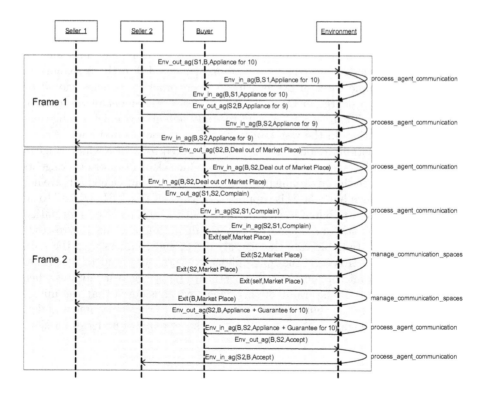

Fig. 7. Scenario Evolution

The sequence follows the two frames of the scenario with our model of environment. In frame 1, all agents are in the market place so that all interactions are overheard. The environment enforces this by sending any message to all other agents in the place. That is the reason why everyone is aware of the concurrence.

In frame 2, S_2 leaves the market and other agents are informed. Then B leaves and only S_1 is informed since S_2 is not anymore in the TS. Finally, the last discussion between S_2 and B is under the default policy of the environment ('none'), so that S_1 is not informed.

6   Discussion

This paper addresses the relationship between overhearing and environment. The adoption of the environment perspective led us to distinguish exchange situations (transfer, communication, and interaction), entity classes (agent and elemental), and to consider overhearing as an indirect transfer.

The environment is a unique part of MAS that obeys to rules different from agent ones. We consider it is independent from direct agent control as it rather reacts to their influences [7], and it 'ignores' agent individual identities, so that it can be thought of as a 'blind impartial referee'. To achieve such a blind performance of the environment functions, we introduced policies and transfer spaces to address agents. The modeling of OH—and other exchanges we refer to—seems realizable in our approach, but a validation is yet to be completed. The example of section 5 consists in a first step in this direction. For instance, the sequence diagram shows all communications pass through the environment. This may be a bottleneck in practical systems if they are implemented directly. Also, current policies define simple cases of overhearing. But in practice, policies should be configurable (*e.g.* a degree of OH) and it requires a refinement of the current model. In this way, it can also be relevant to study potential conflict among rules and their composition, in the way human societies use norms and laws.

Finally, the relations among entities may be refined to treat a wider range of situations. Typically, agents may consume or produce elementals or other agents that can still exist in the environment. Also, we supposed that elementals are not sensitive to OH. Such hypothesis is supported by the fact that OH can lead to an epistemic effect not attributed to elementals: the overhearer receives information that can update her state (*e.g.* beliefs). Also, the definition of elementals restricts interactions to the tangible case that is only direct and conflicts with the indirect nature of OH. However, the 'microphone concern' may lead to reconsider this hypothesis. A microphone reacts to overheard messages as it vibrates when a discussion occurs. In the frame of this paper, we considered that the microphone only mediates the communication as elemental of the environment and so participates to a tangible interaction, but this choice remains under discussion.

7   Conclusion

In this paper, we proposed a model of explicit and active environment to support overhearing (OH), a particular case of indirect interaction that was limited to broadcasting in past MAS research. The approach with an active environment led to preliminary answers to our questions:

- We propose a model of environment with policies and transfer spaces to model the environment neutral role toward agents.
- We describe a preliminary environmental algorithm for the implementation of our model.
- What is the very nature of OH, classified indistinctly as communication or interaction? We elicit a difference between communication and interaction from the environment viewpoint to show that *overhearing is an indirect transfer of information.* (Section 3.1)
- How does the environment contribute to the OH concept? The environment processes OH in MAS, it places agents in an adequate mental state, and it allows system designers to enforce the execution of OH when required. (Section 2)

Beyond the need to consolidate the present work, the distinctions between entities and their interactivity call for refinements. In particular, elementals and 'agents as elementals' can express more information than current models capture. Philosophical studies about the limit of language and the relationship between mind and world [27,4] lead to extend the concept of overhearing (that mostly deals with language) to an *emission* closely related to the environment and we could name *over–sensing*. Improvements and such developments are the topic of our ongoing activity.

References

1. F. Balbo and S. Pinson. Toward a Multi-agent Modelling Approach for Urban Public Transportation Systems. In A. Omicini, P. Petta, and R. Tolksdorf, editors, *Engineering Societies in the Agent World'01*, volume 2203 of *LNAI*, pages 160–174. Springer–Verlag, 2001.
2. P. Busetta, A. Donà, and M. Nori. Channelled multicast for group communications. In *Autonomous Agents and Multi–Agent Systems*, pages 1280–1287. ACM Press, 2002.
3. V. Chevrier. From self-organized models to collective problem solving, 2004. Invited Talk for Engineering Societies in the Agent World 2004.
4. A. Clark. *Being There: Putting Brain, Body, and World Together Again.* The MIT Press, 1997.
5. F. Dignum and G. Vreeswijk. Towards a Testbed for Multi-party Dialogues. In F. Dignum, editor, *Workshop on Agent Communication Languages*, volume 2922 of *LNCS*, pages 212–230. Springer, 2003.
6. M. Etienne. SYLVOPAST: a multiple target role-playing game to assess negotiation processes in sylvopastoral management planning. *Journal of Artificial Societies and Social Simulation*, 6(2), 2003.
7. J. Ferber. *Multi-Agent Systems: An Introduction to Distributed Artificial Intelligence.* Addison-Wesley, 1999.
8. FIPA-ACL Language. http://www.fipa.org/repository/aclspecs.html.
9. D. Gelernter. Generative communication in linda. *ACM Transactions on Programming Languages and Systems*, 7(1):80–112, January 1985.

10. A. Gouaïch and Y. Guiraud. MIC*: Algebraic agent environment. In *Foundations of Intelligent Systems*, volume 2871 of *LNCS*, pages 216–220. Springer–Verlag, 2003.
11. A. Gouaïch, F. Michel, and Y. Guiraud. MIC*: A deployment environment for autonomous agents. In D. Weyns, H. V. D. Parunak, and F. Michel, editors, *Environment for Multi–Agent Systems'04*, volume 3374 of *LNAI*, pages 109–126. Springer–Verlag, 2005.
12. G. A. Kaminka, D. V. Pynadath, and M. Tambe. Monitoring Teams by Overhearing: A Multi-Agent Plan-Recognition Approach. *Journal of Artificial Intelligence Research*, 17:83–135, 2002.
13. N. Karacapilidis and P. Moraïtis. Intelligent Agents for an Artificial Market System. In *Agents'01*, pages 592–599. ACM Press, 2001.
14. F. Legras and C. Tessier. LOTTO: Group Formation by Overhearing in Large Teams. In *Autonomous Agents and Multi–Agent Systems*, pages 425–432. ACM Press, 2003.
15. P. Longman, editor. *Dictionay of Contemporary English*. Pearson Longman, 2003.
16. M. Mamei and F. Zambonelli. Self-Maintained Distributed Tuples for Field-Based Coordination in Dynamic Networks. In *Symposium on Applied Computing*, pages 479–486. ACM Press, 2004.
17. M. Mamei and F. Zambonelli. Motion Coordination in the Quake 3 Arena Environment: a Field-Based Approach. In D. Weyns, H. V. D. Parunak, and F. Michel, editors, *Environment for Multi–Agent Systems'04*, volume 3374 of *LNAI*, pages 264–278. Springer–Verlag, 2005.
18. A. Omicini and F. Zambonelli. Coordination for Internet Application Development. *Journal of Autonomous Agents and Multi-Agent Systems*, 2:251–269, 1999.
19. H. V. D. Parunak, S. Brueckner, and J. Sauter. Digital pheromones for coordination of unmanned vehicles. In D. Weyns, H. V. D. Parunak, and F. Michel, editors, *Environment for Multi–Agent Systems'04*, volume 3374 of *LNAI*, pages 246–263. Springer–Verlag, 2005.
20. E. Platon, N. Sabouret, and S. Honiden. T-Compound Interaction and Listening Agents. In M.-P. Gleizes, A. Omicini, and F. Zambonelli, editors, *Engineering Societies in the Agent World'04*, volume 3451 of *LNAI*, pages 90–105. Springer–Verlag, 2005.
21. A. Ricci, M. Viroli, and A. Omicini. Environment-based coordination through coordination artifacts. In D. Weyns, H. V. D. Parunak, and F. Michel, editors, *Environment for Multi–Agent Systems'04*, volume 3374 of *LNAI*, pages 190–214. Springer–Verlag, 2005.
22. S. Russell and P. Norvig. *Artificial Intelligence: A Modern Approach*. Prentice Hall, Edition 2003.
23. SOAP1.2 specifications. http://www.w3.org/TR/soap/.
24. Unified Modeling Language Specification. http://www.omg.org/technology/documents/formal/uml.htm, version 2005. accessed on August 2005.
25. D. Weyns, H. V. D. Parunak, and F. Michel, editors. *Environments for Multi-Agent Systems'04*, volume 3374 of *LNAI*. Springer-Verlag, 2005.
26. D. Weyns, H. V. D. Parunak, F. Michel, T. Holvoet, and J. Ferber. Environments for Multiagent Systems, State-of-the-Art and Research Challenges. In D. Weyns, H. V. D. Parunak, and F. Michel, editors, *Environment for Multi–Agent Systems'04*, volume 3374 of *LNAI*, pages 1–47. Springer–Verlag, 2005.
27. L. Wittgenstein. *Philosophical Investigations*. Blackwell Publishing (Edition 2001), 1953.
28. P. R. Wurman, M. Wellman, and W. Walsh. The Michigan Internet AuctionBot: A Configurable Auction Server for Human and Software Agents. In *Second International Conference on Autonomous Agents*, pages 301–308. ACM Press, 1998.

Appendix

Algorithm 2. manage_transfer_spaces()

1: **if** the operation is $NewTS(A, rule)$ **then**
2:     **if** operation is authorized **then**
3:         $\{TS\} \leftarrow \{TS\} \cup \{(\{A\}, \emptyset, rule)\}$
4:         *Relations* tree update with the new TS
5:         **for all** agent $\in \{TS\} \cup \{Environment\}$ **do**
6:             $Env\_in\_ag(Environment, agent, 'NewTS(A, rule)\ available')$
7:         **end for**
8:     **else**
9:         $Env\_in\_ag(Environment, A, FAIL)$
10:     **end if**
11: **else if** the operation is $Enter(entity, space)$ **then**
12:     **if** operation is authorized **then**
13:         **if** entity is an agent **then**
14:             $agent\_pop_{space} \leftarrow agent\_pop_{space} \cup \{entity\}$
15:         **else if** entity is an elemental **then**
16:             $elemental\_pop_{space} \leftarrow elemental\_pop_{space} \cup \{entity\}$
17:         **end if**
18:         **for all** agent $\in \{TS\} \cup \{Environment\}$ **do**
19:             $Env\_in\_ag(Environment, agent, 'entity\ entered\ space')$
20:         **end for**
21:     **else**
22:         $Env\_in\_ag(Environment, A, FAIL)$
23:     **end if**
24: **else if** the operation is $Exit(A, space)$ **then**
25:     /*Similar to Enter*/
26: **end if**

This algorithm manages TS in the environment. First on lines 1–9, the algorithm processes the creation of new TS requested by agent A with policy *rule*. If this operation is authorized in the environment policy, the corresponding TS $(\{A\}, \emptyset, rule)$ is added to $Transpace$ (line 3–4). Then, all agents—including A—are informed about the successful creation (elementals cannot use this knowledge). If the operation is forbidden, the environment informs A about a failure on line 8.

Lines 10–22 deal with the entrance of entities in *space*, either a TS or the environment. If this operation is authorized, *entity* is added to the corresponding TS population (lines 12–16). Then the environment informs all agents in *space* about the fact. In case of forbidden operation, a failure message is sent to *entity*.

Finally, the algorithm processes exits from line 23, similarly to entrances, but one singular case is the exit of agents from the environment itself. In this case the entity leaves the system.

This algorithm processes agent transfers, when the received operation has the correct type (line 1). A target list is initialized on line 2 to contain target agents identities. Lines 3–15 determine the target list within TS where the

---

Algorithm 3. process_agent_transfers()

1: **if** the operation is $Env\_out\_ag(FROM, TO, MESSAGE)$ **then**
2:    target_list ← ∅
3:    **for all** space ∈ $\{TS\} \cup \{Environment\}$ where FROM∈ $agent\_pop_{space}$ **do**
4:       **for all** rule ∈ $policy_{space}$ **do**
5:          **if** rule is *none* **then**
6:             **for all** entity ∈ pop_{space} where entity ∈ TO **do**
7:                target_list ← target_list ∪ {entity}
8:             **end for**
9:          **else if** rule is *overhearing* **then**
10:             **for all** agent ∈ $agent\_pop_{space}$ **do**
11:                target_list ← target_list ∪ {agent}
12:             **end for**
13:          **end if**
14:       **end for**
15:    **end for**
16:    **if** target_list = ∅ **then**
17:       $Env\_in\_ag(Environment, FROM, fail)$
18:    **else**
19:       **for all** entity ∈ target_list **do**
20:          **if** entity ∈ $agent\_pop_{space}$ **then**
21:             $Env\_in\_ag(entity, FROM, MESSAGE)$
22:          **else if** entity ∈ $elemental\_pop_{space}$ **then**
23:             $Env\_in\_ele(entity, FROM, MESSAGE)$
24:          **end if**
25:       **end for**
26:    **end if**
27: **end if**

---

source agent $FROM$ is placed. For each of these TS, the environment identifies targets according to the policy. *overhearing* means all agents in the TS are target, whereas *none* means only the intended recipients are target (lines 5–14). The target list is then processed. If empty, the source agent is informed about the failure to identify targets (lines 16–17). Otherwise, the environment sends forward the message to all targets (lines 19–26).

Grounding Social Interactions in the Environment*

Florian Klein** and Holger Giese

Software Engineering Group, University of Paderborn,
Warburger Str. 100, D-33098 Paderborn, Germany
fklein@upb.de, hg@upb.de

Abstract. While agents and environments are two intimately connected concepts, most approaches for multi-agent development focus on the agent-specific part of the system, whereas the handling of concerns related to the environment is often neglected or delegated to implementation level constructs. In this paper we demonstrate that building on an environment specification with expressive semantics is instrumental in designing agents that are capable of flexible and complex interactions. We propose a modeling approach that allows describing the concrete aspects of a multi-agent system as well as its conceptual and cognitive aspects within a single coherent conceptual framework by grounding all aspects in the environment. This framework enables an efficient development process built around the rapid prototyping and iterative refinement of multi-agent system specifications by applying model-driven design techniques to the system in its entirety.

1 Introduction

Agents and environments are two intimately connected concepts. Most widely accepted definitions juxtapose agents with the environment they sense and act on. Wooldridge and Jennings, for example, propose the following as the most basic definition of an agent: 'An agent is a computer system that is *situated* in some *environment*, and that is capable of *autonomous action* in this environment in order to meet its design objectives.' (emphasis theirs) [1]. However, little attention has traditionally been paid to the environment per se, which many approaches dealing with cognitive agents see as a mere stage on which the agents' intelligent behavior unfolds, in essence a necessary evil that should be treated as abstractly as possible.

Consequently, most approaches focus the analysis and design process on the agent-specific part of the system, whereas the handling of concerns related to the environment is delegated to agent frameworks, middleware, and other implementation level constructs. The environment's impact on the cognitive aspects of the system is thus not directly addressed in the model, but mostly implied in the available interfaces.

Research in the area of reactive agents emphasizes the situatedness of agents and generally pays closer attention to the environment and the way agents perceive and affect it. Despite the central role of the environment, however, the philosophy that 'the

---

* This work was developed in the course of the Special Research Initiative 614 - Self-optimizing Concepts and Structures in Mechanical Engineering - University of Paderborn, and was published on its behalf and funded by the Deutsche Forschungsgemeinschaft.
** Supported by the International Graduate School of Dynamic Intelligent Systems.

D. Weyns, H. Van Dyke Parunak, and F. Michel (Eds.): E4MAS 2005, LNAI 3830, pp. 139–162, 2006.

world is its own best model' [2] basically places it outside the scope of explicit modeling. Again, the implications of the environment for the cognitive level are not explored on a theoretical, more abstract level.

Only recently, the idea to view the environment as a first-order abstraction [3] has begun to gain acceptance in the agent community. Especially through work on stigmergy [4,5,6], the idea that using the environment offers great potential for the efficient coordination and control of multi-agent systems has been established.

We believe that building on an environment specification with expressive semantics is instrumental in designing situated cognitive agents that are capable of flexible and complex interactions. Only an adequate exposition of the environment at the modeling level provides a generic mechanism allowing cognitive agents to make effective use of the environment.

Towards this goal, we make two important contributions, extending our previous work [7,8] towards a complete theory and comprehensive methodology:

1. At the conceptual level, we propose a modeling approach that allows describing the concrete aspects of a multi-agent system, i.e. sensing and acting in physical and virtual environments, and its conceptual aspects, i.e. communication, coordination and social structure, within a single coherent conceptual framework by grounding all aspects in the environment.
2. As a practical result, our approach allows applying model-driven design techniques such as automatic code generation and formal model analysis techniques to the system in its entirety, enabling an efficient development process built around the rapid prototyping and iterative refinement of multi-agent system specifications.

At the heart of our conceptual contribution is the set of abstract principles that shape the proposed conceptual framework. While these are independent of any specific notation and formalism, we chose to extensively build on established software engineering techniques for our practical work. We use UML-based diagrams as an accessible graphical formalism to specify both structure and behavior. The formal, operative semantics required for rapid prototyping and verification of our system are provided by the theory of graph transformation systems.

Returning to the basic idea of an agent interacting with an environment through sensors and effectors, our modeling approach starts from an – essentially object-oriented – model of the entities an agent could potentially interact with and the sensors and effectors available for interaction, comprising both structural and dynamic aspects. As a second layer of abstraction, we add services that the environment provides to the agents to the specification. Services are described in terms of and provided through entities, and thus transparently integrated into the environment. Reusable templates allow the quick incorporation of common services or agent frameworks. As the last level, we add a conceptual layer defining social structures and coordination mechanisms. Inspired by the way human interaction works, social rules act on properties and behavior that are observable, as they would otherwise be neither realizable nor enforceable. Nonetheless, the social context may provide conventions for the interpretation of such observations. These allow the derivation of high level concepts such as commitments or group membership, which are useful for more sophisticated reasoning and yet grounded in the observable environment.

Due to the principle of grounding, the environment model plays an important role at any level. As a side effect, exposing the environment to the agents at the model level enables flexible behavior and makes the agents' interactions with and *through* the environment amenable to formal analysis and verification. Finally, grounding combined with the operative semantics of the employed specification technique ensures that all aspects of the system can be operationalized.

The proposed way of modeling does not impose a specific process model, even though the hierarchic layering implies certain dependencies. In order to explore the approach's potential, we present our vision for a model-driven design process built around prototyping and iteration. This design process comprises four phases (see Fig. 1):

Fig. 1. Overview of the proposed process

1. In the *analysis phase*, the environment and the overall requirements are modeled.
2. In the *social design phase*, the requirements are assigned to social structures; roles and norms fulfilling them are defined; and the required services are added to the environment. Formal verification and experimental validation using rapid prototyping techniques allow the evaluation and step-wise improvement of the design at this early stage.
3. In the *agent design phase*, the actual agents are implemented, respecting the constraints of the social specification. The agents can then be evaluated and optimized for performance, again using generated prototypes and a simulated environment.
4. In the *deployment phase*, the agents are tested in their production environment. This requires replacing the implementations of those services, sensors and effectors directly interfacing with the physical environment, but leaves all other aspects of the specification unchanged.

We are currently implementing the tools and frameworks required for bringing this vision to life within the scope of a student project. As our example for validation purposes, we are using an automated warehouse.

Section 2 provides a short introduction to the notation. The proposed conceptual framework is discussed in Sect. 3. The process is treated in more detail in Sect. 4. We present our intermediate results in Sect. 5, followed by a review of related work and an outlook on future work.

2   Foundations

For specifying the structural and behavioral aspects of the system, our approach employs UML-based notations. We chose them because visual specification languages provide an accessible and intuitive way of modeling and because this allows us to build on existing tools and practices from object-oriented software engineering.

We basically use UML class and object diagrams for the structure and employ story patterns, an extended type of UML object diagrams based on the theory of graph transformation systems (cf. [9]), for expressing structural changes and properties.

We provide a formal semantics for the employed concepts that are typically missing from UML-based notations by mapping them to a formal model based on the theory of graph transformations (cf. [10,11]), which serves as the basis for code generation and formal verification.

2.1   Class and Object Diagrams

Class diagrams are the most fundamental UML concept employed in our approach. They allow describing the underlying structure of the problem and solution domain using classes and their relations. Class diagrams have been successfully employed to model complex structures and relationships in the context of software systems. Furthermore, we employ them to describe the physical environment, using attributes to capture physical characteristics such as mass, position, or velocity.

In Fig. 2, an example consisting of a forklift, crates, aisles, and shelves is represented as a class diagram.

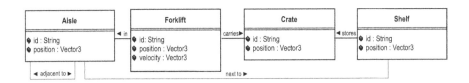

Fig. 2. Elements of a simple warehouse

Object diagrams can be used to depict specific configurations of objects which are valid instances of a given class diagram. This can be employed for describing the topology or the initial configuration of a system, e.g., laying out a warehouse floor and populating the shelves with crates (see Fig. 3).

2.2   Story Patterns

Behavioral aspects and invariants of the system under consideration can then be modeled using *story patterns*. In general, story patterns specify two instance situations, a precondition (left hand side) that needs to be fulfilled before applying the pattern and a postcondition (right hand side) that is fulfilled after the pattern is applied. We first

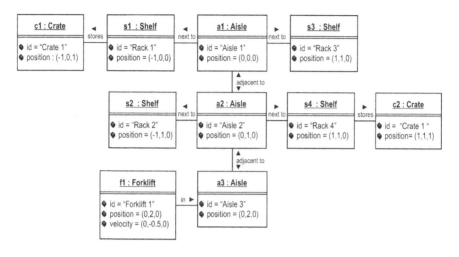

Fig. 3. A simple warehouse layout

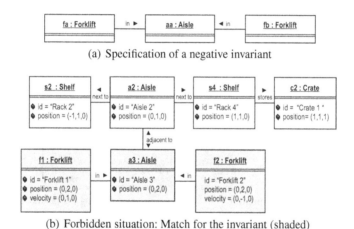

(a) Specification of a negative invariant

(b) Forbidden situation: Match for the invariant (shaded)

Fig. 4. Invariant: Two forklifts may not occupy the same space

look into *invariant story patterns*, where only the left hand side is present and the pattern simply states that the situation should always (positive invariant) or never (negative invariant) hold.

In Fig. 4, we model the constraint that two forklifts may not occupy the same space in an aisle as a negative invariant, an elementary guarantee upheld by the laws of physics. The positive invariant that every shelf is accessible, i.e. next to, an aisle is specified in Fig. 5.

Forbidden elements may be indicated in story patterns by crossing them out. They can be employed to describe rules that only match when no match for any one of their forbidden elements is found, which allows specifying more complex rules.

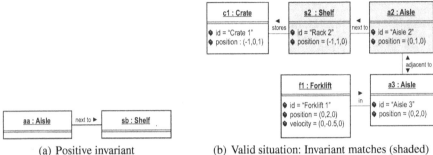

(a) Positive invariant   (b) Valid situation: Invariant matches (shaded)

Fig. 5. Invariant: Every shelf is accessible from an aisle

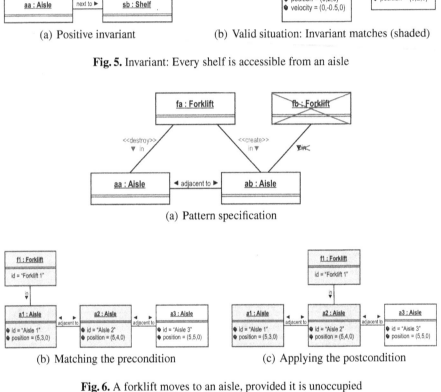

(a) Pattern specification

(b) Matching the precondition   (c) Applying the postcondition

Fig. 6. A forklift moves to an aisle, provided it is unoccupied

If we also provide a right hand side for a rule, we can use it to describe behavior. The right hand side may be integrated into the left hand side by using the stereotypes ≪create≫ and ≪delete≫ for denoting elements which should be created resp. deleted as a side-effect of the rule, which yields a compact representation. An example of such a rule is depicted in Fig. 6, where a forklift moves to another aisle.

2.3 Tool Support

The open source UML CASE tool Fujaba [1] offers state of the art support for the modeling of class diagrams, object diagrams, and story patterns and thus enables model-driven development based on the outlined set of UML concepts.

---

[1] http://www.fujaba.de

The UML concepts introduced above, notably class diagrams and object diagrams, and the proprietary extensions such as story patterns (cf. Fig. 2, 3, 4(a), and 6(a)) have been given a formal semantics based on the theory of *graph transformation systems* (GTS).

This formal semantics enables us to provide sound code generation for these models, which is both useful for deriving simulation prototypes from early models (cf. [9]) and for generating a correct implementation of the production system from the final model that does not introduce implementation errors. Currently, the code generation of Java and C++ source code is supported for all employed diagram types.

Given the formal semantics, we can further employ formal techniques to validate and verify a given model, which is supported from inside the Fujaba CASE tool.

A first option is the GTS model checker GROOVE [12]. GROOVE imports GTS specifications and computes all reachable states of the transformation system, optionally bounded by the occurrence of a forbidden graph. With the help of a converter plug-in, we are able to export models from Fujaba to GROOVE's input format, check them, and visualize identified counterexamples in Fujaba. However, this approach can only be employed to verify finite state models with known initial configurations.

In order to be able to check invariant properties for the more general case of infinite state systems as well, we developed an invariant checker [11,13] which exploits the local character of the graph transformation rules to perform a fully automatic check whether a given set of properties represent an inductive invariant of the system.

3 Approach

We now introduce the elements of the conceptual framework underlying our approach in more detail.

The notion of agents interacting with an environment, be it digital or physical, through sensors and effectors is central to our approach. We therefore make a clear distinction between concrete entities that agents can perceive and/or manipulate directly and conceptual entities that only exist virtually. Conceptual entities are explicitly derived from concrete entities by convention.

The concrete part of the model is predominantly descriptive in nature. Of course, design decisions do have a profound impact on the model, as the choice of sensors and effectors provided to the agents constrains what can be expressed. However, agents in the implemented system can immediately interact with concrete entities, even in heterogeneous open systems. The conceptual part of the model, on the other hand, is engineered deliberately, with the system's design objectives in mind. The way that conceptual entities are grounded in the concrete entities is *not* immediately visible to the agents. In order to allow an agent to interact with the system, this knowledge needs to be made explicitly available to the agents or implied in their implementation. This problem is also touched on by [3], who distinguish between *natural* and *arbitrary* protocols and observe that the more natural protocols are, the easier ensuring interoperability becomes.

In order to structure the design and treat these different concerns separately, we divide the model into submodels that are layered on top of each other.

The environment model describes the environment, the concrete entities it contains, and their behavior. It also specifies the agents (which are themselves concrete entities) with their sensors and effectors.

The service model describes the infrastructure and protocols provided to the agents by the environment. As services are provided and accessed through concrete entities, the service model is predominantly concerned with the concrete parts of the system.

The social model introduces social structures, roles and norms along with the conventions required to connect them to elements of the more concrete layers.

3.1 Environment Model

In the *environment model*, we want to describe all concrete *entities* and environment processes as they are relevant to the agents. We try to model the entities as 'objectively' as possible, i.e. as they are, not as the different agents perceive them, however. Concrete entities can be physical – these entities need to be simulated while prototyping and are later provided by the physical environment – or digital – which means they need to be implemented in software both in the prototypes and the production system. The entities and their attributes are modeled using class diagrams (as in Fig. 2).

We also model environment *processes*, using story patterns. They describe laws of nature (e.g. gravity), the behavior of simple machines (e.g. a conveyor belt), and non-deterministic external influences on the system (e.g. an entity arriving in the environment). They are useful both for simulating the system and reasoning about its expected behavior at the agent level.

The *agents* and their sensors and effectors can now be added to the environment model. Both sensors and effectors can only be applied to a specific *context*, i.e. the subset of all entities that is, e.g., of the right type and physically close enough to the agent. The story patterns that specify the effects of the sensors and effectors limit them to this context.

Sensors transform concrete entities into *perceptions*. When generating perceptions, the sensor usually only retains a subset of an entity's attributes, may transform and aggregate them, may introduce random errors with a specific probability distribution, or may even fail to produce a perception with a given failure probability (see Fig. 7(a)).

Effectors create, manipulate and destroy entities, their attributes and associations. Unlike typical AI-centric agent specifications that usually provide an agent with a set of named actions or performatives, the semantics of the effector actions we specify are fully transparent both for the agent and any formal method we would like to employ at the agent level; i.e. we can seamlessly integrate the environment into our analysis of an agent's behavior. The formalism allows specifying any conceivable state transition of the specified environment and is thus capable of expressing the effects of any effector, now matter how complex (see Fig. 7(a)).

Obviously, in order to obtain a valid model, the specified effects need to stay within the limits of what is reasonable and physically possible. Generally, the validity of any results obtained by means of simulation and formal verification of the model largely depends on the quality of the environment model, i.e., whether it is correct and appropriate. This is less of a problem for digital entities, as – due to the reliance on proven object

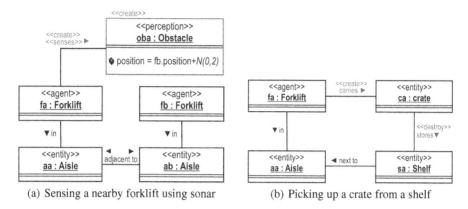

(a) Sensing a nearby forklift using sonar   (b) Picking up a crate from a shelf

Fig. 7. Sensor and Effector specifications

oriented formalisms – they can be represented by their actual design. It is somewhat more problematic for physical entities, where we can only strive to provide as good an approximation as possible. Our approach is better suited to describing structural adaptation than continuous change. We currently only support modeling continuous processes through difference equations, which we consider sufficient for most application areas, though. If an in-depth treatment of the mechanical engineering aspects of the system is essential, it is necessary to additionally apply our techniques for the design of hybrid systems [14].

3.2 Service Model

As we have already suggested with the introduction of environment processes, entities are not limited to being inert, monolithic objects, even if entities in the environment model were limited to rather simple behavior. In principle, entities may be complex and have extensive internal machinery that performs complex actions. The essential distinction is that entities are never autonomous and do not possess internal motivation, i.e. they are passive unless activated by an agent or an environment process.

The *service model* basically describes the infrastructure used by the agents. This infrastructure is implemented as a set of services that are provided through dedicated entities called *facilities*. *Services* can fall into various classes, e.g. life cycle management, resource allocation, scheduling, communication, directory services, persistency, access control, authentication, or application-specific functions. They can reach a high level of sophistication, e.g. a distributed blackboard with consistency management.

Services mostly represent functionality that is normally provided by middleware. Indeed, services will often be implemented using some type of middleware. We can differentiate between production middleware that will be present in the final system, usually providing lookup, messaging and other higher level functions, and prototyping middleware that is mainly concerned with emulating the production environment, providing services that will later be implicitly performed by the physical environment (e.g. computation of the available physical context) or the production hardware (e.g. scheduling).

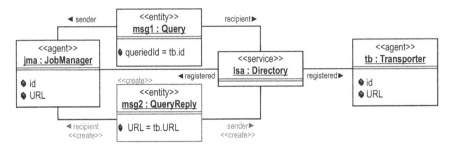

Fig. 8. A directory service replies to a query

As services are specified in terms of entities, we can apply the same object-oriented modeling techniques using story patterns as for entity behavior and effector use (see Fig. 8). However, as services can to some degree be standardized, they offer obvious potential for reuse. Specifying the same services from scratch over and over again would be tedious and inefficient. Templates encoding recurring desing patterns for reuse offer a solution to this problem. Templates may range from simple patterns describing the functionality of a single facility to complex systems of connected facilities representing a whole agent platform, component framework or distributed computing library. This means that after a service description for a particular solution has been modeled once, it can be reused, adapted and combined with other building blocks in a modular manner.

3.3 Social Model

Now, where are the agents, organizations, roles, and communication languages in all this? Frequently, agent-oriented methodologies that closely build on object-oriented software engineering techniques are criticized for focusing on the technical aspects of multi-agent systems and neglecting advanced agent-oriented abstractions, thus providing poor support for the coordination of multi-agent systems and essentially limiting their scope to simple reactive agents. We, however, believe that such abstractions can in fact be supported based on an object-oriented design.

Mentalistic concepts have proven useful for reasoning about autonomous, cognitive agents. It is mainstream in agent-oriented research to assume that agents have intentional stance, assigning beliefs, goals and intentions to them [15]. Despite its unquestionable appeal, formalisms based on intentional stance face some well-documented problems, notably when used in the context of agent communication (languages). Such formalisms often assume a specific implementation of the agents' internals, which severely limits their applicability to real-world scenarios. As the semantics of messages depend on the state of an agent's mind, they may not be decidable from an outside perspective [16]. Besides, the resulting specifications are notoriously complex, and proving the conformance of an implementation may be impossible [17]. One solution that was proposed to solve these problem is to model agents as *observable sources* that expose a well-defined part of their internals in order to allow other agents to reason about their beliefs and intentions [18].

Legal Stance. We propose using the environment to a similar effect, thus providing a generic mechanism that is completely independent of the agents' implementations. The basic principle is to not reason about what an agent actually intends or believes, but what an external observer, or more specifically other agents in the system, can know or reasonably assume the other agent to believe or intend. It is inspired by the way human interaction, or more specifically human laws, work. Courts frequently infer beliefs and intentions from situations, acts, and speech. Legal codes (in the continental tradition) devote significant effort to fixing the exact modalities of how and when a person can profess an intention. In criminal codes, intent is a defining characteristic of various crimes, and the punishment of attempted crimes hinges on establishing the intention (e.g., an unauthorized person breaking into and hotwiring a car could clearly be supposed to intend to steal it). In civil law, what a person should have known (e.g. caveat emptor) and seems to have intended based on the given evidence is a common question. We therefore call this view that is concerned with the *professed intentions* (and professed beliefs) that can be deduced from the environment *legal stance*.

Conventions for interpreting the environment can be attached to any effector or entity type. This specifically includes messages, allowing the specification of agent communication languages, the predominant kind of social convention in current multi-agent system. The implied professed intentions can be used to reason about the system at a higher level of abstraction (see Fig. 12–14). Concepts such as assertions for communicating beliefs, directives as a means of soliciting specific behavior, or commitments for making behavioral guarantees (cf. [19]) help to structure and guide agent behavior.

Just like laws, professed intentions are artificial constructs that are only valid in a specific social context. A group of agents needs to agree on a set of conventions before it can become useful for governing their interaction.

Social Specification. This social context is provided by *communities*, which are – possibly overlapping – groups of agents sharing the same conventions. Research into agent organizations has shown that social structure is essential for designing complex, heterogeneous systems [20]. While our ideas are conceptually close to established work on organizations, we chose the term 'community' in order to avoid confusion because we felt that 'organization' suggests a greater degree of institutionalization, persistence, and complexity than exhibited by many of the communities we have in mind, and, on the other hand, we did not want to try to change established concepts by making additions that are specific to our modeling approach to them.

The conventions used by a community are set down in the corresponding *community type*. The specification of a community type mostly consists of various types of norms, expressed in terms of observable entities by means of story patterns. In detail, a community type defines the following:

- a set of *roles* that can be assumed by agents (Fig. 9(a)),
- a set of *professed intentions* that can be attributed to agents (Fig. 9(b)),
- *instantiation norms* for instantiating communities, as there may be multiple instances (Fig. 10),
- *binding norms* for joining and leaving the community, and for assuming and relinquishing roles (Fig. 11),

- *conventional norms* that specify social conventions, i.e. generate professed intentions from observations (Fig. 12,13(a)),
- *behavioral norms* specifying allowed or required behavior, which need to be compatible to the agents' effector specifications (Fig. 13(b)), and
- a set of *community types* that can be used to form subcommunities contained in the community.

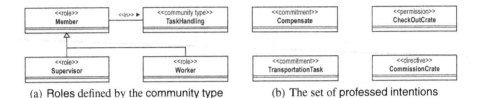

(a) Roles defined by the community type   (b) The set of professed intentions

Fig. 9. Community Type for completing transportation tasks

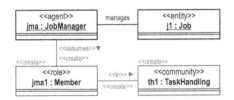

Fig. 10. Instantiation norm instantiating a community

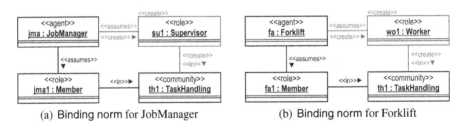

(a) Binding norm for JobManager   (b) Binding norm for Forklift

Fig. 11. Binding member agents to more specific roles by type

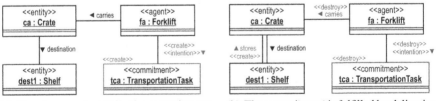

(a) Carrying a crate entails the commitment to transport it to its destination   (b) The commitment is fulfilled by delivering the crate

Fig. 12. Conventional norms for making and fulfilling commitments

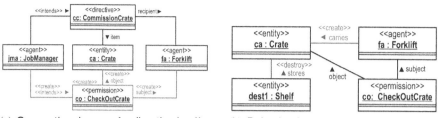

(a) Conventional norm: the directive implies a permission to actually pick up a crate

(b) Behavioral norm requiring this permission as a precondition

Fig. 13. Conventional and Behavioral norms interact to control behavior

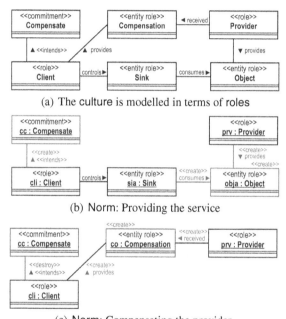

(a) The culture is modelled in terms of roles

(b) Norm: Providing the service

(c) Norm: Compensating the provider

Fig. 14. Culture regulating payment for goods or a service in a generic manner. A concretization is used as a sub-community type inside the above TaskHandling community type by JobManagers (Client) for paying Forklifts (Provider) after delivering a crate.

The specification is expressed entirely in terms of classes and objects, which are marked up with stereotypes in order to indicate their specific semantics. Therefore, it is possible describe community types as graph transformation system, which can be seamlessly integrated with the graph transformation system of the environment model to yield a comprehensive specification of the system's physical and social behavior.

Community types can specify complex organizations, but may as well describe the ad-hoc interaction between a pair of agents. In general, a community type deals with a particular problem, which usually grows in complexity in proportion to the community type's position in the hierarchy.

As there may be commonly recurring subproblems (e.g., collision avoidance, job assignment, coordinating distributed problem solving), we once again propose the use of templates or design patterns. We call these patterns *cultures*. Cultures extract the essence of a community type by abstracting from the concrete environment. This is done by replacing the concrete agent and entity types used in norms (e.g. 'car salesman', 'motorist', 'car') with more generic agent ('buyer', 'seller') and entity ('merchandise') roles (see Fig. 14). A culture can be formally verified in order to prove that it correctly solves a problem, or, more specifically, satisfies a set of requirements using our work on the verification of coordination patterns [21]. It may then be reused in future systems to derive a community type inheriting these properties by binding appropriate concrete types or sets of types from the environment model to these abstract roles.

Even though community types impose requirements and limitations on the capabilities of agents, they do not restrict the actual implementation of agents in any way, making the approach mostly agnostic with respect to their internal architecture. As the specification is only concerned with observable behavior, correctly implementing it comes down to behaving correctly in the environment. The agents have complete 'freedom of thought', even though certain mentalistic notions are certainly implied by particular behavior through conventions, which may require some sort of compatible internal model in order to be able to conform to more intricate behavioral requirements.

4   Process

In order to show how the proposed concepts can benefit the development of situated multi-agent systems, we now describe the process from requirements engineering to deployment as we envision it. As mentioned in the introduction, we divide this process into analysis, social design, agent design and deployment. Figure 15 gives an overview of the phases and their main objectives.

Even though each phase deals with clearly defined aspects of the system, a linear progression through the phases should be seen as an idealization. Each phase builds upon the output of the previous phase. Within the later phases, prototyping is used to enable iterative improvement of the specification. In practice, it will be necessary to revisit previous phases and make adjustments in this context.

4.1   Analysis Phase

The analysis phase is mainly concerned with the specification of the environment model. The structure and behavior of the environment are considered as fixed at this stage. Using methods for the identification of classes from traditional object-oriented analysis, the relevant entities from the system's prospective environment can therefore be identified and modeled. Likewise, the behavior of these entities may be observed and modeled through environment processes. Such services as are already provided by the environment are also recorded at this time. The result is a domain model of the environment which forms the core of the ontology used in later phases. As agents (as physical entities), sensors, and effectors are part of the environment model, they are included in the analysis phase. This is only logical, as any model is, by a common definition, driven by a specific purpose, which in our case is to represent the environment as relevant to the

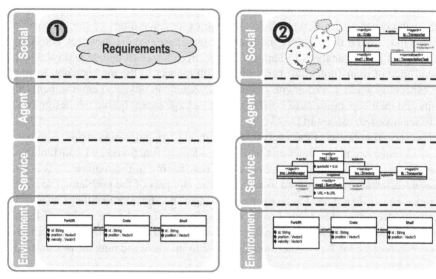

(a) Analysis: Modeling Requirements and the Environment

(b) Social Design: Designing Communities and Services

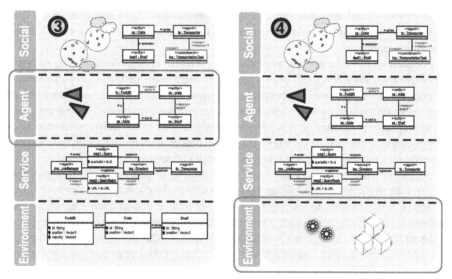

(c) Agent Design: Designing agents' behavior and internals

(d) Deployment: Replacing the simulated environment

Fig. 15. Phases of the proposed process in more detail. The UML diagrams merely serve as iconic representatives for the respective models (see Fig. 12(b), 7(b), 8, and 2 for full-scale versions).

agents. Without at least a basic knowledge of their capabilities, the environment model could not fulfill this purpose. Nonetheless, it could be argued that the agent types and the sensors and effectors available to them are design decisions that have no place in analysis. While it is true that the addition of new agent types may become necessary in the subsequent social design phase, and the exact capabilities of the sensors and effectors may not be fixed before the agent design phase, we do, however, consider it an important part of analysis to identify prospective classes of agents and establish a general idea of their (potential) capabilities with respect to the environment. In practice, especially when working with (mechanical) agents in phyisical environments, the agents and their capabilities are usually given to a large extent before the design of the multi-agent system even starts.

The second concern of the analysis phase are the system *requirements*. Again, established requirements analysis can be used to identify functional and non-functional requirements, as there is nothing inherently agent-specific in the requirements – after all, agent-orientation is supposed to be a solution, not part of the problem. The resulting requirements do not need to be expressed using a specific notation, they can even be informally documented in textual form. If a requirement is to be the subject of formal verification later on, it is however preferable to specify it directly as a story pattern over the environment model. It is furthermore desirable to structure and rank the requirements.

4.2 Social Design Phase

The social design phase begins by taking these requirements, breaking them down into suitable subsets, and assigning them to agent communities. These communities are then responsible for ensuring that the systems meets the requirements in question by defining appropriate norms.

For each set of requirements, a community type which is capable of dealing with this responsibility is then designed. This will usually include the definition of subcommunities concerned with even more specific tasks, which ultimately leads to a hierarchy of community types whose bottom elements are basic interaction patterns dealing with simple, manageable problems. At this time, cultures that address a specific requirement can be applied to the system. As cultures may themselves contain more specific subcultures, instantiating a culture may create a whole hierarchy of community types.

When applying cultures or devising new solutions to problems, the designer will need to take the agents' capabilities (as expressed by their sensors and effectors) into account. It is not helpful to specify behavioral norms that agents cannot enact, or conventional norms that depend on something agents cannot sense. If the physical design of the agent is under the designer's control, it is possible at this point to add new capabilities through new sensors and effectors. The most common way to provide agents with additional capabilities, however, is to specify services that provide them. Also, the idea behind communities *is* using interaction in order to achieve goals beyond the reach of the individual agents. Thus, communities can themselves provide new capabilities that can be used as a bootstrap by other communities. For example, in order to allow every agent in a system to communicate with any other agent, one could introduce a network of access points capable of relaying messages and a community type that requires agents to register with a distributed directory, instead of upgrading the agents' antennas.

Together, the community types need to result in a consistent specification. If the requirements are not orthogonal, i.e., the norms of the community types constrain the same effector or concern the same entities, different community types might be in conflict. E.g., if a community type responsible At this point, we try to spot cases where conforming with all norms is *theoretically* impossible. Other than that, we merely strive to keep dependencies between community types as weak as possible and defer the task of actually reconciling conflicts to the agent design phase.

Once all relevant community types have been specified, the model can be validated. Individual community types can be formally verified: As both their norms and the behavior of the environment can be modeled as a graph transformation system, we can apply the above-mentioned invariant checking techniques [11] in order to prove certain required properties, e.g. the absence of accidents or safety hazards. We can also export the model into GROOVE, which allows us to systematically explore the state space for specific initial configurations up to a certain size. Other aspects such as requirements concerning efficiency and performance or emergent properties of complex systems that cannot be assessed through formal methods require empirical validation by means of a prototype.

As the complete specification, from entities and environment processes to roles, norms, and professed intentions, is expressed by class diagrams and story patterns, it is possible to create an executable prototype using code generation. The environment model simply needs to be run in order to simulate the environment, even though it is usually advisable to make use of some kind of prototyping middleware in the implementation of the model in order to achieve more efficient simulation. As for the social model, the generated implementation tries to apply all applicable norms to the system and keeps track of the result by instantiating explicit representations of communities and professed intentions. For each agent, the system non-deterministically choses an action from the set of enabled sensor and effector applications. This makes it possible to assess whether the system's behavior stays within the intended limits. When a constraint specified by a community type is violated or an agent gets stuck in a state with no valid course of action left, this is detected and reported by the system. It may indicate a conflict within or between communities. As corrections in the model can immediately be tested in a new prototype, iterative, step-wise improvements can be applied to the design quickly and conveniently. Starting from the earliest stages of the design, it is possible to generate prototypes from specifications in order to evaluate them.

4.3   Agent Design Phase

Once the social specification meets all pertinent formal requirements and appears to address all other requirements, the actual agents can be implemented, respectively specified. Even though any architecture producing the appropriate output is acceptable, it is convenient to start from the generated implementation of the social model. For behavioral norms that specify concrete, reactive behavior, adding strategies for intelligently chosing between the available options is a quick way to obtain a reasonable implementation. Behavioral norms that are of a more declarative nature, e.g., concerning the commitment to travel to a specific location by a given deadline, require more elaborate strategies and algorithms that cannot simply be deduced, but need to be designed.

In practice, devising an implementation that respects the constraints of all pertinent communities may not be a trivial task. It is facilitated by the ability to test prototypes of the agents in the simulated environment. The generated social model is reused for monitoring conformance with the specification. This time around, the model does not randomly choose a course of action for the agents, but merely checks whether the exhibited behavior was enabled, flagging violations. Agents can also be benchmarked extensively in order to optimize their performance.

4.4 Deployment Phase

Once the agent design conforms to the social specification and has proven itself in the simulated environment, it can be moved to its production environment for testing. An appealing feature of the proposed approach is that this mainly means replacing the simulated parts of the system with their physical counterparts. Provided that it was modeled correctly, the environment model can simply be dropped. At the service level, the prototyping middleware is replaced by the production middleware. The overall complexity of the software system decreases, as physics, processes and physical constraints (e.g. context) no longer need to be replicated in software; however, the middleware that processes sensor input and interprets effector commands becomes significantly more complex internally.

The model of the actual agents remains unchanged, as their interfaces are unchanged. Using a specific real-time runtime environment supported by Fujaba's code generator, we can actually reuse the exact same code for simulation and hardware tests [22]. Of course, it is nonetheless necessary to perform a sufficient number of tests in order to ensure that there were no errors or oversimplifications in the environment model that lead to significant discrepancies between simulated and actual behavior (cf.[23]).

5 Experiences

In order to evaluate our approach, we intend to apply it to a large, realistic scenario. Implementing a non-trivial example and testing the iterative development process furthermore requires appropriate tool support. Within the scope of the project group *intrapid*, consisting of 18 students and currently in its second and final semester, we are working towards these objectives.

We are basing our work on Fujaba for Eclipse, a port that integrates the Fujaba CASE tool into the Eclipse platform as plugins. We are implementing our extensions as a UML Profile, i.e., we add the appropriate stereotypes from our conceptual framework to the metamodel and define the different variants of story patterns and class diagrams we use with their respective constraints and semantics. We are also adding a configurable translation layer that transforms these diagrams into input for the existing code generation mechanisms by joining them together in the correct manner.

Another important part of the project is the work on 'prototyping' middleware that supports the efficient simulation, visualization and run-time manipulation of environments. At the agent level, a component-based 'production' middleware is providing the internal infrastructure.

The ultimate goal is to use the developed tools and middleware for the design of a large and complex logistics management application. The scenario comprises warehouses and various types of robotic agents moving goods inside and between them. It was chosen because logistics are a common application area of agent-based approaches that offers potential for optimization and exploiting synergies between agents. It also requires relatively simple agents, which, however, need to flexibly interface in different ways.

In order to give the students the opportunity to familiarize themselves with the approach and get a better grasp of the underlying concepts, we implemented a very simple scenario as a prototype. The idea was to keep the application specific part as basic as possible and focus on a sound implementation of the meta model and the infrastructure as a preparation for the work on tools and middleware in the second phase. The prototype was therefore not designed to validate the approach in general, but show the feasibility of some of our ideas and identify challenges.

We use the phases of the development process to structure the presentation of the prototype and our experiences.

5.1   Analysis Phase

The scenario consists of an aquarium containing a swarm of fish hunted by sharks. The environment is extremely simple: there are walls, cylindrical obstacles that may be placed dynamically by the user, sharks, and prey. Sharks and prey have sensors for sensing other fish (sharks have longer range, but a more limited field of vision, prey have a greater field of vision but limited range) and an effector (tail fin) for propulsion (sharks are faster, but prey is more agile). Sharks also have an effector for eating prey fish. The context of this latter effector is limited to fish in close proximity that are, literally, right under a shark's nose. There are no more advanced sensors and effectors, specifically none enabling direct communication.

The requirements were straight-forward: sharks were supposed to eat as many fish as possible, prey was to keep together and try to stay alive.

The main challenge at this level was designing and implementing the modular prototyping middleware needed to simulate the physical behavior of the system, compute the sensors' contexts, visualize the simulation and allow users to place obstacles into the aquarium. See Fig. 16 for a screenshot.

5.2   Social Design Phase

The requirements easily lead to the two community types shoal (for the prey) and pack (for the sharks).

The shoal type is quite basic. The behavioral norms are reactive in nature, describing how fish should react to seeing other fish or shark. They are modeled on the well-known boid paradigm [24], i.e., fish move towards the center of mass of the fish they see, try to keep their distance from neighboring fish and obstacles and match their velocity with other fish. Besides these basic behaviors, they exhibit a strong repulsion from sharks and places where sharks have recently been seen and a weak tendency to keep away from the outer parts of the aquarium. The behavioral norms require only simple processing of the fish and almost directly map sensor input into effector output.

Perhaps contrary to intuition, a large shoal of fish is not represented by a single community. It is rather composed of many smaller communities consisting of a fish playing the 'active' role and every fish it can see, playing the 'passive' role. As visibility

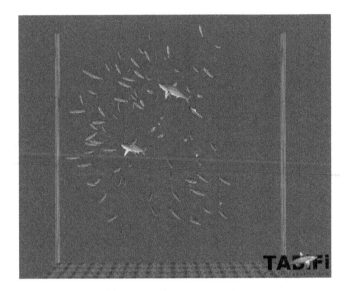

Fig. 16. Screenshot from the prototype

between fish is not a symmetric relation, each of the communities from the same 'shoal' may have slightly different members. The behavioral norms of the community only have implications for the behavior of the 'active' fish at the center. While this may seem like a degenerate case of a community, it illustrates one important principle of community type design: A design that operates by governing behavior based on observable actions and states will only work as intended if it can reasonably be assumed that an agent expected to exhibit a certain behavior can actually make the observation that is supposed to trigger it. More specifically, there needs to be a conventional norm that can generate a professed intention to that effect (in this case the assertion that 'an agent knows what it sees', combined with the sensor context specification). In the example, as all prey fish implement the same community type, behavior is still consistent – 'as if' all fish were in the same community.

The sharks' pack community type is based on similar behavioral norms. Sharks tend to keep greater distances, but match velocities in order to attack the prey in a coordinated manner. Obviously, sharks are strongly attracted by prey. There are simple conventional norms for creating professed intentions for coordinating shark behavior, e.g. determining which fish a shark is currently hunting so that sharks may cooperate in their attacks and do not go after the same fish.

Substantial effort was spent on implementing the shoal community type in the way it will later be automatically generated from the social model. This required creating explicit representations of the relevant meta model elements, namely community types, communities, behavioral norms (for specifying expected behavior), and binding norms (for determining membership in communities). As the behavioral norms are deterministic (unlike in typical future systems, where norms permit non-deterministic choice or may even only state goals that need to be achieved), a conforming implementation of agent behavior could be achieved by explicitly checking and applying behavioral norms.

5.3 Agent Design Phase

The sharks were implemented as simple intelligent agents. They are deliberately not implementing an explicit 'community' concept, but simply conform to the community type specification by implementing the required behavior. This demonstrates both how the approach can be used as a fairly architecture-agnostic specification technique and that the essence of the specification is in the observable behavior.

The prey fish were not implemented at all, as executing the community type specification was already sufficient for obtaining the desired behavior. All that was required was a stub for relaying the commands from the social model to the effector. The community type specification simply applies the behavioral norms to every fish in a fish's community, aggregates the results into a single impulse and passes the result down to the fin effector of the agent stub.

The ability to run a 'prototype' of one type of agent alongside an actual agent implementation only made a small difference in the current context, but should be interesting for the development of more complex systems.

The prototype allowed experimenting on the emergent properties of the system. By changing sensor and effector parameters and varying the thresholds and intensities for the behavioral norms, the balance of the system could be shifted and diverse behavioral patterns be induced.

For obvious reasons, there was now deployment phase.

In all, the prototype has already hinted at the potential of the approach, but has also helped to identify challenges. The efficient evaluation of social norms will be essential for prototyping and monitoring large systems. For truly assessing the added value of the approach on the conceptual level, we will have to wait for the full scale logistics scenario incorporating multiple community types and communication – the current state is already promising, though.

6 Related Work

Even though our methodology is clearly rooted in object-oriented software engineering traditions and techniques, the conceptual framework for grounding social interactions in the environment is based on agent-oriented abstractions and influenced by existing research from the domain.

The idea of the legal stance is both related to work on intentional stance (cf. [1]), the social level [25] and social order [26]. It was inspired by Viroli and Omicini's idea of agents as an *observable source* [18], but goes beyond it by basing the interaction on the environment. This provides a more flexible, general mechanism, at the cost of diminishing the ability to formally reason about the observations from an AI perspective. The categories of professed intentions we use stem from Singh's work on agent communication languages [16].

The concept of social structure was established by Ferber's organizational models [20]. As discussed, Communities combine an intentionally broad interpretation of what constitutes social structure with pattern-based software engineering techniques.

Environments still play a minor role in current multi-agent systems research, even if this is beginning to change. However, there are several papers putting forward similar ideas concerning the role of the environment:

Weyns et al. [3] discuss several functions of environments that are also important to our approach, namely structuring the system (for defining localized communities), providing a shared state (by storing the evidence of professed intentions), providing service support (through facilities), enabling coordination (this, again, is the key idea of legal stance) and acting as a regulating entity (by means of laws implemented as environment processes). The practical work on virtual environments [27,28] could be seen as a real world application of the idea of bootstrapping by means of services. Our main contribution is offering systematic support of such solutions at the level of a model-driven development process.

Recent work by Omicini et al. [29] proposes 'artifacts' as a general way to structure the interaction between agents and the environment. In a way, artifacts and facilities represent similar concepts. However, facilities are rooted in the software engineering perspective and offer concrete, transparent behavioral specifications, whereas artifacts come from an AI background and provide more abstract interfaces based on messages, which facilitates standardization but makes analysis of the services they actually provide harder.

7   Conclusion and Future Work

We have presented a conceptual framework that grounds social interactions in the environment. We have moreover proposed an iterative design process that makes use of the ability to generate executable prototypes from high-level specifications and conduct formal analysis, starting with the early phases.

While the results obtained from our implementation work are encouraging, it is too early to actually draw any conclusions concerning the applicability and validity of our approach. We did, however, establish that our ideas for modeling the concrete parts of the system centered around entities, sensors and effectors, are feasible and work as intended.

We hope to complete our work on the development tools in the foreseeable future and be able to test them on a large multi-agent system using sophisticated coordination mechanisms.

At the same time, we will continue our work on the theoretical underpinnings of our approach. We hope to be able to extend the scope of formal verification techniques in the social model and assist in the identification and reconciliation of conflicts between norms.

References

1. Wooldridge, M., Jennings, N.: Intelligent agents: Theory and practice. Knowledge Engineering Review **10** (1995) 115–152
2. Brooks, R.A.: Intelligence Without Reason. In Myopoulos, J., Reiter, R., eds.: Proceedings of the 12th International Joint Conference on Artificial Intelligence (IJCAI-91), Sydney, Australia, Morgan Kaufmann publishers Inc.: San Mateo, CA, USA (1991) 569–595

3. Weyns, D., Parunak, H.V.D., Michel, F., Holvoet, T., Ferber, J.: Environments for multiagent systems state-of-the-art and research challenges. In Weyns, D., Parunak, H.V.D., Michel, F., eds.: Environment for multi-agent systems: first international workshop, 2004, New York, NY. Volume 3374 of Lecture Notes in Computer Science. (2004) 1–47

4. Bonabeau, E.: Editor's introduction: Stigmergy. Artificial Life **5** (1999) 95–96

5. Fenster, M., Kraus, S., Rosenschein, J.S.: Coordination without communication: Experimental validation of focal point techniques. In: Proc. of the 1st Int. Conf. on Multiagent Systems (ICMAS), San Francisco, CA, USA, The MIT Press (1995) 102–108

6. Parunak, H.V.D., Brueckner, S., Sauter, J.A.: Digital pheromones for coordination of unmanned vehicles. In Weyns, D., Parunak, H.V.D., Michel, F., eds.: Environments for Multi-Agent Systems, First International Workshop, New York, NY, USA, 2004. Volume 3374 of Lecture Notes in Computer Science., Springer (2005) 246–263

7. Klein, F., Giese, H.: Separation of concerns for mechatronic multi-agent systems through dynamic communities. In Choren, R., Garcia, A., Lucena, C., Romanovsky, A., eds.: Software Engineering for Multi-Agent Systems III. Volume 3390 of Lecture Notes in Computer Science (LNCS). Springer Verlag (2005) 272–289

8. Klein, F., Giese, H.: Analysis and Design of Physical and Social Contexts in MultiAgent Systems using UML. In et al., R.C., ed.: Proc. of the 4th Workshop on Software Engineering for Large-Scale Multi-Agent Systems at ISCE, St. Louis, MO, USA, IEEE (2005) 1–7

9. Köhler, H., Nickel, U., Niere, J., Zündorf, A.: Integrating UML Diagrams for Production Control Systems. In: Proc. of the 22nd International Conference on Software Engineering (ICSE), Limerick, Irland, ACM Press (2000) 241–251

10. Zündorf, A.: Rigorous Object Oriented Software Development. Habilitation, University of Paderborn (2001) Available online: http://wwwcs.upb.de/cs/ag-schaefer/Personen/ Ehemalige/Zuendorf/AZRigSoftDraft_0_2.pdf.

11. Giese, H., Schilling, D.: Towards the Automatic Verification of Inductive Invariants for Invinite State UML Models. Technical Report tr-ri-04-252, University of Paderborn, Paderborn, Germany (2004)

12. Rensink, A.: Towards model checking graph grammars. In Leuschel, M., Gruner, S., Presti, S.L., eds.: Workshop on Automated Verification of Critical Systems (AVoCS). Technical Report DSSE–TR–2003–2, University of Southampton (2003) 150–160

13. Becker, B., Giese, H., Schilling, D.: A plugin for checking inductive invariants when modeling with class diagrams and story patterns. In: Proc. of the 3rd International Fujaba Days 2005, Paderborn, Germany. (2005)

14. Burmester, S., Giese, H., Oberschelp, O.: Hybrid UML Components for the Design of Complex Self-optimizing Mechatronic Systems. In: Informatics in Control, Automation and Robotics. Kluwer Academic Publishers (2005) to appear.

15. Rao, A., Georgeff, M.: BDI Agents: From Theory to Practice. In: Proceedings of the 1st International Conference On Multi Agent Systems, San Francisco, USA (1995)

16. Singh, M.P.: On Competitive On-Line Algorithms for the Dynamic Priority-Ordering Problem. IEEE Computer **31** (1998) 40–47

17. Wooldridge, M.: Verifiable semantics for agent communication languages. In: Proceedings of the 3rd International Conference on Multi Agent Systems (ICMAS98), Paris , France. (1998) 349–356

18. Viroli, M., Omicini, A.: A specification language for agents observable behavior. In: Proceedings of the International Conference on Artificial Intelligence (ICAI) 2002 (Las Vegas, US), CSREA Press (2002) 321–327

19. Singh, M.P.: The intentions of teams: Team structure, endodeixis, and exodeixis. In: ECAI. (1998) 303–307

20. Ferber, J., Gutknecht, O.: A meta-model for the analysis and design of organizations in multi-agent systems. In: Proceedings of the 3rd International Conference on Multi Agent Systems (ICMAS98), Paris , France. (1998) 128–135

21. Giese, H., Tichy, M., Burmester, S., Schäfer, W., Flake, S.: Towards the Compositional Verification of Real-Time UML Designs. In: Proc. of the European Software Engineering Conference (ESEC/FSE), Helsinki, Finland, ACM Press (2003) 38–47

22. Burmester, S., Giese, H., Klein, F.: Design and Simulation of Self-Optimizing Mechatronic Systems with Fujaba and CAMeL. In Schürr, A., Zündorf, A., eds.: Proc. of the 2nd International Fujaba Days 2004, Darmstadt, Germany. Volume tr-ri-04-253 of Technical Report., University of Paderborn (2004) 19–22

23. Broeckman, B., Notenboom, E.: Testing Embedded Software. Addison Wesley (2003)

24. Reynolds, C.: Flocks, herds, and schools: A distributed behavioral model. Computer Graphics **21** (1987)

25. Jennings, N.R., Campos, J.R.: Towards a social level characterisation of socially responsible agents. IEE Proceedings on Software Engineering **144** (1997) 11–25

26. Castelfranchi, C.: Engineering social order. In: Engineering Societies in the Agent World, First International Workshop, ESAW 2000, Berlin, Germany, August 21, 2000, Revised Papers. Volume 1972 of Lecture Notes in Computer Science., Springer (2000) 1–18

27. Weyns, D., Schelfthout, K., Holvoet, T., Lefever, T.: Decentralized control of E'GV transportation systems. In Pechoucek, M., Steiner, D., Thompson, S., eds.: 4rd International Joint Conference on Autonomous Agents and Multiagent Systems (AAMAS 2005), July 25-29, 2005, Utrecht, The Netherlands, ACM (2005) 67–74

28. Schelfthout, K., Holvoet, T.: Objectplaces: An environment for situated multi-agent systems. In: 3rd International Joint Conference on Autonomous Agents and Multiagent Systems (AAMAS 2004), 19-23 August 2004, New York, NY, USA, IEEE Computer Society (2004) 1500–1501

29. Omicini, A., Ricci, A., Viroli, M., Castelfranchi, C., Tummolini, L.: Coordination artifacts: Environment-based coordination for intelligent agents. In: 3rd International Joint Conference on Autonomous Agents and Multiagent Systems, 19-23 August 2004, New York, NY, USA. (2004) 286–293

A Survey of Environments and Mechanisms for Human-Human Stigmergy*

H. Van Dyke Parunak

Altarum Institute, 3520 Green Court, Suite 300, Ann Arbor, MI 48105
`van.parunak@altarum.org`

Abstract. Stigmergy (the coordination of agents through signs they make and sense in a shared environment) was originally articulated in the study of social insects. Its basic processes are much simpler than those usually used to model human-level cognition. Thus it is an attractive way to coordinate agents in engineered environments such as robotics or information processing. Stigmergic coordination is not limited to insects. Humans regularly use environmentally-mediated signals to coordinate their activities. This paper develops a schema for analyzing stigmergy among humans, discusses examples (some using a computational environment and others antedating digital computation), and suggests how the use of such mechanisms may be extended.

1 Executive Summary

Human-Human Stigmergy is pervasive. A wide range of pre-computer social systems fit the pattern of stigmergic coordination, and have provided a rich set of metaphors on which a diverse set of computer-enabled systems for enabling human stigmergy have been constructed. It would be more difficult to show a functioning human institution that is not stigmergic, than it is to find examples of human stigmergy.

The reason that human-human stigmergy is so common can be understood from the growing body of experience in constructing large-scale distributed computing systems with resource-constrained elements. Central control of such systems is not feasible, since resource-constrained components cannot cope with the large-scale, distributed aspects of such systems. The central insight of stigmergy is that coordination can be achieved by resource-constrained agents interacting locally in an environment. Two fundamental principles govern the success of this strategy.

1. No matter how large the environment grows, because agents interact only locally, their limited processing capabilities are not overwhelmed.
2. Through the dynamics of self-organization, local interactions can yield a coherent system-level outcome that provides the required control.

The essence of stigmergy is the coordination of bounded agents embedded in a (potentially unbounded) environment, whose state they both sense (to guide their

---

D. Weyns, H. Van Dyke Parunak, and F. Michel (Eds.): E4MAS 2005, LNAI 3830, pp. 163–186, 2006.
© Springer-Verlag Berlin Heidelberg 2006

actions) and modify (as a result of their actions). Section 2 introduces the concept of stigmergy and describes its varieties and characteristics. Section 3 classifies a range of human stigmergic mechanisms, both pre-computational and computational. Section 4 describes ongoing areas of research that will foster applications of human-human stigmergy. Reflecting the interests of the client for whom this report was originally prepared, we focus on military applications.

2   An Introduction to Stigmergy

The French entomologist Grassé coined the term "stigmergy" in the 1950's [32] to describe a broad class of multi-agent coordination mechanisms that rely on information exchange through a shared environment. The term is formed from the Greek words *stigma* "sign" and *ergon* "action," and captures the notion that an agent's actions leave signs in the environment, signs that it and other agents sense and that determine their subsequent actions.

In spite of Grassé's preoccupation with insects, stigmergy is ubiquitous in the human interactions. Our experience with a wide range of distributed systems suggests that it is the only way for members of a large distributed population, whatever their individual cognitive capabilities, to coordinate themselves with bounded computational resources. To set the context for our survey of stigmergy among humans, we outline the basic architecture of stigmergy, then develop a taxonomy of stigmergic interactions that can be used to classify specific instances. We discuss further details on how stigmergic systems can be engineered in [72].

2.1   Architecture of Stigmergy

Fig. 1 summarizes the basic components of a stigmergic system: a population of agents and an environment in which they are immersed.

Each agent has

- an internal state, which generally *is not* directly visible to other agents;
- sensors that give it access to some of the environment's state variables;
- actuators that enable it to change some of the environment's state variables;
- a program (its "dynamics") that maps from its current internal state and its sensor readings to changes in its state and commands given to its sensors and actuators.

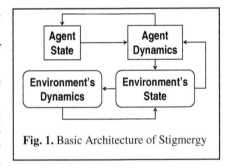

Fig. 1. Basic Architecture of Stigmergy

The environment has

- a state, certain aspects of which generally *are* visible to the agents;
- a program (its "dynamics") that governs the evolution of its state over time.

The most important distinction between agents and the environment is that the internal state of agents is hidden, while the state of the environment is accessible to an agent with appropriate sensors. In most cases, a second distinction can be observed. Each agent is monolithic, a self-contained computational object with a well-defined boundary. Typically, the environment is not monolithic, but is structured according to some topology. Some examples of environmental topologies include

- a Cartesian space (e.g., the surface of the earth);
- a graph structure (e.g., a telecommunications network or social organization);
- a list of disjoint categories (e.g., a list of topics, though these are usually organized into a graph by imposing an ontology).

When the environment is structured in this way, each agent is localized in the environment. That is, its sensors and actuators are confined to one region of the environment. If the agent is mobile, it can change location in the environment, but at any moment it is at one location. This localization of agents within the environment restricts the computational load imposed on the agents, and enables stigmergic systems to scale without exceeding the load on each agent.

While localization in a distributed environment keeps the computational load on each agent manageable, it does not ensure that a reasonable system-level behavior will emerge from the interactions of the agents. Critical support for this objective lies in the interaction of the dynamics of the agents with those of the environment. The dynamics of individual agents are typically nonlinear, and their interactions are often nonlinear as well, resulting in a system that is susceptible to formal chaos. Far from being a disadvantage, such dynamics actually enable self-organization, since they permit the system to explore its state space efficiently. This exploration is a key ingredient of self-organization, other components of which are discussed in [72].

2.2 Varieties of Stigmergic Interaction

We distinguish four varieties of stigmergy, generated by two binary distinctions. One distinction is whether the signs consist of special markers that agents deposit in the environment ("marker-based stigmergy") or whether agents base their actions on the current state of the solution ("sematectonic stigmergy") [9]. The other distinction is whether the signals are a single scalar analogous to a potential field ("quantitative stigmergy") or whether they form a set of discrete options ("qualitative stigmergy") [12]. The two distinctions are orthogonal (Table 1).

The paradigm for marker based stigmergy is the use of pheromones by certain social insects. Some species use multiple pheromone "flavors" [25] and thus use qualitative as well as quantitative decision-making. In engineered systems, stigmergic markers can consist of actual physical chemicals deposited in a

Table 1. Varieties of Stigmergy

	Marker-Based	Sematectonic
Quantitative	Gradient following in a single pheromone field	Ant cemetery clustering
Qualitative	Decisions based on combinations of pheromones	Wasp nest construction

physical landscape, labeled scalar variables stored in a data structure whose topology reflects that of the problem (as in much of our UAV control work), or price signals in a marketplace [17]. The latter metaphor is particularly important in coordinating human interactions, as in our RAPPID system for collaborative design [75-77].

The structure of the domain itself provides sufficient signals for coordinating some insect behaviors, without the need for special markers. Ants cluster corpses in their cemeteries, guided only the density of corpse distribution [7]. This is a quantitative decision, depending only on the distribution of a single type of object. Wasps decide where to add the next cell to their nests based on which of several templates best characterizes the current local shape of the nest, thus making a qualitative distinction. Sematectonic stigmergy is also illustrated by an algorithm that explains how wolves surround their prey [44], by being attracted to the prey while repelled by neighboring wolves. We have applied sematectonic stigmergy to coordination of multiple sensors [69, 73] and the assembly of intelligence information [95].

A subset of stigmergic mechanisms, "coordination fields" or "co-fields" [47, 52, 53, 96], consists of quantitative stigmergy. The scalar field is generated by a combination of attracting and repelling components, and the agents follow gradients in this field, thus tending to avoid repellers and approach attractors. Such techniques have an extended history in controlling individual robots [81].

Whatever the details of the interaction, examples from natural systems show that stigmergic systems can generate robust, complex, intelligent behavior at the system level even when the individual agents are simple and individually non-intelligent. In these systems, intelligence resides not in a single distinguished agent (as in the centralized model) nor in each individual agent (the intelligent agent model), but in the interactions among the agents and the shared dynamical environment.

3   Present Status of Technology

We summarize instances of stigmergic human coordination in two broad categories: those that do not rely on digital computers (though they may be enhanced by them), and those that are distinctively creatures of the computer age. For each category, we document an example, and analyze it in terms of the theoretical categories developed in the previous section, using the template shown in Fig. 2. We first identify the environment, describe its topology, the state variables that it

> **Environment:**
> - Topology:
> - State:
> - Dynamics:
>
> **Agents:**
> - Sensor:
> - Actuator:
> - Dynamics:
>
> **Emergent system behavior:**
>
> **Fig. 2.** Template for Analysis of Examples

supports, and any internal dynamics. Then we identify the agents, discuss how they sense and modify the environment (with attention to the main distinction between sema(tectonic) and marker(-based) stigmergic interaction), and summarize their internal dynamics. Finally, we describe the overall emergent system behavior that the stigmergy achieves.

3.1 Pre-computational

Humans have long coordinated their activities through non-computational environments, though these mechanisms can often be enhanced with computers.

3.1.1 Movement Coordination

Humans have always needed to move in their environment, and have drawn on stigmergic mechanisms both to form their trails and to choose among alternate existing trails.

3.1.1.1 Trail Formation The simplest and most primitive trail formation mechanisms rely on sematectonic stigmergy. Humans wear down vegetation on frequently-used routes, and grass regrows if an old path is not used (Fig. 3). There is an extensive literature on mathematical models for such path formation by "active walkers" [37].

While trails can form entirely with sematectonic stigmergy, humans tend

Environment: Vegetated terrain
- Topology: 2D manifold
- State:
    - Degree of ground cover
    - Obstacles
- Dynamics:
    - Trodden vegetation dies
    - Vegetation regrows on untrodden areas

Agents: People (pedestrians or in vehicles)
- Sensor:
    - Sema: smoothness to path
    - Sema: direction to destination
    - Marker: road signs
- Actuator:
    - Sema: direction of next step
    - Marker: pave the path
    - Marker: set road signs
- Dynamics: optimize smoothness and direction

Emergent system behavior: globally marked paths

Fig. 3. Trail Formation

to enhance them with markers. My college campus was notorious for laying pavement along bare tracks through the grass, turning emergent trails into permanent ones. A common modern example is traffic signs, often maintained locally by a variety of jurisdictions, but Native Americans also used artificial markers, including unnaturally bent trees [23] and petroglyphs [54], to mark trails. While such mechanisms can make trails easier to follow, they also render them less dynamic. It takes longer for a concrete path to crumble than for grass to regrow over an unused dirt path.

3.1.1.2 Traffic Flow Humans not only generate trails stigmergically, but also allocate their movement across alternative routes, both sematectonically and using markers (tolls) (Fig. 4). Note that this behavior builds on the product of a previous stigmergic activity (the formation of the trails themselves).

3.1.2 Market Systems

Adam Smith's "invisible hand" is an example of the self-organizing potential of a stigmergic system, and have the benefit of an immense body of formal study [92].

There are two varieties of open markets. Both are stigmergic, though at different levels.

In an auction-based market (such as a stock market or commodities exchange), the marketplace is the environment in which buyers and sellers interact, using currency as markers (Fig. 5). The markets for individual products are distinct, so the topology of the environment is strictly speaking a set of disjoint categories. However, different products are linked by other processes in the economy (for example, the markets for steel and automobiles), leading to an implicit graph structure.

A less-studied alternative to auction systems is the pattern of Edgeworth barter, in which buyers and sellers interact directly with each other in repeated pairwise transactions, without the benefit of an auctioneer [3] (Fig. 6). In this system, the environment consists entirely of the graph of dependencies among different products induced by patterns of joint use, since it is through these dependencies that individual transactions have an effect on one another.

3.1.3 Elections

An election can be viewed as a market with candidates and issues as commodities and votes as currency. In a single-issue or single-office election, the dynamics are simple. However, many elections involve a series of issues or offices, often linked through political platforms. The ultimate outcome in terms of governance depends on the policies advocated by a candidate. A voter may favor some of those policies and oppose others, but rarely has the opportunity of voting for or against individual policies. Voting for a candidate can be compared to buying a complex product with multiple attributes. For example, in an automobile, one may want high fuel economy, good off-road performance, and low maintenance, but usually must make compromises.

Environment: Trail network
- Topology: Graph
- State:
  - Congestion
  - Toll fees
- Dynamics: Convey traffic across edges of the graph

Agents: People (pedestrians or in vehicles)
- Sensor:
  - Sema: current congestion on edge
  - Sema: direction to destination
  - Marker: requested toll
- Actuator:
  - Sema: choice of edges at each node
  - Marker: pay toll
- Dynamics: optimize speed and economy

Emergent system behavior: more balanced load on different paths

Fig. 4. Traffic Flow

Environment: Product-specific exchanges
- Topology: Categories (though often linked by product dependencies, e.g., steel in autos)
- State: Current bid and ask prices
- Dynamics: integrate offers to compute prices that clear the market

Agents: Buyers and sellers
- Sensor (Marker): Current prices
- Actuator (Marker): State own bid or ask price
- Dynamics: Maximize time integral of revenue over expense

Emergent system behavior: globally optimum allocation of resources

Fig. 5. Auction Market Systems

If an election is like a market, representative government is like an economy. Elected officials themselves participate in numerous legislative actions, including both explicit votes and implicit agreements, to pursue their platforms. Voters often choose a set of representatives in anticipation of the subsequent legislative give-and-take, providing for a balance of power in the overall structure.

Viewed in this way, the topography within which elections take place is a graph with different colors of nodes and edges. Some nodes represent candidates, others represent policies, and still others represent representative divisions (such as geographical regions). Edges link candidates to their regions and the issues they support or oppose. Votes for candidates propagate to the issues associated with them (Fig. 7).

Environment: Pairwise encounters
- Topology: Spatial distribution of traders
- State: Current locations of traders
- Dynamics: Support mixing of traders

Agents: Traders
- Sensor (Marker): Bid and ask price for single entity
- Actuator (Marker): State own ask or bid price
- Dynamics: Integrate information over successive exchanges

Emergent system behavior: In repeated trades, balances supply and demand

Fig. 6. Edgeworth Barter Markets

3.1.4 Document Editing

Joint authorship has always been a stigmergic activity, mediated by the emerging document itself. Each author is stimulated by what previous authors have written to add main-line content or marginal comments. The dynamics of this process have been greatly enhanced by sophisticated word processing software that includes specific facilities for review, comment, and tracking   multiple authors.

While a document may seem to be a static entity, internal semantic relations can change as a result of individual modifications. As a trivial example, consider a document on a sensitive issue. A later reviser adds a tendentious definition to the first page of the document. The structural integrity of the document has the effect of propagating the semantics of this definition to later sections, potentially changing their meaning (Fig. 8).

Environment: Network of districts, candidates, and issues
- Topology: Graph
- State: Connectivity of links
- Dynamics: Population of districts; support for candidates and issues

Agents: Voters
- Sensor (Sema): Affiliation of candidates with issues
- Actuator (Marker): Vote
- Dynamics: Choose policies indirectly through candidates

Emergent system behavior: Set of policies aligned with voter interests

Fig. 7. Elections

An extension of document editing is the development of knowledge in a scientific community. Each paper that is published contributes knowledge that other researchers can use in stimulating their ideas, modifying their research directions, and deriving their results (not to mention the more mundane results of achieving tenure for the authors and thus prolonging their ability to contribute to the field) [57].

3.1.5 Status Boards

Many social settings use a publicly visible display to coordinate activity (Fig. 9). Examples include "in-out" boards indicating which staff are currently in the office, situation boards used in military battle management, and a wide range of bulletin boards advertising items for sale, employment opportunities, services offered, etc.

> **Environment:** A document
> - Topology: Linear or (if structured) hierarchical
> - State: Current content, both mainline and marginal comments
> - Dynamics: Internal semantic propagation
>
> **Agents:** Writers and editors
> - Sensor (Sema): Current state of the document
> - Actuator:
>   - Sema: New content
>   - Marker: Strike-outs, highlighting
> - Dynamics: Adjust content to modulate ambiguity, tune an argument, or advocate a particular position
>
> **Emergent system behavior:** Expression of jointly held consciousness
>
> **Fig. 8.** Document Editing

The emergent behavior mediated by the board depends on its theme. "For sale" boards generate market encounters, usually of the Edgeworth variety. Situation boards enable tactical coordination of military forces. "In-out" boards enable more effective direction of inquiries and assignments to staff who are immediately available.

3.1.6 Viral Marketing

Viral marketing describes "any strategy that encourages individuals to pass on a marketing message to others" [103]. Before the advent of computers, this form of communication was known as "word-of-mouth," and in non-commercial venues was known as "rumors." The speed of digital communication has made it particularly powerful. One classic example is free email such as Hotmail: every message sent by a user includes a system-generated tagline that encourages recipients to get their own Hotmail account, thus opening themselves to follow-on advertisements. Another, less blatant example is the use of planted participants in chat rooms to generate "buzz" in favor of a new music album, film, or book.

The heart of these strategies is the propagation of a message along the

> **Environment:** Modifiable public display
> - Topology: 2-dimensional surface
> - State: Current contents
> - Dynamics: Most current material obscures or replaces older material
>
> **Agents:** People visiting the board
> - Sensor (Sema): Contents of the board
> - Actuator (Sema): New postings
> - Dynamics: Add new postings, remove or regroup old ones
>
> **Emergent system behavior:** Depends on theme of the board (see text)
>
> **Fig. 9.** Status Board

social network of participants (Fig. 10), analogous to the propagation of a disease (thus the name). Like disease propagation, viral marketing depends on several factors [78], including

- the susceptibility of the members of the network to the message (if the message is intrinsically uninteresting, it will die out);
- the connectivity of the infected individuals (if the product of connectivity times susceptibility falls below 1, the infection will die out);

Environment: Social network
- Topology: Graph
- State: Connectivity of participants
- Dynamics: Communication

Agents: Members of network
- Sensor (Sema): Content heard from others
- Actuator (Sema): Repeating content
- Dynamics: Spread of message

Emergent system behavior: Number of individuals who have heard the message increases rapidly.

Fig. 10. Viral Marketing

- the structure of the social network (an infection will die out in a lattice if the percentage of infected individuals falls below a certain threshold, but can persist in a power-law network no matter how small the percentage of infected individuals).

3.2 Computational

The advent of information technology has extended the applicability of stigmergic mechanisms for human coordination, by augmenting human abilities for sensing, communication, and information processing. Each of the examples in this section can be viewed as a descendant of one or more of the pre-computational examples discussed in the previous section.

3.2.1 Intelligent Transportation Systems

The application of computer technology to human movement coordination (Section 3.1.1) has produced the burgeoning field of "Intelligent Transportation Systems" (ITS, also known as "Intelligent Highway Systems," IHS), with extensive government attention [22, 87], independent business groups [42, 43], and dedicated research societies and journals [40].

The field as a whole includes all modes of transportation. Our analysis (Fig. 11) focuses on highway systems.

Computational mechanisms in this domain rely on the existence of road networks that in most

Environment: Highway network
- Topology: Graph
- State:
  o Locations and velocities of vehicles
  o Timing of control signals
- Dynamics: Enable movement of vehicles from one place to another

Agents: Vehicles
- Sensor:
  o Marker: Signals
  o Sema: Local congestion
- Actuator (Sema): Route choices
- Dynamics: Obey signals; minimize local congestion; make progress toward destination

Emergent system behavior: Increased throughput, reduced collisions

Fig. 11. Intelligent Highway System

cases were established using pre-digital stigmergy. Computational enhancements include

- roadbed sensors for real-time estimates of traffic density and velocity;
- improved signal systems (including not only traffic lights but also digital signs) for providing feedback to motorists;
- advanced algorithms [45, 104] for controlling signals on the basis of sensed traffic.

3.2.2 Collaboration Environments

Recognition of the potential of stigmergy for promoting coordination in human organizations [19] has led to a proliferation of systems that support human collaboration in one way or another. These fall under two broad headings: content (technologies that enable a community to assemble knowledge structures that exceed their individual expertise) and process (technologies that enable members of a community to act in coordination with one another). In many ways, these systems can be viewed as a digital extension of the "Status Boards" discussed in Section 3.1.5 above.

Content-oriented collaboration environments can be viewed as digital libraries (a domain with an extensive research literature [21], organizational infrastructure [20, 41], and public-sector support [15, 60]). Their function is to store, index, and provide access to shared materials. Because of the ease with which digital materials can be authored and distributed, these environments can be modified by the same communities to which they provide information, thus closing the stigmergic feedback loop. The computer adds three successive layers of functionality to the traditional library, discussed in the following three sections:

1. Enhanced storage and interlinking of materials, increasingly by the user community
2. Automatic ranking of materials, based on utilization by others
3. Dynamic distribution and sharing of content.

3.2.2.1 Content Storage and Linking
Most computer users today are frequent users of the World-Wide Web (WWW), a worldwide network of interlinked documents to which anyone can add. The notion of such a web of information was initially proposed by Vannevar Bush in 1945 [11]. There were numerous attempts at implementation, but the approach that finally took hold was that devel-

---

Environment: Networked Computers
- Topology: Categories (but linked through cross references)
- State: Current collection of articles
- Dynamics:
  o Web link: Addressing
  o Search engine: Indexing, Ranking, Summarizing

Agents: People
- Sensor:
  o Sema: Entries
  o Marker: Linking Scores (Google)
- Actuator (Sema): Post a document
- Dynamics: Find desired information

Emergent system behavior: Maintain rationalized system of interrelated information

Fig. 12. World-Wide Web

---

oped by Berners-Lee [5], based on a common linking protocol (http) embedded in simple text files.

The strength of the WWW is its open character, enabling it to grow rapidly. As sites link to one another, the web becomes a framework for self-organizing communities [94] (Fig. 12). In fact, one of the first references to appear in response to a Google search on "stigmergy" (as of the date of writing) is a discussion of the collaborate effect of web logs, or blogs [33]. In the military domain, the US Army has made effective use of the emergent character of the WWW to share knowledge and experience among soldiers [88].

For some commercial purposes private file storage and sharing mechanisms are preferred (and often built on top of the WWW). One widely marketed example is Groove [34], which provides a common file repository and a variety of tools for project management to support distributed project teams.

Originally, the only way to modify the WWW was to add a new document that contained links to documents already there. A given document could only be changed by its author. Recent technical developments (most prominently, Wiki [49]) enable the maintenance of web pages that can be edited by anyone with the appropriate access. A prominent example of the potential of this approach is the WikiPedia [101], an encyclopedia of over half a million articles (many of very high quality), maintained entirely by the users. (By way of comparison, the Encyclopaedia Britannica contains about 120,000 articles.) The Wiki technology is an example of tools for social bookmarking [36], by which people can share not only their documents but also their annotations on the documents of others. This dynamic extends to entire libraries the dynamics of shared document editing discussed in Section 3.1.4.

3.2.2.2 Site Ranking In a shared information system such as the WWW or a Wiki, computers store the content, make it available to users, and facilitate changes and additions, but in the original form of such systems the interpretation of the resulting network is based on the human user's perception. Computers can augment this perception, to provide the user with a richer view of the network than would otherwise be possible. For example, the same openness to growth that makes the WWW so powerful can also make it overwhelming. A keyword search can return thousands of documents ("stigmergy," in spite of its rarity, returns 16,500 under Google at the time of writing), far more than a human user can effectively use. A common example of this enhancement is the ranking of web sites.

For example, much of the benefit of the Google indexing system lies in its PageRank^{TM} algorithm [8, 31, 61] (Fig. 13), which assigns each web page a rank based on how many pages point to it, weighted by the ranks of those pages and the number of pages

> **Environment:** Network of hyperlinked documents
> - Topology: Graph
> - State: Connectivity of the graph
> - Dynamics: Maintenance of indices (via web spiders)
>
> **Agents:** Creators of links in pages
> - Sensor (Sema): Content of other relevant pages
> - Actuator (Marker): Insert links to relevant pages
> - Dynamics: Seeks to maximize connectivity of own pages to relevant pages
>
> **Emergent system behavior:** Pages are assigned ranks that guide agents in finding useful material.
>
> **Fig. 13.** Google Page Rank

to which they point. This recursive computation is far beyond the ability of a human to calculate, but can readily be performed by computers, and enables users to find valuable material far more easily than would otherwise be the case. A page's rank under this algorithm is a clear example of an emergent phenomenon generated stigmergically. It guides web page authors seeking material to reference in their own pages, and in turn is modulated by the links that those authors insert to the material they find. Authors who wish to promote their own pages often seek to subvert the stigmergic nature of the system and control their page ranking. Much of Google's effort is devoted to blocking such subversion.

Another system for helping users find useful material is the PackHunter [79]. Users deposit digital pheromones on a map of their web browsing activity, leading other users with similar pheromone patterns to sites likely to be of interest to them. Where PageRank™ focuses on the structure of the network as constructed by its authors, PackHunter takes into account the actions of users. It can be viewed as a form of collaborative filtering (Section 3.2.3) applied to web pages.

3.2.2.3 Peer-to-Peer Computing In the WWW, every document lives on some computer, which must be active to make the content available. If a document is very popular, the computer's individual bandwidth may be overwhelmed, making access slow or impossible. The computer hosting the document is the "server," and computers that access it are "clients."

An alternative strategy, peer-to-peer (P2P) computing, seeks to do away with the client-server distinction. In this strategy, content moves dynamically from one computer to another, and may exist in several places at the same time. When a user seeks a document, the network dynamically retrieves it from the nearest available machine. No single server has a monopoly on any document, and if one source for a document is heavily loaded, others can supply the demand.

Current implementations of P2P, such as Gnutella [30], serve mainly as ways to share content without the need for a central file server, and are popular mechanisms for private users interested in sharing media. LOCKSS [50] applies the P2P approach to preserving digital media by distributing them over multiple machines, and is oriented to the library community. Bit-Torrent [6] provides a general-purpose peer-to-peer distribution system. In

Environment: Computer network
- Topology: Graph
- State: Semantic signature of users at each computer
- Dynamics: Maintain semantic signatures based on documents generated and accessed

Agents: Users at nodes of the network
- Sensor (Sema): Review of accessed documents
- Actuator:
  - Sema: Documents and queries generated
  - Marker: Rewards sent to relevant documents
- Dynamics: User interactively generates and reviews documents

Emergent system behavior: Documents find their way to nodes where they are likely to be of most value

Fig. 14. PARTNER (Smart P2P Document Distribution)

principle, such a framework would be an excellent environment for "smart" information that finds its way to users based on an emergent model of their interests, as in

Altarum's PARTNER technology [64] (Fig. 14) and in a research project currently underway at the Université de Tours in France [57].

The collaboration systems described so far focus on making digital content accessible to users. A further level of collaborative support is represented by systems that help users manage the processes of their work. We briefly describe several examples, beginning with the most mature.

3.2.2.4 BPM: ActionWorks There is an established market in the commercial world for workflow or business process management (BPM) systems. These systems help organizations define and follow standard processes to ensure uniformity of performance. A premier example is the Action-Works system [2] from Action Technologies [1] (Fig. 15). This system analyzes all workflows as built on a basic four-step cycle involving a Customer for whom work is being done and a Performer who does the work.

1. The Customer *prepares* a plan of the work to be done and issues a request.
2. The Customer and Performer *negotiate* the terms of the work.
3. The Performer *performs* the work and reports completion.
4. The Customer evaluates the work and either *accepts* it or identifies what remains to be done.

Each of these steps can in turn be broken down into further cycles until the company's entire business process has been analyzed. The resulting network forms an environment that supports stigmergic interactions among workers, who receive and give local signals concerning the state of their own responsibilities.

Environment: Model of interlocking Prepare-Negotiate-Perform-Accept cycles
- Topology: Graph
- State: Identify of Customer and Performer for each cycle, and current state of the cycle
- Dynamics: Propagate information about the state of each cycle to its sub- and super-cycles

Agents: Workers
- Sensor (Marker): State of current cycle and component subcycles
- Actuator (Marker): Report state of current work package
- Dynamics: Seek to move along cycles in which one is either a Customer or a Performer

Emergent system behavior: Coordinated execution of an overall workflow without missing or duplicative action.

Fig. 15. ActionWorks BPM Framework

Environment: Web site
- Topology: Graph
- State: Information about products offered, seller identity, reputation, and conditions, buyer identity, reputation, and bid, state of the overall auction process
- Dynamics: Maintains and publishes current state of the auction; determines the winner; notifies participants.

Agents: Buyers and sellers
- Sensor (Marker): Current prices
- Actuator (Marker): State own bid or ask price
- Dynamics: Maximize time integral of revenue over expense

Emergent system behavior: globally optimum allocation of resources

Fig. 16. On-Line Auctions

3.2.2.5 On-Line Auctions On-line auctions such as eBay [24] provide a standardized process that guides sellers and buyers in finding one another, engaging in bidding, and concluding deals. The process being automated is essentially a Walrasian auction (Section 3.1.2). The overall system includes WWW structures for organizing products offered for sale and bids offered, a reputation system for enforcing honesty in transactions, and time-based mechanisms for managing the flow of an actual auction (Fig. 16). Similar mechanisms are provided by Amazon in support of the network of used book sellers that advertise through its website, or the Yahoo merchants network.

3.2.2.6 Market-Based Design: RAPPID Altarum's RAPPID technology for distributed electromechanical design [75-77] (Fig. 17) helps designers reach agreement on design specifications at the intersections. RAPPID is based on a generalization of Walrasian market model for coordination (Section 3.1.2). A market exists for each interface parameter (for example, the torque or RPM of a shaft connecting a motor and a transmission), and the goods being traded are the assignments to those parameters. The prices manipulated in the markets are either catalog costs for actual components or "play money" that designers are allocated by the customer and must spend to get the functionality they require from other designers.

Environment: Set of markets on interfaces
- Topology: Graph reflecting product structure
- State: Current bid and ask prices
- Dynamics: Compute prices that clear the markets

Agents: Designers
- Sensor (marker): Current prices
- Actuator (marker): State bid or ask
- Dynamics: Maximize time integral of revenue over expense

Emergent system behavior: Balanced assignments to interacting design variables

Fig. 17. RAPPID

3.2.2.7 Battle Plan Adjustment: Coordinators A current DARPA program, Coordinators [93], focuses on the task of helping fielded military units adapt their mission plans as the situation around them changes. Each unit has a networked computer or personal digital assistant (PDA). Agents representing each unit and running on their computer negotiate with one another to determine the interactions among tasks, the impact of the unfolding battle, and possible adaptive changes such as task timings, task assignments, or adoption of pre-planned contingencies.

One analyst has briefly described guerilla operations from a stigmergic perspective [82].

3.2.3 Recommender Systems

A "recommender system" or "recommendation system" attempts to predict items (such as books, movies, or music) that a user may find interesting, based on the user's profile. Such systems are usually implemented using collaborative filtering [38]. The system (the stigmergic environment) collects a large number of profiles on different users. Each profile is a vector over the universe of items for which recommendations are being made, and the magnitude of each element in a user's profile indicates the attractiveness of that item for that user. To make a recommendation, the system first finds other users whose profiles are similar to that of the user for whom the recommendation is intended (the recommendee). Then it identifies elements in their profiles with high scores, elements for which the recommendee has registered no score.

The big challenge for recommender systems is collecting and maintaining a collection of user profiles. Users typically find it onerous to rank their preferences explicitly. However, their preferences can often be deduced from other actions they take. Perhaps the best known recommender system is that used by Amazon to recommend books to its buyers (Fig. 19). This system functions stigmergically. Every purchase of an item is taken as evidence that the purchaser has a high level of interest in that item, and is registered in that user's profile. Thus individual actions (purchases) leave signs in the environment (the collection of profiles) that are integrated to provide feedback to the individual (what book might be a reasonable next acquisition).

3.2.4 Scheduling and Planning

Many problems of operational importance can be cast as scheduling and planning problems. Abstractly, these problems concern the allocation of scarce resources to a set of tasks over time. Much of the research in Operations Research is devoted to formal algorithms for solving such problems, with special emphasis on guaranteeing the optimality of the solution.

A large body of centralized algorithms has been developed for solving these problems. However, many versions of the problem are NP-complete [27], meaning that for an instance of reasonable size, the time required to

---

Environment: Communication network
- Topology: Graph
- State: Current state of the plan; representation of extraneous events
- Dynamics: Negotiation of plan adjustments among agents

Agents: Warfighters
- Sensor (Sema): Learn of constraints from other warfighters, and recommendations from the agents
- Actuator (Sema): Represent state of the battle and current constraints in to the system
- Dynamics: Report constraints and preferences

Emergent system behavior: Adjusted battle plan that balances requirements of the entire team

Fig. 18. DARPA Coordinators

Environment: Collection of user profiles
- Topology: Colored graph (user and item nodes with links indicating preferences between users and items, and similarities between users)
- State: Degree of preference of each user for each item; degree of similarity among users
- Dynamics: Maintain preference and similarity scores

Agents: Purchasers
- Sensor (Sema): Description of recommended purchase
- Actuator (Sema): Purchase an item
- Dynamics: Spend money on items most likely to be of interest

Emergent system behavior: Identify items most likely to be of interest to the user

Fig. 19. Recommender System (Amazon)

---

compute the solution is too long to complete by the time the plan is needed. To address these problems, a number of agent-oriented solutions have been proposed.

While these methods vary considerably in their details, they tend to share two features. First, they do not guarantee optimal solutions, but use heuristics to obtain "good-enough" solutions in reasonable time. Second, a common heuristic is for the agents to restrict their interactions to other agents that are near them in some problem-specific topology. Thus these systems often qualify as stigmergic (Fig. 20), and frequently draw on recognized stigmergic mechanisms, such as market or pheromone systems. We can illustrate these systems with two examples from the domain of manufacturing planning and scheduling.

AARIA [66, 67] is based on the model of the factory as a marketplace [4, 62]. The participants in the market are the workstations in the factory that can change the state of material, and agents representing each job that moves through the factory. A job agent negotiates with workstations to perform the operations that it requires in the appropriate sequence, using market mechanisms as already discussed in Section 3.1.2.

Environment: Factory conveyance structure
- Topology: Graph
- State: Connectivity between workstations; capabilities and load profile of each workstation
- Dynamics: Maintain load profiles on workstations

Agents: Workstations, Jobs
- Sensor (Marker): Market bids, pheromone levels
- Actuator (Market): Make bids; deposit pheromones; (jobs) select next operation
- Dynamics: Maximize local performance (utilization for a workstation; delivery time for a job)

Emergent system behavior: Reduced overall production time and increased throughput

Fig. 20. Manufacturing Scheduling and Planning

An important innovation in AARIA is the use of a loading profile or "dance card" on each workstation agent [16]. This profile aggregates the expected load on the workstation over time. Job agents search this profile to find relatively unoccupied times when they can be executed, and augment it when they book a reservation on a workstation. Thus the profile behaves like a pheromone over time, leveling the load that each workstation experiences.

The pheromone approach is taken even further in the system described in [9]. Each job sends out a swarm of ghost agents that explore alternative possible routings and record their findings in the form of digital pheromones in a graph representing the factory's conveyance system. The actual job then follows the emergent pheromone trace. Another set of dynamics from insects, based on task allocation in wasps, has also been exploited in support of manufacturing planning and scheduling [14].

Yet another leading effort in stigmergic scheduling and planning applied to manufacturing is the work of the PROSA group at the Katholieke Universiteit Leuven in Belgium [91]. The acronym PROSA stands for "Product, Resource, Order, Staff Architecture," and identifies the main software agents (products, resources, and orders) that interact stigmergically to guide the factory.

David Scheidt of Johns Hopkins University's Advanced Physics Lab reports work on using markets for shipboard power and fluids distribution at JHU/APL, Rockwell Automation, Nutech, and Icosystems [85], but these systems are not documented in the open literature. Work on market mechanisms for power distribution in residential and industrial settings has been published [106, 107]

4 Future Developments

Further technical enablement of human-human stigmergy depends on developments in several enabling technologies, including ubiquitous computing, theoretical foundations, simulation, and privacy and security.

4.1 Computing Hardware

The environment is intrinsic to stigmergy. As computing technology grows smaller, less costly, and lower in power requirements, it can be distributed more widely in the physical environment, increasing the potential for stigmergic interactions.

Embedded sensors in the environment will enable passive tracking of the locations of mobile entities. Roadway sensors that can detect vehicles by their ferrous signature are already a critical component of intelligent transportation systems (Section 3.2.1). RFID [100] provides a way to make less readily sensed objects (including humans) visible, and can provide support for digital pheromones [51]. A new generation of microsensors include limited computational and communications capability. The University of Berkeley is a leading center in the development of this hardware [80].

Today, we think of human interactions with computers as deliberate and explicit, relying on keyboards, display screens, and pointing devices. As sensors, processing, and communications become more tightly integrated with the environment, computers will become invisible [86], yielding "ubiquitous" or "pervasive" computing. Humans will interact with computers via ordinary objects. (A current example is the modern automobile. Most drivers are unaware of the half-dozen or so computers they are manipulating as they drive down the road.) To enhance the transparency of this interaction, human interface devices will be critical. These include

- Heads-up displays to merge computer-generated information unobtrusively with the user's normal field of vision,
- RFID technologies to track a person's location and physiological state without explicit action on the part of the subject,
- Haptic technologies to guide the user through touch and feel.

An important area of research will be the development of power sources for pervasive computers. The smaller and more numerous computing elements become, the less power each will require, but the more impractical conventional power sources (such as batteries) become. In some cases (such as passive RFID), many passive sensors can receive the power they need from a few active readers. More generally, mechanisms such as parasitic power extraction from ambient RF or thermal noise will be come critical to the operation of such systems.

4.2 Foundations

Engineering requirements for ubiquitous computing are radically different from those that support the development, deployment, and maintenance of traditional computer systems [110], and will rely on a new body of theory and software engineering practices that can cope with the large numbers of processing elements, their physical distribution, the nonlinearity of their dynamics, and the nature of emergent behavior. Leading centers for the development of such software engineering methods include the Altarum Institute [63, 72] and the Università di Modena e Reggio Emilia in Italy with its vision of spraying computers onto the physical environment [109].

An important basis for this new theory is likely to be statistical physics, a mature quantitative science that is concerned with the emergence of macro-level system characteristics (such as pressure and temperature) from the behaviors of micro-level elements (atoms and molecules). Some research has been done on transferring insights from statistical physics to self-organizing systems [10, 48, 68, 71, 74, 84], but the field merits much more systematic exploration.

Applying formal methods will require simplified models of the phenomena in question. One important such model in the case of resource allocation is the minority game [70, 83, 84]. Altarum has been a leader in developing this analogy. Another class of models is derived from the new science of network structure [59], where Mark Newman of the University of Michigan is a leader [58]. Understanding better the dynamics of processes constrained to such networks is vital in understanding the spread of stigmergic information, such as the effectiveness of viral marketing.

The recent institution of the Workshop on Environments for Multi-Agent Systems (E4MAS [18, 99]) enables a necessary focus on the agent environment as a first-class engineering object in constructing and maintaining such systems. Recognizing the environment in this way not only facilitates system engineering, but is in fact essential to avoid inconsistencies that otherwise hamper the design [55]. Researchers from Leuven [97] (Danny Weyns), Reims [89] (Fabien Michel), and Ann Arbor [65] (Van Parunak) are the organizers of this series of workshops.

4.3 Integrated System-Social Simulation

Because of their emergent character, stigmergic systems require extensive use of simulation for their design and analysis.

Most simulation platforms used historically to study stigmergy in animals or robotic systems focus on support for large populations of fairly simple agents and the presence of an active environment. The leading simulation platforms in this area are Swarm [46] from the Santa Fe Institute, RePast [90] from the University of Chicago, and NetLogo [102] from Northwestern University.

There is a growing discipline of social simulation that takes account of the richness of human behavior. The University of Surrey in the UK is one leading center [28, 29]. These systems typically do not support large populations or environmentally-mediated interactions. Advances in human-human stigmergy will require simulation tools that combine the features of these two classes of existing systems.

4.4 Security and Privacy

One of the strengths of stigmergy is that information deposited by one agent can be retrieved and acted upon by other agents that visit the same location in the environment where the deposit was made. This openness of information poses a challenge to security and privacy. Adversarial applications (such as commerce or warfare) require guarantees that adversaries will not be able to learn a system's intentions by eavesdropping, or to disrupt its operation by inserting malicious information. More generally, western society rightly places a premium on the rights of the individual human to protect personal information from broad dissemination.

In some respects, stigmergy is more secure than alternatives. Conventional systems for command and control involve messages whose contents provide considerable semantic detail about plans and objectives. Stigmergic messages, by way of contrast, are often numeric (e.g., a digital pheromone deposit). Such messages make sense only in the context of the entire system, making it much more difficult for an adversary either to interpret an intercepted message or to craft a spurious one to achieve a desired disruption. In addition, the stochasticity implicit in many stigmergic designs means that the detailed behavior of the system is unpredictable even to the user, making it even more obscure to an adversary without knowledge of its context.

Nevertheless, because stigmergic systems post information in the environment, responsible deployment will require new advances in security technology. Leading research in security for highly distributed systems is being pursued at many institutions, including IBM [13] and the University of New Mexico [26], and is published in the IEEE Distributed Systems Online e-journal [39] and workshops such as the International Workshop on Security in Distributed Computing Systems [35] and the International Workshop on Security in Systems and Networks [105].

Acknowledgments

This review benefited greatly by responses to a survey mailed to internationally known researchers in this field. We acknowledge the detailed responses provided by the following colleagues: Nicholas Monmarché [56], David Payton, David Scheidt, Paul Valckenaers, Danny Weyns [98], and Franco Zambonelli [108].

References

[1]   Action. Action Technologies. 2005. http://www.actiontech.com/index.cfm.
[2]   Action Technologies. Enabling Business Process Management. Action Technologies, Inc., Oakland, CA, 2005. http://www.actiontech.com/library/documents/ Enabling-BPM.pdf.
[3]   R. Axtell and J. Epstein. Distributed Computation of Economic Equilibria via Bilateral Exchange. Brookings Institution, Washington, DC, 1997.
[4]   A. D. Baker. *Manufacturing Control with a Market Driven Contract Net*. Thesis at Rensselaer Polytechnic Institute, Department of Electrical Engineering, 1991.
[5]   T. Berners-Lee. *Weaving the Web: Origins and Future of the World Wide Web*. Texere Publishing, 1999.
[6]   BitTorrent. The Official BitTorrent Home Page. Web site, 2005. http://www. bittorrent.com/index.html.
[7]   E. Bonabeau, G. Theraulaz, V. Fourcassié, and J.-L. Deneubourg. The Phase-Ordering Kinetics of Cemetery Organization in Ants. *Physical Review E*, 4:4568-4571, 1998.
[8]   S. Brin and L. Page. The anatomy of a large-scale hypertextual Web search engine. *Computer Networks and ISDN Systems*, 30(1-7):101-117, 1998.

[9] S. Brueckner. *Return from the Ant: Synthetic Ecosystems for Manufacturing Control.* Thesis at Humboldt University Berlin, Department of Computer Science, 2000.

[10] S. Brueckner and H. V. D. Parunak. Information-Driven Phase Changes in Multi-Agent Coordination. In *Proceedings of Autonomous Agents and Multi-Agent Systems (AAMAS 2003)*, pages 950-951, 2003.

[11] V. Bush. As We May Think. *The Atlantic Monthly*, vol. 176, pages 101-108, 1945. http://www.theatlantic.com/doc/prem/194507/bush.

[12] S. Camazine, J.-L. Deneubourg, N. R. Franks, J. Sneyd, G. Theraulaz, and E. Bonabeau. *Self-Organization in Biological Systems.* Princeton, NJ, Princeton University Press, 2001.

[13] D. Chess. Massively Distributed Systems. Web site, 2001. http://www.research.ibm.com/massive/.

[14] V. A. Cicirello and S. F. Smith. Wasp-like Agents for Distributed Factory Coordination. *Journal of Autonomous Agents and Multi-Agent Systems*, 8(3 (May)):237-266, 2004.

[15] CIDL. Canadian Initiative on Digital Libraries / Initiative Canadienne sur les Bibliothèques Numériques. Web site, 2004. http://www.collectionscanada.ca/cidl/.

[16] S. J. Clark and H. V. D. Parunak. Density-Based Emergent Scheduling System. USA Patent # 5,953,229, Environmental Research Institute of Michigan, 1999.

[17] S. H. Clearwater, Editor. *Market-Based Control: A Paradigm for Distributed Resource Allocation.* Singapore, World Scientific, 1996.

[18] T. DeWolf. The Second International Workshop on Environments for Multiagent Systems. Web site, 2005. http://www.cs.kuleuven.ac.be/~distrinet/events/e4mas/.

[19] V. Dimitrov. Swarm-Like Dynamics and their Use in Organizations and Management. 2000. http://www.zulenet.com/VladimirDimitrov/pages/swarmanprint.html.

[20] DLF. Digital Library Federation. Web site, 2005. http://www.diglib.org/.

[21] DLib. D-Lib Magazine. Web site, 2005. http://www.dlib.org.

[22] DOT. ITS Joint Program Office Home. 2005. http://www.its.dot.gov.

[23] J. C. Dyer. Indian Trail Trees. 2004. http://home.att.net/~trailtrees/.

[24] eBay. eBay. Web site, 2005. http://www.ebay.com.

[25] A. M. El-Sayed. The Pherobase: Database of Insect Pheromones and Semiochemicals. 2005. http://www.pherobase.com.

[26] S. Forrest. Forrest Home page. Web site, 2005. http://www.cs.unm.edu/~forrest/.

[27] M. R. Garey and D. S. Johnson. *Computers and Intractability.* San Francisco, CA, W.H. Freeman, 1979.

[28] N. Gilbert, Editor. *Journal of Artificial Societies and Social Simulation.* Surrey, UK, University of Surrey, 1998-.

[29] N. Gilbert. Centre for Research on Simulation in the Social Sciences. Web Page, 2001. http://www.soc.surrey.ac.uk/research/simsoc/cress.html.

[30] Gnutella. Gnutella.com. Web site, 2005. http://www.gnutella.com/.

[31] Google. Google Technology. Web site, 2004. http://www.google.com/technology/.

[32] P.-P. Grassé. La Reconstruction du nid et les Coordinations Inter-Individuelles chez *Bellicositermes Natalensis et Cubitermes sp.* La théorie de la Stigmergie: Essai d'interprétation du Comportement des Termites Constructeurs. *Insectes Sociaux*, 6:41-84, 1959.

[33] J. Gregorio. Stigmergy and the World-Wide Web. Blog page, 2002. http://bitworking.org/news/Stigmergy.

[34] Groove Networks. Groove Virtual Office - Virtual office software for sharing files, projects and data. Web Site, 2005. http://www.groove.net/home/index.cfm.

[35] Y. Guan and W. Zhao. 2005 International Workshop on Security in Distributed Computing Systems (SDCS 2005). Web site, 2005. http://securityworkshop.ece.iastate.edu/.

[36] T. Hammond, T. Hannay, B. Lund, and J. Scott. Social Bookmarking Tools (I): A General Review. *D-Lib Magazine*, 11(4 (April)), 2005.

[37] D. Helbing, F. Schweitzer, J. Keltsch, and P. Molnár. Active Walker Model for the Formation of Human and Animal Trail Systems. Institute of Theoretical Physics, Stuttgart, Germany, 1998. http://xxx.lanl.gov/ps/cond-mat/9806097.

[38] F. Heylighen. Collaborative Filtering. Web page, 2001. http://pespmc1.vub.ac.be/COLLFILT.html.

[39] IEEE. IEEE Distributed Systems Online--Security. Web site, 2005. http://dsonline.computer.org/portal/site/dsonline/menuitem.9ed3d9924aeb0dcd82ccc6716bbe36ec/index.jsp?&pName=dso_level1&path=dsonline/topics/security&file=index.xml&xsl=article.xsl&;jsessionid=CGj1WsF77cmpLrdrnLm7558Lpwt8blznMbx075JDjftDV5k57RGf!1502094820.

[40] IEEE. IEEE ITSS Transactions and Society. 2005. http://www.ewh.ieee.org/tc/its/trans.html.

[41] IFLA. Digital Libraries: Resources and Projects. Web site, 2003. http://www.ifla.org/II/diglib.htm.

[42] ITS-STI Canada. ITS - STI Canada - Intelligent Transportation Systems Society of Canada | Systèmes de Transportes Intelligents Société du Canada. 2005. http://www.itscanada.ca/.

[43] ITS America. ITS America Home. 2005. http://www.itsa.org.

[44] R. E. Korf. A Simple Solution to Pursuit Games. In *Proceedings of Eleventh International Workshop on Distributed Artificial Intelligence*, pages 183-194, 1992.

[45] T. J. Lambert, III, M. A. Epelman, and R. L. Smith. A Fictitious Play Approach to Large-Scale Optimization. *Operations Research*, 53(3 (May-June)), 2005.

[46] C. Langton, R. Burkhart, and G. Ropella. The Swarm Simulation System. 1997. http://www.swarm.org.

[47] L. Leonardi, M. Mamei, and F. Zambonelli. Co-Fields: Towards a Unifying Model for Swarm Intelligence. DISMI-UNIMO-3-2002, University of Modena and Reggio Emilia, Modena, Italy, 2002. http://polaris.ing.unimo.it/didattica/curriculum/marco/Web-Co-Fields/stuff/Swarm.pdf.

[48] K. Lerman and A. Galstyan. A General Methodology for Mathematical Analysis of Multi-Agent Systems. ISI-TR-529, USC Information Sciences Institute, Marina del Rey, CA, 2001. http://www.isi.edu/%7Elerman/papers/isitr529.pdf.

[49] B. Leuf and W. Cunningham. Wiki: Welcome Visitors. Web site, 2002. http://wiki.org/.

[50] LOCKSS. LOCKSS Program Home. Web site, 2005. http://lockss.stanford.edu/.

[51] M. Mamei and F. Zambonelli. Spreading Pheromones in Everyday Environments via RFID Technologies. In *Proceedings of 2nd IEEE Symposium on Swarm Intelligence*, IEEE, 2005.

[52] M. Mamei, F. Zambonelli, and L. Leonardi. A Physically Grounded Approach to Coordinate Movements in a Team. In *Proceedings of First International Workshop on Mobile Teamwork (at ICDCS)*, IEEE CS Press, 2002.

[53] M. Mamei, F. Zambonelli, and L. Leonardi. Distributed Motion Coordination with Co-Fields: A Case Study in Urban Traffic Management. In *Proceedings of 6th IEEE Symposium on Autonomous Decentralized Systems (ISADS 2003)*, IEEE CS Press, 2003.

[54] L. Martineau. *The Rocks Begin to Speak*. Las Vegas, NV, KC Publications, 1973.

[55] F. Michel. *Formalisme, méthodologie et outils pour la modélisation et la simulation de systèmes multi-agents*. Thesis at Université des Sciences et Techniques du Languedoc, Department of Informatique, 2004.

[56] N. Monmarché. HaNT Web Site: Nicholas Monmarché. Web site, 2005. http://www.hant.li.univ-tours.fr/webhant/index.php?pageid=16.

[57] N. Monmarché. Personal Communication. 2005.

[58] M. Newman. Mark Newman. Web site, 2005. http://www-personal.umich.edu/~mejn/.

[59] M. E. J. Newman. The structure and function of complex networks. *SIAM Review*, 45:167-256, 2003.

[60] NSF. Digital Libraries Initiative Phase 2. Web site, 2003. http://www.dli2.nsf.gov/.

[61] L. Page, S. Brin, R. Motwani, and T. Winograd. The PageRank Citation Ranking: Bringing Order to the Web. Stanford Digital Library Technologies Project, Palo Alto, CA, 1998. http://citeseer.ist.psu.edu/page98pagerank.html.

[62] H. V. D. Parunak. Manufacturing Experience with the Contract Net. In M. N. Huhns, Editor, *Distributed Artificial Intelligence*, pages 285-310. Pitman, London, 1987.

[63] H. V. D. Parunak. Making Swarming Happen. In *Proceedings of Swarming and Network-Enabled C4ISR*, ASD C3I, 2003.

[64] H. V. D. Parunak. Challenging Old Assumptions in Global Information Management. In *Proceedings of ONR Conference on Collaborative Decision-Support Systems*, CADRC, California Polytechnic Institute, 2004.

[65] H. V. D. Parunak. Home page of H. Van Dyke Parunak. 2005. http://www.altarum.net/~vparunak/.

[66] H. V. D. Parunak, A. D. Baker, and S. J. Clark. The AARIA Agent Architecture: From Manufacturing Requirements to Agent-Based System Design. *Integrated Computer-Aided Engineering*, 8(1):45-58, 2001.

[67] H. V. D. Parunak and L. Barto. Agent-based Models and Manufacturing Processes. In *Proceedings of Embracing Complexity: The 1999 Colloquium on the Application of Complex Adaptive Systems to Business*, pages 109-118, Ernst & Young Center for Business Innovation, 1999.

[68] H. V. D. Parunak and S. Brueckner. Entropy and Self-Organization in Multi-Agent Systems. In *Proceedings of The Fifth International Conference on Autonomous Agents (Agents 2001)*, pages 124-130, ACM, 2001.

[69] H. V. D. Parunak and S. Brueckner. Swarming Coordination of Multiple UAV's for Collaborative Sensing. In *Proceedings of Second AIAA "Unmanned Unlimited" Systems, Technologies, and Operations Conference*, AIAA, 2003.

[70] H. V. D. Parunak, S. Brueckner, J. Sauter, and R. Savit. Effort Profiles in Multi-Agent Resource Allocation. In *Proceedings of Autonomous Agents and Multi-Agent Systems (AAMAS02)*, pages 248-255, 2002.

[71] H. V. D. Parunak, S. Brueckner, and R. Savit. Universality in Multi-Agent Systems. In *Proceedings of Third International Joint Conference on Autonomous Agents and Multi-Agent Systems (AAMAS 2004)*, pages 930-937, IEEE, 2004.

[72] H. V. D. Parunak and S. A. Brueckner. Engineering Swarming Systems. In F. Bergenti, M.-P. Gleizes, and F. Zambonelli, Editors, *Methodologies and Software Engineering for Agent Systems*, pages 341-376. Kluwer, 2004.

[73] H. V. D. Parunak, S. A. Brueckner, and J. Odell. Swarming Pattern Detection in Sensor and Robot Networks. In *Proceedings of 10th International Conference on Robotics and Remote Systems for Hazardous Environments*, American Nuclear Society (ANS), 2004.

[74] H. V. D. Parunak, S. A. Brueckner, J. A. Sauter, and R. Matthews. Global Convergence of Local Agent Behaviors. In *Proceedings of Fourth International Joint Conference on Autonomous Agents and Multi-Agent Systems (AAMAS05)*, pages 305-312, 2005.

[75] H. V. D. Parunak, A. C. Ward, M. Fleischer, and J. A. Sauter. The RAPPID Project: Symbiosis between Industrial Requirements and MAS Research. *Autonomous Agents and Multi-Agent Systems*, 2:2 (June):111-140, 1999.

[76] H. V. D. Parunak, A. C. Ward, and J. A. Sauter. A Systematic Market Approach to Distributed Constraint Problems. In *Proceedings of International Conference on Multi-Agent Systems (ICMAS'98)*, pages 455-456, American Association for Artificial Intelligence, 1998.

[77] H. V. D. Parunak, A. C. Ward, and J. A. Sauter. The MarCon Algorithm: A Systematic Market Approach to Distributed Constraint Problems. *AI-EDAM: Artificial Intelligence for Engineering Design, Analysis and Manufacturing*, 13(3):217-234, 1999.

[78] R. Pastor-Satorras and A. Vespignani. Epidemic Spreading in Scale-Free Networks. *Physical Review Letters*, 86:3200-3203, 2001.

[79] D. Payton, M. Daily, and K. Martin. Dynamic collaborator discovery in information intensive environments. *ACM Computing Surveys*, 31(2 (June)), 1999.

[80] K. Pister. Smart Dust: Autonomous sensing and communication in a cubic millimeter. Web Page, 2001. http://robotics.eecs.berkeley.edu/~pister/SmartDust/.

[81] E. Rimon and D. E. Kodischek. Exact Robot Navigation Using Artificial Potential Functions. *IEEE Transactions on Robotics and Automation*, 8(5 (October)):501-518, 1992.

[82] J. Robb. Stigmergic Learning and Global Guerillas. Web page, 2004. http://globalguerrillas.typepad.com/globalguerrillas/2004/07/stigmergic_syst.html.

[83] R. Savit, S. A. Brueckner, H. V. D. Parunak, and J. Sauter. Phase Structure of Resource Allocation Games. *Physics Letters A*, 311:359-364, 2002.

[84] R. Savit, S. A. Brueckner, H. V. D. Parunak, and J. Sauter. General Structure of a Class of Resource Allocation Games. *Physica A*, 345:676-704, 2005.

[85] D. Scheidt. Personal Communication. 2005.

[86] N. Streitz and P. Nixon. Special Issue on The Disappearing Computer. *Communications of the ACM*, vol. 48, pages 32-71, 2005.

[87] Transport Canada. Intelligent Transportation Systems. 2005. http://www.its-sti.gc.ca/en/menu.htm.

[88] U.S. Army. Army Knowledge Online. 2005. https://www.us.army.mil/suite/login/welcome.html#.

[89] Université de Reims. CReSTIC: Centre de Recherche en Sciences et Technologies de l'Information et de la Communication. 2005. http://crestic.univ-reims.fr/.

[90] University of Chicago. RePast: An Agent Based Modelling Toolkit for Java. Web Page, 2003. http://repast.sourceforge.net/.

[91] P. Valckenaers, H. V. Brussel, K. Hadeli, O. Bochmann, B. S. Germain, and C. Zamfirescu. On the design of emergent systems: an investigation of integration and interoperability issues. *Engineering Applications of Artificial Intelligence*, 16:377-393, 2003.

[92] H. Varian. *Intermediate Microeconomics*. Fifth ed. New York, NY, W. W. Norton, 1999.

[93] T. Wagner. Coordinators. Web site, 2004. http://www.darpa.mil/ipto/Programs/coordinators/index.htm.

[94] F. Wang. Self-Organizing Communities Formed by Middle Agents. In *Proceedings of First International Conference on Autonomous Agents and Multi-Agent Systems (AAMAS 2002)*, pages 1333-1339, 2002.

[95] P. Weinstein, H. V. D. Parunak, P. Chiusano, and S. Brueckner. Agents Swarming in Semantic Spaces to Corroborate Hypotheses. In *Proceedings of AAMAS 2004*, pages 1488-1489, 2004.

[96] F. Weiskopf and D. Scheidt. Cooperative Autonomous UAV Team. *Presentation at Swarming Entities – Joint C4ISR DSC Study Plan Conference*, Johns Hopkins University Applied Physics Laboratory, Laurel, MD, 2002.

[97] D. Weyns. Homepage of Danny Weyns. Web page, 2005. http://www.cs.kuleuven.ac.be/~danny/home.html.

[98] D. Weyns. Homepage of Danny Weyns. Web site, 2005. http://www.cs.kuleuven.ac.be/~danny/home.html.

[99] D. Weyns, H. V. D. Parunak, F. Michel, T. Holvoet, and J. Ferber. Multiagent Systems, State-of-the-Art and Research Challenges. In *Proceedings of Workshop on Environments for Multi-Agent Systems (E4MAS 2004)*, pages 1-47, Springer, 2004.

[100] Wikipedia. RFID. Web page, 2005. http://en.wikipedia.org/wiki/RFID.

[101] Wikipedia. Wikipedia, The Free Encyclopedia. Web site, 2005. http://en.wikipedia.org/wiki/Main_Page.

[102] U. Wilensky. NetLogo. Web site, 1999. http://ccl.northwestern.edu/netlogo.

[103] R. F. Wilson. The Six Simple Principles of Viral Marketing. *Web Marketing Today*, 2000. http://www.wilsonweb.com/wmt5/viral-principles.htm.

[104] K. Wunderlich, D. Kaufman, and R. L. Smith. Link Travel Time Prediction for Decentralized Route Guidance Architectures. *IEEE Transactions on Intelligent Transportation Systems*, 1(1 (March)):4-14, 2000.

[105] C.-Z. Xu and X. Zhou. The First International Workshop on Security in Systems and Networks (SSN2005). Web site, 2005. http://www.cs.uccs.edu/~SNS/sns2005.html.

[106] F. Ygge and H. Akkermans. Power Load Management as a Computational Market. In *Proceedings of Second International Conference on Multi-Agent Systems (ICMAS-96)*, pages 393-400, AAAI, 1996.

[107] F. Ygge and H. Akkermans. Decentralized Markets versus Central Control: A Comparative Study. *Journal of Artificial Intelligence Research*, 11:301-333, 1999.

[108] F. Zambonelli. Home page for Franco Zambonelli. Web site, 2005. http://www.dismi.unimo.it/Members/fzambonelli.

[109] F. Zambonelli, M. P. Gleizes, M. Mamei, and R. Tolksdorf. Spray Computers: Explorations in Self-Organization. *Journal of Pervasive and Mobile Computing*, 1(1 (March)), 2005.

[110] F. Zambonelli and V. Parunak. Towards a Paradigm Change in Computer Science and Software Engineering: a Synthesis. *The Knowledge Engineering Review*, (forthcoming), 2004.

Augmenting the Physical Environment Through Embedded Wireless Technologies

Marco Mamei and Franco Zambonelli

Dipartimento di Scienze e Metodi dell'Ingegneria,
University of Modena and Reggio Emilia,
Via Allegri 13, 42100 Reggio Emilia, Italy
{mamei.marco, franco.zambonelli}@unimo.it

Abstract. Emerging pervasive computing technologies such as sensor networks and RFID tags can be embedded in our everyday environment to digitally store and elaborate a variety of information about the surrounding. By having application agents access in a dynamic and wireless way such distributed information, it is possible to enforce a notable degree of context-awareness in applications, increase the capabilities of interacting with the physical world, and eventually give a concrete meaning to the abstract concept of agent situatedness. This paper discusses how both sensor networks and RFID tags can be used to that purpose, outlining the respective advantages and drawbacks of these technologies. Then, to ground the discussion, it presents a multiagent application for physical object tracking, facilitating the finding of "forgot-somewhere" objects in an environment.

1 Introduction

The never ending technological progresses in miniaturization of electronic devices and in wireless communication technologies are making possible to enrich our everyday environments (and any objects in them) with sensing, computation, and communication capabilities [1]. Overall, this may end up in an increased capability of interacting with the physical world by acquiring, in a digital form and in a wireless way, a number of information beyond the normal sensing capabilities of humans and robots, as well as in the possibility of exploiting the devices embedded in the environment as a pervasive platform for distributed computing and communication.

With reference to the multiagent systems paradigm and to agent-oriented software engineering [2], the advent of such pervasive computing technologies notably impacts on the concept of *situatedness*. Agents have always been assumed – by very definition [3] – as entities whose activities are related to some sensing and effective of the properties of some environment in which they situate for execution. However, despite this, the concept of environment has always been an overlooked topic, and a few proposals for agent languages and architectures explicitly deal with this concept in a constructive way [4]. Pervasive computing

D. Weyns, H. Van Dyke Parunak, and F. Michel (Eds.): E4MAS 2005, LNAI 3830, pp. 187–204, 2006.

technologies, by making available to application agents expressive digital information about the environment, can leverage the concept of situatedness from a mere conceptual definition to a practical useful feature.

Starting from the above considerations, this paper discusses which technologies can be actually used to this purpose. In particular, this paper shortly presents both sensor network technologies [1] and RFID technologies [5], and discusses how they can be exploited to augment the physical environments with the possibility of easily accessing digital information, as well as with the possibility of enforcing forms of stigmergic (i.e., environment-mediated) interactions across the physical environment. A comparative analysis of these two technologies outlines their respective advantages and limitations, and their potentials in pervasive multiagent system applications.

To ground the discussion, we presents our own experience in the implementation of a multiagent application for stigmergic physical object tracking, allowing agents (whether in the form of autonomous robots or computer-assisted humans) to find "forgot-somewhere" objects in an environment. The application relies on pheromone-based interaction, and exploit RFID tags as a physically distributed memory infrastructure in which agents can deploy pheromones and that agents can access for reading pheromone paths spread in the environment.

The rest of this paper is organized as follows. Section 2 introduces in general the concept of situatedness and the problem of interacting with physical environment. Section 3 presents and discusses sensor network technologies, while Section 4 presents and discusses RFID technologies. Section 5 presents our experience in RFID-based object tracking. Section 6 concludes and outlines open directions.

2   Situatedness and Physical Environments

While the concept of situatedness plays a fundamental role in the engineering of multiagent systems, the practical application of the concept cannot abstract from what actual infrastructures are available to model the environment and to interact with it. In this section, after having discussed the various facets of situatedness, we analyse how pervasive computing technologies can be used to somehow "augment" a physical environment to facilitate agents in interacting with it.

2.1   Computational vs. Physical Environments

Software systems are rarely developed to be deployed as stand-alone, isolated systems. Rather, in most practical cases, software systems (and multiagent systems specifically) are designed for being deployed in some sort of existing computational or physical environments, and have to necessarily interact with such environments to properly accomplish their tasks [6].

As far as computational environments are concerned, modern distributed applications are always built to interact with an existing world of data, services, and computational resources, and have to get advantage of them. For instance, in multiagent systems for Web-based applications agents are deployed in the Web and have to mine Web data to exploit available services in order to achieve specific goals [7]. In the Grid, agents have to interact and negotiate for accessing computational and memory resources [8]. In P2P systems, networks of autonomous components (that can be assimilated to agents) have to connect and interact with each other in order to provide access to large set of shared files [9,10].

As far as physical environments are concerned, the market is more and more demanding for a strict inter-twining of software and the physical world. Firstly, mobile computing technologies, enabling us to stay connected 24 by 7 from wherever, require context-awareness and context-dependency, to have our computer-supported activities properly adapted to the physical context and situation from which we are performing them [11]. Secondly, more and more autonomous software systems (or, which is the same, systems of autonomous robots [12]) are in need to be deployed to monitor and/or control processes occurring in the physical world, e.g., system for control of manufacturing processes [13] or of human activities [14].

2.2 Environment-Mediated Interactions

The considerations in the above subsection justify the adoption of situatedness as a central concept in the engineering of multiagent systems. However, whether one consider computational or physical environments, the role of the environment does not simply reduce to a source of information and services, or to a set of entities that should be controlled by the multiagent system itself. Rather, the environment can also play the active central role of interaction medium, i.e., of infrastructural support for agent interactions that can occur with the active mediation of some sort of environment.

Environment-mediated interaction (aka stigmergic interaction [15]) plays an important role in nature. Indeed, the spreading and sensing of pheromones in an environment to organize the activities of ant colonies, the process of morphogenesis as enforced by diffusion of chemicals in the embryo, the movement of masses induced by gravitational fields, are all examples of stigmergic interactions [16]. In the last few years, however, stigmergic models of interactions have been recognized as very powerful to facilitate interactions in dynamic distributed systems. Indeed, stigmergic models of interactions, whether relying on synthetic pheromones, on diffusion of digital chemicals, or on spreading of virtual computational fields, are being proposed to facilitate the enforcement of adaptive interaction patterns in dynamic distributed systems and to promote self-organization and self-adaptation of activities [15,9,14]. Thus, the presence of some environment in which multiagent systems situates can also be exploited to support stigmergic forms of interactions.

2.3 Augmenting Physical Environments

In the case of agents situated in a computational environment (e.g., the Web, a P2P network, or the Grid), supporting the interaction of agents with such an environment is a rather natural process. Simply, multiagent systems are computational entities the same as the environment, and once proper data formats and interaction protocols are established, the access to the computational environment (and possibly the exploitation of such environment as an infrastructure in which to store the units of stigmergic interactions) becomes rather easy: the "sensors" and the "effectors" that the agents may use to interact reduce to a set of APIs or programming constructs.

The problem is totally different in the case of a physical environment. In this case, to access the physical environment, agents must be somehow be capable of perceiving and affecting physical properties. To this extent, an agent (whether in the form of an autonomous robot, or of an embedded controller, or of some software running on a mobile devices) must be necessarily supported by some hardware sensors and effectors to properly interact with the world.

Traditionally, most approaches for physically situated agents, assume that agents are augmented with the necessary capabilities for sensing and effecting the physical world. For instance, in the case of autonomous robots, traditional approaches assume that the robot itself is equipped with videocameras, temperature sensors, location sensors (e.g., GPS), and robotic hands. Such approach tends to notably increase the internal complexity of agents. In fact, agents not only have to perform the computational activities associated to deciding how to accomplish a goal, but have also to take care of properly internalizing and interpreting the data coming form the associated sensors, and of properly controlling their effectors to actualize their actions.

Another drawback of the above approach is that the physical environment can hardly be used to support stigmergic models of interactions, unless one adopt rather tricky solutions. If the environment is purely physical, in fact, stigmergic interactions should occur by physically affecting the properties of the environment. For example, to mimic the behavior of ants, robots would be forced to actually pollute the environment with some kind of marker, and would have to be equipped with sensor to perceive such marks [17].

The advent of pervasive computing technologies dramatically changes this scenarios. The availability of small-scale and low-cost devices that can be distributed in physical environment in a non intrusive way, that can be devoted to sense (or affect) specific properties in the environment, and that enable to interact with them in a wireless way (a capability to be easily provided to agents), enables agents to externalize all the activities devoted to interpret and control their physical activities. Simply, sensing and effecting the environment reduces in properly accessing some digital services. The result is in a notable reduction of complexity in agents, both at the hardware and at the software level.

In addition, the presence in an environment of embedded computational resources, as those that can be provided by the embedded computing devices, can be fruitfully exploited as an infrastructure to support stigmergic models of interactions. In fact, stigmergy can take place without actually affecting the physical environment, but simply by exploiting the distributed embedded resources as stores for those data structures that are at the basis of stigmergy, e.g., pheromones, fields, etc.

Clearly, depending on the specific technologies and devices adopted, the interactions with the environment and the support of stigmergic coordination models can be more or less facilitated. In the following of this paper, we analyze in detail two different classes of devices (sensor networks and RFID tags), discuss how they can be exploited, and outline their respective advantages and drawbacks.

3   Ad-Hoc and Sensor Network

As proved in the context of the Smart Dust project at Berkeley [18,19], it is already possible to produce fully-fledged computer-based systems of a few cm^3, and even much smaller ones will be produced in the next few years. Such computers, which can be enriched with communication capabilities (radio or optical), local sensing (e.g., optical, thermal, or inertial) and local effecting (e.g., optical and mechanical) capabilities, are the basic ingredients of the sensor network scenario (see Fig. 1-top).

Such a scenario implies spreading (i.e., deploying) a large number of these sensing devices across an environment, letting them create an ad-hoc wireless network by communicating with each other and perform some kind of distributed application. Traditional applications can vary from monitoring of physical parameters (e.g., monitoring weather) and distributed surveillance (e.g., tracking vehicles crossing a specific area) (see Fig. 1-bottom).

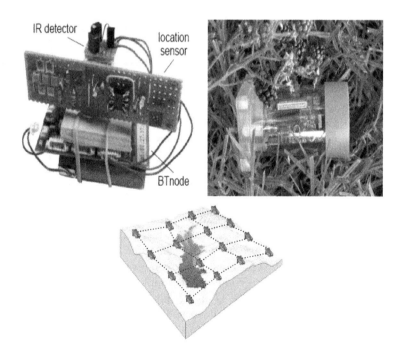

Fig. 1. (top) Wireless sensor devices. (bottom) sensor network in an environment.

3.1 Deploying Digital Information

In general terms, sensor networks are an ideal platform to augment the physical environment with digital information.

- Sensors can store data to represent some kind of contextual information. Moreover, they can deliver such data to agents (e.g., users with PDA) passing nearby.
- Sensors can perform computations to support and facilitate the agents' fruition to that data. For example, sensors can propagate and diffuse data across the network. They can automatically delete old and possibly corrupted information. They can combine and transform data to let it become more expressive and easy to use.

Sensors can provide agents with the data they collect to support context-awareness. For example, an agent getting an extremely-high temperature reading from a sensor nearby can infer the presence of fire and act consequently. Sensors provided with GPS devices or running a beacon-based localization algorithm [20] can provide location information. An agent getting the location of sensors nearby can infer its own actual position.

Other than providing contextual information coming from the "outside" world, sensor network can also be used to store and convey information produced by the agent themselves. Following this approach, the sensor network acts as a coordination media supporting agents' decoupled interactions and coordination [21,22]. For example, the sensors can act as a collection of distributed tuple spaces that can be accessed by agents for the sake of enforcing coordination [23].

Moreover, relying on the sensor networking capabilities it is possible to spread distributed data structures across the environment. Data structures can be injected in the sensor network by agents and then propagate across. In addition, sensors can run maintenance algorithms to fix the data structure to account for changing conditions and dynamic networks [24].

To clarify these concepts let us focus on the problem of coordinating the movements of some autonomous agents in a distributed environment. In particular, we focus on the simple application of having two persons, provided with a PDA, moving across an environment instrumented with a sensor network infrastructure. The goal of the application is to allow one person to be guided by the PDA, to follow the other person. A simple solution based distributed data structures is the let the person to-be-followed to spread in the environment (i.e., sensor network) a data structure that increases an integer value by one at every hop as it gets farther from the source. This creates a sort of gradient that can be followed downhill by the other person to complete the application [25] (see Fig. 2(a)). If the person to-be-followed moves, it is important that the data structure adjust its shape accordingly, so that the gradient leads to that person anyway (see Fig. 2(b)). To this end, sensor nodes can run specific maintenance algorithms to keep the data structure consistent.

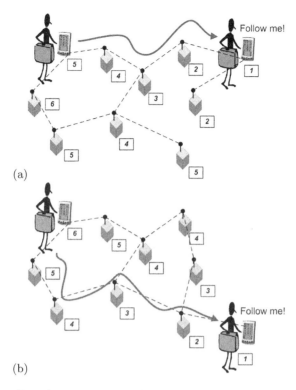

Fig. 2. (a) A gradient data structure enables an agent to follow another one. (b) The data structure is updated to reflect the new agent position.

3.2 Pros and Cons

The power of this approach is that the distributed data structure provides expressive contextual information tailored for that specific task. The agent running on the PDA does not need to know any map of the environment, nor it has to execute complex algorithms to decide where to go. It just blindly follows the data structure. All the complexity of the application is moved away form from the agents and diverted into the environment-infrastructure.

Sensor networks are a powerful technology to support environment abstractions in multi-agent systems. In the long run, once current technological problems will be properly addressed, it will be the leading infrastructure of environment applications. Its main strength is that it is an *active* infrastructure: sensor nodes can run (distributed) algorithms to process data as required. For example, sensor nodes can proactively delete old information or run algorithm to aggregate data on needs. At present, however, this is also sensor network main weakness. Nodes suffer, in fact, from battery-exhaustion problems, they are costly and failure prone.

3.3   Related Work

A number of recent proposals address the problem of defining supporting environments for the development of adaptive, dynamic, context-aware distributed applications, suitable for pervasive computing.

The TinyLime middleware [26] proposes accessing the environmental data collected by a sensor network via an associative tuple-based mechanisms. When a user with a mobile device "walks-through" a network of distributed sensors, all the data collected by the in-range sensors automatically feeds a local tuple space of the mobile device, which thus can perceive sensorial data collected by sensors simply by reading in the local tuple space.

ObjectPlaces [27] is an interesting middleware infrastructure that offers support to exchange and share information among nodes in mobile and ad-hoc networks. Specifically, in ObjectPlaces, agents communicate indirectly through the exchange of objects that can be temporarily stored across suitable object-places (that are virtual containers stored in the ad-hoc network itself). Agents invoke operations to add and remove objects, or to observe the content of a specific object-place (via a pattern-matching process). Agents can also create object-places dynamically, and link them together to form a graph-like environment connecting related object-places.

TOTA [24] and Smart Messages [28] are two architectures for computation and communication in large networks of embedded systems. Communication is realized by sending "smart tuples" in the network, i.e., tuples which include code to be executed at each hop in the network path. These models comply with the general idea of putting intelligence in the network by letting tuples and messages execute hop-by-hop small chunk of code to determine their propagation.

Lime [29] and XMIDDLE [30] exploits transiently tuple spaces as the basis for interaction in dynamic network scenario. Each mobile device, as well as each network nodes, owns a private tuple space. Upon connection with other devices or with network nodes, the privately owned tuple spaces can merge in a federated tuple space, to be used as a common data space to exchange information.

4   RFID Technology

Advances in miniaturization and manufacturing have yielded postage-stamp sized radio transceivers called Radio Frequency Identification (RFID) tags that can be attached unobtrusively to objects as small as a toothbrush. The tags are wireless and battery free. Each tag is marked with an unique identifier and provided with a tiny memory, up to some KB for advanced models, allowing to store data. Tags can be purchased off the shelf, cost roughly 0.20 Euro each and can withstand day-to-day use for years (being battery-free, they do not have power-exhaustion problems). Suitable devices, called RFID readers, can access RFID tags by radio, either for read and write operations. The tags respond or store data accordingly using power scavenged from the signal coming from the RFID reader. RFID readers divide into short- and long-range depending on the distance within which they can access RFID tags. Such distance may vary from few centimeters up to some meters. Deploying RFID technology requires that a number of places in the environment (e.g. doors, corridors, etc.) or objects (e.g. beds, washing machines, etc.) are tagged with RFID tags. Tagging a place or an object involves sticking an RFID tag on it, and making a database entry mapping the tag ID to a name. It is worth emphasizing that current trends indicate that within a few years, many household objects and furniture may be RFID-tagged before purchase, thus eliminating the overhead of tagging [31]. Moreover, some handheld devices start to be provided with RFID read and write capabilities (the Nokia 5140 phone can be already equipped with a RFID reader [32]).

4.1 Deploying Digital Information

The set of RFID tags deployed across the environment can be regarded as an infrastructure to store and deliver digital information.

From a general perspective, accessing the RFID tags nearby is a powerful source of context information. For example, RFID tags can reveal the location of agents in that tags can be associated to uniquely identified places. So reading the tag associated with "Prof. Smith desk" can let an agent infer its location as "Prof. Smith office". More in general, the knowledge of RFID tags (and thus objects) nearby can possibly identify a specific application context (e.g. reading a LCD-projector tag, and a microphone tag can let the agent infer of being in a meeting room).

In addition, given the fact that RFID tags can be written on-the-fly, agents can use the tags as a distributed shared memory with which to exchange information. For example, RFID tags can be accessed as if they were distributed tuple spaces [33]. A particulary significant development of this idea is related to spreading pheromone-inspired distributed data structures across the tags in the environment. The basic scenario consists of human users and robots carrying handheld computing devices, provided with a RFID reader, and running an agent-based application. The agent, unobtrusively from the user, continuously detects in range tags as the user roams across the environment. Moreover, the agent controls the RFID reader to write pheromone data structures (consisting at least in a pheromone ID) in all the tags encountered. This process creates a digital pheromone trail distributed across the tags. More formally, let us call $L(t)$ the set of tags being sensed at time t. It is easy to see that the agent can infer that the user is moving if $L(t) \neq L(t-1)$. If instructed to spread pheromone O, the agent will write O in all the $L(t)$-$L(t-1)$ tags as it moves across the environment. For the majority of applications a pheromone trail, consisting of only an ID, is not very useful. Like in ant foraging, most applications involve agents to follow each other pheromone trails to reach the location where the agents that originally laid down the trail were directed (or, on the contrary, to reach the location where they came from). Unfortunately, an agent crossing an-only-ID-trail would not be able to choose in which direction the agent that laid down that trail was directed. From the agent point of view, this situation is like crossing a road without knowing whether to turn left or right. To overcome this problem, the agent stores in the tags also an ever increasing hop-counter associated with O - we will call this counter $C(O)$. In particular, if an agent decides to spread pheromone O at time t, the agent reads also the counter C(O) in the L(t) set (if C(O) is not present, the agent sets C(O) to a fixed value zero). Upon a movement, the agent will store O and C(O)+1 in the tags belonging to L(t+1) that do not have O or have a lower C(O). In addition, the basic pheromone idea requires a pheromone evaporation mechanism to discard old - possibly corrupted - trails. To this end we store in the tag also a value T(O) representing the time where the pheromone O has been stored.

To read pheromones, an agent trivially accesses neighbor RFID tags reading their memories. Since RFID read operations are quite unreliable, the agent actually performs a reading cycle merging the results obtained at each iteration. Given the result, the agent will decide how to act on the basis of the perceived pheromone configuration. To realize pheromone evaporation, after reading a tag, an agent checks, for each pheromone, whether the associated timestamp is, accordingly to the agent local time, older than a certain threshold T. If it is so, the agent deletes that pheromone from the tag. This kind of pheromone evaporation leads to two key advantages:

1. Since the data space in RFID tags is severely limited, it would be most useful to store only those pheromone trails that are important for the application at a given time; old, unused pheromones can be removed.
2. If an agent does not carry its personal digital assistant or if it has been switched off, it is possible that some actions will be undertaken without leaving the corresponding pheromone trails. This cause old-pheromone trails to be possibly out-of-date, and eventually corrupted. In this context, it is of course fundamental to design a mechanism to reinforce relevant pheromones not to let them evaporate.

With this regard, an agent spreading pheromone O, will overwrite O-pheromones having an older T(O). From these considerations, it should be clear that the threshold T has to be tuned for each application, to represent the time-frame after which the pheromone is considered useless or possibly corrupted.

4.2 Pros and Cons

The main point in favor of this approach is its extremely low cost since it uses technologies (RFID) that are likely to be soon embedded in the scenario independently of this application. Relying on such an implementation, a wide range of application scenarios based on pheromone interaction can be realized ranging from multi-robot coordination [34], to monitoring of human activities [35].

The main problem with this approach is related to current limitations of RFID technology. Accessing tags for reading and writing operations can fail for a number of hardly controllable issues (electromagnetic disturbances, metallic objects nearby, interferences and collisions, etc.). Moreover, in the next section, we will present and discuss some limitations in our RFID implementation of the pheromone evaporation mechanism.

4.3 Related Work

Several proposals, as well as ours, consider the idea of having mobile devices integrated with a RFID reader, thus having the capability of accessing RFID tags around, as sorts of digital contextual information stores. However, rather than considering the possibility of storing new information in RFID tags and enforcing coordination through them, most approaches exploit RFID tags only for reading pre-existent environmental/contextual information. For instance, the system described in [36] proposes associating location information with tags (e.g., "I am the tag of the living room") that can be read by mobile robots carrying on a RFID reader to roughly localize themselves.

The system described in [35] exploits RFID tags for inferring information about contextual activity in an environment. Users are assumed to wear an RFID reader connected with a Wi-Fi portable device so that, when the user moves and acts in the environment, the type and the sequence of tags read by the reader can suggest what the user is doing. For example, reading the tag associated to the user boss and of a video projector can let infer that the user is in a sort of important meeting with his/her boss.

Pheromones spread in the environment can enable a group of users (both humans and robotics) to coordinate their respective movements. An exemplary application would be distributed environment exploration. Users could decide to explore a specific area if there are not pheromones pointing in that direction (the area is truly unexplored). In this context, it is important to remark that this approach clearly requires the presence of RFID tags before pheromones can be spread. If the environment does not contain tags at all, this approach could not be used. However, on the one hand, RFID tags are likely to be soon densely present in everywhere (embedded in tiles, bricks, furniture, etc.). On the other hand, it is possible to conceive solutions where agents physically deploy RFID tags while exploring the environment to be used for subsequent coordination. For instance, future development in plastic (and printable) RFID technology [37] let us envision the possibility of enriching an agent with a simple RFID printer to dynamically print in pavements, walls, or any type of surface, RFID tags.

5 Pheromone-Based Object Tracking

In this section, to ground the discussion, we present a concrete application to test the introduced RFID approach. It consists in an agent-based application to easily find everyday objects (glasses, keys, etc.) forgot somewhere in our homes. The application allows everyday objects to leave virtual pheromone trails across our homes to be easily tracked afterwards.

5.1 Overview

Overall, the object tracking application work as follows:

- The objects to be tracked need to be tagged. For sake of clarity, we will refer to these tags as object-tags to distinguish them from the tags identifying places in the environment.

- Agents (either robotic or humans) are provided with a handheld computing
  device, connected to a RFID reader, and running an agent-based application.
- The agent-based application can detect, via the RFID reader, object-tags
  carried on by the user. Exploiting the mechanism described in the previous
  section, it can spread a pheromone identifying such objects into the available
  memory of near tags.
- This allows the object to leave a pheromone trail across the tags in the
  environment.
- When looking for an object, a user can instruct the agent to read in-range
  tags searching the object's pheromone in their memory. If such pheromone
  is found, the user can follow it to reach the object current location.
- Once the object has been reached, if it moves with the user (i.e. the user
  grabbed it), the agent automatically starts spreading again the object associated pheromone, to keep consistency with the new object location.

This application naturally suits a multi-user scenario where an user (or a
robot), looking for an object moved by another user, can suddenly cross the
pheromone trail the object left while moved by the other user.

5.2   Spreading Pheromones to Track Object

To spread pheromones, the agent needs first to understand which objects are
currently being carried (i.e. moved around) by the user. To perform this task
unobtrusively, it accesses the RFID reader to detect in-range RFID tags once a
second. Let us call $O(t)$ the set of object-tags being sensed at time t, $L(t)$ the
set of tags being sensed at time t. If the agent senses an object-tag O such that
$O \in O(t)$, $O \notin O(t-1)$, but $L(t) \neq L(t-1)$, then the agent can infer that the user
picked-up the object O and the object is moving around. In this situation, the
agent has to spread O pheromone in the new location. To this end, the agent
writes O in the available memory space of all the $L(t)$ tags that do not already
contain O. This operation is performed, for every object O, upon every subsequent movement. Similarly, if the agent senses that an object-tag $O \in O(t-1)$,
but $O \notin O(t)$, then the agent infers that the user left object O. When this situation is detected the agent stops spreading O pheromone. These operations create
pheromone trails of the object being moved around.

  Once requested to track an object O the agent will start reading, once per
second, nearby tags looking for an O-pheromone within the sensed tags $L(t)$. If
such a pheromone is found, this implies that the user crossed a suitable pheromone trail. There are two alternatives: either in $L(t)$ there are two tags having
O-pheromones with different $C(O)$, or $L(t)$ contains only one tag. In the former
(lucky) case, the agent notifies the user about the fact it has crossed a pheromone
trail and it suggest to move towards those tag having the higher $C(O)$. In the
following, we will refer to this as grad-search, since it is like following a gradient
uphill. In the latter (unlucky) case, the agent notifies the user about the fact it
has crossed a pheromone trail, but nothing else. In such situation, the user has
to move in the neighborhood, trying to find higher $C(O)$ indicating the right

direction to be followed (this is like dowsing – i.e. finding underground water with a forked stick – but it works!). In the following, we will refer to this as local-search. Following the agent advices, the user gets closer and closer to the object by following its pheromone trail, until reaching it.

5.3   Implementation and Experiments

To assess the validity of the presented approach and the effectiveness of the object tracking application, we developed a number of experiments, both adopting the real implementation and an ad-hoc simulation (to test on the large scale).

Implementation. The real implementation consisted in tagging places and objects within our department. Overall, we tagged 100 locations within the building (doors, hallways, corridors, desks, etc.) and 50 objects (books, laptops, cd-cases, etc.). Locations have been tagged with ISO15693 RFID tags, each with a storage capacity of 512 bits (each tag contains 30 slots, 1 byte each, thus it is able to

a)   b)

c)

Fig. 3. (a) Our test-bed hardware implementation. (b) Some tagged objects. (c) The Lego Mindstorms robots performing pheromone search.

store 10 pheromones). Objects have been tagged with ISO14443B RFID tags, each with a storage capacity of 176 bits (each tag contains only the object ID) [38]. In addition, we set up three HP IPAQ 36xx running Familiar Linux 0.72 and J2ME (CVM - Personal Profile). Each IPAQ is provided with a WLAN card and a M21xH RFID reader. Each IPAQ runs the described agent-based application. Finally, a mobile robot has been realized by installing one of our wireless IPAQ (connected to a RFID reader) on a Lego Mindstorms robot (see Fig. 3).

To test on the large scale, we realized a JAVA-based simulation of the above scenario. The simulation is based on a random graph of places (each associated to a tag), and on a number of objects (each associated to an object-tag) randomly deployed in the locations-graph. Each tag has been simply realized by an array of integer values. A number of agents wanders randomly across the locations-graph collecting objects, releasing objects, and spreading pheromones accordingly. At the same time, other agents look for objects in the environment eventually exploiting pheromone trails previously laid down by other agents. For the sake of comparison, we implemented 3 search algorithms: in blind-search, an agent explores the locations-graph disregarding pheromones. In local-search, the agent perceives the pheromones in its current node, but it cannot see the direction in which the pheromones increase. In grad-search, the agent perceives pheromones together with the directions in which they increase. The simulator, allows to perform a number of experiments changing a number of parameters such as the graph size, the number of objects, the number of agents involved, the storage capacity of the tags, etc.

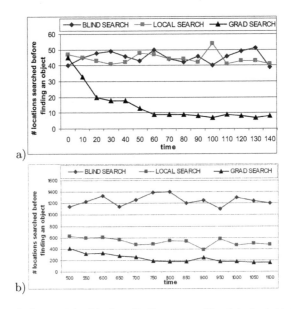

Fig. 4. Number of places visited before finding a specific object plotted over time. (a) 100 tagged places. (b) 2500 tagged places.

Experiments. A first group of experiments (reported in Fig. 4) aims at verifying the effectiveness of the application. Specifically, we set up two environments: one consisting of 100 tagged places with 100 objects (Fig. 4-a) and another consisting of 2500 tagged places with 500 objects (Fig. 4-b). 10 agents populate these environments wandering around moving objects and spreading pheromones and, at the same time, looking for specific objects. In the experiments, we report the number of places visited (i.e. number of tags perceived) before finding specific objects, for different search methods, plotted over time. These results are the average of a number (over 300) of simulated experiments and verified - on a smaller scale - on the real implementation.

The more time passes the more pheromone trails get deployed. It is easy to see that blind-search does not take advantage of pheromone trails and in fact objects are found after visiting on-average half of the places. Grad-search takes a great advantage of pheromones, in fact, after several pheromone trails have been deployed, less than 10% of the places need to be visited before finding the object. Local-search is useful only in large scenarios: the time taken wandering randomly in a neighborhood, looking for the direction where a pheromone increases, hides pheromone benefits in small environments.

A second group of experiments aims at exploring the effects of RFID tag storage saturation upon pheromone spread. This of course represents a big problem, in fact, it can happen that pheromone trails can be interrupted, because there is not available space left on neighbor tags, while the object to be tracked moves away. This create a broken pheromone trail leading to a place that is not the actual location of the object.

In Fig. 5, we report an experiment conducted in the 100-tagged-places-environment described before. This time the tag capacity has been fixed to 50 pheromones (150 bytes), and we plot the number of places visited before finding specific objects, for different search methods, over time. Let us focus again on the grad-search behavior. It is easy to see that, when time is close to zero, grad-search works equal to blind-search, since no pheromone trails have been already laid down. After some time, grad-search works considerably better than blind-search, since pheromone trails drive agents. However, as time passes, tags capacity tend to saturate, the objects are moved, but no pheromone trails can be deployed. This situation rapidly trashes performance leading back to blind-search performance.

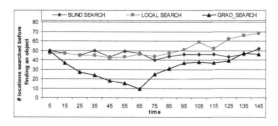

Fig. 5. Number of visited places before finding a specific object plotted over time, when tags tend to saturate

We get two main lessons from the above experiments.

First Lesson: in small environments grad-searches work considerably better than local-searches. However, this is not longer true in large environments, where the two methods have almost the same performance. This is clearly because the cost of "orienting" in a local neighborhood becomes negligible when the environment is large. Moreover, the drawback of grad-searches is the need for longer-range (more costly) RFID reader: the reader, in fact, must be capable of reading tags in a "one-hop" neighborhood. On the contrary local-searches can work with shorter-range (cheaper) RFID reader as well. Overall, the experiments conducted show that in near-future environments (with thousands of objects and places being tagged) local-search is a promising approach.

Second Lesson: the limited storage capacity of the RFID tags is a big problem. Basically, if the number of objects to be tracked is greater than the available slots on the RFID tag, in the long run the problem is unavoidable. Sooner or later, a new object will cross to an already full tag, breaking the pheromone trail. We still do not have a solution for this problem. Our research with regard to this topic is leading in two main directions: (i) we are currently researching more advanced pheromone evaporation mechanisms. (ii) We are considering the idea of spreading pheromone trails not only in tags but also on object-tags. The advantage would be that the more objects are in the system, the more storage space is available for pheromones, letting the system to scale naturally. The problem is how to manage the fact that object-tags containing pheromones can be moved around, breaking the pheromone trail structure. As a partial relief from this problem, it is worth reporting that, recent RFID tags have a storage capacity in the order of the KB, making possible to track thousands of objects without changing our application.

6   Conclusion and Future Work

This paper presented the role of sensor network and RFID-based infrastructures to support environment abstraction in pervasive computing scenarios. These infrastructures not only allow agents to acquire context information, but also can serve as suitable media to support their coordination activities.

Our future work in this direction is twofold. On the one hand, we will try to solve technological problems related to current hardware limitations (e.g. the RFID saturation problem). On the other hand, we will try to apply environment abstractions and situatedness to several pervasive computing scenarios.

References

1. Estrin, D., Culler, D., Pister, K., Sukjatme, G.: Connecting the physical world with pervasive networks. IEEE Pervasive Computing 1 (2002) 59 – 69
2. Zambonelli, F., Jennings, N.R., Wooldridge, M.: Developing multiagent systems: the gaia methodology. ACM Transactions on Software Engineering and Methodology 12 (2003) 417 – 470

3. Wooldridge, M., Jennings, N.R.: Intelligent agents: Theory and practice. The Knowledge Engineering Review **10** (1995) 115–152
4. Weyns, D., Parunak, V., Michel, F., Holvoet, T., Ferber, J.: Environments for Multiagent Systems, State-of-the-art and Research Challenges. Springer Verlag - LNAI 3374 (2005)
5. Want, R.: Enabling ubiquitous sensing with rfid. IEEE Computer **37** (2004) 84 – 84
6. Zambonelli, F., Parunak, H.V.D.: Signs of a revolution in computer science and software engineering. In: 3rd International Workshop on Engineering Societies in the Agents World. Volume 2577 of LNCS. Springer Verlag (2003) 13–28
7. Berners-Lee, T., Hendler, J., Lassila, O.: The semantic web. Scientific American (2001)
8. Foster, I., Kesselman), C.: The Grid: Blueprint for a New Computing Infrastructure. Morgan Kaufmann, San Francisco (CA) (1999)
9. Babaoglu, O., Meling, H., Montresor, A.: A framework for the development of agent-based peer-to-peer systems. In: 22nd International Conference on Distributed Computing Systems. IEEE CS Press, Vienna, Austria (2002) 15 – 22
10. Ripeani, M., Iamnitchi, A., Foster, I.: Mapping the gnutella network. IEEE Internet Computing **6** (2002) 50–57
11. Davies, N., Cheverst, K., Mitchell, K., Efrat, A.: Using and determining location in a context-sensitive tour guide. IEEE Computer **34** (2001) 35 – 41
12. Nourbakhsh, I., Sycara, K., Koes, M., Yong, M., Lewis, M., Burion, S.: Human-robot teaming for search and rescue. IEEE Pervasive Computing **4** (2005) 72 – 78
13. Bussmann, S.: Agent-oriented programming of manifacturing control tasks. In: Proceedings of the 3rd International Conference on Multi-Agent Systems. IEEE CS Press, Paris (F) (1998) 57–63
14. Mamei, M., Zambonelli, F.: Physical deployment of digital pheromones through rfid technology. In: IEEE Swarm Symposium. IEEE CS Press, Pasadena (CA), USA (2005)
15. Parunak, V.: Go to the ant: Engineering principles from natural agent systems. Annals of Operations Research **75** (1997) 69–101
16. Bonabeau, E., Dorigo, M., Theraulaz, G.: Swarm Intelligence. From Natural to Artificial Systems. Oxford University Press, Oxford (UK) (1999)
17. Svennebring, J., Koenig, S.: Building terrain covering ant robots: a feasibility study. Autonomous Robots **16** (2004) 313 – 332
18. Berlin, A., Gabriel, K.: Distributed mems: New challenges for computation. Computing in Science and Engineering **4** (1997) 12 – 16
19. Pister, K.: On the limits and applicability of mems technology (2000) Defense Science Study Group Report.
20. Nagpal, R., Shrobe, H., Bachrach, J.: Organizing a global coordinate system from local information on an ad hoc sensor network. In: Proceedings of the International Workshop on Information Processing in Sensor Networks. Number 2634 in LNCS. Springer-Verlag, Palo Alto, California, USA (2003)
21. Gelernter, D., N.Carriero: Coordination languages and their significance. Communication of the ACM **35** (1992) 96 – 107
22. Cabri, G., Leonardi, L., Zambonelli, F.: Engineering mobile agent applications via context-dependent coordination. IEEE Transaction on Software Engineering **28** (2002) 1040 – 1056
23. Cabri, G., Leonardi, L., Mamei, M., Zambonelli, F.: Location-dependent services for mobile users. IEEE Transactions on Systems, Man, and Cybernetics **33** (2003) 667 – 681

204   M. Mamei and F. Zambonelli

24. Mamei, M., Zambonelli, F.: Programming pervasive and mobile computing applications with the tota middleware. In: Proceedings of the International Conference On Pervasive Computing (Percom). IEEE CS Press, Orlando, Florida, USA (2004)
25. Mamei, M., Zambonelli, F., Leonardi, L.: Co-fields: A physically inspired approach to distributed motion coordination. IEEE Pervasive Computing **3** (2004) 52 – 61
26. Curino, C., Giani, M., Giorgetta, M., Giusti, A., Murphy, A., Picco, G.: Tinylime: Bridging mobile and sensor networks through middleware. IEEE CS Press (2005)
27. Weyns, D., Schelfthout, K., Holvoet, T.: Exploiting a virtual environment in a real-world application. In: Proceedings of the International Workshop on Environments for Multiagent Systems, Utrecht, NL (2005)
28. Borcea, C., Iyer, D., Kang, P., Saxena, A., Iftode, L.: Cooperative computing for distributed embedded systems. In: Proceedings of the International Conference on Distributed Computing Systems. IEEE CS Press, Wien, Austria (2002)
29. Picco, G., Murphy, A., Roman, G.: Lime: a middleware for logical and physical mobility. In: Proceedings of the International Conference on Distributed Computing Systems. IEEE CS Press, Providence, Rhode Island, USA (2001)
30. Mascolo, C., Capra, L., Zachariadis, Z., Emmerich, W.: Xmiddle: A data-sharing middleware for mobile computing. Wireless Personal Communications **21** (2002) 77 – 103
31. (Smart-Mobs) http://www.smartmobs.com.
32. (Nokia-Mobile-RFID-Kit) http://www.nokia.com/nokia/0,,55738,00.html.
33. Mamei, M., Quaglieri, R., Zambonelli, F.: Making tuple spaces physical with rfid tags. In: Proceedings of the Symposium on Applied Computing (SAC). ACM Press, Dijon, France (2006)
34. Payton, D., Daily, M., Estowski, R., Howard, M., Lee, C.: Pheromone robotics. Autonoumous Robots **11** (2001) 319 – 324
35. Philipose, M., Fishkin, K., Perkowitz, M., Patterson, D., Fox, D., Kautz, H., Hahnel, D.: (Inferring activities from interactions with objects)
36. Kulyukin, V., Gharpure, C., Nicholson, J., Pavithran, S.: Rfid in robot-assisted indoor navigation for visually impaired. In: Proceedings of the International Conference on Intelligent Robots and Systems. IEEE CS Press (2004)
37. Collins, G.: Next stretch for plastic electronics. Scientific American (2004)
38. (Autentiweb) http://www.autentiweb.com.

The Environment: An Essential Abstraction for Managing Complexity in MAS-Based Manufacturing Control

Paul Valckenaers[1] and Tom Holvoet[2]

[1] K.U. Leuven, Dept. of Mechanical Engineering,
B-3001 Heverlee, Belgium
Paul.Valckenaers@mech.kuleuven.be
http://www.mech.kuleuven.be/macc/
[2] K.U. Leuven, Dept. of Computer Science,
B-3001 Heverlee, Belgium
Tom.Holvoet@cs.kuleuven.ac.be

Abstract. This paper analyses the concept of an environment for multi-agent systems from the perspective of a class of manufacturing control systems using stigmergy. The discussion reveals that significant responsibilities can be attributed to the environment as an essential abstraction in MAS. Analysis shows that the environment is well positioned to manage functionalities of multi-agent systems that otherwise would be scattered over the agents, execution platform and communication infrastructure. Importantly, the environment represents a significant contribution handling the complexity of manufacturing control applications and providing a common repository for subsystems originating from different parties.

1 Introduction

This paper presents insights and results originating from research on multi-agent manufacturing control, in particular concerning environments for multi-agent systems. Manufacturing control systems supervise process control systems and handle factory operations. A manufacturing control system decides about the routes that the products follow, it decides when and where operations on the products start, when the machines receive preventive maintenance, etc. In contrast, it does not deal with the production processes themselves. After initiating processing, process control takes over and reports the result. Manufacturing control must handle all possible processing outcomes, some of which disturb the manufacturing operations significantly - e.g. process failures causing the need for a repair.

Manufacturing control is a complex task because of the non-linear nature of the underlying production system, the uncertainties stemming from the environment and the production processes, and the combinatorial growth of the decision space. Schedules and plans, originating from higher levels in a manufacturing organization, are known to become ineffectual within minutes on a factory

D. Weyns, H. Van Dyke Parunak, and F. Michel (Eds.): E4MAS 2005, LNAI 3830, pp. 205–217, 2006.

floor. Manufacturing is a very dynamic environment and handling changes and disturbances is high on its list of research challenges.

The performance of a manufacturing system affects the competitiveness of manufacturing organizations. The aspect of a production system that determines actual performance - the bottleneck - is subject to change. Indeed, this bottleneck normally is the prime target for investments and system enhancements, after which something else becomes this critical aspect. Likewise, market demand fluctuations may switch the control system's objective from throughput maximization toward lead-time minimization. This represents a formidable challenge to the decision-optimizing components of a manufacturing control system, and implies that changing the decision-making mechanism must not create an avalanche of software maintenance work.

The research - discussed in this paper - targets the above challenges and in particular the handling of changes and disturbances, a common weakness of the existing control systems in industrial practice. It also aims for a software system architecture in which the decision-making is confined to system components that can be modified without causing an avalanche of software maintenance involving other parts of the manufacturing control system.

This paper discusses a specific multi-agent manufacturing control system, based on the PROSA architecture [1] and employing bio-inspired coordination mechanisms [2]. This design heavily relies on indirect coordination and communication - i.e. stigmergy [3]. Moreover, the design addresses the requirement to shield most of the software from unavoidable and frequent changes [4], especially concerning the decision-making, resulting in software components that reflect parts of the relevant reality as much as possible (analogous to using maps in navigation systems).

Note however that this manufacturing control system design is not the main contribution of the paper. The core issue in this paper is the environment as a first-class abstraction in multi-agent systems. Indeed, the heavy use of indirect coordination, the presence of a complex physical environment (production system), and the system design approach [4] to facilitate the survival of changes by the software components, naturally lead to assigning the concept of an environment a key role in MAS.

The focus of this paper is to reformulate the manufacturing control approach using the environment concept and, doing so, to show how this helps in dealing with the complexity faced by the developers of multi-agent manufacturing control (and similar) systems. Through this exercise, the paper identifies functionalities of an environment for MAS targeted at this application domain (coordination and control of activities in a macroscopic physical world in which resource allocation is a key issue) and validates and/or evaluates recent theoretical claims on environments for MAS.

This paper first discusses the multi-agent manufacturing control systems. Next, it concisely discusses what the responsibilities are that can be attributed to a MAS environment. Finally, the MAS environment for multi-agent manufacturing control is addressed, followed by conclusions.

2   Multi-agent Manufacturing Control and Ants

This section presents the multi-agent manufacturing control system design. This is background material for the subsequent sections and the reader is referred to the proper references [1][2][4] for more details. Therefore, there is no comparison of this research to work by others. This section aims to keep this paper readable by itself. In short, we can say that the design delivers different functionality in comparison to related work that addresses decision-making components as their main concern [5][6][7][8]. In contrast, the control systems in this paper postpone that aspect (i.e. how to make decisions) as much as possible. As an analogy in the domain of navigation, the work by others focuses on generating route descriptions whereas the work in this paper focuses on creating maps. Importantly, it develops a subsystem that predicts near-future system states given the decision-making mechanisms. The reader should keep this property of these multi-agent manufacturing control systems in mind to avoid confusion when looking for the decision-making components in the design.

2.1   PROSA

The manufacturing control systems in this paper implement the PROSA reference architecture. This acronym denotes Product-Resource-Order-Staff Architecture [1]. The structure of systems designed along the PROSA architecture is composed of three types of basic agents:

1. Resource agents correspond to a physical part - e.g. a production resource in the manufacturing system - and contain an information processing part that controls their resource. They offer processing capacity and functionality to the surrounding agents. In manufacturing control systems, a resource agent is an abstraction of the production means such as machines, conveyors, pallets, raw materials, tool holders, material storage, personnel, floor space, etc. Each resource agent reflects a physical resource, is able to drive this resource, and keeps its resource-state-reflecting internal model synchronized with this resource's actual state.

2. Order agents represent tasks in the underlying system. They are responsible for performing the assigned work correctly and on time. In manufacturing control systems, an order agent manages the physical product being produced, the product state model, and all logistic information processing related to the job. An order agent may represent customer orders, make-to-stock orders, prototype-making orders, orders to maintain and repair resources, etc.

3. Product agents hold the process and product knowledge to assure the correct making of a product with sufficient quality. As such, they contain the "product model" of their product type, not the "product state model" of one physical product instance being produced. The product agent acts as an information server to the other agents, delivering the right recipes in the right place. It knows how to make a product without making any decisions about

when and where production takes place. In object-oriented terminology, a
product agent corresponds to a product class, an order agent to a product
instance (or more precisely a product being instantiated).

These basic agents are structured through aggregation and specialization. An
agent may belong to several aggregations and aggregated agents can dynamically
change their contents. For instance, membership of a batch order agent may
depend on the timely arrival of the prospective members. Aggregated agents may
emerge out of the self-organizing interaction of agents or they may be designed
up front. The number of aggregation levels depends on the specific needs of a
certain system, and is not dictated by the architecture. Aggregation reduces
exposure of the individual agents and increases software reuse. For instance, a
shopping list agent simply creates new agents for each item on the shopping list
and manages the aggregate; the production of the individual items is delegated
to the corresponding item agents.

Specialization allows a layered implementation of the agents, where the higher
layers can be shared and, more importantly, used as interfaces to the remainder
of the coordination and control system. For instance, in a manufacturing control
system there will be a specialization hierarchy starting from agent along resource
agent, transport resource agent, toward conveyor belt agent. Importantly, any
agent working with resource agents will perform its duties regardless of which
more specialized kinds of resource agents it is interacting with.

Staff agents, as in human organizations, can be added to assist the basic
agents with expert knowledge. These agents often reflect functions such as planning systems. However, they only produce advice and never hold final responsibilities concerning command and control of the underlying system. In certain
ways, these agents reflect information rather than being a function. The weak
coupling (advice-only) effectively limits the mutual exposure of the agents and
eases integration.

Furthermore, relentless usage of delegation characterizes the interaction
amongst the basic PROSA agents, which limits their exposure to system properties outside their own scope. Product agents never accept to manage state
information about ongoing tasks and delegate this to the order agent. Product
agents receive an object representing the state of a task from the corresponding
order agent whenever they need this information to perform their tasks. Likewise, order agents always consult product agents about possible ways to proceed
with their task.

2.2 Coordination and Stigmergy

Stigmergy. The basic PROSA design has been augmented to support stigmergy.
Grassé introduced this word to describe how signs in the environment are used
to coordinate activities of social insects, replacing direct communication [3]. The
display of goods with price labels in shops is an example of manmade stigmergy;
road signs are another example. To support stigmergy, information spaces are
attached to the basic PROSA agents. In the current systems, only information

spaces attached to resource agents are relevant. Any agent acquainted with a resource agent is able to place, retrieve and modify software objects on its attached information space, somewhat analogous to medical staff using clipboards attached to hospital beds in old movies.

The information on these boards has a finite lifetime. When the information progresses beyond a given age, it is discarded. Agents must refresh information on these boards fast enough if they want it to remain available for other agents observing the information space. This is a generic mechanism to handle changes: any stale information simply disappears when it becomes too old. The frequency at which information is refreshed and the upper bound on its lifetime determine how fast the system will observe changes. Hence, a system designer must trade communication and computing effort against the delay at which changes become known throughout the manufacturing control system.

Coordination. Historically, the control system design originated out of inspiration by the coordination through stigmergy in food-foraging ant colonies [9]. However, the design has evolved significantly and, presently, the analogy with social insects often confuses rather than helps the discussion. Nonetheless, our terminology still reflects this source of inspiration. In an ant colony, ants deposit information in their environment (pheromones) informing other ants about remote facts (how to find food). The PROSA agents create agents for similar purposes (i.e. system-wide coordination; see below). These agents are called ant agents or simply ants in the remainder of this text.

In the current designs, ant agents are associated to a resource agent, which is their current position. The ant agents query their resource agent about its connections to neighboring resource agents and use this to virtually navigate through the manufacturing system, more precisely through the network of resource agents reflecting the manufacturing system. Ant agents get their initial position - association to a resource agent - at creation time. Ant agents typically originate from basic PROSA agents, and perform an information retrieval and dissemination task on behalf of the PROSA agent. Ant agents are created at a given rate, among others, to refresh information before it expires on the information spaces.

The manufacturing control systems all contain three types of ant agents (specific implementations may use additional ant types for other coordination purposes). Feasibility ants constitute a first type of ant agents. They put signposts on the information spaces enabling order agents to decide locally which routing options are available to them. Resource agents that correspond to a product shipping area (factory exits) create feasibility ants at a suitable frequency. These ant agents virtually navigate through the factory in the opposite direction of the production flows (i.e. upstream). During their journey, the feasibility ants query resources, which they visit, about their processing capabilities, collecting information that describes all possible process plans that can be executed downstream from the current position. In addition, the ant agents deposit their information on the information spaces that they encounter on their journey, merging it with information from other ant agents of their own generation. This information constitutes signposts for other agents representing the hard constraints in the manufacturing system. If an order agent obeys these signposts, it will eventually get produced in a technically correct manner. Note that such signposts permit a product agent to determine which part of the process plan can be executed downstream. Locally available information describes non-local system properties.

Secondly, order agents create at a regular frequency ant agents that will scout for possible solutions. Such an exploring ant generates one possible feasible solution by traveling virtually through the factory and by making the resource agents virtually perform the required processing steps. The exploring ant is created at the location of its order agent. It queries the associated resource agent about the ongoing activity. For instance, the order is queued on a conveyor belt and the conveyor belt agent reports the estimated time when the order will reach the end of the belt. The ant agent virtually moves to the end of the conveyor belt and progresses its virtual clock to this estimated time. At the end of the conveyor belt, the exploring ant retrieves the signposts, placed by the feasibility ants, and presents them to the associated product agent to learn the available routing options. The exploring ant selects one of the available options and continues its virtual journey. When the exploring ant arrives on a processing unit, it retrieves the processing capabilities from the resource agent and presents them to the product agent to discover which processing steps can be performed. In addition, the signpost information is used to decide whether leaving the processing unit is already an option. Again, the ant agent selects and virtually executes an option that is available. Importantly, exploring ants rely on resource agents to provide sound estimates for the duration of transport and processing steps. To this end, resource agents have a 'reservations department' that answers queries about capacity availability. However, this 'reservations department' cannot properly answer queries without an informed estimate of future usage of the resource; it needs future visitors to book (make a reservation).

The third type of ant agents, the intention ants, performs this task. Intention ants reserve capacity at the resources on behalf of their order agent. When an exploring ant finds a solution, it reports back to the order agent. This order agent evaluates the performance of this solution (e.g. rush orders rank solutions by their estimated finishing time) and it maintains a small collection of attractive solutions. At a given moment, the order agent selects the most attractive solution to become its intention, and starts to create intention ants at a regular frequency. Intention ants behave in the same manner as the exploring ants except for two aspects. First, it follows the route specified by the order intention and reports back the estimated performance of this intention, accounting for the consequences of any changes in the system (e.g. a machine breakdown). Second, the intention ant informs all the resource agents on its journey of the order intentions. In other words, it books the required capacity on the resource. Thus, the resource agents receive the necessary information to calculate a short-term forecast of their utilization. This enables the resource agents to give accurate answers to the queries by exploring and intention ants alike. Importantly, bookings must be refreshed regularly. Otherwise, the reservation is discarded and becomes available for other users.

The above combination of exploring and intention ants provides both order agents and resource agents with short-term forecasts. Again, this paper does not discuss the merits and limitations of this system design. The purpose is to reveal how this class of systems benefits from having the environment as a first-class abstraction in MAS.

3   The Environment

"Environments for multi-agent systems" is an emerging research topic [10][11]. Although discussions are only recently setting off, some attributes and aspects are already emerging. Weyns and Holvoet distinguish an initial list of characteristics [10]:

1. Independent and actively self-supporting,
2. Offering support services for the situated agents therein to pursue their goals,
3. Possibly having maintenance goals, but never one-shot achievement goals,
4. Coordination medium for the situated agents therein,
5. Enforcing system-wide constraints (laws),
6. Unbounded and open,
7. Observable and actuate-able.

This list of characteristics is helpful in mentally identifying what an environment for MAS is, but it does not constitute a sound starting ground for the development of environment entities. Certainly, it was not usable for mapping responsibilities from the multi-agent manufacturing control systems onto environment entities. To this end, the initial list of features of environments is more helpful [10]:

1. Structuring: the environment acts as a structuring entity for the multi-agent system. This structuring can be spatial, organizational,... and it defines the rules governing the relationships facilitated by the structuring features.
2. Resources: the environment provides resource management in a broad sense.
3. Ontology: agents must be able to understand their environment.
4. Communication: the environment facilitates and regulates the communication activities.
5. Action processing: the environment is the natural medium through which agents can act upon the world. Note that this aspect is largely an unexplored field offering many non-trivial research challenges.
6. Perception: the agents observe the world through the environment in manners similar to action processing, sharing the need for extensive further research.
7. Environmental processes: the environment handles choice-free but possibly stochastic ongoing processes (e.g. evaporation of pheromones).

Observing the agent community's research activities and results from the perspective of manufacturing, especially the last three items represent almost virgin territory in which formidable but rewarding research challenges can be found. Note that these features probably cannot be tackled independently, especially in the situation where the agents face constraints concerning the observe-ability and actuate-ability of the (physical and/or manufacturing) environment.

The above list of features proved to be a workable structure to identify responsibilities that can be assigned to the environment and environment entities, seen from the perspective of the multi-agent manufacturing control systems discussed earlier. The next section discusses this in detail.

4   Environments for Manufacturing Control MAS

This section roughly follows the list of features for environments and environment entities proposed by Weyns and Holvoet; it first addresses the structure-related issues followed by the activity-related ones [10]. The discussion reveals that it is indeed possible to lift out environment entities. Implicitly, this reveals how explicit support thereof will significantly ease the development and implementation of the multi-agent manufacturing control systems, if only because the effort can be shared with other developments. It also facilitates integration of software that was developed independently but targeting the same MAS environment.

4.1   Structure-Related Features

Structuring. The environment embedded in the multi-agent manufacturing control systems supports a lumped graph model of the real world - i.e. a manufacturing plant and the entities therein. The factory floor/building constitutes the root node of the graph. Each entity - machine, product part - in the factory is another node in this graph. Each node has a finite number of exits and entries (node attributes). Entries connected to exits constitute an edge in this graph model of the world; these are peer-to-peer edges. Another type of edges corresponds to parent-child relations between entities; examples are a workpiece (child) located on a machine (parent) and a machine (child) on the factory floor (parent).

The graph changes over time according to the laws of this environment. For instance, when a machine enters the factory, a parent-child edge is created between the root and this machine; the attributes of the edge include its position. When machine entries or exits are hooked up to exits or entries of neighboring equipment, peer-to-peer edges are created. When a part or a tool arrives on the machine, a parent-child edge is created, attributed by its position. The environment maintains this graph model and keeps it synchronized with reality.

This environment provides a lumped model of the world in contrast to geometrical and/or physical models. Physical and geometrical properties are supported through attributes or functions/methods associated to the nodes and edges in the graph. For instance, the location of a machine on the factory floor is an attribute of the parent-child edge connecting these two nodes. The main motivation is efficiency. An explicit geometrical/physical model currently is beyond the state-of-the-art. Note that in a rigid-body world, the state vector of an entity has 12 coordinates -comprising position, orientation, linear velocity and rotational momentum - in addition to body geometry and weight distribution. Moreover, non-rigid body properties often are relevant (elasticity, friction, resonance frequencies. . .). In a competitive environment, failure to account for such a property will be fatal when it determines a critical aspect of the overall system performance. And, many factories are working on the edge of what is technically feasible. The lumped model, with its ad hoc augmentations, is a flexible solution: it can be elaborated in detail wherever it counts. A downside is the need for discipline and standardization to avoid multiple representations for the same aspect.

Resources. The PROSA architecture explicitly acknowledges the fact that the environment comprises a collection of resources, which have structure and explicit resource management. The explicit presence of and support for environment entities partitions a PROSA resource agent into an environment resource entity accompanied by a pure resource agent. The resource entity reflects what is present in the real world while the resource agent encapsulates all decision-making aspects of the PROSA resource agent. Indeed, making the environment entities 'choice-free' (except for purely representational aspects) has important integration advantages. When choice-free entities reflect some part of the real world, there will be no serious conflict amongst them simply because they reflect a world that is coherent, consistent and integrated. Road maps are sample choice-free artefacts: a map developer simply looks at reality to know what to do. In contrast, developing a set of traffic regulations or a programming language involves making a lot of (basically arbitrary) choices.

Ontology. The PROSA architecture partitions the agent community such that they have a limited exposure to the overall system. As a consequence, there is no need for a powerful comprehensive global ontology, known and agreed upon by the entire MAS. In contrast, there will be a multitude of small agent communities with a specialized local ontology covering their technical jargon; for instance, only a few product agents and resource agents are involved in 5-axes milling operations. The global ontology mostly covers invariant and generic concepts such as time, space, ownership, etc.

The application domain imposes nonetheless severe demands on such a local ontology concerning the life cycle of the ontology itself. It is imperative that a local ontology can change at run-time (= normal operating mode). It must be possible to add concepts and deprecate concepts as required by the application. These changes often will be quick-and-dirty at first, requiring support for cleaning up and restructuring at some later time.

The current manufacturing control prototypes do not explicitly support ontologies. An environment for MAS, providing such support, will make such manufacturing control MAS a much more open community. For instance, a third-party product agent will be able to assess what the processing capabilities of the manufacturing resources are without the need for a mapping between the capabilities representation of a resource agent and the capabilities representation used by this product agent. Notice that at such an encounter, the local ontologies of the respective parties need to be reconciled and/or merged [12].

4.2   Activity-Related Features

Communication. The manufacturing control system employs two modes of communication. In a first mode, the agents know the other agents' address and send messages directly. There are two main methods to acquire the address of other agents. First, when one agent creates another (ant) agent, they mutually know each other's address. Second, the agents can deposit and retrieve addresses on the lumped graph model supported by the environment.

The second communication mechanism is stigmergy [3]. All nodes in the lumped graph model posses an information space on which information can be placed, observed and modified. By default, this information evaporates and needs to be refreshed if it is to remain available. Some parts of these information spaces are only observable and modifiable through the responsible local environment entity (or agent?). For instance, resources have a 'reservation register' in which visitors cannot write themselves. Note that also reservations evaporate. Moreover, agent sub-societies can obtain a unique identifier to ensure that they have their own sub-space of information spread over the environment. Access control is an issue that remains to be investigated.

There is no explicit support (or usage) of shared/distributed spaces or subscribe/distribute services in the current implementations. Adding those does however not pose any problem (there is no conflict with the other mechanisms).

Action Processing. The manufacturing control system triggers actions in the underlying production system and observes the outcome. In this context, the MAS environment must regulate and support the link to the real world in a systematic manner. In addition, the application domain has a requirement for being able to control an emulated world without requiring modifications to the MAS manufacturing control system (in addition to controlling the real world system). Furthermore, at the level of a single (lumped) node, there is a requirement for a 'what-if self-modeling' capability. For instance, a conveyor belt (a resource) should provide estimates on how long it will take a part to be transported from its entry to its exit.

In other words, the manufacturing control application domain is able to benefit from a MAS environment and environment entities that systematize this aspect of the overall system. Again, a key criterion for putting functionality in the environment entities versus the agents should be whether the functionality requires decision-making (choice). If not, it is a candidate for becoming part of the MAS environment.

Perception and Actuation. Concerning this aspect, the application domain presents a specific issue: to maintain the consistency between the lumped graph model - in which each node is enriched with capabilities, attributes and functionalities as required - and the real world. This is far from trivial because sensors and actuators often are very expensive and/or unreliable. As a consequence, there will be relevant aspects of the manufacturing system that cannot be observed directly and actuators that cannot guarantee specific outcomes. For instance, the system may not be able to observe whether an operator manually changes the sequence of pallets/parts on a conveyor belt. This creates uncertainty for the control system, which can be challenging.

Functionality in the environment that alleviates this problem is certainly valuable. Raising the intelligence in the manufacturing control system to the point where probability representation formats are common knowledge might be necessary to get adequate solutions in this area. This is definitely an open research issue where it is even hard to judge how much can be achieved.

Environmental Processes. There is a strong relationship with the previous topic. In practice, modeling and predicting what the system state will be compensates for the limited availability of sensors. For instance, a conveyor belt only senses arrival and departure of parts on top of it. It must calculate the position of these parts based on its speed setting. As stated before, when an operator changes the position or, worse, the sequence of the parts on top of the conveyor belt without informing the system, a disaster may happen. The environment cannot assume that this calculated system state information is correct and need to correct/merge with new sensor readings as they emerge, even if they conflict with the expectations. Likewise, contradictory sensor readings are part of normal life in industry and need to be handled. Again, there is a real research challenge but without an obvious solution at present.

4.3   Other Issues

The MAS manufacturing control systems present a number of additional issues, which do not directly fit the list of features presented in [10]. These include:

1. Support for agent sub-societies and agent teams.
2. Support for social control, ensuring that agents obey a given set of rules.
3. Register past behavior and estimate what constitutes normal performance and behavior.
4. Support for agent accreditation, agent reputations.

This list is evidently non-exhaustive. In particular, the environment may be able to support making a MAS more autonomic by helping to identify and detect abnormal situations and behavior, to diagnose what the possible sources are, and to facilitate directed action against the cause of the problem.

Also, note that in stigmergic designs, like the MAS manufacturing control systems, the environment and the agents are likely to interact and cooperate in specific patterns in which information flows from the environment through the agents and vice versa.

For instance, an agent may propagate its near-future resource requirements in the environment; a unique identifier marks this information. The environment propagates this information to agents currently owning (some of) these resources. These agents propagate this information in turn. When at some point the information reaches its origin again, an indication of an impending deadlock possibility becomes apparent. Clearly, such a scheme needs further detailing and needs to be accompanied by a similar scheme to discourage agents from entering a cycle that is approaching a deadlock situation. The main point is that the environment entities are unlikely to provide almost all useful functionality on their own. Many kinds of useful functionality require a choreography involving both agents and environment entities.

5   Conclusions

This paper illuminates the aspects of an environment for multi-agent systems that are directly relevant for a class of manufacturing control systems using stigmergy. The initial list of environment features proposed in [10] serves as a guidance to identify which environment entities and functionality represents a valuable contribution to the application domain. The confrontation reveals that explicitly recognizing the different responsibilities that can be attributed to the environment allows to better manage functionalities of MAS systems that were otherwise scattered in the agents, the underlying execution platform, the communication infrastructure, and so on. In particular, the environment facilitates the development of subsystems by different parties and supports managing to a large extent the application domain's complexity.

The paper identifies some aspects outside the initial list of features (as understood by the authors), which cover concerns about the agent societies and about functionality that requires an interaction pattern between agents and environment entities. Nonetheless, the analysis in this paper clearly supports the usefulness of considering the environment as a first-class entity with well-defined responsibilities.

Acknowledgements

This work was supported by the K.U.Leuven research council (GOA-AgCo2).

References

1. Van brussel, H., Wyns, J., Valckenaers, P., Bongaerts, L., Peeters, P.: Reference architecture for holonic manufacturing systems: Prosa. COMPUTERS IN INDUSTRY **37**(3) (1998) 255 – 274
2. Valckenaers, P., Saint Germain, B., Verstraete, P., Hadeli, Zamfirescu, C., Van Brussel, H.: Ant colony engineering in coordination and control: How to engineer an emergent short-term forecasting system. In: Proceedings IWES2004, Budapest. (May 24-25, 2004)
3. Grassé, P.P.: La reconstruction du nid et les coordinations interindividuelle chez bellicositermes natalensis et cubitermes. la theorie de la stigmergie: Essai dinterpretation des termites constructeurs. Insectes Sociaux **6** (1959) 4183
4. Valckenaers, P., Van brussel, H., Hadeli, Bochmann, O., Saint germain, B., Zamfirescu, C.: On the design of emergent systems: an investigation of integration and interoperability issues. ENGINEERING APPLICATIONS OF ARTIFICIAL INTELLIGENCE **16**(4) (2003) 377 – 393

5. Bussmann, S., Sieverding, J.: Holonic control of an engine assembly plant, an industrial evaluation. In: Proceedings of the 2001 IEEE Systems, Man, and Cybernetics Conference. (2001) 169 – 174
6. Bussmann, S., Schild, K.: An agent-based approach to the control of flexible production systems. In: Proceedings of the 8th IEEE Intern. Conf. on Emergent Technologies and Factory Automation. (2001) 481–488
7. Parunak, H., Baker, A., Clark, S.: The aaria agent architecture: From manufacturing requirements to agent-based system design. INTEGRATED COMPUTER-AIDED ENGINEERING **8**(1) (2001) 45 – 58
8. Brueckner, S.: Return from the Ant - Synthetic Ecosystems for Manufacturing Control. PhD thesis, Humboldt University, Berlin (2000)
9. Mueller, J.P., Parunak, H.: Multi-agent systems and manufacturing. In: Proceedings of INCOM98, IFAC. (1998) 165–170
10. Weyns, D., Holvoet, T.: On environments in multi-agent systems. AgentLink News **16** (December 2004) 18–19
11. Weyns, D., Parunak, H., Michel, F., Holvoet, T., Ferber, J.: Environments for multiagent systems state-of-the-art and research challenges. ENVIRONMENTS FOR MULTI-AGENT SYSTEMS **3374** (2005) 1 – 47
12. Carpenter, M., Gledson, A., Mehandjiev, N.: Support for dynamic ontologies in open business systems. In: Proceedings of the AAMAS'04 Agent-Oriented Information Systems Workshop. (2004)

Exploiting a Virtual Environment in a Real-World Application

Danny Weyns, Kurt Schelfthout, and Tom Holvoet

AgentWise, DistriNet,
Department of Computer Science, K.U. Leuven,
Celestijnenlaan 200 A, B-3001 Leuven, Belgium
{Danny.Weyns, Kurt.Schelfthout, Tom.Holvoet}@cs.kuleuven.be

Abstract. In situated multi-agent systems (situated MASs), agents are explicitly placed in an environment. A situated agent does not not use long-term planning to decide what action sequence should be executed, but selects actions on the basis of its current position, the world it perceives and limited internal state. Situated agents exploit the environment to coordinate their behavior and to reach a common goal. In a recent project, we applied situated MASs to the control of an automated transportation system that uses automatic guided vehicles (AGVs) to transport loads in a warehouse. In contrast to traditional approaches where the AGVs are controlled by a central server, in this project we model the AGVs as agents in a situated MAS, aiming to improve flexibility and openness. Since the physical environment of AGVs is very restricted, it offers little opportunities for agents to use the environment. We introduce a virtual environment for agents to live in. This virtual environment (1) offers a medium that agents can use to exchange information and coordinate their behavior, and (2) serves as a suitable abstraction to shield low-level physical processing from the AGV agents. Since the only infrastructure available to the AGVs is a wireless network, the virtual environment is necessarily distributed over the AGVs. Synchronization of the state of the virtual environment is provided by ObjectPlaces, a middleware infrastructure that offers support to exchange and share information among nodes in mobile and ad-hoc networks. In this paper, we demonstrate how the environment is used creatively in the design of a MAS solution, helping to manage the complexity of engineering a complex real-world application.

1 Introduction

In the last fifteen years, multi-agent systems (MASs) have been put forward as a paradigm to tackle the increasing complexity of distributed applications. Our research focusses on situated MASs, i.e. MASs in which agents are explicitly placed in an environment. In situated MASs, agents and the environment are first-order abstractions [15]. Situated agents exploit the environment to coordinate their behavior and to reach a common goal. Example mechanisms for environmental coordination are marks [4], gradient fields [6] and digital pheromones [10].

In [16], M. Wooldridge lists benefits of situated MAS including efficiency, robustness and flexibility, but he also points to a number of limitations of situated MASs.

D. Weyns, H. Van Dyke Parunak, and F. Michel (Eds.): E4MAS 2005, LNAI 3830, pp. 218–234, 2006.

Wooldridge argues that situated agents take into account only local, current information and thus inherently must take a "short-time" view for decision making. However, complex problem domains suitable to apply agent-technology, such as ad-hoc networks or manufacturing control, are by their very nature distributed and highly dynamic. In such domains it is questionable whether it is feasible or even useful for agents to collect global information or have a "long-term" view on the situation. Another problem raised by Wooldridge is that there is no methodology to engineer situated agents, in particular with respect to desired overall behavior of the system. The relationship between local interactions of agents on the one hand and global behavior of the MAS on the other hand is indeed a complex open problem in need of extensive further research. An interesting approach is proposed in [3].

Situated MASs have been applied with success in practical applications over a broad range of domains. Some examples are: manufacturing control [9], supply chains systems [12], social simulation [5] and network management [1]. In an ongoing R&D project with Egemin[1], we apply the paradigm of situated MASs to the control of automatic guided vehicles (AGVs) that have to transport loads in a warehouse. In contrast to traditional approaches where the AGVs are controlled by a central server, in this project we model the AGVs as agents in a situated MAS, aiming to improve flexibility and openness. Flexibility refers to a system's capability to adapt its behavior with different environmental situations, and openness enables a system to cope with expansion (new agents that join the system) and reduction (agents that leave the system). Since the physical environment of AGVs is very restricted, it offers little opportunities for agents to use the environment. We introduce a virtual environment for agents to live in. This virtual environment (1) offers a medium that AGV agents can use to exchange information and coordinate their behavior, and (2) serves as a suitable abstraction to shield low-level physical processing from the AGV agents. Since the only infrastructure available to the AGVs is a wireless network, the virtual environment is necessarily distributed over the AGVs. Synchronization of the state of the virtual environment is provided by ObjectPlaces, a middleware infrastructure that offers support to exchange and share information among nodes in mobile and ad-hoc networks. In this paper, we demonstrate how the environment is used creatively in the design of a MAS solution, helping to manage the complexity of engineering a complex real-world application.

This paper is structured as follows. In Sect. 2, we elaborate on situated MASs, and we discuss opportunities that environments offer for situated MASs. Section 3 introduces the AGV application. We discuss the traditional centralized solution briefly, and then explain how we have modelled this application as a situated MAS. In Sect. 4, we zoom in on the virtual environment and illustrate how AGV agents exploit this environment to coordinate their behavior. Finally, in Sect. 5 we draw conclusions.

2   Situated MASs and Environments

2.1   Situated MASs

A situated MAS consists of a (distributed) environment populated with a set of agents that cooperate to solve a complex problem in a decentralized way. Situated agents have

---
[1] http://www.egemin.com/

local access to the environment, i.e. each agent is placed in a local context which it can perceive and in which it can act and interact with other agents. A situated agent does not use long-term planning to decide what action sequence should be executed, but selects actions on the basis of its current position, the state of the world it perceives and limited internal state. Intelligence in a situated MAS originates from the interactions between the agents, rather than from their individual capabilities.

Situated agents exploit the environment to share information and coordinate their actions. A digital pheromone, for example, is a dynamic structure in the environment that aggregates with additional pheromone that is dropped, diffuses in space and evaporates over time. Agents can use pheromones to dynamically form pheromone paths to locations of interest. Another example is a gradient field that propagates through the environment and changes in strength the further it is propagated. Agents can use a gradient field as a guiding beacon. The environment is thus a crucial part of any situated MAS: both agent and environment are first-order abstractions.

2.2 Opportunities for Exploiting the Environment

Inspired by research and our own experiences with situated MAS, we discuss opportunities that environments offer for MASs [15].

1. Structuring entity: the agents as well as the objects and resources of a MAS are dynamically related to each other. It is the role of the environment to define the rules under which these relationships can exist and can evolve. As such the environment acts as a structuring entity for the MAS. For MASs with an explicit spatial structure, the layout as well as the constraints associated with this layout are part of the environment.
2. Maintenance of shared state: an environment can serve as a robust, self-revising, shared memory for agents. This unburdens the individual agents from continuously keeping track of their knowledge about the system. The state of digital pheromones is an example of shared state that is maintained by the environment.
3. Service support: the environment can provide services for the situated agents to pursue their assigned goals. For example, the environment can provide support to propagate and maintain gradient fields in a distributed environment.
4. Coordination: the environment enables situated agents to coordinate their interactions. Communication required to coordinate can take very different forms: agents can communicate directly via message transfer, or communicate anonymously via a shared space, or communicate indirectly through marks in the environment.
5. Regulating entity: the environment can serve as a means to enforce system-wide constraints (laws) on all agents within a MAS. The environment, e.g., regulates the access to resources. In general, the environment defines the rules for, and enforces the effects of, the agents' actions.

3   The AGV Transportation System

We apply the approach of situated MASs to a real-world application in the domain of automating logistics services in warehouses and manufactories. This application is investigated in a joint R&D research project between the AgentWise research group and

Egemin, a manufacturer of automated warehouse systems. In this section, we first introduce the application and list the required functionalities. We discuss the traditional centralized solution briefly. Next, we discuss new quality requirements for the application and we give a high-level overview of the decentralized solution with a situated MAS. We introduce the virtual environment and illustrate how AGV agents exploit this environment to coordinate their behavior. In the next section, we explain the virtual environment in depth.

3.1   The AGV Application

An AGV transportation system uses unmanned vehicles (AGVs) to transport *loads* through a warehouse. Typical applications are repackaging and distributing incoming goods to various branches, or distributing manufactured products to storage locations. An AGV uses a battery as its energy source. AGVs can move through a warehouse, following a physical path on the factory floor, guided by a laser navigation system, or by magnets or cables that are fixed in the floor. An AGV can pick a load at a certain location and drop it at another location. An AGV can also park at particular locations when it is idle, and charge its battery at a charging station.

Functionalities. The main functionality the system should perform is handling *transports*, i.e. moving loads from one place to another. Transports are generated by *client systems*. Client systems are typically business management programs, but can also be other logistic machines, employees or service operators. A transport is composed out of multiple *jobs*: a job is a simple task that can be assigned to an AGV. For example, picking a load is a pick job, dropping it is a drop job and moving over a specific distance is a move job. A transport typically starts with a pick job, followed by a series of move jobs (probably interrupted by one or more wait jobs) and ends with a drop job.

In order to execute transports, the main functionalities the system has to perform are:

1. Transport assignment: transports are generated by client systems and have to be assigned to AGVs that can execute them.
2. Routing: AGVs must route efficiently through the layout of the warehouse when executing their transports.
3. Gathering traffic information: although the layout of the system is static, the best route for the AGVs in general is dynamic, and depends on the current conditions in the system. For example, some paths may be busy and cause more delay than a longer path that is not busy. Gathering traffic information concerns the monitoring of the current traffic status of the system to adapt the routing of the AGVs to these dynamic conditions.
4. Collision avoidance: obviously, AGVs may not collide. AGVs can not cross the same intersection at the same moment, however, safety measures are also necessary when AGVs pass each other on closely located paths.
5. Deadlock prevention: since AGVs are relatively constrained in their movement (they cannot divert from their path), the system must ensure that at least one of the necessary conditions for deadlock can never hold.

When an AGV is idle it can park at a neighboring park location; when the AGV runs out of energy, it has to charge its battery at one of the charging stations.

3.2   Traditional Approach

Traditionally, vehicles are controlled by one central server, using wireless communication. The server has global knowledge of the system and plans routes for AGVs according to incoming transports and instructs AGVs to perform the jobs. The server continuously polls the AGVs about their status. The low-level control of the AGVs, in terms of actuators, sensors, etc., is handled by the AGV control software called E'nsor[2]. To this end, the layout of the factory is divided into logical elements: *segments* and *nodes*. A logical segment typically corresponds to a physical part of a path of three to five meters. E'nsor is able to steer the AGV per segment, and the AGV can stop on every node, possibly to change direction. E'nsor understands five basic actions:

- Move(segment): instructs E'nsor to drive the AGV over the given segment. Each segment and node is identified by a unique identifier.
- Pick(segment): instructs E'nsor to drive the AGV over the given segment and to pick the load at the end of it.
- Drop(segment): the same as pick, but drops a load the AGV is carrying.
- Park(segment): instructs E'nsor to drive the AGV over the given segment and to park at the end of the segment.
- Charge(segment): instructs E'nsor to drive the AGV over a given segment to a battery charge station and start charging batteries there.

The physical execution of these actions, such as staying on track on a segment, turning, and manipulation of loads are handled by E'nsor. Reading out specific sensor data, such as the current position and the battery level is also provided by E'nsor. When the transport is finished, the server reports the completion of the transport to the corresponding client system.

New Quality Requirements for AGV Transportation Systems. The centralized approach has successfully been applied in numerous practical systems. The main quality properties of the traditional approach are efficiency, configurability and predictability. However, the evolution of the market put forward new requirements for AGV transportation systems.

First, customers request for flexibility of the transportation systems, AGVs should adapt their behavior with changing circumstances. In particular, AGVs should be able to exploit opportunities, e.g., when an AGV is assigned a transport and moves toward the load, it should be possible for this AGV to switch tasks along the way if a more interesting transport pops up. AGVs should also be able to anticipate possible difficulties, e.g., when the battery level of the AGV decreases, the AGV should prefer a zone close to a charge station. Another desired property is that AGVs should be able to cope with particular situations, e.g., when a truck with loads arrives at the factory, the system should be able to reorganize smoothly.

Second, customers expect that the AGV transportation system is open, i.e., the system should be able to deal with leaving AGVs, or new AGVs entering the system. One example is maintenance. Currently, maintenance of AGVs is based on fixed worst-case

---

[2] E'nsor ® is an acronym for Egemin Navigation System On Robot.

rules. However, the time an AGV should go into maintenance depends on the number of movements (turns, picks, drops, . . .) the AGV has executed. Since this information can be locally collected on each AGV, it is more precise (and efficient) to allow each AGV to decide individually whether to go into maintenance or not. AGVs can then leave and enter the system at arbitrary moments. As another example of openness, some customers want to interact with the AGVs on the factory floor, by directly assigning a job to a particular AGV.

In summary, flexibility and openness are high-ranking quality requirements for to-day's AGV transportation systems.

3.3   A Decentralized Solution with a Situated MAS

The general idea of the decentralized approach is to put more autonomy in the AGVs allowing for improved flexibility and openness. In the decentralized solution, vehicles become autonomous agents which make decisions based on their current situation, and who coordinate with other agents to ensure the system as a whole processes transports.

Decentralized control of automated warehouse transportation systems is an active area of research. In [7], Ong gives an extensive overview of decentralized agent-based manufacturing control and compares the pros and cons of centralized versus decentralized control. According to Ong, the advantages of decentralized control are: (1) it is more economical w.r.t. required processing power, and (2) it is more reliable. Disadvantages of decentralization are: (1) performance of the system may be affected by the communication links between nodes, (2) while the distributed approach is designed to cope with disturbances, there is, in general, a trade-off between its performance and the reactivity of the system to disturbances, and (3) myopic decision may occur due to the lack of global information. Examples of other recent decentralized approaches are [8] that discusses a decentralized cognitive planning approach for collision-free movements of vehicles, and [2] that discusses a behavior-based approach for decentralized control of automatic guided vehicles. However, both approaches are validated only in simulations under a number of simplifying assumptions. In general, applications of decentralized control of automated transportation systems in real industrial settings are rarely discussed in literature.

Besides the advantages of decentralization listed by Ong, we believe that in principle, a MAS-based AGV transportation system also becomes more flexible. Since each AGV acts locally, it can better exploit opportunities and adapt its behavior under changing circumstances. On the other hand, the benefits of a decentralized approach do not come for free. Since an all knowing entity in the system does not exist, inter-AGV coordination becomes complex. Bandwidth must be considered carefully to ensure that the communication network does not become a bottleneck. Another important consequence of decentralization, not mentioned by Ong, is an increased complexity of debugging.

The general challenge in the project is to support the current functionality, while aiming to improve flexibility and openness, and keeping in mind the benefits of the centralized approach. So far, we have implemented AGV routing, information sharing and collision avoidance. We have validated the solution in a test setup with two physical AGVs, and in a number of advanced simulation cases with up to six AGVs. Many challenges lie ahead. Currently, we are developing architectural models to cope with order assignment and deadlock prevention. Only when these models are implemented and tested, we can start the validation of the integral solution in an advanced setup.

High-Level Model of the Situated MAS. The situated MAS consists of two kinds of agents, *transport agents* and *AGV agents*. Transport agents are located at *transport bases*. AGV agents are located in AGVs that are situated on the factory floor. Figure 1 depicts a high-level model of the situated MAS with one transport base and two AGVs. A transport agent represents a transport that needs to be handled by an AGV. AGV

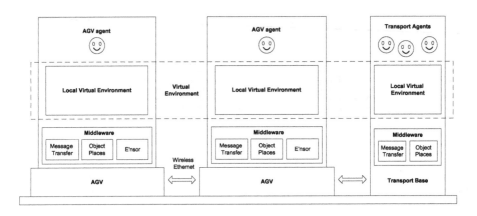

Fig. 1. High-level model of the AGV transportation system

agents are responsible for executing the assigned transports. We fully reused the E'nsor software that deals with the low-level control of the AGVs. As such, the AGV agents control the movement and actions of AGVs on a fairly high level. The communication infrastructure provides a wired network that connects client systems and transport bases, and a wireless network that enables mobile AGVs to communicate with each other and with transport agents on transport bases.

AGVs are situated in a physical environment, however, this environment is very constrained: AGVs cannot manipulate the environment, except by picking and dropping loads. This restricts how AGV agents can exploit their environment. We introduce a virtual environment for agents to live in. This virtual environment offers a medium that agents can use to exchange information and coordinate their behavior. Besides, the virtual environment serves as a suitable abstraction that shields the AGV agents from low-level issues, such as the physical control of the AGV.

In the AGV application, the only physical infrastructure available to the AGVs is a wireless network for communication. In other words, the virtual environment is necessarily distributed over the AGVs and transport bases. In effect, each AGV and each transport base maintains a *local virtual environment*, which is a local manifestation of the virtual environment. Local virtual environments are merged with other local virtual environments opportunistically, as the need arises. In other words, *the* virtual environment as a software entity does not exist; rather, there are as many local virtual environments as there are AGVs and transport bases. Some of these local virtual environments may recently be synchronized with each other, while others may not. From the agent perspective, the virtual environment appears as one entity. The synchronization of the state of neighboring local virtual environments is supported by the ObjectPlaces middleware [11]. We elaborate on state management in the virtual environment in Sect. 4.

Responsibilities of Agents and the Environment. To describe how we apply a situated MAS to control an AGV system, we revisit the five core functionalities of the AGV application described in Sect. 3.1. We describe the main responsibilities of the two types of agents in the MAS, as well as the responsibilities of the virtual environment.

Transport Assignment. As stated above, transports are represented by transport agents that reside on transport bases. Transport bases receive transports from client systems. For each new transport, a new transport agent is created that is responsible to assign the transport to an AGV and to ensure that the transport is completed correctly. Each transport has a priority that depends on the kind of transport, the pending time since its creation, and the nature of other transports in the system. Therefore, transport agents interact with other related transport agents to determine the correct priority over time. Transport agents use the virtual environment to find AGV agents to assign the transports, and to follow the progress of the assigned transports. To assign a transport, the transport agent negotiates with AGV agents of AGVs near to the pick location of the load. Once the transport is assigned, the awarded AGV handles the transport. As soon as the transport is completed, the AGV agent informs the transport agent, that in its turn informs the client system after which the transport agent is removed. The transport agent guarantees the persistence of the transport in the system. If for some reason the assigned AGV is unable to complete the transport, the transport agent may negotiate with other AGVs to reassign the order.

Routing. For routing purposes, the virtual environment has a static map of the paths through the warehouse. This graph-like map corresponds to the layout used by E'nsor. To allow agents to find their way through the warehouse efficiently, the virtual environment provides signs on the map that the agents use to find their way to a given destination. These signs can be compared to traffic signs by the road that provide directions to drivers. At each node in the map, a sign in the virtual environment represents the cost to a given destination for each outgoing segment. The cost of the path is the sum of the static costs of the segments in the path. The cost per segment is based on the average time it takes for an AGV to drive over the segment. The agent perceives the signs in its environment, and uses them to determine which segment it will take next.

Gathering Traffic Information. Besides the static routing cost associated with each segment, the cost is also dependent on dynamic factors, such as congestion of a segment. To warn other agents that certain paths are blocked or have a long waiting time, agents mark segments with a dynamic cost on a *traffic map* in the virtual environment. Agents mark the traffic map by dropping pheromones on the applicable segments. When AGVs come in each others neighborhood, the information of the traffic maps is exchanged and merged to provide up-to-date information to the AGV agents. Since pheromones evaporate over time, outdated information automatically vanishes over time. AGV agents take the information on the traffic map into account when they decide how to drive through the warehouse.

Collision Avoidance. AGV agents avoid collisions by coordinating with other agents through the virtual environment. AGV agents mark the path they are going to drive in their environment using *hulls*. The hull of an AGV is the physical area the AGV occupies. A series of hulls then describes the physical area an AGV occupies along a certain path. If the area is not marked by other hulls (the AGV's own hulls do not intersect with others), the AGV can move along and actually drive over the reserved path. Afterwards, the AGV removes the markings in the virtual environment. We zoom in on collision avoidance in Sect. 4.4.

Deadlock Prevention. The basic mechanisms for deadlock prevention provided in the traditional approach can be adopted in the MAS approach. E.g., when an AGV approaches a bidirectional path in the layout, the AGV agent can lock that path via the hull reservation mechanism, or when an AGV reaches an entry point of a critical area where only a limited number of AGVs are allowed, the AGV agent can instruct the AGV to wait there until the area is accessible. However, those rules only provide a partial solution to avoid deadlock. Currently, we study two additional tracks to deal with deadlock, one with a supervising MAS that monitors the AGV movements and provides feedback to the AGV agents, and another where AGVs themselves monitor their neighborhood and exchange information regarding deadlock threats via the environment.

4   A Virtual Environment for AGV Agents

This section describes the virtual environment in the AGV transportation application. We focus on the virtual environment from the viewpoint of AGV agents. First we give a broad overview of the structure of the virtual environment, in three parts. The first part gives a brief overview of the high-level model of an AGV and situates the virtual environment in this model. The second part describes how the local virtual environment synchronizes its state with other local virtual environments. The third part describes how the virtual environment handles perception, action and communication. Concluding with an example, we describe how the virtual environment is exploited by the AGV agents to avoid collisions.

4.1   High-Level Model of an AGV

Figure 2 depicts an overview of an AGV. The AGV agent is shown in the top layer of the model. We do not elaborate on the architecture of the AGV agent; it is based on the reference architecture discussed in [13] and [14]. The AGV agent is situated in the virtual environment, shown as a layer below the top layer. The virtual environment uses the middleware layer, that is composed of a Message Transfer System, the ObjectPlaces middleware [11] (both discussed later) and E'nsor. The operating system is located below the middleware. Finally, the bottom layer represents the physical infrastructure of the AGV, including a processor, communication infrastructure, actuators and sensors. We further elaborate on the virtual environment and the supporting middleware hereafter.

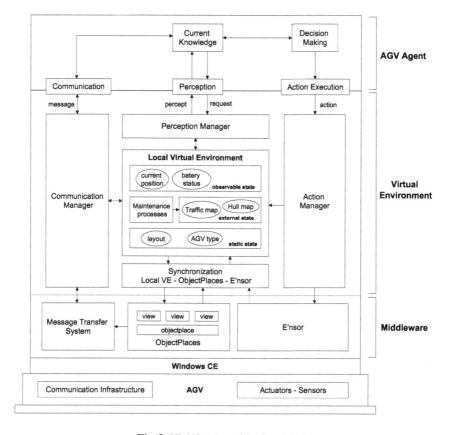

Fig. 2. High-level model of an AGV

4.2   Managing State in the Virtual Environment

Since the virtual environment is necessarily distributed over the AGVs and transport bases, each local virtual environment is responsible to keep its state synchronized with other local virtual environments. The state of the local virtual environment on an AGV is divided into three categories:

1. Static state: this is state that does not change over time. A typical example is the layout of the factory floor, which is needed for the AGV to navigate. Static state must never be exchanged between local virtual environments, since it is common knowledge and never changes.
2. Observable state: this is state that can be changed in one local virtual environment, while other local virtual environments can only observe the state. An AGV typically obtains this kind of state from its sensors directly. An example is an AGV's position. Local virtual environments are able to observe another AGV's position, but only the local virtual environment on the AGV itself is able to read it from its sensor, and change the representation of the position in the local virtual environment. No

conflict ever arises between two local virtual environments concerning the update of observable state.

3. Shared state: this is state that can be modified in two local virtual environments concurrently. So, two or more local virtual environments can conflict on what is the "right" state. The traffic map, containing dynamic costs associated with segments, is an example of shared state. Several AGV agents can modify the cost on the same segment concurrently. When the local virtual environments on these AGVs synchronize, costs of the local virtual environments' traffic maps are mutually exchanged and conflicts are resolved to generate an up-to-date traffic map in both local virtual environments.

In order to manage and maintain this state, the local virtual environment performs three basic activities. We describe each of these in turn.

The first activity is synchronizing the state of the local virtual environment with the AGV's sensors. The local virtual environment uses E'nsor to regularly poll the vehicles's current status and adjust its own state appropriately. For example, if the AGV's position has changed, the AGV position in the local virtual environment is updated.

The second activity the virtual environment performs is synchronizing the state of the local virtual environment with other AGVs. This is supported by the ObjectPlaces middleware. ObjectPlaces offers high-level abstractions to deal with communication in mobile and ad hoc networks. The local virtual environment uses the middleware by sharing objects in a tuplespace-like container, called an *objectplace*. Every AGV has one objectplace locally available. Objects in objectplaces on remote AGVs can be gathered using a *view*. The local virtual environment can define a view by (1) specifying which AGVs' objectplaces need to be included in the view (e.g. the objectplaces of all AGVs within a specific range), and (2) specifying what objects need to be included in the view (e.g. hull objects). Based on these specifications, the ObjectPlaces middleware then builds a local collection of objects reflecting the current contents of the remote objectplaces. In other words, a local virtual environment shares data with other AGVs by putting objects in the local virtual environment's objectplace. Local virtual environments gather data from other AGVs by defining a view on the objectplaces of those AGVs. For example, when an AGV agent marks a hull in the environment, this hull is published in the local virtual environment's objectplace. When the AGV agent wants to perceive hulls in its vicinity, the local virtual environment defines a view on all hull objects in objectplaces of AGVs within a certain physical distance from the AGV. The middleware then gathers the hull objects from the objectplaces on the appropriate AGVs. The local virtual environment can then use the hull objects to determine whether the requested path is free or not and return this results to the agent.

The third and last activity is maintaining the state of the virtual environment locally. This is done by *maintenance processes* in the local virtual environment itself. An example is the maintenance of pheromones. A change of local state possibly triggers an update of state in the local virtual environment's objectplaces, so that other virtual environments can synchronize with the new state.

In summary, the virtual environment deals with the management of state in the distributed system, hiding many aspects of distribution from the AGV agent. Agents can act and perceive in the local virtual environment, which in turn contacts local environments on other AGVs to synchronize state.

4.3   Perceiving, Acting and Communicating

The virtual environment offers abilities for perception, action and communication to the AGV agent, shielding low-level details from the agent.

Perception is handled by the *perception manager*. The perception manager's task is straightforward: when the agent requests a percept, for example the current positions of neighboring AGVs, the perception manager queries the necessary information from the local virtual environment and returns it to the agent.

Actions are handled by the *action manager*. A first kind of actions concerns the physical actions of the AGV, for example moving over a segment or picking a load. These actions are handled fairly easily by passing them on to the E'nsor control software. A second kind of actions does not actually have an effect on the behavior of the AGV, but manipulates the virtual environment. Marking hulls is one example of this, which is described in detail in Sect. 4.4. Another is dropping a virtual pheromone. In general, an action can be handled by passing it down to Ensor, and/or by changing the local virtual environment which in turn may change the content of the objectplace.

Communication is handled by the *communication manager*. Agents can communicate directly with other agents through the virtual environment. A typical example is an AGV agent that communicates with a transport agent. Another example is an AGV agent that requests the AGV agent of a waiting AGV to move out of the way. The virtual environment is responsible for translating high level messages to messages that can be sent through the network (resolving agent names to IP numbers for example). For this, it uses the *message transfer system* in the middleware layer.

In summary, the virtual environment offers high level primitives to the AGV agent to act in the world, perceive the world, and communicate with other agents. The virtual environment shields the agent from having to deal with lower level issues.

4.4   A Specific Scenario: Collision Avoidance

We now describe a specific scenario, to illustrate how collision avoidance works. In the centralized approach, collision avoidance is realized as follows: for each AGV in the system, a series of *hulls* are calculated along the path each AGV is going to drive. When two or more such *hull projections* overlap, AGVs are on a collision course and all except one AGV are commanded to wait.

In a decentralized architecture, a central arbitrator does not exist. However, the virtual environment enables the agents to act as if they are situated in a shared environment, while the virtual environment takes on the burden of coordination. Figure 3 shows a series of screenshots of a simulation run in a realistic map. In Fig. 3(a), two AGVs are approaching one another. We call the AGV approaching from the top AGV A, and the other AGV B. Both are projecting hulls in the environment. At this point, no conflict is

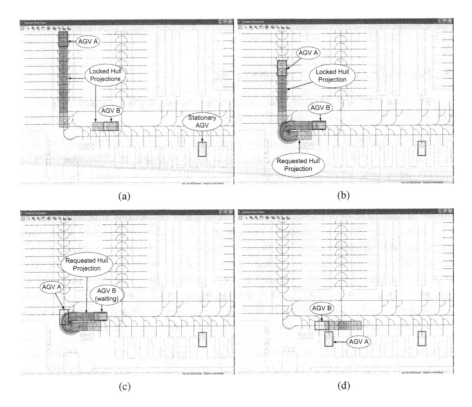

(a)   (b)

(c)   (d)

Fig. 3. (a) Two AGVs approaching, (b) A conflict is detected, (c) One AGV passes safely, (d) The second AGV can pass as well

detected. In Fig. 3(b), AGV B has projected further ahead, and is now in conflict with the hull projection of AGV A. However, since AGV A's hull projection was already locked, AGV B must wait. In Fig. 3(c), AGV A is taking the curve, passing AGV B. Finally, in Fig. 3(d), AGV A has parked at the bottom, and AGV B can start moving.

We now describe the collision avoidance mechanism in more detail. First, we focus on how the agent avoids collision without being aware of the actual underlying collision avoidance protocol, then we study the work behind the scenes (i.e. the protocol) in the virtual environment.

In order to drive, the agent takes the following actions:

1. The agent determines the path it intends to follow over the layout. The agent determines how much of this path it wants to lock. This is determined by a safe stopping distance on the one hand, and the application of basic rules for deadlock avoidance on the other hand. As an example of the latter, if the AGV tries to lock a bidirectional path, it must lock that path until the end, since otherwise another AGV might enter it from the other direction, leading directly to a deadlock situation.

2. The agent marks the path it intends to drive with a *requested hull projection*. This projection contains the agents id and a priority, that depends on the current transport the AGV is handling.

3. The agent perceives the environment to observe the result of its action.
4. The agent examines the perceived result. There are two possibilities:
   (a) The hull is marked as "locked" in the environment; it is safe to drive.
   (b) The hull is not marked as locked. This means that the agent's hull projection conflicted with that of another agent. The agent may not pass; at this point the agent may decide to wait and look again at a later time, or remove its hull projection and take another path altogether.

The virtual environment plays an important role in this coordination approach: it must make sure that a hull projection becomes locked eventually. To this end, the local virtual environment of the AGV agent that requests a new hull projection, executes a collision avoidance protocol with local virtual environments of nearby AGVs.

It is desirable to make the set of nearby AGVs not larger than necessary, since it is not scalable to interact with every AGV in the system. On the other hand, the set must include all AGVs with which a collision is possible: safety must be guaranteed.

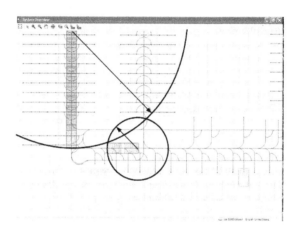

Fig. 4. Determining nearby AGVs

A solution to this problem is shown in Fig. 4. The local virtual environment of a *requesting AGV* will interact with the local virtual environments of other AGVs whose *hull projection circle* overlaps with the hull projection of the requesting AGV. The hull projection circle is defined by a center point, which is the position of the AGV itself, and a radius, which is equal to the distance from the AGV to the furthest point on its hull projection. If two such circles overlap, this indicates (to a first approximation) that the two AGVs might collide. We call the set of AGVs with overlapping hull projection circles the *requested AGVs*.

The local virtual environment of the requesting AGV executes the following protocol with the local virtual environment's of requested AGVs. The protocol is a variant on well-known mutual exclusion protocols based on voting.

1. The local virtual environment of the requesting AGV sends the requested hull projection to the local environments of all requested AGVs.

2. The local environments of requested AGVs check whether the projection overlaps with their hull projection. There are three possibilities for each of the requested AGVs:

   (a) No hull projections overlap. The local virtual environment of the requested AGV sends an "allowed" message to the local virtual environment of the requesting AGV.

   (b) The requesting AGV's hull projection overlaps with the requested AGV's hull projection, and the requested AGV's hull is already locked. The local virtual environment of the requested AGV sends a "forbidden" message to the local virtual environment of the requesting AGV.

   (c) The requesting AGV's hull projection overlaps with the requested AGV's hull projection, and the requested AGV's hull is not locked. Since each of the requested hulls contains a priority, the local virtual environment of the requested AGV can check which hull projection has precedence. If the hull projection of the requesting AGV has a higher priority than that of the requested AGV, the local virtual environment of the requested AGV replies "allowed"; it replies "forbidden" otherwise.

3. The local virtual environment of the requesting AGV waits for all "votes" to come in. If all local virtual environments of the requested AGVs have voted "allowed", the hull projection can be locked and the local virtual environment is updated. If not, the local virtual environment of the requesting AGV waits a random amount of time and then tries again from step 1.

If at any time, the agent removes the requested hull from the virtual environment, the protocol is aborted.

In this scenario, the virtual environment serves as a flexible coordination medium, which hides much of the distribution of the system from the agents: agents coordinate by putting marks in the environment, and observing marks from other agents.

5   Conclusions

Situated agents exploit the environment to coordinate their behavior and reach their goals. Research in this area almost invariably assumes the existence of an exploitable environment a priori that is accessible for all agents, either by centralizing or by providing infrastructural support especially for environments. A possible critique on this research is that it takes the access to the environment as a common shared entity for granted, whereas the absence of such an entity is the essence of many multi-agent based systems. On the contrary, we have shown that an environment does not need to be a common shared entity to be useful. We introduced the concept of virtual environment, a *decentralized* entity in an application where a centralized approach is undesirable and no shared infrastructure is available to deploy an environment as a common accessible entity. We also showed that offering an observable and moldable environment to agents living in a constrained physical environment, strengthens the MAS approach instead of diluting it. The virtual environment is a first-order abstraction in the designed solution of the AGV transportation application.

So far, we have implemented AGV routing, information sharing and collision avoidance. We have validated the solution in a test setup with two physical AGVs, and in a number of advanced simulation cases. The next challenges are order assignment and deadlock avoidance. With respect to order assignment we study two different tracks, one with an adaptive version of the Contract-Net protocol and one with a gradient field based approach. In this latter approach, each transport agent emits a gradient field in the virtual environment that attracts interested AGVs to the pick location of the load, while each interested AGV emits a gradient field that repels other competitor AGVs. The gradient fields guide idle AGVs toward the most appropriate transports, ensuring maximal flexibility (e.g., AGVs take into account opportunities –new transports that pop up– when they drive toward a load). To deal with deadlock, we also follow two possible approaches, one with a supervising MAS that monitors the AGV movements and provides feedback to the AGV agents, and another where AGVs themselves monitor their neighborhood and exchange information regarding deadlock threats via the virtual environment.

We are convinced that exploiting the environment in our ongoing AGV research case is an asset, and will continue our validation of situated MAS in this complex real-world application.

References

1. Bonabeau, E., Henaux, F., Guérin, S., Snyers, D., Kuntz P., Theraulaz, G.: Routing in Telecommunications Networks with "Smart" Ant-Like Agents. Intelligent Agents for Telecommunications Applications (1998)
2. Berman, S., Edan, Y., Jamshidi, M.: Decentralized autonomous Automatic Guided Vehicles in material handling. Transactions on Robotics and Automation 19(4) (2003)
3. De Wolf, T., Samaey, G., Holvoet, T., Roose, D.: Decentralised autonomic computing: Analysing self-organising emergent behaviour using advanced numerical methods. 2th International Conference on Autonomic Computing. IEEE (2005)
4. Ferber, J.: Multiagent Systems: An Introduction to Distributed Artificail Intelligence. Addison-Wesley (1999) 439-445
5. Macy, M., Willer, R.: From Factors to Actors: Computational Sociology and Agent-Based Modeling. Annual Review of Sociology 28 (2002)
6. Mamei, M., Zambonelli, F.: Programming Pervasive and Mobile Computing Applications with the TOTA Middleware. International Conference on Pervasive Computing and Communication (2004)
7. Ong, L.: An investigation of an agent-based scheduling in decentralised manufacturing control. Ph.D Disseration University of Cambridge (2003)
8. Pallottino, L., Scordio, V.G., Frazzoli, E., Bicchi, A.: Decentralized cooperative conflict resolution for multiple nonholonomic vehicles. AIAA Conference on Guidance, Navigation and Control (2005)
9. Parunak, H.V.D., Baker, A.D., Clark, S.J.: The AARIA Agent Architecture: From Manufacturing Requirements to Agent-Based System Design. Workshop on Agent-Based Manufacturing (1998)
10. Parunak, H.V.D., Brueckner, S., Sauter, J.: Digital Pheromones ofr Coordination of Unmanned Vehicles. Post-proceedings of the First International Workshop on Environments for Multiagent Systems, Lecture Notes in Computer Science Series, Vol. 3374 (2005)

11. Schelfthout, K., Holvoet, T., Berbers, Y.: Views: Customizable abstractions for context-aware applications in MANETs. Proceedings of the fourth international workshop on Software engineering for large-scale multi-agent systems, St. Louis, USA. ACM Press (2005).

12. Sauter, J.A., Parunak, H.V.D.: ANTS in the Supply Chain. Workshop on Agent based Decision Support for Managing the Internet-Enabled Supply Chain, Seattle, WA (1999)

13. Weyns, D., Holvoet, T.: A Formal Model for Situated Multi-agent Systems. Formal Approaches for Multi-Agent Systems, R. Verbrugge and B. Dunin-Keplicz Eds., Special Issue of Fundamenta Informaticae 63(2-3) (2004)

14. Weyns, D., Steegmans, E., Holvoet, T.: Protocol Based Communication for Situated Multi-agent Systems. 3th International Joint Conference on Autonomous Agents and Multi-Agent Systems, New York (2004)

15. Weyns, D., Parunak, H.V.D., Michel, F., Holvoet, T., Ferber, J.: Environments for Multi-agent Systems, State-of-the-art and Research Challenges. First International Workshop on Environments for Multiagent Systems, Lecture Notes in Computer Science Series, Vol. 3374 (2005)

16. Wooldridge, M.: An Introduction to MultiAgent Systems. John Wiley and Sons, UK (2002)

Web Sites as Agents' Environments: General Framework and Applications

Stefania Bandini, Sara Manzoni, and Giuseppe Vizzari

Dipartimento di Informatica, Sistemistica e Comunicazione,
Università degli Studi di Milano–Bicocca,
Via Bicocca degli Arcimboldi 8 20126 Milan, Italy
Tel.: +39 02 64487835; fax: +39 02 64487839
{bandini, manzoni, vizzari}@disco.unimib.it

Abstract. A web site presents an intrinsic graph–like spatial structure composed of pages connected by hyperlinks. This structure may represent an environment in which agents related to visitors of the web site are positioned and moved in order to track their navigation. To consider this structure and to keep track of these movements allows the monitoring of the site and its visitors, in order to support the enhancement of the site itself through forms of adaptivity, but also to introduce new forms of interaction among registered visitors. This paper presents a model supporting the collection of information related to user's behaviour in a web site, and an application supporting the proposal of hyperlinks based on the history of user's movement in the web site environment. Moreover the paper briefly describes a system implementing a context-aware form of interaction, supporting the communication among visitors of a web site through the exploitation of its structure.

1   Introduction

A web site presents an intrinsic graph–like spatial structure composed of pages connected by hyperlinks. However, this structure is generally not considered by web servers, which essentially act as a sort of extended and specific File Transfer Protocol servers [1], receiving requests for specific contents and supplying the related data. Several web–based applications instead exploit the structure of the sites itself to support users in their navigation, generating awareness of their position. For instance, many e–commerce sites emphasize the hierarchical structure linking pages related to categories (and possibly subcategories), included products and their specific views, and remind users' relative position (i.e. links to higher level nodes in the tree structure). Some specific web–based applications, mainly bulletin boards and forums (see, e.g., phpBB[1]), are also able to inform users about the presence of other visitors of the web site or even, more precisely, of the specific area of the site that they are currently viewing. Web site structure and users' context represent thus pieces of information that can be exploited to supply visitors a more effective presentation of site contents.

---

[1] http://www.phpbb.com/

D. Weyns, H. Van Dyke Parunak, and F. Michel (Eds.): E4MAS 2005, LNAI 3830, pp. 235–250, 2006.
© Springer-Verlag Berlin Heidelberg 2006

Different visitors, however, may have very different goals and needs, especially with reference to large web sites made up of several categories and subcategories. This consideration is the main motivation for the research in the area of adaptive web sites [2]. The various forms of adaptation may provide a customization of site's presentation for an individual user or even an optimization of the site for all users. There are various approaches supporting these adaptation activities, but they are generally based on the analysis of log files which store low–level requests to the web server: this kind of file is generally made up of entries including the address of the machine that originated the request, the indication of the time and the resource associated to the request. In order to obtain meaningful information on users' activities these raw data must be processed (see, e.g., [3]), for instance in order to collapse requests related to various elements of a single web page (e.g. composing frames and images) into a single entry. Moreover this kind of information must be further processed to detect groups of requests that indicate the path (web pages connected by hyperlinks) that a user followed in the navigation. Recent results [4] show that this kind of analysis, also referred to as web usage mining, could benefit from the consideration of site contents and structure.

This paper proposes to exploit the graph-like structure of a web site as a Multi–Agent System (MAS) environment [5] on which agents representing visitors of the web site are positioned and moved according to their navigation. In particular, in this case, the environment is a virtual structure which allows the gathering of information on user's activities in a more structured way, simplifying subsequent phases of analysis and adaptation of site contents. Furthermore, part of the adaptivity could be carried out without the need of an off-line analysis, but could be the result of a more dynamic monitoring of users' activities. In particular, the paths that are followed by users are often related to recurrent patterns of navigation which may indicate that the user could benefit from the proposal of additional links providing shortcuts to the terminal web pages. Index pages may thus be enhanced by the inclusion of links representing shortcuts to the typical destinations of the user in the navigation of the web site. Users without a relevant history (and also anonymous or unrecognized ones) may instead exploit the paths that are most commonly followed by site visitors. Moreover such an information could also be communicated to the webmaster suggesting possible modifications to the static predefined structure of the site. This approach provides thus both a support for site optimization, but also for the customization to specific visitor's needs and preferences.

The metaphor of a web site as an environment on which users move in search for information is not new (see, e.g., [6] but also more recent approaches such as [7]), and its application to web site adaptation resembles the emergent, collective phenomenon of trail formation [8] which is can be identified in several biological systems. However this proposal provides more than just gather information on users' behaviours for sake of web pages adaptation or navigation support, but exploits the MAS environment to provide users a means for mutual perception and interaction. In fact information related to users' positions on the environment representing the web site can also be used to supply them awareness information on other visitors which are currently browsing the same page or area of the site. Moreover to keep track of this information allows the conception of a form of interaction among users that is based on their positions on the site. Essentially, more than just showing a user the other registered visitors that are "nearby" (i.e. viewing the same page or adjacent ones), the system should also allow to communicate with them. This form of interaction clearly requires the adoption of a supporting technology that goes beyond the request/response form (e.g. a Java applet). This kind of interaction represents a hybrid between a common web site and an instant messenger (see, e.g., ICQ2Go![2]).

The following section describes the general framework of this approach, the mapping between the web site structure and agents' environment, while Section 3 describes the kind of gathered information on agents' movement in their environment. Section 4 describes an application providing the exploitation of this kind of information for the adaptation of web pages, both for customization and optimization, while Section 5 briefly introduces a system supporting a context-aware form of interaction among visitors of the same web site. Concluding remarks and future developments will end the paper.

2   Site Structure and Agents' Positions

A web site is made up of a set of HTML pages (generally including multimedia contents) connected by means of hyperlinks. It is possible to obtain a graph-like structure mapping pages to nodes and hyperlinks to edges interconnecting these nodes. This kind of spatial structure could be exploited as an *environment* on which agents related to site visitors are placed and move according to the related users' activities. A diagram showing a sample mapping among a web site and this kind of structure is shown in Figure 1.

This structure can be either static or dynamic: for instance it could vary according to specific rules and information stored in a database (i.e. database driven web sites). However, this kind of structure (both for static and dynamic web sites) can generally be obtained by means of a crawler (see, e.g., Sphinx [9] and the related WebSphinx project[3]); then it could be maintained by having periodic updates.

Given this spatial structure, a multi-agent model allowing an explicit representation of this aspect of agents' environment is needed to represent and exploit this kind of information. Environments for Multi Agent Systems [10] and situated agents represent promising topics in the context of MAS research, aimed at providing first class abstractions for agents environment (which can be more than just a message transport system), towards a clearer definition of concepts such as *locality* and *perception*. There are not many models for situated agents, which provide an explicit representation of agent's environment. Some of them are mainly focused on providing mechanisms for coordinating situated agent's

---

[2] http://go.icq.com/
[3] http://www-2.cs.cmu.edu/ rcm/websphinx/

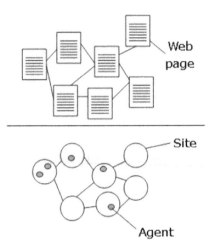

Fig. 1. The diagram shows a mapping between a web site structure and an agent environment

actions [11], other provide the interaction among agents through a modification of the shared environment (see, e.g., [12,13]). An interesting approach that we adopted for this work is represented by the Multilayered Multi Agent Situated Systems (MMASS) [14] model. MMASS allows the explicit representation of agents' environment through a set of interconnected layers whose structure is an undirected graph of nodes (also referred to as sites in the model terminology; from now on we will use the term node to avoid confusion with web sites). The model was adopted given the similarity among the defined spatial structure of the environment and the structure underlying a web site. Moreover the model defines a set of allowed actions for agents' behavioural specification (including a primitive for agents' movement); for this specific application, however, the constraint which limits the number of agents positioned in a node was relaxed. In fact there is no limit to the number of users that are viewing the same web page.

Moreover a platform for the specification and execution of simulations based on the MMASS model [15] was exploited to implement the part of the system devoted to the management of agents in their environments. The definition of spatial structure of the environment was supplied by the previously introduced crawler, while agents' movement is guided by external inputs generated by the requests issued by the related web site visitor. The general architecture of the system is shown in Figure 2: the *Agent server* module is implemented through the MMASS platform, while the *Web server* is represented by Snip-Snap[4], a Java-based weblog and wiki software. The highlighted *Tracker* module is a implemented through a Java Servlet, which is invoked by every page of the site but does not produce a visible effect on the related web page. Contents created through the SnipSnap page creation facility automatically include this

---

[4] http://snipsnap.org

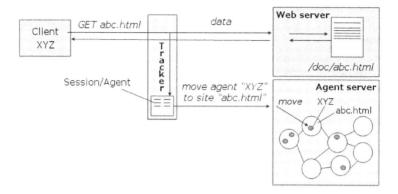

Fig. 2. A diagram showing how user actions influence the related agent through the capture of requests by the Tracker module

invocation, which is specified in the template for new pages, while other contents (e.g. specific HTML pages, Java Server Pages) should explicitly state it in order to be included in the site spatial structure. The Tracker is responsible for the management of user authentication and requests, but it is also responsible for the creation of agents related to visitors and for the triggering of their movement in the environment related to the web site.

In particular, when a user makes his/her first page request, the Tracker tries to set a cookie on the client including the session information. If the cookie is accepted, then it is possible to use the session information and the *Referer* parameter of the HTTP request header to track user's movement in the graph related to the web site. Requests from clients not accepting cookies will thus not be monitored.

Moreover, the management of agents creation and movement is not as simple as its intuitive description might indicate. In fact, the same user could be using different browser pages or tabs to simultaneously view distinct pages of the site. In other words, a user might be simultaneously following different trajectories in his/her web site navigation. In order to manage these situations, a user can be related to different agents, and his/her requests must be associated to the correct agent (possibly a new one). Finally, agents related to finished (or interrupted) user navigation should be eliminated by the system, storing the relevant part of their state in a persistent way, until the related user requires again a page of the site. In particular, remote users' requests may be divided into two main classes, according to their effects on the Tracker and Agent server:

– *creating a new agent*: whenever a new user requires a web page, the Tracker will invoke the Agent Server requiring the creation of an agent whose starting position is the node related to the required page; the same effect is generated by a request coming from an already registered user which was not present in the system, but in this case information related to previous user agents must be retrieved in order to determine the new agent's state; finally, when

an already registered and active user requires a page that is not adjacent to
its current one, a new agent related to the new browsing activity must also
be created;

– *generating the movement of an agent*: when the viewer of a page follows one
of the provided links, the related web browser will generate a request for
a page that is adjacent to one of the related agents which must be moved
to the node related to the required page; whenever there are two or more
agents in positions that are adjacent to the required page, in order to solve
the ambiguity and choose the agent to be moved, the Tracker will invoke
the Session object in which it stores the current URL related to the viewed
page.

Finally, the Tracker can also represent a resource in the management of the
spatial structure of the environment. Whenever the high dynamism of the structure (and in particular the addition of new pages) or particular architectural
choices or web server configurations prevent the adoption of the web crawler
solution, the Tracker can actually create sites related to pages that were not previously present in the environment, interacting with the Agent Server. Figure 3
shows a sample situation in which the spatial structure of the environment is
not present until actual requests are captured by the Tracker. In (a) no page of
the web site is still present in the environment, while in (b) a user just requested
the page A. The latter was analyzed and outgoing links were identified, so three
sites were created, respectively related to pages A, B and C; user's request of
page C generates in turn the situation shown in (c), that is, the creation of sites
related to pages D, E and F.

A prototype implementation of this approach to the creation and management of the spatial structure of the web site (as well as the web crawling solution)
was realized and tested in a small scale web site, but it must be noted that this
work is not meant as a contribution to solving the "invisible web" [16] issues (i.e.
pages on the World Wide Web that are not simply indexed by common search
engines and related technologies). It represents instead a possible approach to
the design and development of web sites exploiting a MAS architecture support-

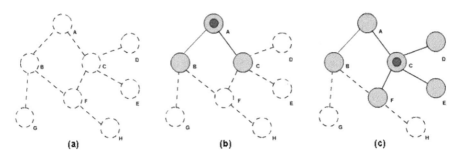

Fig. 3. The diagram shows the dynamic management of the web space according to
actual requests captured by the Tracker

ing a novel form of users' monitoring, a simple adaptation approach and a new form interaction among users.

The following section will describe how the raw information that can be gathered thanks to the above described framework can be processed in order to obtain higher level indications on users' behaviours.

3   Gathered Information: Users' Traces

This system allows to gather and exploit two kinds of information: first of all situated agents related to web site visitors have a perception of their local context, both in terms of relative position, adjacent nodes and presence of other visitors; second, agents may gather information related to the paths defined by the browsing activities or the related user in the site itself.

There are inherent issues in determining in a precise way the actual users' activities on the web site, due to the underlying request/response model: the only available indications on these activities can be obtained by requests captured by the Tracker. In particular, we have an indication of the page that was required by a user and the time-stamp of the request. Starting from this raw information we can try to detect *emerging links*, which are hyperlinks that are not provided by the structure of the site but can be derived by the behaviour of specific visitors. To this purpose, the concept of *trace* was introduced as a higher level information describing the behaviour of a user. A trace synthesizes a path followed by a user, from the web page representing his/her entry point, to a different point of the environment (i.e. another web page) which may represent an interesting destination. Every agent related to a visiting user is associated to a *temporary* trace, and it may generate several actual traces (also called *closed* traces) in the course of its movement in the environment.

Formally a trace is a three-tuple $\langle A_{Id}, Start, Dest \rangle$, where A_{Id} represents the identifier of the agent to which the trace is related, while $Start$ and $Dest$ indicate the starting and destination node related to the browsing sequence which generated the trace. A new trace is generated when a user enters the site, triggering the creation of a related agent. The starting trace has a null value for the destination node. Subsequent requests by the user generated following hyperlinks will bring the related agent to an adjacent node, and the the $Dest$ field of the corresponding trace will be modified in order to reflect user's current position. Non trivial traces provide $Start$ and $Dest$ nodes that are not directly connected by means of a hyperlink.

There are two relevant exceptions to the basic rule for trace update, that are related respectively to the *duplication* of a trace and to its *closing*. According to the previously introduced informal definition, a trace should be coherent in time and space. In fact, whenever the same user requires simultaneously two or more different pages he/she is probably following distinct search trajectories, possibly even related to different goals. In this case, as previously introduced, the Tracker will detect this situation and create additional agents that refer to the same user. Figure 4 shows two sample situations providing respectively trace

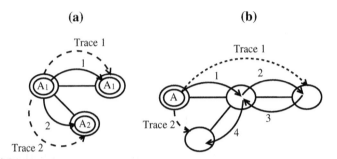

Fig. 4. A diagram describing two traces that are derived by a sequence of user requests

duplication and closing: in (a) the user has chosen to open a hyperlink in a new browser page (request 1) and then has followed another link in the first browser page (request 2). According to the previously described Tracker behaviour, two agents are now associated to the user, and they are associated to different traces sharing the *Start* field.

In (b), instead, the user has followed links 1 and 2 from the starting page, then he/she made a step back (request 3) and eventually moved to the last known position (request 4). The step back causes the closure of the temporary trace associated to the agent (Trace 1 in the Figure), and the creation of a new temporary one with the same *Start* field (Trace 2). In this case the step back may have different interpretations: it could refer to a negative evaluation of the page contents but it could also indicate the fact that the user has found what he/she was searching for. An information that could be exploited to determine if the *Dest* field of the trace was interesting for the user is the time interval between request 2 and 3: for instance, given Δt_d a threshold indicating the minimum time required to reasonably inspect the content of a specific web page, if $timestamp(3) - timestamp(2) < \Delta t_d$ then Trace 1 could be ignored. However, the mere interval between the two requests is not a safe indicator of the fact that the page was actually viewed and considered interesting.

In fact, the time spent on a web page is also important in order to determine when a temporary trace must be closed. In fact, whenever a user does not issue requests for a certain time we could consider that his/her browsing activity has stopped, possibly because he/she is reading the page related to the *Dest* field of the trace associated to the related agent. In other words, every agent has a timer, set to the previously introduced threshold Δt_d, which is set when the agent is created and it is reset whenever it moves. The action associated to this timer specifies that its temporary trace becomes closed, and a new timer is set: the action associated to this second timer caused the disappearance of the agent from the system, and the storage of the related state.

It is important to note that even anonymous visitors (i.e. non authenticated ones) whose clients are accepting cookies, can be tracked and can thus generate traces, although anonymous ones. The latter can be exploited for sake of web optimization but are not relevant for sake of user specific site customization.

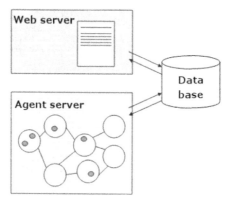

Fig. 5. Users' actions, captured by the related agents, influence the construction of subsequent web pages

Figure 5 shows how the information generated by user agents, and in particular traces, can be used to influence the new pages that will be generated by the Web server, and more precisely by the SnipSnap based Content Management system. In fact the latter uses information stored in a database to compose the required web pages; agents store information related to closed traces into this database, and a specific dynamic user interface element exploits this information to propose links that are not included in the basic structure of the site that are considered interesting, according to the previous user's behaviour. The following section will more thoroughly discuss the application of this framework for web site adaptivity.

4   Web Site Adaptation

4.1   Proposed Approach

The adopted instrument for the dynamic generation of web pages based on the content of a database organizes the structure of pages in blocks. The implemented system provides a static header block, including relevant areas of the web site, a left column providing dynamic additional information, such as the current user position in the structure of the web site and relevant links, and a main central area in which the specific current content is shown in details. The area which is interested in the first experimentation of this approach to content adaptivity is included in the left column. It is aimed at showing a visitor emerging links, that are hyperlinks not included in the predefined structure of the site but are considered interesting according to the history of the related user. These emerging links have some kind of relationship with the previously introduced traces, which represent behaviours and movements of a user in a web site. The strategy which is adopted to select the most relevant traces to be presented to a given user in a given situation represents the behavior of an interface agent whose responsibility is the management of this adaptive sub-block of the user interface related to the web site. Figure 6 presents a screenshot of a sample

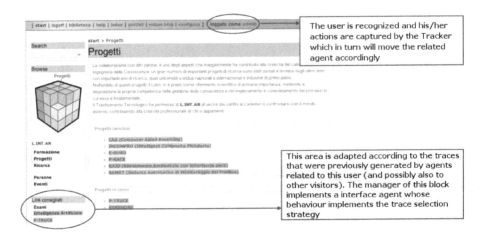

Fig. 6. A screenshot of a web page adapted according to gathered traces and interface agent selection strategy

adapted web page: the visitor is recognized and his/her movement are monitored by the Tracker. The lower part of the left column presents three links related to stored traces related to the same user.

A first element of this strategy is adopted when new users (or non authenticated ones) enter the site. In this case the user has no previous history (or it is not possible to correlate the user with his/her history), and the adopted strategy considers all stored traces, not considering the user which generated them. An additional information that is stored with traces is the number of times that the related trace was effectively selected and shown to a user and the number of times that the related link was effectively exploited by a user. This kind of information allows to obtain an indication of the success rate of the hyperlinks that were chosen by the interface agent, and can be exploited by this agent to select the traces to be shown in the adaptive block. Furthermore this success rate can be used by the web master to consider which traces should be considered as emerging links to be included in the predefined site structure. Summarizing, the interface agent, in order to select which traces must be proposed as emerging links, considers two kinds of information: the occurrence of trace generation and the success rate of the traces that were proposed.

When the interface agent has an indication of the user which issued the request, it may focus the selection activity to those traces that compose the history of user's activities in the web site, in a web customization framework. In fact traces include an indication of the agent which generated them, and in turn agents are related to registered users. As for the anonymous or new user case, also this strategy must consider both the occurrence of traces and their success rate. Moreover, in order to focus on a specific user's history but do not waste the chance to exploit other users' experiences, just two of the three available slots for emergent links are devoted to traces that were generated by that user and one is selected according to the strategy adopted for anonymous or new users.

These strategies for the exploitation of the gathered and stored traces, based on users' behaviours and movement in the web site environment, represent a very simple way of exploiting this kind of information without requiring an off-line analysis of the logs generated by the web server. The design, implementation and test of more complex strategies, for instanced based on details of the outcomes of emerging link proposals (e.g. which user effectively followed the suggested adaptive hyperlink) are object of future works.

4.2   Related Works

There are several approaches and relevant experiences in the area web site adaptation. The Avanti project [17] provides an automated customization of web site contents, basing on user modelling techniques and analysis of their behaviours. It also provided a specific attention to specific needs of elderly and partially disabled users.

The Footprints system [6] instead provides a site optimization through the metaphor of site visitors leaving traces in their navigation. These signals accumulate in the environment, generating awareness information on the most frequently visited areas of the web site. No user profile is needed, as visitors are essentially provided this information which could represent an indicator of the most interesting pages to visit. The metaphor of the structure of the web site as an environment on which visitors move in their search for information is very similar to the one on which the proposed framework is based, but we also propose the exploitation of the gathered information on users' paths for user specific customization.

Other approaches provide instead the generation of index pages [3], that are pages containing links to other pages covering a specific topic. These pages, resulting from an analysis of access logs aimed at finding clusters grouping together pages related to a topic, are proposed to web masters in a computer-assisted site optimization scheme. A different approach provides the real-time generation of shortcut links [18], through a predictive model of web usage based on statistical techniques and the concept of expected saving of a shortcut, which considers both the probability that the generated link will be effectively used and the amount of effort saved (i.e. intermediate links to follow). In particular this framework is very similar to the one proposed here with reference to the aims of the overall system, but it incorporates a complex algorithm for off-line analysis of logs, while the proposed approach provides a light and dynamic generation of most probable useful links and the storage of these proposals and high level information on site usage for a possible further off-line analysis.

In the agent area, a relevant approach provides the adoption of information agents supporting users in their navigation [19], considering both his/her specific behaviour and the actions of other visitors and adopting multiple strategies for making recommendations (e.g. similarity, proximity, access frequency to specific documents).

A different approach to web site adaptation provides the adoption of a learning network to model the evolution of a distributed hypertext network, such as a web site [20]. Also in this case the adaptation provides a modification in the structure of a web site, and the concept of emergent link and the underlying mechanisms present a similarity with the learning rules adopted for that kind of learning network. However that approach also provides a modification in the architecture of the site and modifications in the web protocols, while this work aims at providing a solution that can be easily integrated with a traditional web architecture.

From this point of view, the introduced system supporting web site adaptation seems more similar to a recommendation system. A relevant type of recommender exploiting users' behaviours to decide which contents could be interesting for a certain visitor is represented by the collaborative filter approach [21]. The latter has been adopted in different recommendation systems, filtering mail messages, newsgroup articles and web contents in general, but typically requires users to rate these items. Moreover it generally provides a concept of explicit users descriptions through profiles which can be compared to determine similarity among them. The idea is that contents that received a high rating by a certain user could be considered interesting by a similar user. The introduced system instead does not require an explicit rating of contents, but it rather observes the frequency of specific navigation paths, and exploits emergent links for customization or optimization of site structure. However, the adaptive block of the page can include emerging links that are not related to the specific visitor who is currently browsing that page, but were generated by other users which frequently followed paths that the current one still did not follow. From this point of view, the system provides a very basic collaborative browsing scheme, but a more through analysis of a possible integration with this approach is object of current and future works.

5   Towards New Forms of Interaction

The metaphor of a web site as an environment on which agents related to visitors move according to their browsing activity allows to gather and exploit information on users' behaviours for sake of web pages adaptation in a collaborative agents framework. Another interesting possibility offered by this framework provides the exploitation of this structure and information to provide users a of context aware interaction form. While several web based applications are able to provide users an awareness information related to their position on the web site (e.g. the category of products their are currently viewing in an e-commerce site), and also an indication of other users that are currently viewing the same page, we propose to exploit this information on user context to support user interaction. Such a system represents a hybrid among a web application and an instant messenger, and could be fruitfully exploited in sites related to relatively small communities. In fact, the number of visitors that are viewing a single web page may be relatively high and difficult to present[5] in an effective and usable way in a block of a web page or in a separate page that however should not

---

[5] See, e.g., the "What's Going On?" section of RPGnet forums (http://forum.rpg.net).

occupy a large portion of user screen. In order to support this new form of interaction among web site visitors, the general architecture of the system must be
modified. In particular, a client-side component able to establish and maintain
a connection with the Agent server must be included. A possible approach to
tackle this problem provides the inclusion of an applet as a block of the web page
structure which is constantly presented to the users (see Figure 7 for a diagram
of the modification of the general architecture).

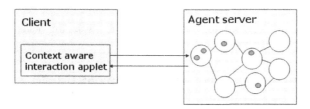

Fig. 7. In order to support interaction among web page visitors a client-side component
(Context aware interaction applet) must be included in the system architecture

The proposed form of interaction is context aware as a visitor is able to
perceive other users currently viewing the same web page or adjacent ones and
can try to interact with them. The perception of other users and the interaction is
thus mediated by the environment, and given the fact that generally the structure
of a web site reflects an underlying semantics (e.g. index pages which connect
elements of a category) the concept of adjacency can be a relevant contextual
element.

The MMASS multi-agent model provides both a concept of agent perception
and two mechanisms for interaction: a direct form of interaction among adjacent
agents is provided through the *reaction* operation, but agents are also able to
emit fields which propagate in the spatial structure of the environment and
may be perceived by other agents. The first mechanism may be invoked by a
user which tries to establish an interaction with another one, provided that a
preliminary agreement phase is successfully carried out. This phase represents
a possibility for a user to ignore incoming interaction requests. The other form
of interaction instead provides the diffusion of an information conveyed by a
field which may represent a message of general interest for visitors of a specific
area of the site. Such message could represent a help request to other visitors of
the area which could be interested in the same subject. In this framework, the
design of diffusion strategies for this kind of field should take into account the
underlying conceptual structure of the web site. For instance, in an e-commerce
site, fields generated in a page related to a product could be related to a request
of information on that subject. These fields should thus be diffused in pages
related to the product category and other instances of that category, but should
probably not be diffused into areas related to other categories. Figure 8 shows
this sample diffusion strategy.

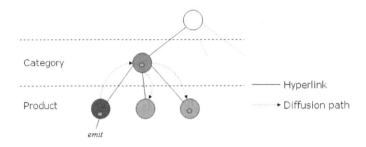

Fig. 8. A sample diffusion strategy in an e-commerce web site: fields are propagated inside a category but do not reach other ones

In addition to the agreement phase which precedes the effective reaction, the model provides the definition of the perceptive capabilities of every agent, and thus of every user. The actual sensitivity to fields also depends on agent state, so there is the possibility to model and implement different levels of availability of a user to incoming interaction requests. For instance, in the e-commerce example, some agents could be related to operators of the product support service, and could thus be more sensitive to help requests, while the casual visitor of the site could be less sensitive to these messages.

6 Conclusions and Future Developments

This paper introduced a general framework providing the adoption of a web site as an environment on which agents related to visitors move and possibly interact. This approach allows the gathering of a more structured form of information on users' behaviours and activities in the web site. The concept of emerging links and traces have been introduced in order to support an application exploiting information on users' browsing history for sake of web pages adaptation. The introduced framework and the application to web site adaptation have been designed and implemented, exploiting a platform supporting systems based on the MMASS model.

A campaign of tests aimed at evaluating the effectiveness of the adaptation approach, and also for sake of tuning the involved parameters (e.g. timings, number of presented possible emerging links) is under way, in the context of a collaboration with the Italian company Cosmovision Srl. This evaluation will provide both forms for user interviews and the exploitation of the gathered information of the success rate of proposed adaptive hyperlinks. The results of this evaluation might also lead to consider the modelling, design and implementation of more complex trace selection strategies, and thus a more complex behaviour for the interface agent.

An application exploiting the data gathered by the system in order to support the monitoring and visualization of the web site structure and utilization is currently being developed. Future works will be focused on the introduction and exploitation of higher level semantic information related to the site structure and contents, and thus agents' environment, aimed at providing additional forms of adaptation, including images and multimedia contents. A further development provides the design and implementation of a prototype supporting the context-aware interaction among web site visitors.

References

1. Tanenbaum, A.S.: Computer Networks - third edition. Prentice Hall (1996)
2. Perkowitz, M., Etzioni, O.: Adaptive Web Sites: an AI Challenge. In: Proceedings of the Fifteenth International Joint Conference on Artificial Intelligence. (1997) 16–23
3. Perkowitz, M., Etzioni, O.: Adaptive Web Sites. Communications of the ACM **43** (2000) 152–158
4. Cooley, R.: The Use of Web Structure and Content to Identify Subjectively Interesting Web Usage Patterns. ACM Transactions on Internet Technology **3** (2003)
5. Weyns, D., Van Dyke Parunak, H., Michel, F., Holvoet, T., Ferber, J.: Environments for Multiagent Systems State-of-the-Art and Research Challenges. In: Environments for Multi-Agent Systems, First International Workshop (E4MAS 2004). Volume 3374 of Lecture Notes in Computer Science., Springer–Verlag (2005) 1–47
6. Wexelblat, A., Maes, P.: Footprints: History-Rich Tools for Information Foraging. In: Proceedings of the SIGCHI conference on Human factors in computing systems, ACM Press (1999) 270–277
7. Liu, J., Zhang, S., Yang, J.: Characterizing Web Usage Regularities with Information Foraging Agents. IEEE Transactions Knowledge and Data Engineering **16** (2004) 566–584
8. Helbing, D., Schweitzer, F., Keltsch, J., Molnár, P.: Active Walker Model for the Formation of Human and Animal Trail Systems. Physical Review E **56** (1997) 2527–2539
9. Miller, R.C., Bharat, K.: Sphinx: a Framework for Creating Personal, Site-Specific Web Crawlers. Computer Networks and ISDN Systems **30** (1998) 119–130
10. Weyns, D., Michel, F., Van Dyke Parunak, H., eds.: Environments for Multi-Agent Systems, First International Workshop (E4MAS 2004). Volume 3374 of Lecture Notes in Artificial Intelligence., Springer–Verlag (2004)
11. Weyns, D., Holvoet, T.: Model for Simultaneous Actions in Situated Multi-Agent Systems. In: First International German Conference on Multi-Agent System Technologies, MATES. Volume 2831 of Lecture Notes in Computer Science., Springer–Verlag (2003) 105–119
12. Mamei, M., Zambonelli, F., Leonardi, L.: Co-fields: Towards a Unifying Approach to the Engineering of Swarm Intelligent Systems. In: Engineering Societies in the Agents World III: Third International Workshop (ESAW2002). Volume 2577 of Lecture Notes in Artificial Intelligence., Springer–Verlag (2002) 68–81
13. Hadeli, K., Valckenaers, P., Zamfirescu, C., Van Brussel, H., Saint Germain, B., Hoelvoet, T., Steegmans, E.: Self-Organising in Multi-Agent Coordination and Control Using Stigmergy. In: Engineering Self-Organising Systems: Nature-Inspired Approaches to Software Engineering. Volume 2977 of Lecture Notes in Computer Science., Springer–Verlag (2004) 105–123

14. Bandini, S., Manzoni, S., Simone, C.: Dealing with Space in Multi–Agent Systems: a Model for Situated MAS. In: Proceedings of the First International Joint Conference on Autonomous Agents and Multiagent Systems, ACM Press (2002) 1183–1190

15. Bandini, S., Manzoni, S., Vizzari, G.: Towards a Specification and Execution Environment for Simulations Based on MMASS: Managing At–a–distance Interaction. In Trappl, R., ed.: Proceedings of the 17th European Meeting on Cybernetics and Systems Research, Austrian Society for Cybernetic Studies (2004) 636–641

16. Sherman, C., Price, G.: The Invisible Web: Uncovering Information Sources Search Engines Can't See. CyberAge Books (2001)

17. Fink, J., Kobsa, A., Nill, A.: User-Oriented Adaptivity and Adaptability in the Avanti Project. Technical report, Microsoft Usability Group (1996)

18. Anderson, C.R., Domingos, P., Weld, D.S.: Adaptive Web Navigation for Wireless Devices. In: Proceedings of the Seventeenth International Joint Conference on Artificial Intelligence. (2001) 879–884

19. Pazzani, M.J., Billsus, D.: Adaptive Web Site Agents. Autonomous Agents and Multi-Agent Systems **5** (2002) 205–218

20. Bollen, J., Heylighen, F.: Algorithms for the Self-Organisation of Distributed, Multi-User Networks. Possible Application to the Future World Wide Web. In Trappl, R., ed.: Proceedings of the 13th European Meeting on Cybernetics and Systems Research, Austrian Society for Cybernetic Studies (1996) 911–916

21. Resnick, P., Iacovou, N., Suchak, M., Bergstrom, P., Riedl, J.: Grouplens: an Open Architecture for Collaborative Filtering of Netnews. In: CSCW '94: Proceedings of the 1994 ACM conference on Computer Supported Cooperative Work, ACM Press (1994) 175–186

Environment Organization of Roles Using Polymorphism

Derek Messie and Jae C. Oh

Department of Electrical Engineering and Computer Science,
Syracuse University, Syracuse, NY 13244, USA
{dsmessie, jcoh}@syr.edu

Abstract. In the field of multi-agent systems, there has lately been a growing interest on ways in which the environment can better be exploited to coordinate agent behavior and manage complex problems. This paper describes an environment that is able to organize and adapt agent roles as conditions warrant. Roles are adapted using polymorphism as directed by the environment. The design combines strategies from game theory and other biologically inspired models to address fault mitigation in large-scale, real-time, distributed systems. It is implemented on a prototype of the data acquisition system for BTeV, a High Energy Physics experiment consisting of 2500 digital signal processors. Results show environment organization of roles for the lightweight agents embedded within each of the individual processors.

1 Introduction

A major research theme for multi-agent systems is on investigating various architectures and methodologies that promote effective organization and coordination within large-scale, complex, distributed systems [1, 2]. Specifically, the interest is in developing approaches that can be implemented within multi-agent systems to produce some desirable emergent behavior that coordinates individual actors in a system competing for resources such as bandwidth, computing power, and data.

The *environment* is increasingly being explored as an underutilized resource for engineering these complex systems. Most researchers overlook opportunities to integrate the environment as a primary abstraction in models and tools for multi-agent systems, or minimize its responsibilities [3]. This paper explores various design techniques that rely on the environment to facilitate organization within the system.

Multi-agent systems methodologies that exhibit self-* (self-organizing, self-managing, self-optimizing, self-protecting) attributes are of particular value [4, 5]. This paper introduces *polymorphic* self-* agents that are capable of multiple roles as directed by the environment. A working definition of polymorphic agents is provided. These agents evolve an optimum core set of roles for which they are responsible, while still possessing the ability to take on alternate roles as environmental demands change. They are directly implementable in computer systems applications.

D. Weyns, H. Van Dyke Parunak, and F. Michel (Eds.): E4MAS 2005, LNAI 3830, pp. 251–269, 2006.

The approach adapts polymorphic agents to the environment using *stigmergy*, a concept that explains organization and coordination within social insect societies that rely strictly on environmental cues for indirect communication between individuals. It is implemented on RTES/BTeV, a data acquisition system developed by the Real-Time Embedded Systems (RTES) group for a particle accelerator-based High Energy Physics (HEP) experiment currently under development at Fermi National Accelerator Laboratory. Multiple layers of polymorphic, very lightweight agents (VLAs) are embedded within 2500 Digital Signal Processors (DSPs) to handle fault mitigation across the system. The primary challenge is to determine the frequency at which VLAs should perform specific monitoring tasks. Results show how polymorphic self-* VLAs evolve independently to find the optimum rate at which monitoring and fault mitigation tasks should occur. SWARM multi-agent simulation software is used to model RTES/BTeV.

The paper is divided into four separate sections. First, some background on self-* systems, polymorphism and stigmergy, along with the RTES/BTeV experiment itself is provided. A description of VLAs embedded within Level 1 of the RTES/BTeV environment is provided, followed by an explanation of current challenges and other motivating factors. Section 3 then introduces a working definition for polymorphic agents, and provides details on the design. Next, results of a SWARM simulation of the RTES/BTeV environment that implements the polymorphic self-* approach are evaluated in Sect. 4. Finally, next steps and a conclusion are provided.

2   Background and Motivation

2.1   Self-* Systems

Distributed AI research has been increasingly interested in techniques and methodologies that promote self-* (self-organizing, self-managing, self-optimizing, self-protecting) behavior within computing systems. Several international conferences and workshops that focus specifically on this issue have formed in the past few years (SOAS, ESOA, SELF-STAR, WOSS).

Self-organization is defined formally as a 'dynamical and adaptive process where systems acquire and maintain structure themselves, without external control' [6]. Other similar definitions refer to systems that are self-organizing, self-managing, self-optimizing, and self-protecting as being capable of dynamically changing their functionality and structure without direct intervention to meet changing conditions within the environment. Self-* systems typically changes progressively, in non-linear fashion, until a state is reached where system requirements are satisfied. These systems continually adapt to changing conditions and requirements.

While self-organization and adaptation have been studied intensively in control theory, systems theory, adaptive complex systems, robotics, etc., they are relatively new concepts for computing systems [7]. Since computing systems are basically artificial entities, they are usually difficult to apply to conventional

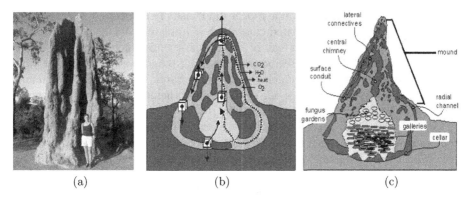

(a)   (b)   (c)

Fig. 1. (a) Large termite mound commonly found in subsaharan Africa. (b) The mounds act as respiratory devices, built from the surrounding soil by the termites in a colony. The mound powers ventilation of the subterranean nest by capturing energy from the wind. (c) Air shafts lead to underground spaces where larvae, food, and fungus is stored.

principles or approaches for self-organization and adaptation aimed at physical laws governed systems. Unlike the frameworks established for understanding and engineering self-organization and adaptation in systems governed by physical laws, the framework for self-organization and adaptation in artificial systems has yet to be established.

2.2   Polymorphism and Stigmergy

In many of the self-* architectures and methodologies developed, inspiration is often derived from biological systems [8, 9]. The approach introduced in this paper is largely based on two behaviors commonly found in social insect societies.

Concepts of polymorphism and stigmergy are founded in biology and the study of self-organization within social insects. The term *polymorphism* is used in describing ants and other social biological systems, and is defined as the occurrence of different forms, stages, or types in individual organisms or in organisms of the same species, independent of sexual variations [10, 11]. Within an individual colony consisting of ants with the same basic genetic wiring, two or more castes belonging to the same sex can be found. A caste here is defined as a differentiated morphological form with a specialized function, or at least the infrequent relict of such a form. The function or role that any individual ant takes on is dictated by cues from the environment [12].

The agents described in detail in Sect. 3 of this paper adhere to this definition of polymorphism in that they are genetically identical, yet each evolve distinct roles that they play as demanded of them through changes in the environment.

The concept of polymorphic agents presented in this paper is different from other definitions of polymorphism that have surfaced in computer science. In object-oriented programming, polymorphism is usually associated with the ability of objects to override inherited class method implementations [13]. The term has also arisen in other subareas of computer science, including some agent designs [14], but generally describes a templating based system or similar variation of the object-oriented model. On the other hand, techniques that attempt to evolve specialized agents are one of the central themes under investigation in the field of large-scale multi-agent systems [15].

Stigmergy was introduced by biologist Pierre-Paul Grasse to describe indirect communication that takes place between individuals in social insect societies [16]. The theory explains how organization and coordination of the building of termite nests is mainly controlled by the nest itself, and not the individual termite workers involved. It views the process of emergent cooperation as a result of participants altering the environment and reacting to the environment as they pass through it. The canonical example of stigmergy is ants leaving pheromones in ways that help them find the shortest, safest distance to food or to build nests. Ant colony optimization methods alone have had a wide impact on coordination within multi-agent systems, addressing various adaptive network routing and load balancing problems [17, 18].

A stigmergic approach to fault mitigation is introduced in this paper. Individual agents communicate indirectly through errors that they find (or do not find) in the environment. This indirect communication is manifested through actions that each agent takes as cued by the environment. Results show how the local actions of agents allow self-* global behavior to emerge.

2.3   RTES/BTeV

BTeV (B-physics experiment at the Tevatron Collider) is a proposed particle accelerator-based High Energy Physics (HEP) experiment currently under development at Fermi National Accelerator Laboratory. The goal is to study charge-parity violation, mixing, and rare decays of particles known as beauty and charm hadrons, in order to learn more about matter-antimatter asymmetries that exist in the universe today [19]. An aerial view of the particle collider located at Fermi National Laboratory is shown in Fig. 2.

The experiment uses approximately 30 planar silicon pixel detectors that are connected to specialized field-programmable gate arrays (FPGAs). The FPGAs are connected to approximately 2500 digital signal processors (DSPs) that filter incoming data at the extremely high rate of approximately 1.5 Terabytes per second from a total of 20×10^6 data channels. A three tier hierarchical trigger architecture will be used to handle this high rate [19]. An overview of the BTeV triggering and data acquisition system is shown in Fig. 3, including a magnified view of the L1 Vertex Trigger responsible for Level 1 filtering consisting of 2500 Worker nodes (2000 Track Farms and 500 Vertex Farms).

There are many Worker level tasks that the Farmlet VLA (FVLA) is responsible for monitoring. A traditional hierarchical approach would assign one (or more) distinct DSPs the role of the FVLA, with the responsibility of monitoring the state of other Worker DSPs on the node [20]. However, this leaves the

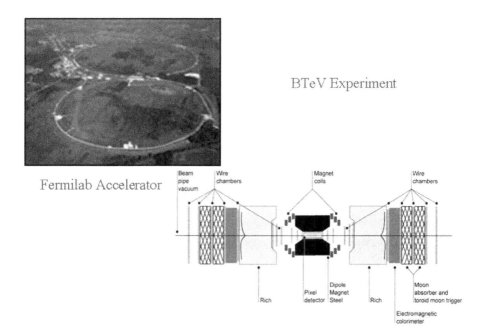

Fig. 2. Aerial view of the Fermilab Tevatron, the world's highest-energy particle collider. Beams of protons and antiprotons are collided to examine the basic building blocks of matter.

system with only very few possible points of failure before critical tasks are left unattended.

Another approach would be to assign a single redundant DSP (or more) to each and every Worker DSP, to act as the FVLA [21]. However, since 2500 Worker DSPs are projected, this would prove expensive and may still not fully protect all DSPs given even a low number of system failures.

The events that are actually accepted within this system occur very infrequently, and the cost of operating this environment is high. The extremely large streams of data resulting from the BTeV environment must be processed realtime with highly resilient adaptive fault tolerant systems [22]. For these reasons, a Real-Time Embedded Systems Collaboration (RTES) was formed with the purpose of designing real-time embedded intelligent software to ensure data integrity and fault-tolerance within this data acquisition system.

2.4 Very Lightweight Agents (VLAs)

Multiple levels of very lightweight agents (VLAs) [23] are one of the primary components responsible for fault mitigation across RTES/BTeV.

The primary objective of the VLA is to provide the RTES/BTeV environment with a lightweight, adaptive layer of fault mitigation. One of the latest phases of work at Syracuse University has involved implementing embedded proactive and reactive rules to handle specific system failure scenarios.

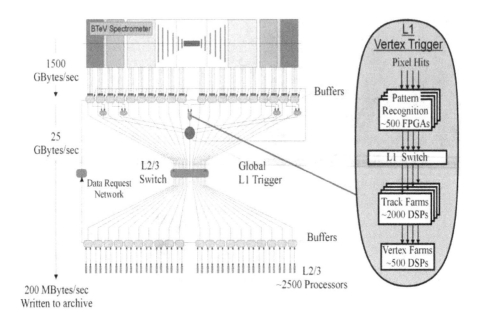

1500
GBytes/sec

25
GBytes/sec

200 MBytes/sec
Written to archive

Fig. 3. The BTeV triggering and data acquisition system showing (left side) detector, buffer memories, L1, L2, L3 clusters and their interconnects and (right side) a magnified figure of the L1 Vertex trigger

A scaled prototype of the Level 1 RTES/BTeV environment was presented at the SuperComputing 2003 (SC2003) conference [24]. Reactive and proactive VLA rules were integrated within this Level 1 prototype and served a primary role in demonstrating the embedded fault tolerant capabilities of the system.

Since the physics application (PA) at the worker level is responsible for the critical overall objective of Level 1 data filtering, it is extremely important that DSP usage by the VLA at the worker level is minimal, and only occurs either when the PA is not utilizing the DSP, or when emergency fault mitigative action is required. For this reason, the prototype worker VLA is implemented as an Interrupt Service Routine (ISR) that is triggered only when expected PA processing time thresholds are exceeded. The TI T6711 DSP processor used within the prototype has 15 hardware interrupts (HWIs). HWI 15 is assigned Timer 1, and HWI 14 is assigned Timer 0. The VLA prototype uses HWI 15 (Timer 1).

A list of ten possible BTeV error scenarios, along with a list of associated likely causes, is listed in Tab. 1. One of the fault scenarios modeled within the prototype occurs when the DSP is found to be over the estimated time budget on crossing processing (e1). In this scenario, HWI 15 (Timer 1) is used by the VLA to monitor PA crossing processing times, and trigger the VLA ISR if the time threshold is exceeded. At the start of processing each crossing, the PA provides the VLA with a time estimate as to the maximum time that it should take to process the current crossing. The Timer 1 Period Register (T1PR) is assigned this estimated value, and timer counting is enabled. If the PA completes crossing

Table 1. List of 10 BTeV error scenarios, along with list of associated likely causes

e1	DSP over time budget on crossing processing.	Crossing was too complex to complete and developer was not careful to give up in time.
e2	PA is stuck in a loop (within software timer control).	Improper error handling caused the program to go into an infinite loop.
e3	DSP application enters a loop (outside of software timer control).	Logic error in code that manipulates the boards communications facilities.
e4	DSP application branches to an illegal instruction.	Logic error any place in the code that causes corruption of memory.
e5	Processing times per crossing are too long.	SAF reported crossing processing times are consistently falling out of range.
e6	Too many track segments. Not necessarily a fault at the source.	The front-end hardware is malfunctioning; more particles collided than can be managed; bug in the upstream algorithms.
e7	Corrupt data in a crossing (truncated, misaligned, or bad header).	Bad checksum or incorrect header data in a crossing due to transmission failure or upstream logic error.
e8	Corrupt data - no such channels in the detector.	Logic error in front-end electronics or firmware (byte swapping).
e9	Crossing data lost.	DSP was reset or reboot while an event was being processed; FPGA input queue overflow; FPGA output queue overflow.
e10	Failed to transfer results down the DSP L1 buffer link (buffer ready flag not set in time).	The level-1 buffers were not ready to receive data; the farmlet output queues overflowed.

processing as expected prior to the timer expiring, then the timer is stopped and reset when the PA begins processing the next crossing. If on the other hand, the timer expires before the PA has completed processing, then the VLA ISR is called. The first time that the VLA ISR is triggered, the VLA notifies the PA of the time threshold violation, and resets the timer for a set grace period. The PA then attempts to cleanup any remaining processing that it has to complete. If successful, the PA stops the timer, and continues on to the next crossing. If the cleanup is unsuccessful, the VLA ISR is again called, and this time, it either attempts to reset the PA itself (if it has authority), or sends communication up to the next level of VLA (in this case the Farmlet VLA) for remedial action.

In addition to taking direct fault mitigative actions on various system components, multiple layers of VLAs are also responsible for communicating specific error messages to higher layers within the system.

2.5   Challenges

While the SC2003 prototype was effective for demonstrating the real-time fault mitigation capabilities of VLAs on limited hardware utilizing 16 DSPs, one of the major challenges is to find out how the behavior of the various levels of VLAs will scale when implemented across the 2500 DSPs projected for

RTES/BTeV [25]. In particular, how frequently should these monitoring tasks be performed to optimize processing time, and what affect does this have on other components and the overall behavior of a large-scale real-time embedded system like RTES/BTeV.

Given the number of components and countless fault scenarios involved, it is infeasible to design an 'expert system' that applies mitigative actions triggered from a central processing unit acting on rules capturing every possible system state. Instead, a distributed approach using self-organizing VLAs accomplishes fault mitigation within the large-scale real-time RTES/BTeV environment.

2.6 SWARM

SWARM (http://www.swarm.org), distributed under the GNU General Public License, is software available as a Java or Objective-C development kit that allows for the multi-agent simulation of complex systems [26, 27]. It consists of a set of libraries that facilitate implementation of agent-based models. SWARM has previously been used by the RTES team in simulations that model the RTES/BTeV environment [28].

3 Polymorphic Agents

3.1 A Working Definition

Some initial supporting terminology from the field of multi-agent systems will first be reviewed before a definition for polymorphic agents is presented:

Agent -
Finding a single universally accepted definition of an *agent* has been as difficult for the agent-based computing community, as defining *intelligence* has been for the mainstream AI community [29]. However, a few of the core properties of agents that have been widely accepted include :

- *autonomy*: agents operate without the direct intervention of humans or others, and have some kind of control over their actions and internal state;
- *social ability*: agents interact with other agents;
- *reactivity*: agents respond to changes in their environment;
- *pro-activeness*: agents exhibit goal-directed behavior.

The VLAs embedded within each of the DSPs in the RTES/BTeV environment possess each of these core properties.

Environment -
Similarly, robust definitions of *environments* in multi-agent systems can be even more challenging to find than those for *agents*. In very general terms, environments 'provide the conditions under which an entity (agent or object) exists' [3].

A growing amount of research has turned attention to the role of the environment in system design. The recognition is that the distributed AI community has failed to treat the environment as a *first-class entity* [30]. Here, a *first-class entity* is seen as an independent piece of software which provides an abstraction that can be modified without requiring a change to other software components. The approach presented in this paper implements the environment as a first-class entity responsible for indirect communication between agents.

Roles -

In multi-agent systems, roles are generally viewed as 'an abstract representation of an agents function, service, or identification within a group' [31]. A role can be viewed as a class that defines some normative behavioral repertoire of an agent [32]. They provide both the building blocks for agent social systems and the requirements by which agents interact.

Roles are derived from the functional requirements of the system, and act to link agents together. They define a set of actions that are permitted for a certain class of agents. For example, an agent that is assigned the role of a customer may request a certain set of goods, but not supply them. An agent assigned the supplier role on other hand, has the opposite requirements.

A single agent may be assigned multiple roles, and can change roles as conditions warrant. Roles are found in countless different forms for grouping tasks or responsibilities. In database systems, roles are assigned to individual users (or groups of users) as a way to allow access to certain categories of information. For example, a role may be created that allows read-write access to a set of three specific accounting tables. Individual users that are assigned this role, then have read-write access to those tables. Other users that are not assigned this role, will not have access to the tables.

In autonomous robots, roles are assigned to different components of the system as a way to compartmentalize tasks required for the overall desired behavior of the system. A single sensor on the base of the robot may be responsible for avoiding objects, while a sound recognition system may simultaneously move the robot towards music playing in another room.

In the RTES/BTeV environment, roles are used to group together related fault mitigation tasks. Individual VLAs adapt the set of roles for which they are responsible as environmental conditions change. For example, as described in more detail below, a single VLA may be primarily responsible for one set of fault mitigation tasks (role A) at one moment, and responsible for a completely different set (role B) shortly later in time.

Research concerning other static definitions for roles, role formation and configuration, and the dynamic interactions among roles have been examined quite extensively in recent years [33, 34, 35].

Polymorphic Agents -

As described earlier, *polymorphism* is defined in biology as:

'the occurrence of different forms, stages, or types in individual organisms or in organisms of the same species, independent of sexual variations' [10, 11].

For the definition of *polymorphic agents* in multi-agent systems proposed in this paper, *organisms* are replaced by *agents*, and agent *roles* (function, service, or identification) are used in place of *forms*, *stages*, and *types* of organisms. The environment in this new definition in many ways remains unchanged.

This leads to the following working definition for *polymorphic agents* within the field of multi-agent systems:

'Individual agents within groups of similar or identical agents that are capable of adapting roles based on their perceived environment.'

Polymorphic VLAs are described in detail in the next section.

3.2   Design Overview

This paper introduces a stigmergic multi-agent systems approach that uses polymorphic self-* agents to address the weaknesses inherent in traditional hierarchical fault mitigation designs. Rather than hard-wiring the assignment of FVLA roles to specific VLAs embedded within individual DSPs, VLAs are made *polymorphic* so that *every* VLA is equipped to play the role of FVLA for *any* DSP on the same node.

Since the FVLA is responsible for a wide range of monitoring tasks, this means that we must build the capability of performing each task into every Worker Level VLA. The classic problem this presents in traditional hierarchical approaches is how to process all of the data necessary for all of these tasks in time for a useful response [29]. However, since these agents are polymorphic and evolve roles gradually over time, there is only a small set of tasks for which each agent is responsible for at any given point in time.

Stigmergy is used to determine which set of tasks any given VLA performs. Errors found (or not found) in the environment by an individual VLA increase (decrease) the sensitivity of that VLA to that particular type of error. Agents start out by monitoring each type of error at a fixed rate. Then, based entirely on what is encountered in the environment, each develops a core set of roles for which it takes responsibility. For example, a single VLA embedded within a DSP monitors each particular error at some unique rate. When an individual VLA performs a monitoring task on some DSP, it either finds an error and performs mitigative action, or does not find an error and does nothing. If it finds an error, it increases its own sensitivity to that type of error on the corresponding DSP. If it does not find an error, its sensitivity to the error decreases slightly. Results show how, over time, this produces an optimal distribution of monitoring tasks across all VLAs, with each VLA evolving responsibility for a unique core set of monitoring tasks.

The overall emergent behavior of this design results in self-organization of FVLA responsibilities based on the state and workload of all DSPs within the node. A certain set of VLAs may perform specific FVLA tasks at one moment, and another set (which may or may not include VLAs from the original set) can be found performing these same tasks later in time. The organization occurs automatically within the system as environmental cues fluctuate. This eliminates the financial and efficiency costs associated with having specialized FVLAs that at times sit idle as Worker DSPs operate at full capacity and fall behind on event processing. It also increases the efficiency of Worker DSPs that may be wasting idle time when crossing processing rates are low. In effect, a fully connected network of FVLAs is created that continue to provide effective fault mitigation when exposed to a high volume of system failures.

There are two key characteristics of this model. The first is that it requires no central management or global processing. Second, it is optimally reliable since FVLA monitoring tasks are distributed across all DSPs, and can be adapted based on changes in the environment. The next section explains implementation details on how each individual agent uses only cues from the environment to determine necessary actions.

3.3   Utility Value Drives Real-Time Scheduling

As described above, distributed VLAs within Worker level DSPs are used to accomplish the fault monitoring tasks that the FVLA is responsible for. However, these are the same DSPs that are responsible for the critical overall objective of Level 1 physics application (PA) data filtering [19]. It is therefore extremely important that DSP usage by each Worker VLA is minimal, and only occurs either when the PA is not fully utilizing the DSP, or when critical fault mitigative action is required.

Game theory has been applied to a wide range of problems, and is used here to coordinate the amount of DSP clock cycle that is allocated between the PA and the VLA. Both the PA and VLA wish to maximize the number of clock cycles during which they have control. If the VLA takes too many DSP cycles, then the PA will be unable to process the incoming data at a high enough rate to prevent the buffers from overflowing, resulting in a loss of data continuity. This is often fatal for the experiment since this lost data could very well contain portions of vital characteristics of the physics properties being evaluated. If on the other hand, the PA takes too many DSP cycles, then it runs the risk that system faults will go undetected, resulting in acceptance of corrupt data, and/or incremental bottlenecks that again cause buffer overflows.

An efficient adaptive scheduling algorithm is required that will effectively establish scheduling priorities between the PA and VLA. Mandatory costs associated with the Kernel/Command Processor, including clock cycle costs for context switching must be factored in. An analysis of the worst-case behavior of tasks (both VLA and PA) can be done to determine the amount of time that must be allotted to each process. However, there must be a way for the system to adaptively modify these values when environmental conditions change. That is, if during every interval T, the HEP applications and the operating system use T_{PA} and T_{OS} time units, respectively, then the VLA will be allowed to use $T - T_{PA} - T_{OS}$ every T time units [23].

An analysis of best-case behavior of tasks (VLA and PA) requires the use of a *utility value* in order for each DSP to determine locally precisely when the PA or VLA should relinquish control [36]. A reward system based on a combination of the amount of data processed, along with the frequency of VLA maintenance checks, is used by each DSP for each error in calculating the following local utility value :

DSP Utility Value $= Dw^{-1} + cF^{-1}$, where

$D =$ Expected amount of data that DSP could process
    during a given time interval (T).
$w =$ Current data buffer watermark.
$F =$ Total number of clock cycles elapsed since last
    FVLA check on neighboring DSPs.
$c =$ Adaptive constant representing weight to place on
    FVLA checks.

Since the amount of data that any single DSP can process (D) over a given time interval is fixed, the utility value essentially involves summing the inverse of the current data buffer watermark (w^{-1}) with a weighted value for the inverse of the time elapsed since individual FVLA tasks were last performed (F^{-1}).

The task currently active (PA or VLA) calculates the optimum expected utility value for the DSP at a time interval based on the criticality of each error. If the active process determines that a higher DSP utility value is received by remaining active, then the active task will continue. However, if a higher utility value can be gained by passing control to the currently inactive process, then that is what does. For example, if the PA is currently active, the input data buffer for a given DSP is low, and FVLA monitoring responsibilities for a specific error have not been performed on a particular DSP in a long time, then the VLA task will be made active. If however, the VLA was currently active under these conditions, then the VLA would simply maintain control for another T time steps, at which time corresponding utility values would again be calculated. This is equivalent to determining :

$$\max(w, 2 \times ((1 / (1 + e^{-dF})) - .5)$$

the maximum value of either w or $2 \times$ ((sigmoid function value for F) - .5). Here, $2 \times ((1 / (1 + e^{-dF})) - .5)$ is an adjusted sigmoid function for F which represent F as a weighted value between 0 and 1.

It is important to note here that the value assigned to d determines the steepness of the sigmoid function, and hence the sensitivity of the agent to a given error. In other words, the higher the value of d, the higher the adjusted sigmoid value of F, and the higher the sensitivity (the frequency of checks) of the VLA to a particular error.

This is where the polymorphic behavior of the VLA is introduced. Any time that an individual VLA finds a specific error while performing FVLA monitoring tasks, the d value for that error on that particular node is increased. Any time that an individual VLA performs a monitoring task and does *not* find an error, the d value is slightly decreased.

A high value for F means that FVLA tasks are performed more frequently (high sensitivity), whereas a low value for F means they are performed less often (low sensitivity). The PA is passed (or maintains) control if w is higher than this adjusted sigmoid function value for F, otherwise the VLA is passed (maintains) control. For example, if the PA is currently active, the input data buffer watermark for a given DSP is about half full (w=.5), and FVLA functions have recently been performed (the adjusted sigmoid function value for F is, say, .15) then the PA will remain active.

4   Results

SWARM simulates Farmlet data buffer queues that are populated at a rate consistent with the behavior of the incoming physics crossing data. Each DSP within a given Farmlet processes a fixed amount of data at each discrete time step. Three distinct types of errors are introduced randomly within each Worker DSP at a variable rate using a Multiply With Carry (RWC8gen) random number generator with a fixed seed. Any time a software or hardware error is encountered within the simulation, the processing rate for that DSP decreases a set amount depending on the type of error. The error is cleared when any DSP within the same Farmlet performs FVLA checks against the DSP for the error type present. However, there is a time cost associated with performing these checks. As detailed above describing the self-organizing model, the DSP must decide whether or not it is worth taking time to perform FVLA monitoring tasks against neighboring DSPs. If checks are performed too frequently, then the time available for data crossing processing is limited. On the other hand, if they are not performed frequently enough, then the chance that other DSPs within the same Farmlet are experiencing errors is high. As described, a high error rate will also lead to slow processing rates.

The formula designed for these experiments calculates the frequency of performing FVLA tasks for neighboring DSPs as a sigmoid function adjusted to a value between 0.0 and 1.0. The fullness of the crossing data buffer queue is also a value between 0.0 and 1.0 representing the data watermark percentage. These two values are weighed against each other, and the DSP makes a decision on where to devote its energy as described earlier.

The decision of whether the VLA or PA has control of the DSP is made by each DSP at each time step in the SWARM simulation. In this way, the monitoring tasks required by the environment are always met, but not necessarily by one (or a few) designated DSPs. Instead, these tasks are performed by any polymorphic DSP within the Farmlet as dictated by the changing needs of the environment.

Currently, a relatively rudimentary method is used to adapt the d-value (sensitivity) of each agent to a particular type of error. The approach relies only on a very limited amount of local information that is gathered from the environment at the time FVLA monitoring tasks are performed. The DSPs themselves self-organize as different DSPs within the Farmlet take on the necessary monitoring

tasks at different points in time as required by the environment. If a DSP performs FVLA monitoring tasks for a given type of error on a neighboring DSP,
it will either determine that the error is not present, or it will find the error
and perform the designated mitigative actions. In the case where an error is
found, the d-value for that particular error on the specific DSP is increased. As
described in detail earlier, this essentially increases the sensitivity of the VLA
for this type of error. On the other hand, if no error is found, then the d-value
(sensitivity) is slightly decreased.

As detailed next, Fig. 4 shows how the local action performed by each VLA
over a short period of time results in VLAs evolving responsibility for a core set
of fault monitoring tasks. Over the 100000 time steps for which the SWARM
simulation is run, the 5 VLAs (1 per DSP) can be seen taking on distinct roles
that lead to an efficient global fault mitigation strategy for monitoring errors on
DSP1. These roles are evolved using local information only, and rely on stigmergy
within the environment for indirect coordination with other VLAs.

The simulation fluctuates the error rate at various intervals in order to
demonstrate the affect changes in error rate can have on polymorphic behavior. A moderate error rate (5×10^{-4}) is used for the first 35000 time steps, a low
error rate (5×10^{-6}) for the next 35000 time steps (35001-70000), and the last

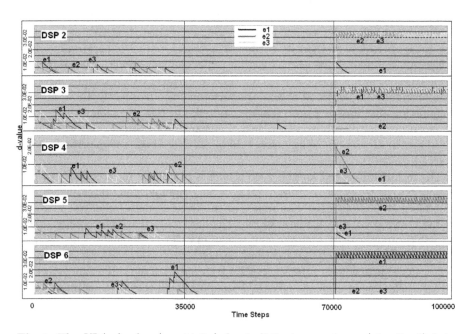

Fig. 4. The VLA d-value (sensitivity) for 3 distinct error types (e1, e2, e3) being
monitored on DSP1. Each of the 5 graphs represent the d-value adapted over time by
each of the remaining 5 DSPs (DSP2 - DSP6) on the same Farmlet. The simulation
fluctuated the error rate between a moderate rate (5×10^{-4}) for the first 35000 time
steps, a low rate (5×10^{-6}) for the next 35000 time steps (35001 - 70000), and a high
rate (5×10^{-3}) for the last 30000 time steps (70000 - 100000).

30000 time steps (70001-100000) use a high rate (5 x 10 $^{-3}$). Fig. 4 shows how all of the VLAs are able to adjust sensitivity to errors on DSP1 based on these fluctuating error rates over time. For example, the d-value (sensitivity) to individual errors on DSP1 for all 5 VLAs (embedded within DSP2 - DSP6) can be seen dropping starting around time step 35000, and then increasing dramatically again at time step 70000 during the significant increase in error rate.

Polymorphism is demonstrated clearly in Fig. 4 which displays the VLA d-value (sensitivity) for 3 distinct error types being monitored on DSP1 within a single Farmlet. The d-values evolved by each of the VLAs within the 5 DSPs (DSP2-DSP6) monitoring DSP1 within the same Farmlet are shown. When the error rate is high (from time steps 70000-100000), the VLAs embedded within DSP3 and DSP6 develop a high sensitivity for error type 1 (e1), while the sensitivity for e1 of the VLAs in the remaining DSPs remains low. Similarly, the VLAs on DSP2 and DSP5 have a high sensitivity for error type 2 (e2), and VLAs for DSP2 and DSP3 are highly sensitive to e3.

The moderate error rate used for the first 35000 time steps reveals additional polymorphic characteristics of this approach. Here, the error rate is not quite high enough for any single VLA to evolve long term responsibility for an individual error type on DSP1. Instead, 1 or 2 VLAs can be seen monitoring a single error type at one moment, and then a separate VLA (or group of VLAs) can be seen monitoring the same error type a short time later. This is due to the fact that the error rate is too low to stimulate high sensitivity in a single VLA. Sensitivity for the error type drops to a level comparable with other available VLAs on the Farmlet. For example, the VLAs on DSP 3 and DSP 4 develop a modest level of sensitivity for e1 early on (time steps 0-15000), but the role is taken over by VLAs on DSP 5 (time steps 15000-28000) and later DSP6 (28000-35000).

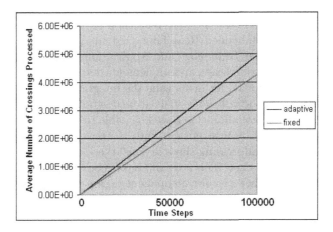

Fig. 5. Average number of crossings processed per DSP resulting from the stigmergic approach using polymorphic agents(adaptive), compared against the same simulation using a fixed monitoring rate (d-value fixed at .01)

Fig. 5 shows the average data processing rate per DSP for the stigmergic approach using polymorphic agents, as compared to the same simulation using a fixed monitoring rate (d-value fixed at .01) for each agent. The polymorphic agents in the stigmergic approach adapt an optimum monitoring rate for each error based strictly on the demands of the environment at any given time. This results in a higher number of crossings processed since, as described in detail earlier, less time is wasted performing needless monitoring tasks or missing critical errors.

5 Next Steps

The next phase of this project will expand the number of different types of errors handled, along with the amount of fluctuation in error rates. It will also focus further on how sensitivity (d-value) is adapted for each VLA. Currently, a rudimentary method is used that slightly increases (or decreases) sensitivity based on the presence (or absense) of an error. Other variables could be considered in determining the amount of change to apply, such as factoring in the severity level of the error, or looking at the consequences of other recently taken actions. An enhanced evaluation methodology to better demonstrate the performance advantage of this approach as compared to other traditional methodologies is also necessary.

Another issue being investigated is how to handle communication between agents when one agent has information that may be relevant to other agents, but it does not know to which other agent the information is relevant. This is a problem encountered in many large-scale multi-agent systems [15], and is especially an issue in fault mitigation where trends in information received across agents can provide valuable warning signs.

At the same time, another scaled prototype of the actual projected RTES/ BTeV software and hardware environment based on the SC2003 demonstration system is also being developed, and will integrate the VLA self-* model. This prototype will be presented at the 2nd Workshop on High-Performance Fault-Adaptive Large-Scale Embedded Real-Time Systems (FALSE-II) in the IEEE Real-Time and Embedded Technology and Applications Symposium (RTAS05).

As described earlier, the design and implementation of the SC2003 prototype was an important step for RTES in showing the integration of many of the component designs and tools that have been developed across the collaboration. Each of the teams within the collaboration have been able to take away some valuable lessons learned that will be incorporated into the development process moving forward. In addition to addressing these lessons, there are many other challenging goals that RTES has set. The next phase of modeling tools are also being developed that will further support component design and implementation.

6 Conclusion

This paper has described a multi-agent systems design approach that uses the environment to facilitate organization and coordination of agents. It details a fully distributed stigmergic approach to fault mitigation in large-scale real-time systems using lightweight, polymorphic, self-* agents embedded within individual DSPs. Stigmergy facilitates indirect communication and coordination between agents using cues from the environment, and concepts from game theory and polymorphism allow individual agents to evolve a core set of roles for which it is responsible. Agents adapt these roles as environmental demands change. The approach is implemented on a SWARM simulation of BTeV, a High Energy Physics experiment consisting of 2500 DSPs.

Results demonstrate the polymorphic nature of the agents, and display the performance and reliability advantages of this approach. The next phase of this project will increase the number of possible error types, and add more fluctuation to individual error rates.More sophisticated ways of adapting error sensitivity among agents will also be investigated, along with more elaborate performance evaluation metrics.

Acknowledgements

The research conducted was sponsored by the National Science Foundation in conjunction with Fermi National Laboratories, under the BTeV Project, and in association with RTES, the Real-time, Embedded Systems Group. This work has been performed under NSF grant # ACI-0121658.

References

1. Estrin, D., Govindan, R., Heidemann, J., Kumar, S.: Next century challenges: Scalable coordination in sensor networks. In: Mobile Computing and Networking. (1999) 263–270
2. Brazier, F., Mobach, D., Overeinder, B., Wijngaards, N.: Supporting life cycle coordination in open agent systems (2002)
3. Weyns, D., Dyke, H.V., Michel, F., Holvoet, T., Ferber, J.: Environments for Multiagent Systems, State-of-the-art and Research Challenges, Post-proceedings of the First International Workshop on Environments for Multiagent Systems, Lecture Notes in Computer Science Series, Volume 3374 (2005)
4. Dowling, J., Cunningham, R., Curran, E., Cahill, V.: Component and system-wide self-* properties in decentralized distributed systems, Self-Star: International Workshop on Self-* Properties in Complex Information Systems, University of Bologna, Italy (2004)
5. Li, Z., Liu, H., Parashar, M.: Enabling autonomic, self-managing grid applications (2004)
6. DeWolf, T., Holvoet, T.: Emergence Versus Self-Organisation: Different Concepts But Promising When Combined, Engineering Self Organising Systems: Methodologies and Applications (Bruecker, S. and Di Marzo Serugendo, G. and Karageorgos, A. and Nagpal, R., eds.). Lecture Notes in Artificial Intelligence vol. 3464 (2005)
7. Serugendo, G.D.M., Karageorgos, A., Rana, O., Zambonelli, F.: Engineering Self-Organising Systems, Nature-Inspired Approaches to Software Engineering, Workshop on Engineering Self-Organising Applications (ESOA), in the International Conference on Autonomous Agents and Multi-Agent Systems (AAMAS) (2003)

8. Ridge, E., Kudenko, D., Kazakov, D., Curry, E.: Moving Nature-Inspired Algorithms to Parallel, Asynchronous and Decentralised Environments, International Conference on Self-Organization and Adaptation of Multi-agent and Grid Systems (SOAS05) (2005)
9. Timmis, J., de Lemos, R., Ayara, M., Duncan, R.: Towards Immune Inspired Fault Tolerance in Embedded Systems, Proceedings of 9th International Conference on Neural Information Processing (2002) 1459–1463
10. Wilson, E.O.: The Origin and Evolution of Polymorphism in Ants. Quarterly Review of Biology **28** (1953) pages 136–156
11. Law, J.H., Wilson, W.O., McCloskey, J.: Biochemical Polymorphism in Ants. Science **149** (1965) pages 544–6
12. Wheeler, D.E.: Developmental and Physiological Determinants of Caste in Social Hymenoptera: Evolutionary Implications. American Naturalist **128** (1986) pages 13–34
13. Josuttis, N.M.: Object Oriented Programming in C++. John Wiley & Sons; 1st edition (2002)
14. Barbat, B., Zamfirescu, C.: Polymorphic Agents for Modelling E-Business Users, International NAISO Congress on Information Science Innovations, Symposium on E-Business and Beyond (EBB), Dubai (2000)
15. Scerri, P., Vincent, R., Mailler, R.: Comparing Three Approaches to Large Scale Coordination, Proceedings of the First Workshop on the Challenges in the Coordination of Large Scale Multi-agent Systems, in the 3rd International Joint Conference on Autonmous Agents and Multi-Agent Systems (AAMAS), New York, NY USA (2004)
16. Grassé, P.P.: La reconstruction du nid et les coordinations inter-individuelles chez Bellicosi-termes natalensis et Cubitermes sp. La theorie de la stigmergie: Essai d'interpretation des termites constructeurs. Insectes Sociaux **6** (1959) pages 41–83
17. Caro, G.D., Dorigo, M.: Ant Colonies for Adaptive Routing in Packet-Switched Communications Networks. Lecture Notes in Computer Science **1498** (1998) 673–683
18. Dorigo, M., Stotzle, T.: Ant Colony Optimization. Bradford Books (MIT Press) (2004)
19. Kwan, S.: The BTeV Pixel Detector and Trigger System, FERMILAB-Conf-02/313 (2002)
20. Cristian, F.: Abstractions for fault-tolerance. In Duncan, K., Krueger, K., eds.: Proceedings of the IFIP 13th World Computer Congress. Volume 3 : Linkage and Developing Countries, Amsterdam, The Netherlands, Elsevier Science Publishers (1994) 278–286
21. Heimerdinger, W., Weinstock, C.: A conceptual framework for system fault tolerance. Software engineering institute, carnegie mellon university, cmu/sei-92-tr-33, esc-tr-92-033 (October, 1992)
22. et. al, J.B.: Fault Tolerant Issues in the BTeV Trigger, FERMILAB-Conf-01/427 (2002)
23. Oh, J., Mosse, D., Tamhankar, S.: Design of Very Lightweight Agents for Reactive Embedded Systems, IEEE Conference on the Engineering of Computer Based Systems (ECBS), Huntsville, Alabama (2003)
24. Messie et al., D.: Prototype of Fault Adaptive Embedded Software for Large-Scale Real-Time Systems, 2nd Workshop on Engineering of Autonomic Systems (EASe), in the 12th Annual IEEE International Conference and Workshop on the Engineering of Computer Based Systems (ECBS), Washington, DC USA (2005)

25. Kowalkowski, J.: Understanding and Coping with Hardware and Software Failures in a Very Large Trigger Farm, Conference for Computing in High Energy and Nuclear Physics (CHEP) (2003)
26. Burkhart, R.: Schedules of Activity in the SWARM Simulation System, Position Paper for OOPSLA Workshop on OO Behavioral Semantics (1997)
27. Daniels, M.: An Open Framework for Agent-based Modeling, Applications of Multi-Agent Systems in Defense Analysis, a workshop held at Los Alamos Labs (2000)
28. Messie, D., Oh, J.: SWARM Simulation of Multi-Agent Fault Mitigation in Large-Scale, Real-Time Embedded Systems, High Performance Computing and Simulation (HPC&S) Conference, Magdeburg, Germany (2004)
29. Wooldridge, M., Jennings, N.R.: Intelligent agents: Theory and practice. HTTP://www.doc.mmu.ac.uk/STAFF/mike/ker95/ker95-html.h (Hypertext version of Knowledge Engineering Review paper) (1994)
30. Weyns, D., Schumacher, M., Ricci, A., Viroli, M., Holvoet, T.: Environments for Multiagent Systems. Knowledge Engineer Review **to appear** (2005)
31. Odell, J., Parunak, H., Fleischer, M., Breuckner, S.: Modeling Agents and their Environment. Lecture Notes in Computer Science **2585** (2002) pages 16–31
32. Odell, J., Parunak, H., Breuckner, S., Fleischer, M.: Temporal Aspects of Dynamic Role Assignment. Lecture Notes in Computer Science **2935** (2004)
33. Ferber, J., O. Gutknecht, e.a.: Agent/Group/Roles: Simulating with Organizations, Fourth International Workshop on Agent-Based Simulation (ABS), Montpellier, France (2003)
34. Castelfranchi, C.: Engineering Social Order. Engineering Societies in the Agent World **1972** (2000) pages 1–18
35. Parunak, H., Odell, J.: Representing Social Structure using UML, Proceedings of the Agent-Oriented Software Engineering Workshop, in the Agents 2001 Conference, Montreal, Canada, Springer (2001)
36. Rapoport, A., Zwick, R.: Game Theory. In A.E. Kazdin, Encyclopedia of Psychology (pp. 424-426). New York: Oxford University Press (2000)

Testing AGVs in Dynamic Warehouse Environments

Alexander Helleboogh, Tom Holvoet, and Yolande Berbers

AgentWise, DistriNet, Department of Computer Science K.U. Leuven University, Belgium
{Alexander.Helleboogh, Tom.Holvoet,
Yolande.Berbers}@cs.kuleuven.be

Abstract. Automatic Guided Vehicles (AGVs) are unmanned vehicles that can transport loads in a warehouse. AGVs are instructed by on-board AGV control software. As multiple AGVs operate in a decentralized manner in the warehouse environment, conflicts may arise. Consequently, it is crucial to test thoroughly whether the AGV control software actually handles the potential conflicts in the appropriate way.

In this paper, we employ a simulated warehouse environment to test the AGV control software. The AGV control software is embedded and activated in the simulated warehouse environment. The simulated warehouse environment provides support for testing by means of (1) representing dynamism in the warehouse environment in an explicit manner, and (2) detecting conflicts of dynamism in an automated way. The approach is illustrated for the case of testing collision avoidance.

1 Introduction

Since March 2004 the AgentWise research group is involved a joint R&D project, called *Egemin Modular Controls Concept* (EMC^2) in cooperation with Egemin, an industrial expert in automating warehouse transportation systems [1]. An AGV transportation system is an industrial transport system using several automatic guided vehicles (AGVs). Typical applications are repackaging and distributing incoming goods to various branches, or distributing manufactured products to storage locations. An AGV is an unmanned, computer-controlled transportation vehicle using a battery as its energy source. AGVs have to perform transports. A transport consists of picking up a load at a particular spot in the warehouse and bringing it to its destination. Transports are generated by client systems, for example business management programs, particular machines, employees or service operators.

Traditionally, AGVs in a warehouse are directly controlled by a central server. AGVs have limited autonomy: the server plans the schedule for the system as a whole, dispatches commands to the AGVs and continually polls their status. This system architecture has successfully been deployed in numerous practical installations. The centralized server architecture has two main benefits. The control software can be customized easily to the needs of a particular project, since the server is a central configuration point. This allows for specific per-project optimizations. A second benefit is that the system is deterministic and predictable.

D. Weyns, H. Van Dyke Parunak, and F. Michel (Eds.): E4MAS 2005, LNAI 3830, pp. 270–290, 2006.

In the EMC^2 project, we are investigating the feasibility of a decentralized system architecture [2, 3] to improve the flexibility of the system. We use concepts from *situated multi-agent systems* (situated MAS) [4]. In our approach, each AGV is controlled by a situated agent. The agents cooperate to ensure the functionality of the system. In contrast to the centralized server architecture, each agent of the situated MAS takes decisions based on local information only. Situated agents deal with opportunities and tackle problems in a decentralized manner.

The warehouse environment the agents are situated in, is inherently dynamic. It contains different AGVs that are constantly driving around, sending messages and manipulating loads. Consequently, conflicts may arise locally between different AGVs each acting autonomously. Examples of conflicts are collisions between AGVs and communication loss because of congestion of the communication channel.

It is evident to test the situated agents thoroughly before they are deployed on real AGVs. In decentralized systems, testing is necessary to determine whether the situated agents actually handle potential conflicts in the appropriate way. Formal approaches are practically infeasible to verify the behavior of decentralized systems [5], such as a situated MAS. This emphasizes the importance of simulation as a means to verify the behavior of decentralized systems [6, 7].

In this paper, we employ a *simulated warehouse environment* to test the situated agents that control the AGVs. The simulated warehouse environment is a model of the real warehouse environment, and contains simulated AGVs. The agents are tested by deploying and activating them in the simulated environment [8]. The simulated warehouse environment facilitates testing by offering a means to (1) represent dynamism in the warehouse environment in an explicit manner, and (2) detect conflicts of dynamism in an automated way. The approach is illustrated for the case of testing collision avoidance between AGVs in the presence of unreliable communication.

The remainder of this paper is structured as follows. In Sect. 2, we elaborate on the real warehouse environment. In Sect. 3, we describe the model of the simulated warehouse environment that was developed to represent the real warehouse environment. In Sect. 4, we explain how the simulated environment supports testing collision avoidance. We evaluate the approach in Sect. 5 and draw conclusions in Sect. 6

2   The Real Warehouse Environment

We focus on two parts of the warehouse environment: the warehouse layout and the AGVs. The warehouse layout is discussed in Sect. 2.1. In Sect. 2.2, we focus on the architecture of an AGV. Section 2.3 analyzes how collisions can occur in the warehouse environment. The requirements for avoiding collisions are specified in Sect. 2.4.

2.1   The Warehouse Layout

The warehouse layout typically contains various loads positioned at various locations in the warehouse. Loads are typically stored in racks. Racks are used to hold loads and are positioned across the warehouse layout, usually according a geometrical pattern that combines easy accessibility of the loads, as well as efficient use of the available room for storage purposes. Typically, also one or several battery chargers for the AGVs are positioned at particular locations on the warehouse layout.

To support AGVs, the warehouse layout is usually customized. This typically involves a custom configuration of the racks. In addition, a complex layout of magnet strips is built into the warehouse floor to guide the AGVs to move from one spot in the warehouse to another. This *magnet track* allows AGVs to maneuver in an accurate manner according to predefined pathways. Moreover, as magnets are inexpensive and can be installed easily, magnet guided navigation is relatively cost-effective.

2.2   Architecture of an AGV

In Fig. 1, the architecture of an AGV is depicted. Each AGV consists of both hardware and software. The hardware of an AGV comprises a number of hardware modules. *AGV sensor modules* represent the sensors to detect the position and battery level of the AGV. *AGV actuator modules* represent the various actuators, such as the engines to move and the lift to pick loads. The *AGV WiFi module* represents the wireless communication infrastructure to send and receive messages. The software of an AGV comprises two main modules: the *AGV controller* and the *AGV agent*.

The *AGV agent* encapsulates the logic to steer the AGV. The AGV agent uses the AGV controller to steer the AGV. The *AGV controller* takes care of all interfacing with the hardware, and determines the granularity of control that can be used to steer an AGV.

The granularity of control offered by the AGV controller is determined by a *logical map* that is a representation of the magnet track, but is expressed in the AGV controller in terms of road segments connected by stations:

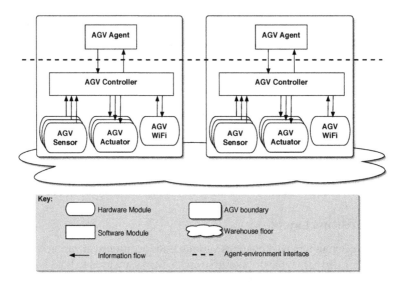

Fig. 1. The architecture of AGVs

- *Road segments.* A road segment corresponds to a particular part of the magnet track, and has a unique identifier. The granularity of road segments is typically chosen such that they represent a physical distance of three to five meters. Road segments can be unidirectional or bidirectional.
- *Stations.* Stations are the logical nodes at the beginning and end of road segments. A station corresponds to a particular spot on the magnet track. A station indicates a special-purpose location for AGVs. A particular station can offer a location for a subset of the following purposes:
  - *Routing.* A station can serve as a location that connects various road segments and allows AGVs to choose alternative routes.
  - *Storage.* A station can serve as a location where loads can be picked up or put down.
  - *Battery charging.* In case a station is positioned at the location of a battery charger, it can offer an AGV the possibility to charge its battery.
  - *Parking.* A station can serve as a location where AGVs can park temporarily, e.g. in case there are no more pending transportation tasks.

The AGV controller allows an AGV agent to steer the AGV *per segment*: the AGV can stop on every station, where it can be instructed to change direction. The AGV controller uses the low-level instructions of the hardware of an AGV in order to stay on the magnet track until the next station is reached. The AGV controller offers the following actions to steer the AGV:

- move(segment): this instructs the AGV controller to drive the AGV over the given segment until the next station is reached.
- pick(segment): instructs the AGV controller to drive the AGV over the given segment and pick up a load at the station at the end of it.
- drop(segment): the same as pick, but drops a load the AGV is carrying.
- park(segment): instructs the AGV controller to drive the AGV over the given segment and park at the station at the end of that segment.
- charge(segment): instructs the AGV controller to drive the AGV over a given segment and start charging batteries at the station at the end of that segment.
- sendBroadcast(message): instructs the AGV controller to broadcast a given message using onboard wireless communication infrastructure.
- sendUnicast(message, receiver): instructs the AGV controller to send a given message to a given receiver.

Furthermore, the AGV controller can be used to perform the following perceptions to inspect the status of an AGV.

- getPosition(): instructs the AGV controller to determine the current position of the AGV. This is the position of a particular reference point situated on the robot.
- getBatteryLevel(): instructs the AGV controller to read out the remaining energy level of the battery of the AGV.
- getMessage(): instructs the AGV controller to return the next message in the inbox of the AGV, which contains all messages received.
- isLoaded(): instructs the AGV controller to check whether the AGV is currently holding a load.
- getAction(): instructs the AGV controller to inspect which action the AGV is currently performing, i.e. busy driving, picking, dropping or charging.

2.3 Collisions in the Warehouse Environment

The warehouse environment in which the agents are situated, is highly dynamic. A dynamic environment is an environment that changes in ways beyond an agent's control [9]. Each agent experiences dynamism in the environment, primarily originating from other AGVs that are constantly driving around, sending messages and manipulating loads. Consequently, there is the possibility that conflicts arise between AGVs in the warehouse environment. The conflicts of interest in this paper are collisions of AGVs.

The movement of an AGV on the warehouse floor over a road segment towards another station can be initiated using a `move`, `pick`, `drop`, `park` or `charge` action. In the dynamic warehouse environment, the movement of an AGV can cause collisions in the following ways:

- *With other AGVs.* Although the layout of road segments is static, the traffic load caused by other AGVs on the layout changes continuously. Consequently, the road segment over which an AGV is driving can become obstructed because of the movement of another AGV. This can lead to collisions.
- *With obstacles.* In a warehouse environment, all kinds of obstacles can appear on the road segments. Examples of obstacles are loads that fall off of AGVs, other AGVs that are out of order because they have collided, broken down or ran out of energy. AGVs can collide into obstacles, as obstacles typically hinder passage on particular road segments.

Agents typically rely on communication to anticipate collisions. However, the unreliability of the communication channel is an important factor that has to be taken into account by the agents. The transmission of communication messages can be initiated by using a `sendUnicast` or `sendBroadcast` action. In the dynamic warehouse environment, the transmission of messages is not reliable and can affected in the following ways:

- *Limited communication range.* The AGV's wireless on-board communication infrastructure can only send and receive messages within a limited range. Consequently, communication is affected as soon as AGVs are moving out of each other's range.
- *Interference of transmission.* The transmission of a communication message can be hindered or delayed by concurrent transmissions of other AGVs within range, or by external sources working on the same channel.

2.4 Requirements for Avoiding Collisions

For an AGV transportation system, the AGV control software has to adhere requirements that specify how AGVs should cope with potential conflicts. We focus on *collision avoidance* in the presence of *unreliable communication*.

The movements of AGVs are not allowed to cause conflicts in the warehouse environment. It is required that the situated agents prevent the AGVs from colliding with each other or with obstacles. The central concept in preventing collisions is the *minimal safety distance*. For each AGV, the agent has to maintain a minimal safety distance at all times with respect to obstacles or other AGVs. This minimal safety distance takes into account the maximum deviation of an AGV with respect to the path of the magnet strip it follows. For AGVs the minimal safety distance is typically about 10 centimeters[1]. It is physically possible that an AGV can pass at a distance smaller than the minimal safety distance. However, it is required that the minimal safety distance is respected in order to guarantee a safe passage *at all times*.

An important factor that has to be taken into account with respect to collision avoidance, is the unreliability of the communication between AGVs. AGVs are required to maintain the minimal safety distance, even in the presence of unreliable communication. A number of quality-of-service attributes specify the worst-case communication characteristics under which correct and safe functioning of the AGVs is required. For the AGVs, a worst-case quality is typically characterized by about 40 percent message loss and 2 seconds transmission delay. Safe and normal operation of the AGVs is required as long as the quality of service is better than the worst-case's. In case the wireless communication quality drops beneath the worst-case's, AGVs are allowed to go into a safe mode, typically suspending any further movements to prevent unsafe situations.

3   The Simulated Warehouse Environment

In this section, we describe the simulated warehouse environment we have developed. A simulated environment is a model of the real environment [10]. We first explain how the situated agents are embedded in the simulated warehouse environment in Sect. 3.1. Then we describe the model of the simulated warehouse environment. In the model of the simulated warehouse environment, we make a distinction between two concerns: state and dynamism. The state (see Sect. 3.2) is concerned with modeling a snapshot at a particular point in time of all parts that constitute the warehouse environment. Dynamism (see Sect. 3.3) is concerned with representing in an explicit manner the evolution of the simulated warehouse environment over time. In Sect. 4, we illustrate how the model is used to test collision avoidance.

3.1   Embedding Situated Agents in the Simulated Warehouse Environment

From Fig.1, it is clear that agents are software modules that are embedded in physical AGVs. From the viewpoint of an agent program, all interaction with the environment is mediated by the interface provided by the AGV controller. Consequently, the simulated warehouse environment has to provide the same interface to the agents. However, instead of being wired to the AGV controller of a real AGV, the simulated warehouse environment redirects the agents' invocations on the interface into actions and perceptions performed by a simulated AGV.

Each agent autonomously decides at what time to invoke an action on the AGV controller. The amount of time it takes an agent to decide upon what to do, results in a delay for all its subsequent actions. To deduce the precise moment in time an action is invoked, we need to determine how long an agent has been thinking or waiting. We developed an approach to map the internal process of an agent to simulation time. The

---

[1] The order of magnitude of numerical data used throughout this paper is based on typical data from several industrial AGV projects.

approach relies on aspect weaving to insert all code to maintain, update and synchronize the logical clocks in a transparent way [11].

3.2   Modeling State

The state of the simulated warehouse environment contains all information to describe the actual state of affairs in the real warehouse environment at a given point in time. A state description is always considered at a particular point in time [12]. The state of the simulated warehouse environment is comprised of *environmental entities* and *environmental relationships*. Figure 2 shows a simplified example of the state of the simulated warehouse environment at a particular point in time.

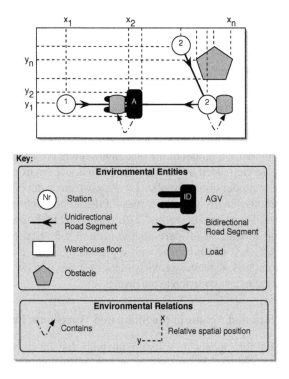

Fig. 2. The state of the simulated warehouse environment

Environmental Entities. Environmental entities are characterized by their own, distinct existence in the environment. The following environmental entities of the warehouse environment are modeled in the simulated environment:

- *AGVs*. AGVs are characterized by a bounding volume to represent the physical size, a battery level, an inbox and an outbox for the wireless communication infrastructure.
- *Loads*. Loads are characterized by a bounding volume that represents the size of the load.
- *Obstacles*. Obstacles are characterized by a bounding volume that represents the size of the obstacle.

- *Warehouse floor*. The warehouse floor is characterized by a two-dimensional area with given size.
- *Road segments*. The magnet track is modeled in terms of the logical map representation that is employed by the AGVs, i.e. in terms of road segments and stations. A road segment can be unidirectional or bidirectional. In the simulated warehouse environment, each road segment is characterized by a direction and a length.
- *Stations*. Stations are locations that connect adjacent road segments. Each station is annotated with the purposes it can be used for, i.e. a location for routing, storage of loads, parking and/or battery charging.

Environmental Relations. An environmental relation is a particular relation between several environmental entities that expresses how these entities are related to each other at a given point in time.

- *Spatial relations*. All environmental entities are spatially related to each other [13]. The spatial relations of all entities are expressed relative to the warehouse floor, using a two-dimensional continuous coordinate system.
- *Containment relations*. Containment relations are used with respect to loads. A containment relation is used to indicate in an explicit manner whether a specific AGV is holding a particular load. For example, a containment relation indicates that a load that is still contained by a particular station and is not yet picked up by an AGV. As soon as an AGV picks up the load, the containment relation indicates the load as being contained by that AGV.

3.3 Dynamism

Until now, we focussed on the static description of the simulated environment. We now elaborate on the way the environment evolves *over time*.

Dynamism as Activities. Dynamism is the evolution of environmental entities and environmental relations over time. An example of dynamism in the warehouse environment is the movement of an AGV driving over a road segment. In the simulated warehouse environment, dynamism is represented as a first-order abstraction, by means of *activities* [14]. An activity represents a well-specified evolution of a particular environmental entity or relation, that happens over a specific time interval. Consequently, the description of an activity comprises the following:

- *A specification of the time interval*. Dynamism happens over time. The time interval of an activity specifies the point in time a particular activity starts and how much time it takes until the evolution completes. The time interval is custom for each activity and can be configured in correspondence to the characteristics measured in the real world.
- *The environmental entity or relation involved*. Dynamism is related to particular environmental entities or relations. Consequently, each activity incorporates a description of the part of the environment it describes the evolution of.
- *An evolution strategy*. Dynamism evolves in a particular, gradual way. Consequently, each activity incorporates a description of the specific evolution as a function of time within the time interval of the activity.

Initiation of Activities. Agents perform actions by invoking methods in the interface of the AGV controller. The invocations on the AGV controller typically initiate activities in the simulated warehouse environment. As such, the invocation of a method by the agent on the interface of the AGV controller, is decoupled from the activity that is initiated in the simulated warehouse environment as the result of the invocation. The time at which an agent triggers the AGV controller (see Sect. 3.1) corresponds to the start of the time interval of the activity it initiates.

Activities in the Simulated Warehouse Environment. In the simulated warehouse environment, activities are used to represent driving, sending messages, lifting and putting down loads, charging the battery, etc. We describe the activity that represents the driving of an AGV in detail:

- `DriveActivity`. A drive activity represents the driving of a particular AGV.
  - *Initiation.* A drive activity can be initiated in case the agent invokes a `move`, `pick`, `drop`, `park` and `charge` action on the AGV controller.
  - *Time Interval.* The time interval of the drive activity is calculated in terms of the physical performance of the AGV en the length of the road segment.
  - *The environmental entity or relation involved.* A drive activity describes the evolution of two parts of the state of the simulated environment: (1) the environmental relation that describes the position of the AGV on the warehouse floor and (2) the battery level of the simulated AGV.

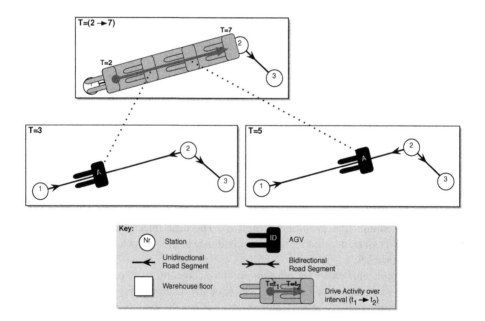

Fig. 3. Example of a drive activity in the simulated warehouse environment

- *Evolution strategy.* The position of an AGV describes the path over the road segment. The position changes over time, approximated by a model of a constant velocity of 2 meters each second. However, during the first 4 seconds of each drive activity, the speed of the AGV increases linearly to represent its acceleration, whereas during the last 2 seconds, its speed decreases linearly to represent the AGV's deceleration. The evolution of the battery level of an AGV is approximated by a model describing a linear decrease according to the distance travelled.

In Fig. 3, an example of a drive activity of AGV A over time interval $(2 \rightarrow 7)$ is depicted. We depict each drive activity as a hull that wraps the intermediate positions that are taken by the AGV over time. In Fig. 3, the evolution represented by the drive activity is illustrated using two snapshots of the state within time interval $(2 \rightarrow 7)$: at time $T = 3$ and $T = 5$, showing the instant position of the AGV.

4 Testing Collision Avoidance

It is crucial to test whether the situated agents handle collision avoidance as required. This requires testing whether the AGVs maintain a minimal safety distance at all times, in the presence of unreliable communication (see Sect. 2.4). In Sect. 4.1, we describe an example scenario performed by a number of agents in a particular warehouse environment. In Sect. 4.2, we focus on how a collision can be detected in an automated way.

4.1 An Example Scenario

In Fig. 4, a fragment of an example layout of a warehouse is depicted. It consists of 10 stations and 12 road segments. Time is expressed in seconds. Initially, 5 AGVs are positioned as depicted on the upper part of of Fig. 4:

- AGV A is positioned at `station 10`.
- AGV B is positioned at `station 6`.
- AGV C is positioned at `station 2`.
- AGV D is positioned at `station 8`.
- AGV E is positioned at `station 4`.

The quality-of-service attributes of the communication are set to the worst-case of 40 percent message loss and 2 seconds transmission delay.

Starting from this initial setup, the agents of the AGVs are embedded in the simulated warehouse environment and activated. During 12 seconds, i.e. over time interval $(0 \rightarrow 12)$, agents are allowed to perform a number of actions. The actions performed by the agents result in activities depicted on the lower part of Fig. 4:

- At time $T = 2$, the agent of AGV A invokes a move action to drive from `station 10` to `station 9`. This results in a `drive activity` over time interval $(2 \rightarrow 10)$, representing the movement AGV A as a result of the action.
- At time $T = 4$, the agent of AGV B invokes a move action to drive from `station 6` to `station 1`. This results in a `drive activity` over time interval $(4 \rightarrow 9)$, representing the movement AGV B as a result of the action.

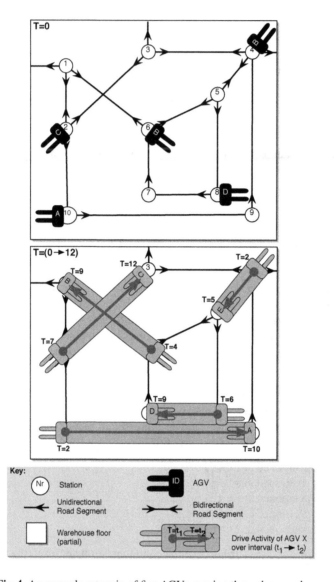

Fig. 4. An example scenario of five AGVs moving through a warehouse

- At time $T = 7$, the agent of AGV C invokes a move action to drive from station 2 to station 3. This results in a drive activity over time interval $(7 \rightarrow 12)$, representing the movement AGV C as a result of the action.
- At time $T = 6$, the agent of AGV D invokes a move action to drive from station 8 to station 7. This results in a drive activity over time interval $(6 \rightarrow 9)$, representing the movement AGV D as a result of the action.

- At time $T = 2$, the agent of AGV E invokes a move action to drive from station 4 to station 5. This results in a drive activity over time interval $(2 \rightarrow 5)$, representing the movement AGV E as a result of the action.

We now focus on detecting whether the minimal safety distance is violated in this scenario.

4.2   The Collision Detection Law

A *collision detection law* is a rule that checks whether drive activities proceed safely. For each drive activity, the collision detection law is able to detect two kinds of interference: violations of the safety distance by entities that are stationary, and violations of the safety distance by entities that are non-stationary.

Entities are stationary over a particular time interval in case they are not involved in any drive activity during that time interval. Otherwise, the entity is non-stationary over that time interval. Obstacles are always stationary. AGVs are stationary during the time intervals they are *not* involved in a drive activity.

A code-fragment of the collision detection law is given in Fig. 5, and will be explained next.

Detecting Interference with Stationary Entities. We first focus on the case of detecting for a particular drive activity whether it violates the minimal safety distance with respect to entities that are stationary during the time interval of that activity. The *activity perimeter* is central in checking interference. The activity perimeter represents the safety distance around the aggregate of all intermediate positions of an AGV during a drive activity as a whole. As an example, consider the drive activity of AGV E in Fig. 4. The activity perimeter for this drive activity is depicted in Fig. 6.

A necessary condition for a particular drive activity to be safe, is that all entities that are stationary over the time interval of that activity, have no overlap with the activity perimeter. This condition is checked in lines 15 to 20 in Fig. 5.

The collision detection law will detect whether stationary entities violate the activity perimeter. When considering the drive activity of AGV E, it is clear from Fig. 4 that AGV C and AGV D are the only stationary entities during the time interval $(2 \rightarrow 5)$. As AGV C and AGV D are both entirely outside the activity perimeter of the drive activity of AGV E, stationary entities do not compromise the safety of AGV E.

Detecting Interference with Non-stationary Entities. Until now, we only considered entities that are stationary during a drive activity. We now focus on the case of detecting for a particular drive activity whether it violates the minimal safety distance with respect to entities that are non-stationary during the time interval of that activity. All other AGVs involved in drive activities during the time interval of the drive activity under investigation, are non-stationary.

Checking the non-stationary entities is performed in lines 21 to 37 of Fig. 5.

As an example, consider the drive activity of AGV B in Fig. 4. The activity perimeter to detect interference with stationary entities is depicted on the left hand side of Fig. 7. Note that no interference with stationary entities is detected, as no AGV is stationary during time interval $(4 \rightarrow 9)$.

```
1    /**
2     * Check the collisions of a given drive activity
3     * @param act the drive activity
4     * @param entities the entities to check collisions with
5     * @return a vector containing the collisions
6     */
7    public Vector checkCollisions(DriveActivity act, Vector entities){
8        Vector result = new Vector();
9        TimeInterval interval = act.getTimeInterval();
10       BoundingBox perimeter = act.getActivityPerimeter();
11       //a loop to check each entity
12       for (int i=0; i < entities.size(); i++)
13       {
14           Entity ent = (Entity)entities.get(i);
15           if (ent.isStationaryDuring(interval))
16           { //in case the entity is stationary:
17               //do one check for the perimeter of the whole activity
18               result.add(checkOverlap(perimeter,
19                   ent.getBoundingBox(interval.getBegin()))));
20           }
21           else //in case the entitiy is non-stationary
22           {
23               //get all activities of the entity that happen during the interval
24               Vector activities = ent.getDriveActivities(interval);
25               //a loop for each activity of the entity
26               for(int j=0; j < activities.size(); j++)
27               {
28                   DriveActivity otherAct = (DriveActivity)activities.get(i);
29                   //test whether the activity perimeters of both activities overlap
30                   if(checkOverlap(perimeter,otheract.getActivityPerimeter())!=null)
31                   { //in case the activity perimeters overlap
32                       //take snapshots in the common interval of both activities
33                       TimeInterval common = otherAct.getTimeInterval().getIntersection(interval);
34                       for(Time t=common.getBegin(); t.before(common.getEnd()); t.increment())
35                           //do the check for one snapshot
36                           result.add(checkOverlap(act.getEntityPerimeterAt(t),
37                               otherAct.getEntityBoundingBoxAt(t)));
38                   }
39               }
40           }
41       }
42       return result;
43   }
```

Fig. 5. Code fragment of the collision detection law

To determine the safety of a particular drive activity, a detailed investigation of all non-stationary entities that cross the activity perimeter is needed. In the example of Fig. 7, the activity perimeter of AGV B overlaps with the drive activity of AGV C. In Fig. 5, this is checked in line 30. To determine the interference of a particular drive activity with another drive activity, we only consider the common time interval between both. In Fig. 5, the common time interval is determined in line 33. In our example of the drive activities of AGV B and AGV C, the common time interval is $(7 \to 9)$. This is depicted on the right hand side of Fig. 7.

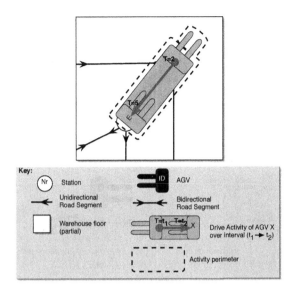

Fig. 6. The activity perimeter of the drive activity of AGV E

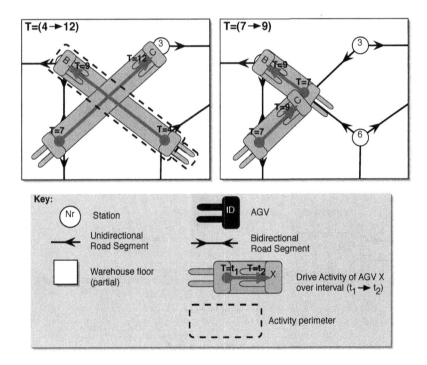

Fig. 7. The drive activity of AGV B. The activity perimeter is depicted on the left part hand side, the common time interval with the drive activity of AGV C is depicted on the right hand side.

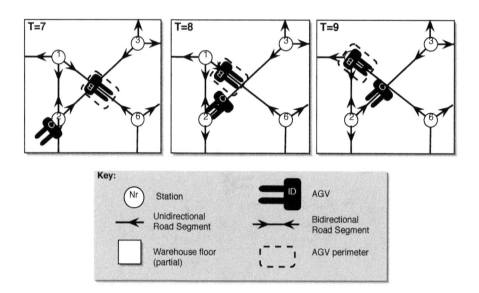

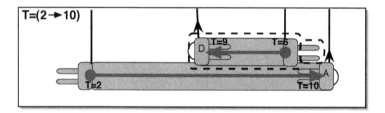

Fig. 8. Checking the drive activity of AGV B. The check for non-stationary entities over time interval $(7 \rightarrow 9)$, on the right of Fig. 7, is analyzed using three state snapshots at $T = 7$, $T = 8$ and $T = 9$.

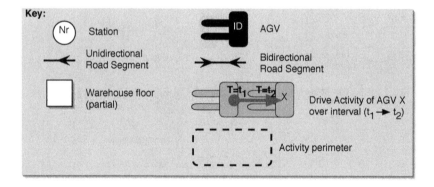

Fig. 9. The activity perimeter of the drive activity of AGV D

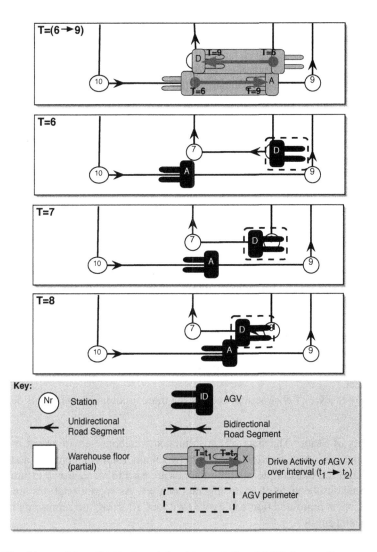

Fig. 10. The drive activity of AGV D and the drive activity of AGV A over the common time interval $(6 \rightarrow 9)$. The interference of both activities is detected using state snapshots at $T = 6$, $T = 7$ and $T = 8$, at which the safety perimeter of AGV D is violated.

Detecting interference between two drive activities over a common time interval is done by taking a number of state snapshots, see Fig. 8. For each state snapshot, it is checked wither the other AGVs is completely outside the safety perimeter of the former AGV. In case of Fig. 8 this is always the case, so AGV C does not compromise the safety of the drive activity of AGV B. In Fig. 5, the snapshots over the common time interval are checked in lines 34 to 37.

A Collision Detection Example. Finally, consider the drive activity of AGV D in Fig. 4. The activity perimeter is depicted in Fig. 9.

- *Interference with stationary entities.* From the activity interference perimeter it is clear that the drive activity of AGV D does not interfere with any entities that are stationary.
- *Interference with non-stationary entities.* The drive activity of AGV A crosses the activity perimeter. Figure 10 illustrates the analysis of the drive activities of AGV D and AGV A over their common time interval $(6 \rightarrow 9)$. In Fig. 10 it is also illustrated how at time $T = 8$, AGV A violates the safety perimeter of AGV D.

5   Discussion and Evaluation

We elaborate on two important characteristics of the simulated warehouse environment we developed: modularity and performance.

5.1   Modularity

Modularity is applied extensively throughout the model of the simulated warehouse environment. Modularity is crucial as it allows *separation of concerns*, a ground rule for decent software engineering. At the highest level of abstraction, the simulated warehouse environment is decomposed in three modular parts: (1) a representation of the *state* of the simulated warehouse environment, (2) a representation of the *dynamism* in the simulated warehouse environment and (3) a representation of *detection laws* describing rules to detect when the consistency is broken in the simulated warehouse environment.

At a lower level of abstraction, each of the three modular parts is itself designed in a modular way.

Modularity of State. The state of the simulated warehouse environment is designed in a modular way. A distinction is made between environmental entities and environmental relations. For example, spatial relations are easy to manage as they are not scattered throughout the state of environmental entities. As spatial relations are modeled separately, their representation can evolve without affecting the representation of the environmental entities.

Modularity of Dynamism. Dynamism is designed in a modular way, clearly separated from the state. Activities encapsulate all characteristics of a particular kind of dynamism happening in the warehouse environment. The characteristics of various activities can be adjusted in a modular way, to suit the characteristics in the real warehouse environment. For example, the acceleration and deceleration characteristics of an individual AGV can be adjusted in the evolution strategy, to accurately reflect the performance of the real AGVs.

Modularity of Detection. The detection laws that check for inconsistencies happening in the simulated environment are developed in a modular way. Detection laws avoid the use of a uniform, global granularity that crosscuts the whole simulation. Instead, each detection law employs its own granularity, customized according to the required accuracy to detect particular inconsistencies. For example, detecting collisions can be done by a collision detection law that uses snapshots with a granularity of 1 second to check interference with non-stationary entities. Obtaining a higher accuracy of detection involves an adjustment applied locally in the collision detection law, e.g. a change in the granularity from 1 second to 5 milliseconds.

5.2   Performance of Collision Detection

We now elaborate on the performance of collision detection based on our approach. We compare the performance of collision detection using a collision detection law (see Sect. 4.2) with the performance of detecting collisions using a global time step. As a performance measure, we employ the number of perimeter checks to detect violations of the safety perimeter.

We compare both approaches using the scenario of Fig. 4. Suppose the required accuracy to detect perimeter violations is 1 centimeter, and that the maximum velocity of an AGV is 2 meter per second.

Collision Detection Using a Global Time Step. In this approach, collision detection happens by evolving the simulation according to a common, system-wide time step. We first determine the step size to check for perimeter violations with the required accuracy. Driving at its maximum speed of 2 meters per second, it takes an AGV 5 milliseconds to move over 1 centimeter. As two AGVs can travel at top speed, their relative position changes at a maximum rate of 4 meters per second. Consequently, to detect collisions with an accuracy of 1 centimeter, a perimeter check must happen at least every 2.5 milliseconds. This means 400 perimeter checks are needed to check violations of the safety perimeter of an AGV driving during 1 second.

We now determine the number of perimeter checks for the scenario of Fig. 4:

- AGV A: to check the drive activity over time interval $(2 \rightarrow 10)$, $400 \times 8 = 3200$ checks are needed with *each* of the other four AGVs. This results in $3200 \times 4 = 12800$ checks.
- AGV B: to check the drive activity over time interval $(4 \rightarrow 9)$, $400 \times 5 = 2000$ checks are needed with each of the other four AGVs. This results in $2000 \times 4 = 8000$ checks.
- AGV C: to check the drive activity over time interval $(7 \rightarrow 12)$, $400 \times 5 = 2000$ checks are needed with each of the other four AGVs. This results in $2000 \times 4 = 8000$ checks.
- AGV D: to check the drive activity over time interval $(6 \rightarrow 9)$, $400 \times 3 = 1200$ checks are needed with each of the other four AGVs. This results in $1200 \times 4 = 4800$ checks.
- AGV E: to check the drive activity over time interval $(2 \rightarrow 5)$, $400 \times 3 = 1200$ checks are needed with each of the other four AGVs. This results in $1200 \times 4 = 4800$ checks.

This means a total of 38400 perimeter checks are needed for the scenario.

Collision Detection Using a Collision Detection Law. We now focus on the number of perimeter checks using the collision detection law that inspects drive activities. In analogy with the previous approach, 400 perimeter checks are needed to check violations of the safety perimeter of a single AGV driving during 1 second.

We now determine the number of perimeter checks for in case of Fig. 4. The number of checks needed for each activity is as follows:

- AGV A: checking the drive activity over time interval $(2 \rightarrow 10)$. There are no stationary entities during this time interval: all four other AGVs are non-stationary. Consequently, the activity perimeter check of line 30 in Fig. 5 is performed 4 times. However, only the activity perimeter of the drive activity of AGV D actually overlaps with the one of AGV A. As the common time interval of both activities is $(6 \rightarrow 9)$, the check in the loop at line 36–37 in Fig. 5 is executed $400 \times 3 = 1200$ times. The total number of perimeter checks needed is $4 + 1200 = 1204$.

- AGV B: checking the drive activity over time interval $(4 \rightarrow 9)$. There are no stationary entities during this time interval: all four other AGVs are non-stationary. Consequently, the activity perimeter check of line 30 in Fig. 5 is performed 4 times. However, only the activity perimeter of the drive activity of AGV C actually overlaps with the one of AGV B. As the common time interval of both activities is $(7 \rightarrow 9)$, the check in the loop at line 36–37 in Fig. 5 is executed $400 \times 2 = 800$ times. The total number of perimeter checks needed is $4 + 800 = 804$.

- AGV C: checking the drive activity over time interval $(7 \rightarrow 12)$. AGV E is stationary during this time interval, resulting in one check performed at line 18–19 in Fig. 5. All three other AGVs are non-stationary. Consequently, the activity perimeter check of line 30 in Fig. 5 is performed 3 times. However, only the activity perimeter of the drive activity of AGV B actually overlaps with the one of AGV C. As the common time interval of both activities is $(7 \rightarrow 9)$, the check in the loop at line 36–37 in Fig. 5 is executed $400 \times 2 = 800$ times. The total number of perimeter checks needed is $1 + 3 + 800 = 804$.

- AGV D: checking the drive activity over time interval $(6 \rightarrow 9)$. AGV C and AGV E are stationary during this time interval, resulting in 2 checks performed at line 18–19 in Fig. 5. The two other AGVs are non-stationary. Consequently, the activity perimeter check of line 30 in Fig. 5 is performed 2 times. However, only the activity perimeter of the drive activity of AGV A actually overlaps with the one of AGV D. As the common time interval of both activities is $(6 \rightarrow 9)$, the check in the loop at line 36–37 in Fig. 5 is executed $400 \times 3 = 1200$ times. The total number of perimeter checks needed is $2 + 2 + 1200 = 1204$.

- AGV E: checking the drive activity over time interval $(2 \rightarrow 5)$. AGV C and AGV D are stationary during this time interval, resulting in 2 checks performed at line 18–19 in Fig. 5. The two other AGVs are non-stationary. Consequently, the activity perimeter check of line 30 in Fig. 5 is performed 2 times. However, none of the activity perimeters of the activities of AGV A and AGV B overlap with the one of AGV E. Consequently, the loop at line 34–37 in Fig. 5 is not executed. The total number of perimeter checks needed is $2 + 2 = 4$.

This means a total of 4020 perimeter checks are needed for the scenario, which is only about 10% of the checks needed in the previous approach.

The number of checks needed by the collision detection law is highly dependent upon the density of AGVs in the warehouse environment. The layout fragment used in Fig. 4 is kept small for demonstration purposes, and hence the density of AGVs is high. The complete layout of a warehouse is much more expanded, and has a lower density of AGVs. For example, for 5 AGVs the number of stations and road segments in an industrial layout typically ranges from 50 to 500, instead of the 10 or 12 in our example. In a layout with a lower density of AGVs, it will be likely that the collision detection law needs to take into account non-stationary entities less often, reducing the number of perimeter checks. For the approach of detecting collisions based on a global time-step, the number of perimeter checks always remains the same, irrespective of the density of AGVs.

6   Conclusion

In this paper, we described a simulated warehouse environment that can be used to test AGV control software. To support testing, the simulated warehouse environment is decomposed in three parts, each with their own responsibility:

– The *state* is responsible to represent snapshots of the warehouse environment at a particular moment in time.
– The model of *dynamism* represents in an explicit manner the evolution of the simulated warehouse environment over time.
– *Detection laws* are responsible to detect for the occurrence of conflicts.

We illustrated the use of the simulated warehouse environment to test collision avoidance. The approach employed a collision detection law that relies on inspection of drive activities to detect whether the minimal safety distance is maintained at all times.

We refer to [15] for further information on the AGV-simulator that was developed and supports the approach described in this paper.

References

1. Egemin International NV: (http://www.egemin.com/) Home page of Egemin International NV. Date of publication: 2002. Date retrieved: December 1, 2005. Date last modified: 2005.
2. Weyns, D., Schelfthout, K., Holvoet, T., Lefever, T., Wielemans, J.: Architecture-centric development of an AGV transportation system. In: Multi-Agent Systems and Applications IV. Volume 3690 of Lecture Notes in Computer Science., Springer Verlag Berlin Heidelberg New York (2005) 640–645
3. Weyns, D., Schelfthout, K., Holvoet, T., Lefever, T.: Decentralized control of E'GV transportation systems. In: Autonomous Agents and Multiagent Systems, Industry Track, University of Utrecht, ACM (2005) 67–74
4. Weyns, D., Holvoet, T.: A formal model for situated multi-agent systems. Fundamenta Informaticae **63** (2004) 125–158
5. Wegner, P.: Why Interaction is More Powerful than Algorithms. Communications of the ACM **40** (1997) 80–91
6. De Wolf, T., Samaey, G., Holvoet, T.: Engineering self-organising emergent systems with simulation-based scientific analysis. In: Proceedings of the Fourth International Workshop on Engineering Self-Organising Applications, Universiteit Utrecht (2005) 146–160

7. Uhrmacher, A.: Simulation for agent-oriented software engineering. In Lunceford, W., Page, E., eds.: First International Conference on Grand Challenges for Modeling and Simulation, SCS, San Diego (2002)

8. Uhrmacher, A.M., Kullick, B.G.: "Plug and test": software agents in virtual environments. In: WSC '00: Proceedings of the 32nd conference on Winter simulation, San Diego, CA, USA, Society for Computer Simulation International (2000) 1722–1729

9. Russell, S., Norvig, P.: Artificial Intelligence: A Modern Approach. Prentice-Hall, Englewood Cliffs, NJ (1995)

10. Klügl, F., Fehler, M., Herrler, R.: About the role of the environment in multi-agent simulations. In: Environments for multi-agent systems. Volume 3374 of Lecture Notes in Computer Science., Springer-Verlag (2005) 127–149

11. Helleboogh, A., Holvoet, T., Weyns, D., Berbers, Y.: Extending time management support for multi-agent systems. In: Multi-Agent and Multi-Agent-Based Simulation: Joint Workshop MABS 2004, New York, NY, USA, July 19, 2004, Revised Selected Papers. Volume 3415 / 2005 of Lecture Notes in Computer Science., Springer-Verlag, GmbH (2005) 37–48

12. Carson, J.S.: Introduction to simulation: introduction to modeling and simulation. In: Winter Simulation Conference. (2003) 7–13

13. Bandini, S., Manzoni, S., Simone, C.: Dealing with space in multi–agent systems: a model for situated mas. In: AAMAS '02: Proceedings of the first international joint conference on Autonomous agents and multiagent systems, New York, NY, USA, ACM Press (2002) 1183–1190

14. Helleboogh, A., Holvoet, T., Berbers, Y.: Simulating actions in dynamic environments. In Barros, F., Bruzzone, A., Frydman, C., Giambiasi, N., eds.: Conceptual Modeling and Simulation Conference, LSIS, Université Paul Cézanne Aix Marseille III (2005) 123–129

15. AgentWise Taskforce, KULeuven: (http://www.cs.kuleuven.ac.be/~distrinet/taskforces/agentwise/agvsimulator/) Home page of the AGV Simulator. Date of publication: 2005. Date retrieved: December 1, 2005. Date last modified: 2005.

Author Index

Lecture Notes in Artificial Intelligence (LNAI)

Vol. 3642: D. Ślęzak, J. Yao, J.F. Peters, W. Ziarko, X. Hu (Eds.), Rough Sets, Fuzzy Sets, Data Mining, and Granular Computing, Part II. XXIII, 738 pages. 2005.

Vol. 3641: D. Ślęzak, G. Wang, M. Szczuka, I. Düntsch, Y. Yao (Eds.), Rough Sets, Fuzzy Sets, Data Mining, and Granular Computing, Part I. XXIV, 742 pages. 2005.

Vol. 3635: J.R. Winkler, M. Niranjan, N.D. Lawrence (Eds.), Deterministic and Statistical Methods in Machine Learning. VIII, 341 pages. 2005.

Vol. 3632: R. Nieuwenhuis (Ed.), Automated Deduction – CADE-20. XIII, 459 pages. 2005.

Vol. 3630: M.S. Capcarrère, A.A. Freitas, P.J. Bentley, C.G. Johnson, J. Timmis (Eds.), Advances in Artificial Life. XIX, 949 pages. 2005.

Vol. 3626: B. Ganter, G. Stumme, R. Wille (Eds.), Formal Concept Analysis. X, 349 pages. 2005.

Vol. 3625: S. Kramer, B. Pfahringer (Eds.), Inductive Logic Programming. XIII, 427 pages. 2005.

Vol. 3620: H. Muñoz-Ávila, F. Ricci (Eds.), Case-Based Reasoning Research and Development. XV, 654 pages. 2005.

Vol. 3614: L. Wang, Y. Jin (Eds.), Fuzzy Systems and Knowledge Discovery, Part II. XLI, 1314 pages. 2005.

Vol. 3613: L. Wang, Y. Jin (Eds.), Fuzzy Systems and Knowledge Discovery, Part I. XLI, 1334 pages. 2005.

Vol. 3607: J.-D. Zucker, L. Saitta (Eds.), Abstraction, Reformulation and Approximation. XII, 376 pages. 2005.

Vol. 3601: G. Moro, S. Bergamaschi, K. Aberer (Eds.), Agents and Peer-to-Peer Computing. XII, 245 pages. 2005.

Vol. 3600: F. Wiedijk (Ed.), The Seventeen Provers of the World. XVI, 159 pages. 2006.

Vol. 3596: F. Dau, M.-L. Mugnier, G. Stumme (Eds.), Conceptual Structures: Common Semantics for Sharing Knowledge. XI, 467 pages. 2005.

Vol. 3593: V. Mařík, R. W. Brennan, M. Pěchouček (Eds.), Holonic and Multi-Agent Systems for Manufacturing. XI, 269 pages. 2005.

Vol. 3587: P. Perner, A. Imiya (Eds.), Machine Learning and Data Mining in Pattern Recognition. XVII, 695 pages. 2005.

Vol. 3584: X. Li, S. Wang, Z.Y. Dong (Eds.), Advanced Data Mining and Applications. XIX, 835 pages. 2005.

Vol. 3581: S. Miksch, J. Hunter, E.T. Keravnou (Eds.), Artificial Intelligence in Medicine. XVII, 547 pages. 2005.

Vol. 3577: R. Falcone, S. Barber, J. Sabater-Mir, M.P. Singh (Eds.), Trusting Agents for Trusting Electronic Societies. VIII, 235 pages. 2005.

Vol. 3575: S. Wermter, G. Palm, M. Elshaw (Eds.), Biomimetic Neural Learning for Intelligent Robots. IX, 383 pages. 2005.

Vol. 3571: L. Godo (Ed.), Symbolic and Quantitative Approaches to Reasoning with Uncertainty. XVI, 1028 pages. 2005.

Vol. 3559: P. Auer, R. Meir (Eds.), Learning Theory. XI, 692 pages. 2005.

Vol. 3558: V. Torra, Y. Narukawa, S. Miyamoto (Eds.), Modeling Decisions for Artificial Intelligence. XII, 470 pages. 2005.

Vol. 3554: A.K. Dey, B. Kokinov, D.B. Leake, R. Turner (Eds.), Modeling and Using Context. XIV, 572 pages. 2005.

Vol. 3550: T. Eymann, F. Klügl, W. Lamersdorf, M. Klusch, M.N. Huhns (Eds.), Multiagent System Technologies. XI, 246 pages. 2005.

Vol. 3539: K. Morik, J.-F. Boulicaut, A. Siebes (Eds.), Local Pattern Detection. XI, 233 pages. 2005.

Vol. 3538: L. Ardissono, P. Brna, A. Mitrović (Eds.), User Modeling 2005. XVI, 533 pages. 2005.

Vol. 3533: M. Ali, F. Esposito (Eds.), Innovations in Applied Artificial Intelligence. XX, 858 pages. 2005.

Vol. 3528: P.S. Szczepaniak, J. Kacprzyk, A. Niewiadomski (Eds.), Advances in Web Intelligence. XVII, 513 pages. 2005.

Vol. 3518: T.-B. Ho, D. Cheung, H. Liu (Eds.), Advances in Knowledge Discovery and Data Mining. XXI, 864 pages. 2005.

Vol. 3508: P. Bresciani, P. Giorgini, B. Henderson-Sellers, G. Low, M. Winikoff (Eds.), Agent-Oriented Information Systems II. X, 227 pages. 2005.

Vol. 3505: V. Gorodetsky, J. Liu, V.A. Skormin (Eds.), Autonomous Intelligent Systems: Agents and Data Mining. XIII, 303 pages. 2005.

Vol. 3501: B. Kégl, G. Lapalme (Eds.), Advances in Artificial Intelligence. XV, 458 pages. 2005.

Vol. 3492: P. Blache, E.P. Stabler, J.V. Busquets, R. Moot (Eds.), Logical Aspects of Computational Linguistics. X, 363 pages. 2005.

Vol. 3490: L. Bolc, Z. Michalewicz, T. Nishida (Eds.), Intelligent Media Technology for Communicative Intelligence. X, 259 pages. 2005.

Vol. 3488: M.-S. Hacid, N.V. Murray, Z.W. Raś, S. Tsumoto (Eds.), Foundations of Intelligent Systems. XIII, 700 pages. 2005.

Vol. 3487: J.A. Leite, P. Torroni (Eds.), Computational Logic in Multi-Agent Systems. XII, 281 pages. 2005.

Vol. 3476: J.A. Leite, A. Omicini, P. Torroni, P. Yolum (Eds.), Declarative Agent Languages and Technologies II. XII, 289 pages. 2005.

Vol. 3464: S.A. Brueckner, G.D.M. Serugendo, A. Karageorgos, R. Nagpal (Eds.), Engineering Self-Organising Systems. XIII, 299 pages. 2005.

Vol. 3452: F. Baader, A. Voronkov (Eds.), Logic for Programming, Artificial Intelligence, and Reasoning. XI, 562 pages. 2005.

Vol. 3451: M.-P. Gleizes, A. Omicini, F. Zambonelli (Eds.), Engineering Societies in the Agents World V. XIII, 349 pages. 2005.

Vol. 3446: T. Ishida, L. Gasser, H. Nakashima (Eds.), Massively Multi-Agent Systems I. XI, 349 pages. 2005.

Vol. 3445: G. Chollet, A. Esposito, M. Faúndez-Zanuy, M. Marinaro (Eds.), Nonlinear Speech Modeling and Applications. XIII, 433 pages. 2005.